RESISTING THE NUCLEAR

Critical Ethnic Studies and Visual Culture

Laura Kina, Series Editor

RESISTING THE NUCLEAR

ART AND ACTIVISM ACROSS THE PACIFIC

EDITED BY ELYSSA FAISON AND ALISON FIELDS

University of Washington Press *Seattle*

Financial support for *Resisting the Nuclear* was provided by the Office of the Vice President for Research and Partnerships, the Office of the Provost, the Dodge Family College of Arts and Sciences, and the Department of History at the University of Oklahoma.

Additional support was provided by the Samuel and Althea Stroum Endowed Book Fund.

Design by Erin Kirk
Composed in Warnock Pro, typeface designed by Robert Slimbach

28 27 26 25 24 5 4 3 2 1

Printed and bound in the United States of America

UNIVERSITY OF WASHINGTON PRESS
uwapress.uw.edu

LIBRARY OF CONGRESS CATALOGING-IN-PUBLICATION DATA

Names: Faison, Elyssa, 1965– editor. | Fields, Alison, 1979– editor.
Title: Resisting the nuclear : art and activism across the Pacific / edited by Elyssa Faison and Alison Fields.
Description: Seattle : University of Washington Press, [2023] | Series: Critical ethnic studies and visual culture | Includes bibliographical references and index.
Identifiers: LCCN 2023030770 (print) | LCCN 2023030771 (ebook) | ISBN 9780295752341 (paperback) | ISBN 9780295752358 (ebook)
Subjects: LCSH: Antinuclear movement —Pacific Area. | Art and social action —Pacific Area.
Classification: LCC JZ5584.P14 R47 2023 (print) | LCC JZ5584.P14 (ebook) | DDC 327.1/747 —dc23/eng/20230811
LC record available at https://lccn.loc.gov/2023030770
LC ebook record available at https://lccn.loc.gov/2023030771

♾ This paper meets the requirements of ANSI/NISO Z39.48-1992 (Permanence of Paper).

Contents

PART TWO. LEGACIES OF THE BIKINI TEST

PART THREE. TRANSPACIFIC ACTIVISMS

Acknowledgments

This volume had its origins in our cotaught Presidential Dream Course, Nuclear Legacies, offered at the University of Oklahoma in 2016. Our course explored the American deployment of atomic bombs in Japan during World War II, ensuing nuclear energy initiatives and antinuclear peace movements, and the global impact of nuclear testing. The course's guest speakers, who represented the fields of history, art, filmmaking, and photography, included volume participants Ran Zwigenberg, Shinpei Takeda, and Will Wilson, as well as filmmaker Linda Hoagland, who was unable to be part of the volume. We are grateful to the University of Oklahoma Presidential Dream Course program for enabling this productive interdisciplinary exchange.

In the years that followed, our vision for *Resisting the Nuclear: Art and Activism across the Pacific* expanded to include essays by historians, artists, and activists working in the American West, Japan, and the Marshall Islands. In late 2019, just after our initial volume submission, five contributors participated in the panel "Nuclear After-Effects: US Atomic Policies in the American West, the Marshall Islands, and Japan" at the American Studies Association Annual Meeting in Honolulu, Hawai'i.

We are grateful to our contributors for remaining committed to this volume as the global pandemic reconfigured scholarly production. We would also like to especially thank University of Washington Press editorial director Larin McLauglin, whose commitment was central to bringing this volume to publication, along with the entire editorial and production team. We are also grateful to our anonymous peer reviewers for strengthening the depth and scope of this volume, as well as the incredibly helpful feedback of series editor Laura Kina. We are honored to be the inaugural volume in Kina's series, Critical Ethnic Studies and Visual Culture.

We acknowledge the many artists who granted permission to include their work in this volume, as well as participated in interviews. Financial support for image reproduction was provided from the Office of the Vice President for Research and Partnerships, the Office of the Provost, the Dodge Family College of Arts and Sciences, and the Department of History at the University of Oklahoma. Finally, we wish to thank our colleagues in the Department of History and the School of Visual Arts, along with our families, who supported this project through to completion.

Note on Naming and Orthography

Names of all contributors to this volume, including those who are Japanese, are rendered in "given name, family name" order. Japanese names that appear within the text, however, use the Japanese convention of family name followed by given name.

Marshallese language orthography has many variations. For the Marshallese atoll we have used Enewetak in the text but have reproduced other variants, such as Eniwetok, when they appear in cited material.

RESISTING THE NUCLEAR

Introduction

Visuality, Temporality, Geography

ELYSSA FAISON AND ALISON FIELDS

Part of the Enewetak Atoll of the Marshall Islands, site of US nuclear testing between 1946 and 1958, the low-lying Runit Island became home to a nuclear waste depository starting in 1979. The depository, known locally as "the Tomb," was intended as a temporary measure. Its cracked concrete dome covers a massive crater caused by the 1958 Cactus nuclear test that houses over 110,000 cubic yards of radioactively contaminated soil and debris. The permeable soil at the crater's base has allowed seawater into the depository, leaching plutonium into the surrounding marine environment. In *Nuclear Hemorrhage: Enewetak Does Not Forget* (2017), artist Joy Enomoto (Kanaka Maoli) transformed the inadequate nuclear waste storage solution on Runit Island into a sea fan, a soft coral with a flattened, branching form. Enomoto's delicately extending branches, created with watercolor and thread, take on the appearance of blood vessels, stemming from a placenta-like base to the dome above. In Enomoto's work, the containment structure is reimagined as a living organism, with a ring of green around the dome signaling "the hope of restoration and the memory of what existed."[1]

Thousands of miles away, the Navajo Nation served as the hub of the US uranium boom from the 1940s to the 1960s and a site of continued commercial mining until the 1980s. Beginning with the Manhattan Project, the mines played a critical role in nuclear weapons development while creating dangerous working conditions for Navajo miners and poisoning land and water. As part of the installation *When They Came Home*, Jane Benale (Diné) created a weaving that addresses toxic waste, memory, and healing on Navajo land. The base of the dyed-wool weaving is layered to represent brown earth and underground turquoise water, with red lines like ochre rock, "thin bloodlines of strata in earth's history; bloodlines from the lives lived."[2] Green lines, suggesting growth and healing medicinal plants, give way to the transformative yellow of daylight, the color of both sacred corn pollen and radioactive uranium dust. Benale's weaving was the inspiration for the installation's accompanying garments and jewelry, created in collaboration by Ann Collier, Kim Hahn (Korean), and Malcolm Benally (Diné), referencing how Navajo women "must wear the memories of how their lives were changed."[3]

Both *Nuclear Hemorrhage: Enewetak Does Not Forget* and *When They Came Home*, juxtaposed in *Exposure: Native Art and Political Ecology*, a 2021–22 exhibition at the Institute of American Indian Arts' (IAIA) Museum of Contemporary Native Arts, creatively depict lasting memories of nuclear contamination, as well as hopes for growth and renewal. The exhibition, which features works of international Indigenous artists responding to nuclear testing, nuclear accidents, and uranium mining in their communities, underscores the links among history, visuality, and activism. When asked about her goal for the exhibition, cocurator Erin Vink described her hope that the artworks would generate an emotional response to prompt further research and, in turn, a "reevaluating [of] your own actions and what you are doing that can help heal the land."[4] By making visible often hidden and traumatic histories and generating imaginative responses to complex problems, artists prompt social action and enact nuclear resistance.

In this volume, we recognize nuclear resistance as multipronged. In addition to considering more familiar modes of political and legal activism, we highlight the visual arts as an understudied space of creative resistance. While many theories of resistance exist, Stellan Vinthagen and Anna Johansson write, they all define resistance as an *oppositional act*. "Like all acts, resistance is situated in certain time, space and relations, and engages with different (types of) actors, techniques and discourses."[5] In response to nuclear trauma, impacted groups have adopted a wide variety of political, legal, and creative strategies of resistance. For instance, following nuclear testing on the Bikini and Enewetak Atolls, the Marshallese engaged many tactics of resistance, including lawsuits, negotiations, demonstrations, petitions, and public hearings to demand acknowledgment and compensation.[6] As historian Martha Smith-Norris writes, despite the vast power differential in facing the US government, Indigenous Marshall Islanders

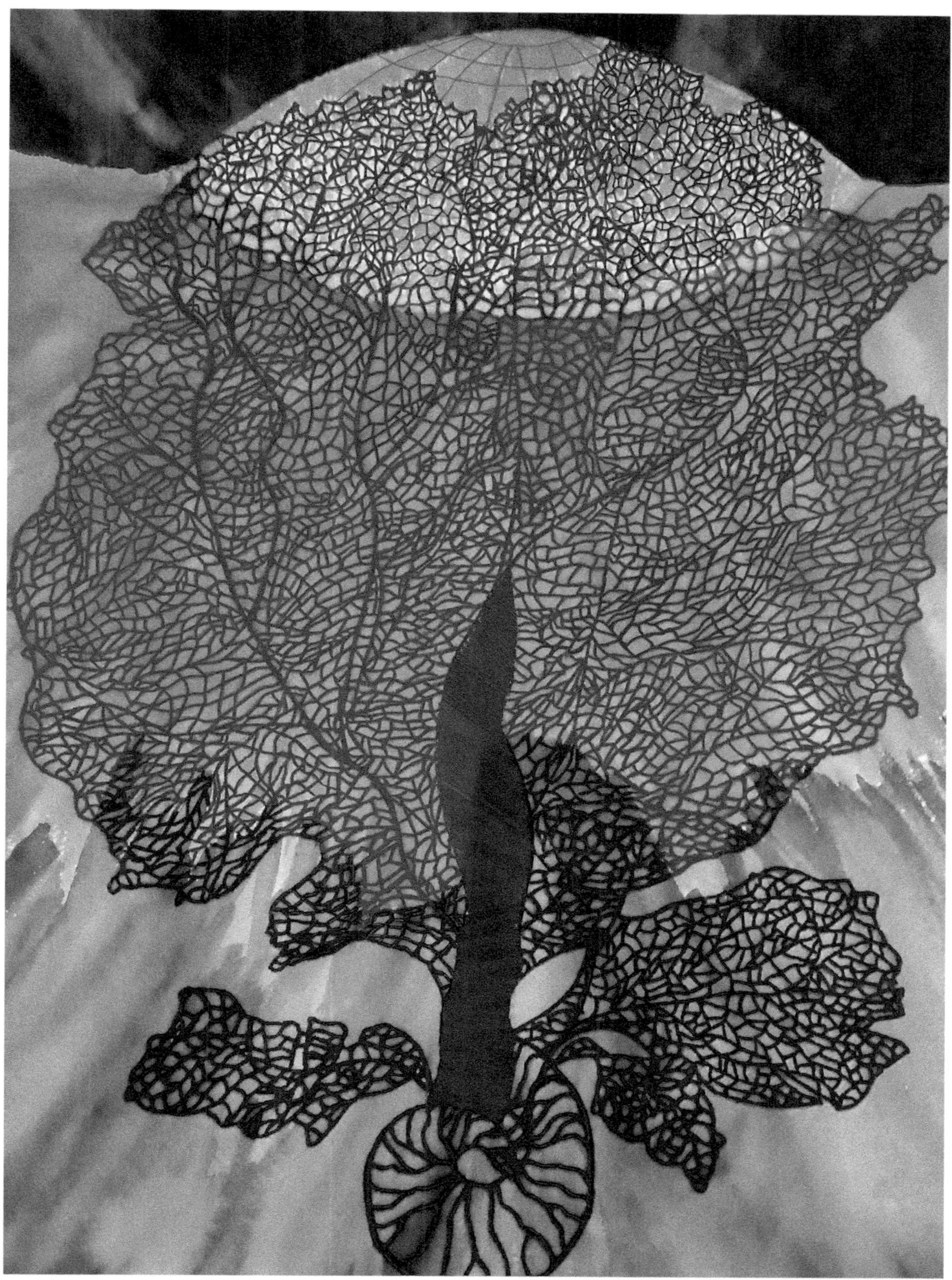

FIGURE 0.1. Joy Enomoto (Kanaka Maoli), *Nuclear Hemorrhage: Enewetak Does Not Forget*, 2017, watercolor and thread, 16 × 12 in. (unframed). Collection of Brandy Nālani McDougall. Image courtesy of Joy Lehuanani Enomoto. See also plate 1.

were able to secure modest economic and political gains through these open forms of resistance.[7]

N. A. J. Taylor and Robert Jacobs note that during the Cold War, nuclear scholarship focused on serving as a warning against catastrophe, to the extent that the people and places discussed were subsumed by symbolism. Today, scholarship in the emerging field of nuclear humanities, an "inclusive and diverse scholarly approach" to nuclear subjects, is better positioned to highlight localized and lived experiences of nuclear development, testing, and warfare. Following Taylor and Jacobs, in this volume contributions in the arts "have been considered just as crucial as knowledge derived by the humanities and social sciences."[8] By considering both artistic production and connected histories of activism, our intention is not to create a dichotomy *between* art and activism, but rather to include artistic production and critique as an essential *part* of what constitutes nuclear resistance. To that end, this book includes discussions and presentations of a wide variety of forms of artistic expression, including fine art, poetry, and activist art. It also includes analysis of visual culture, including monuments (and antimonuments) and memorials, and interventions from the fields of museum studies, arts education, cultural studies, and digital humanities.

The artists featured in *Exposure* focus on land that has been colonized and used for the purpose of developing nuclear weapons and nuclear energy, as well as people whose ties to that land are long and enduring. Rather than focusing entirely on destruction, Enomoto and Benale turn instead to the generative power of the people and the land. Indigenous people like the Marshall Islanders and the peoples of the many Native nations of North America have suffered some of the worst environmental and disease effects of America's push to become and remain the preeminent nuclear superpower in the world. Their lands have been used for the testing and production of nuclear weapons and the mining and waste disposal that support it. The results have included contaminated food sources on land and in the sea, spaces formerly home to small and large communities made unlivable due to high levels of radiation, and ongoing issues with disease. Sustained exposure to elevated levels of radiation have caused various cancers and other diseases, while displacement from homelands and the inability to maintain subsistence levels of fishing, hunting, and farming have created an epidemic of diabetes and other diseases resulting from a dependence on commercial processed foods.

Women have suffered disproportionately from the effects of nuclear testing, nuclear production, and nuclear waste disposal. Women are susceptible to the physical effects of radiation, such as miscarriages, fetal deformities, and cancers of the reproductive organs. But women have also faced social stigma resulting from their own physical deformities and their association with reproductive maladies, which have sometimes compromised employment and marriage prospects—one of the best-known cases being that of the twenty-five "Hiroshima Maidens" who were brought to the United States for plastic surgery treatment in 1955.

These effects have been felt not only among the Indigenous communities of the Marshall Islands and the American West, where nuclear testing, uranium mining to support such testing, and nuclear waste disposal have taken place since the 1940s, but also among diverse populations from New Mexico and Nevada to the Pacific Northwest. Among the first nuclear victims in the world were those unwittingly exposed to the Trinity test in Nevada in July 1945 ("Trinity downwinders") and the many tens of thousands of victims of the wartime atomic bombings of Hiroshima and Nagasaki the following month. In addition, Japanese fishermen operating throughout the Pacific Ocean, as well as the entirety of the Japanese population, found themselves potentially exposed to irradiated fish caught by those fishermen after the Bravo hydrogen bomb test at Bikini Atoll in the Marshall Islands in 1954.

By making these histories visible, artists and activists have played particularly important roles in resisting nuclear regimes. As the *Exposure* exhibition suggests, building awareness can spur social action. Through painting, photography, film, printmaking, sculpture, and installation art, visual artists have recentered the victims of nuclear technologies and those who deployed them, insisting that they be seen and heard. Artists have also documented the work of antinuclear activists, amplifying their efforts.[9] Since World War II, activists have engaged in petition drives, filed lawsuits, and pressed for recognition and treatment of radiation- and other nuclear-related medical conditions.

Nuclear narratives have been, to borrow a phrase from historian John Dower, both "triumphal and tragic."[10] There are those who have hailed the dawn of the nuclear era as creating the possibility for the end of the Second World War and for ushering in a bright era of clean energy production. Such narratives highlight security, defense, and progress, minimizing harmful impacts on bodies and lands. Yet there are many others who point to the environmental and human costs of these "triumphs," which have been borne disproportionately by people on the margins. Nuclear resistance focuses on these costs and often involves resistance to settler colonialism, criticism of American global hegemony during the Cold War, and the production of counternarratives to the orthodox discourses produced by the state.

By exploring both art and histories of activism, along with their intersections, we push against dominant narratives of resistance to the nuclear. These narratives have centered on national and international peace, along with antinuclear organizations and the state-directed nuclear activities—such as nuclear weapons production and testing, as well as the development and deployment of nuclear power technologies—they have opposed.[11] In this volume, we focus on those who have been relegated to the margins of this dominant discourse, while always having been at the center of experiences of nuclearism and resistance to it. This includes Marshall Islanders facing exile due to nuclear testing, Native North Americans living on land contaminated by uranium mining, Japanese women managing concerns about food safety, and Japanese fishermen and their families who were squeezed between the need to maintain their livelihood and to minimize their exposure to radiation.

Our geographic focus is the Pacific, particularly those regions with American nuclear power at its center. Between 1945 and the signing of the Test Ban Treaty in 1963, atmospheric and underground tests were conducted by the United States, the Soviet Union, the United Kingdom, and France in over a dozen sites across the globe. Subsequently China, India, Pakistan, North Korea, and Israel acquired nuclear weapons capabilities. In addition to Marshall Islands testing undertaken by the United States, Oceania has also been used as a site for extensive testing by France, which tested throughout French Polynesia, and the United Kingdom, which has performed nuclear tests at Maralinga in south Australia and at Malden and Christmas Islands (today part of the Republic of Kiribati).

In this volume we have chosen to focus on the "American Pacific," construed as inclusive of the Marshall Islands, Japan, and the American West, because of the rich connections made by artists and activists whose lives have been shaped directly by American Cold War policies and the nuclear programs that have undergirded them. American technological and military dominance led to development of the first atomic bombs, the first atomic test at Alamogordo, New Mexico, the first and only use of atomic weapons in wartime against the Japanese cities of Hiroshima and Nagasaki, and the first test of a hydrogen bomb at Bikini Atoll in the American military–controlled Marshall Islands. The United States has been responsible for more than half of the world's total 2,056 underground and atmospheric tests.[12] The production of these weapons and the development of nuclear reactors for energy production have depended on resource extraction, labor, and testing throughout the North American West and American-controlled Pacific territories, and have coincided with an American-led occupation of Japan and the subsequent emergence of Japanese individuals and organizations as founders and leaders of global antinuclear movements.

Resisting the Nuclear

The idea for this collection of essays emerged from a class titled "Nuclear Legacies" that we taught at the University of Oklahoma in 2016, for which we were able to invite historians and artists to campus as guest speakers. As a historian of Japan and an American studies scholar and art historian, the editors both research and write on atomic/nuclear issues. This volume includes essays by historians, artists, and activists working in (or researching and creating about) Japan, North America, and the Pacific region, all of whom deal in some way with resistance to nuclear regimes. Through the personal testimonies of survivors, lawsuits filed to demand compensation, community education programs that raise historical awareness, and artistic projects that provide social commentary, this volume illustrates that nuclear resistance can come in many forms.

The essays in this volume include contributions from the fields of anthropology, sociology, art history, arts education, environmental management, history, art, and photography, allowing for an exploration of the varied methods of resisting nuclear regimes. Each section, through a combination of interviews, scholarly essays, and discussions of contemporary art, provides layered insight into histories of activism and the arts. In each section, discussions between scholars and arts practitioners serve as a connective tissue linking theory and practice, history and artistic production. While the majority of these chapters deal explicitly with art or visual culture, some of them, such as Takemine's essay on Marshallese political resistance to nuclear testing on their lands and waters, broaden the activist context for others—in this case, the interview conducted by Holly Barker with Marshallese arts educator Ariana Tibon in the next chapter.

While this volume focuses on art and activism related to nuclear legacies, nuclear memory must also be seen within the broader context of the Pacific War. We thus begin with an essay by Margo Machida, "Targeting the Pacific," which examines artistic production related to the war, focusing on topics ranging from the internment of Japanese and Japanese Americans to the complicated legacies of the Battle of Okinawa, the wartime experience on the Japanese home front, the US Pacific War as experienced and remembered by minoritized Asian Americans and Pacific Islanders, and the effects of the atomic bomb. Machida's essay reminds us of the need to situate antinuclear activism, and artistic production that resists nuclearism, not only within a Cold War framework but also as the culmination and continuation of creative resistance to wartime.

Machida's contribution also reminds us that narratives of the Pacific War, its nuclear legacies, and the cultural and artistic production that has come from it cannot be contained by a strictly linear temporality. Nuclear histories and histories of resistance to them involve contemporary politics and social identities, the production of collective memory, and genealogies of war, technology, and social movements. This book is thus configured in a way that relates geography to chronology—in sometimes unexpected ways. Part 1, "Remembering Originary Moments: Trinity, Hiroshima, Nagasaki," focuses on the locations of the first atomic explosions and places special emphasis on exhibition and display in public discourses. Melanie Armstrong's chapter positions us at the Trinity Site in New Mexico, the location of the first test of an atomic bomb. But her essay focuses not on the chronological details of that first test but rather on contemporary tourism (and parodies of tourism) and the ways artistic and other forms of commemoration of the Trinity Site allow visitors to react to existing narratives of the legacies of the test explosion and create their own. Armstrong's chapter offers an investigation of the Trinity Monument as visual and material culture and poses important questions about the extent to which nuclear tourism can be a site for the production of nuclear resistance and counternarratives. In an interview with artist Sarah Kanouse and geographer Shiloh Krupar in the following chapter, Armstrong builds on her discussion to address the *People's Atlas of Colorado*, a digital public humanities project that uses the atlas format, including essays and artworks, to provide layered context to the thousands of nuclear sites that dot the map of Colorado.

Historian Ran Zwigenberg's essay takes us to Hiroshima to explore *hibakusha* (atomic bomb survivor) opposition to the growing embrace of nuclear power in the 1950s. His essay examines the *Atoms for Peace* exhibit at the Hiroshima Peace Museum, which effectively reduced opposition to nuclear power in Japan. Artist Shinpei Takeda also interrogates the importance of art exhibits in creating and challenging narratives about atomic bomb experiences. Takeda centers the stories of Nagasaki survivors while exploring the global contexts of his own artistic work related to Nagasaki, as his *Antimonument* exhibition travels from that originary atomic city to cities in Mexico and Germany. Takeda then engages members of the Antimonument Research Collective to address his related project, *Memory Undertow*, marking the seventy-fifth anniversary of the atomic bombing at the Hypocenter Park in Nagasaki. Takeda's *Antimonument* exhibition and the collective's reflections attempt to find new strategies of remembrance that can address traumatic histories in the present day.

Finally, Jen Richter and Sherri Wasserman argue that since 1945, the development of nuclear technologies has produced political, cultural, and environmental insecurity, while simultaneously promising increased national security. They explore the origins of this paradox of the production of nuclear in/security using documents produced by the Strategic Bombing Survey (SBS) after the United States detonated nuclear bombs over Hiroshima and Nagasaki during World War II, as well as images and videos produced during the early 1950s to introduce the public to atomic energy and foreclose public resistance to nuclear development.

Part 2, "Legacies of the Bikini Test," centers on the important March 1, 1954, nuclear test conducted by the United States at Bikini Atoll in the Marshall Islands, which provides either the backdrop or the focal point for many of the essays in this section. Nuclear testing in the Marshall Islands began well before 1954 and included atolls and islands other than Bikini, most notably Enewetak Atoll, which saw the largest number of nuclear tests (forty-three test blasts between 1948 and 1958). But the March 1, 1954, nuclear test at Bikini known as the Castle Bravo shot had significant implications and elicited a global response for a number of reasons. Castle Bravo was one of the first detonations of a thermonuclear weapon (the first was Ivy Mike in 1952) and the most powerful nuclear weapon detonated up to that time. Its strength and destructive capacity would be exceeded only once, by the Tsar Bomba tested in 1961 by the Soviet Union. The exposure of Japanese fishermen to radioactive fallout from the Bravo shot, most famously those on the tuna trawler *Lucky Dragon No. 5*, led to broader recognition of hibakusha suffering in Japan and eventually to the coalescing of a global antinuclear movement with Japanese witness-survivors at its center.[13] Chapters in this section explore the various geographical and temporal impacts of the Bikini test and examine its effect on women's movements for peace in 1950s Tokyo, Japanese fishermen's advocacy for compensation after the test blast severely impacted their livelihood, and antinuclear activism among the Marshallese people, whose home islands were the site of this and other nuclear tests.

Providing historical context, Seiichirō Takemine closely examines the Marshall Islanders protest movement that emerged after US nuclear testing began in 1954 and its impact on US policy. Holly Barker, who serves as a commissioner to the Republic of the Marshall Islands' National Nuclear Commission (NNC), conducted an interview with Marshallese arts educator Ariana Tibon, the NNC's director for education and outreach. They were joined by NNC research assistants Leimamo Wase and Jasmine Alik and secretary Keyoka Kabua to discuss the role of community and youth art as a response to the nuclear legacy. Building on his groundbreaking 1991 book, *Nuclear Landscapes*, Atomic Photographers Guild member Peter Goin contrasts the physical remains of Marshall Islands detonation sites with Mesoamerican pyramids in Mexico and Guatemala. He imagines human legacies of the nuclear age through a photographic meditation on the nuclear monuments left in the Marshall Islands. The nuclear age, he contends, constitutes our human legacy; what we will leave behind us in the postcivilized world will be these nuclear sites. Finally, Akiko Takenaka and Yuka Tsuchiya Moriguchi rethink conventional narratives of how antinuclear activism was established in Japan following the *Lucky Dragon* incident. Takenaka argues that an emphasis on the participation of women served to depoliticize peace activism, while Moriguchi explores the fishermen's silence in the decades following this incident, questioning what prompted a small minority finally to dissent.

Part 3, "Transpacific Activisms," explores political and artistic antinuclear activism that crosses borders in Cold War and post–Cold War contexts. Naoko Wake examines the persistent racism and ableism directed at American hibakusha, which led to failed efforts to pass bills to support them medically and their exclusion from the Radiation Exposure Compensation Act. Elyssa Faison pairs the work of American antinuclear activist Barbara Reynolds with Hiroshima activist Kawamoto Ichirō, demonstrating the limits of international antinuclear cooperation in the Cold War era. Alison Fields conducts an interview with Diné artist Will Wilson, whose *Auto Immune Response* series features the cultivation of indigenous plants in postnuclear landscapes in the American Southwest. Fields compares this work with artists who reimagine food cultivation following the nuclear disaster in Fukushima.

Like other work in the nuclear humanities, this book eschews analysis of nuclear policy, national security, and nuclear science and technology, in favor of what historian Robert Jacobs describes as "the real-world presence of nuclear technologies and their impact on lives and communities." Jacobs describes the period between 1946 and 1991, during which over two thousand nuclear weapons were tested globally, as a time of "limited nuclear war." Thousands of people became "global hibakusha," victims of atomic blasts who suffered from radioactive fallout.[14] Others exposed to radiation through uranium mining, nuclear materials processing, and nuclear waste storage are also among the global hibakusha. These global hibakusha are at the center of nuclear resistance as artists and as activists. They are agents of such resistance, as well as the subjects of artistic and documentary reflection. This volume centers their experiences by focusing on political acts and political art. The legacies of nuclear regimes—as well as attempts to erase or obscure those legacies—always remind us that we will forever live in a nuclear world, and that every remembrance, erasure, intervention, act of resistance, or act of representation of the nuclear will always be political.

Notes

1. Text panel, *Exposure: Native Art and Political Ecology*, IAIA Museum of Contemporary Native Arts, Santa Fe, New Mexico, August 20, 2021–July 10, 2022.
2. Text panel, *Exposure: Native Art and Political Ecology.*
3. Text panel, *Exposure: Native Art and Political Ecology.*
4. "Curate: A Discussion with 'Exposure' Co-curator Erin Vink," *YouTube*, October 25, 2021, https://www.youtube.com/watch?v=ysxPcXYu2Ro.
5. Stellan Vinthagen and Anna Johansson, "Everyday Resistance: Exploration of a Concept and Its Theories," *Resistance Studies Magazine*, no. 1 (2013): 1.
6. Martha Smith-Norris, *Domination and Resistance: The United States and the Marshall Islands during the Cold War* (Honolulu: University of Hawai'i Press, 2016), 7.
7. Smith-Norris, *Domination and Resistance*, 12.
8. N. A. J. Taylor and Robert Jacobs, "Introduction: On Hiroshima Becoming History," in *Reimagining Hiroshima and Nagasaki: Nuclear Humanities in the Post–Cold War*, ed. N. A. J. Taylor and Robert Jacobs (New York: Routledge, 2020).
9. See, for example, Akiko Takenaka's discussion of the Hiroshima Panels in this volume.
10. John Dower, "Triumphal and Tragic Narratives of the War in Asia," in *Living with the Bomb: American and Japanese Cultural Conflicts in the Nuclear Age*, ed. Laura Hein and Mark Selden (Armonk, NY: M. E. Sharpe, 1997), 37–51.
11. See, for example, Lawrence Wittner's important three-volume work *The Struggle against the Bomb* (Stanford, CA: Stanford University Press, 1993–2003).
12. Arms Control Association Fact Sheets and Briefs, https://www.armscontrol.org/factsheets/nucleartesttally.
13. See, for example, chapter 1 in Lawrence Wittner, *The Struggle against the Bomb*, vol. 2, *Resisting the Bomb: A History of the World Nuclear Disarmament Movement, 1954–1970* (Stanford, CA: Stanford University Press, 1997); chapter 3 in James Orr, *The Victim as Hero: Ideologies of Peace and National Identity in Postwar Japan* (Honolulu: University of Hawai'i Press, 2001); and Ran Zwigenberg, *Hiroshima: The Origins of Global Memory Culture* (New York: Cambridge University Press, 2014).
14. Robert A. Jacobs, *Nuclear Bodies: The Global Hibakusha* (New Haven, CT: Yale University Press, 2022), xvi, 14–15.

Targeting the Pacific

World War II in Asian American and Pacific Islander Art

MARGO MACHIDA

World War II is considered the deadliest and most destructive conflict in human history. Affecting entire regions, this far-ranging contest created new geographic realities, birthed the nuclear age, and ushered in decades of struggle and instability under a radically altered postwar global political structure. While warfare swept across Europe, Africa, and Asia, major combat between the United States and Japan mainly occurred in the Pacific Ocean. In an immense maritime expanse with more islands than are found in all other seas combined, Japan's challenge and the US response entailed a fierce struggle for strategically located Pacific islands.

As demonstrated by this volume, the arts play a dynamic role in memorializing and bearing witness to atomic legacies. But this difficult history and the artistic expressions it elicits exist within a larger continuum of experience and cultural production, both wartime and postwar. This chapter examines the many-sided reverberations of the Pacific War and the ongoing impact of the US presence in the Pacific as compelling themes for artists of Asian American, Asian, and Pacific Islander heritage. Throughout, visual art provides a prominent platform for subaltern voices to address the wartime era and the effects of atomic warfare and bomb development—including actions heralding the conflict and the continued imprint of the United States and other Western militaries in this vast transoceanic arena, from the distinctive vantage points of firsthand witnesses and their descendants.

For Japanese American communities, America's entry into the Second World War was a defining moment. As Japan sought hegemony over the Asia Pacific region, by the end of 1942 the Japanese Empire's advance reached its farthest extent by occupying and attacking territories as far afield as Alaska's Aleutian Islands, Australia, and the borders of India. Amid intensifying domestic hysteria generated by Japan's 1941 air assault on Pearl Harbor and seizure of European and US colonial possessions in East and Southeast Asia, over 110,000 Japanese Americans—men, women, and children—were forcibly relocated from the US Pacific coast to remote camps scattered from California to Arkansas.

The 1942 to 1945 internment under Executive Order 9066 exacted a tremendous psychic and material toll on US citizens of Japanese heritage, who were left deeply traumatized and destitute long after the war ended. It also extended to encompass ethnic Japanese expelled from Canada, South America and the Caribbean, and even an Indigenous Alaskan group. While the internment is pivotal for Japanese Americans, Asian American and Asian artists of Korean, Chinese, and Filipino heritage frequently cite Japan's colonization of Korea and Taiwan, the war against China, the occupation of the Philippines, and the unfathomably brutal policies of the Japanese military: mass killings, forced labor, and institutionalized sexual slavery.

To shift attention from a predominantly continental and domestic American focus, contemporary Asian American, Asian, and Asian diasporic artists are placed in conversation with Indigenous Pacific counterparts. Assembling projects by artists typically not seen together underscores the generative possibilities offered by transpacific conceptual frames. Significantly, this wider focus also points to moves by artists from Japan to access and engage diverse audiences around shared histories of conflict and contact. Extending from Hawai'i and the Aleutian Islands to Japan, Okinawa, the Philippines, Tahiti, Guam, and the Marianas, these artists' projects bring forward multilocated perspectives that gesture to complex histories of contact, circulation, and conflict.

Internments and Wartime Propaganda

Antic and mordant in equal measure, the satiric imagery of Japanese American painter, printmaker, and performance artist Roger Shimomura, born in Seattle in 1939, is emblematic of the pernicious effects of xenophobia and stereotyping on Japanese American communities. Shimomura's prodigious output is replete with Pop Art–like mash-ups involving cross-cultural encounters between Asians and white Americans, drawn from an eclectic array of sources, including advertising, comics, cartoons, animation, and traditional Japanese woodblock prints.

The artist's concerns are indelibly shaped by a World War II childhood during which his family was interned. Beginning in 1978, Shimomura produced paintings and prints to address the mass imprisonment, including a long-running series based on the poignant camp diary of his grandmother. Self-imagery also features strongly in Shimomura's projects, where the artist depicts himself in prototypically American and Asian guises as superheroes, villains, and martial artists. Underlining these citations of popular icons is the preoccupation of a US-born artist steeped in American culture yet regarded as forever foreign because of Asian ancestry. Offering a stark contrast between imposed stereotypes and actual individuals, Shimomura's *Different Citizens* (2009) juxtaposes a somber self-portrait against a caricatured image of the Japanese emperor Hirohito, drawn from his extensive collection of US war propaganda.[1] The format echoes a 1941 *Life* magazine photo essay, "How To Tell Japs from the Chinese," which instructed Americans on how to distinguish "friendly" Asian allies from the new Japanese enemy.[2] Presenting Prime Minister Tōjō Hideki as "typical," Japanese are assigned "primitive" cartoonish features while Chinese are styled as closer to a Eurocentric ideal.

The 2002 painting *Remember Pearl Harbor,* based on Shimomura's numerous encounters with "racial insensitivity," underscores the significance of the 1941 surprise assault in shaping domestic perceptions of Japanese long into the postwar period.[3] Alluding to the artist's resentment over a mid-1960s encounter in which an elderly white woman screamed, "You Japs ought to go back to where you came from," Shimomura sardonically portrays a Japanese pilot dive-bombing a scowling Caucasian woman.[4]

While the World War II internment in the continental United States is extensively documented, California-based artist Shizu Saldamando's (b. 1978) mixed media installation *Farewell to Honouliuli* (2017) points to the lesser known imprisonment of a portion of Hawai'i's Japanese American population from 1943 to 1946. The title refers to the name of the largest confinement site in the Hawaiian Islands. Staged in Honolulu, Hawai'i, this participatory art project was developed for *'Ae Kai: A Culture Lab*

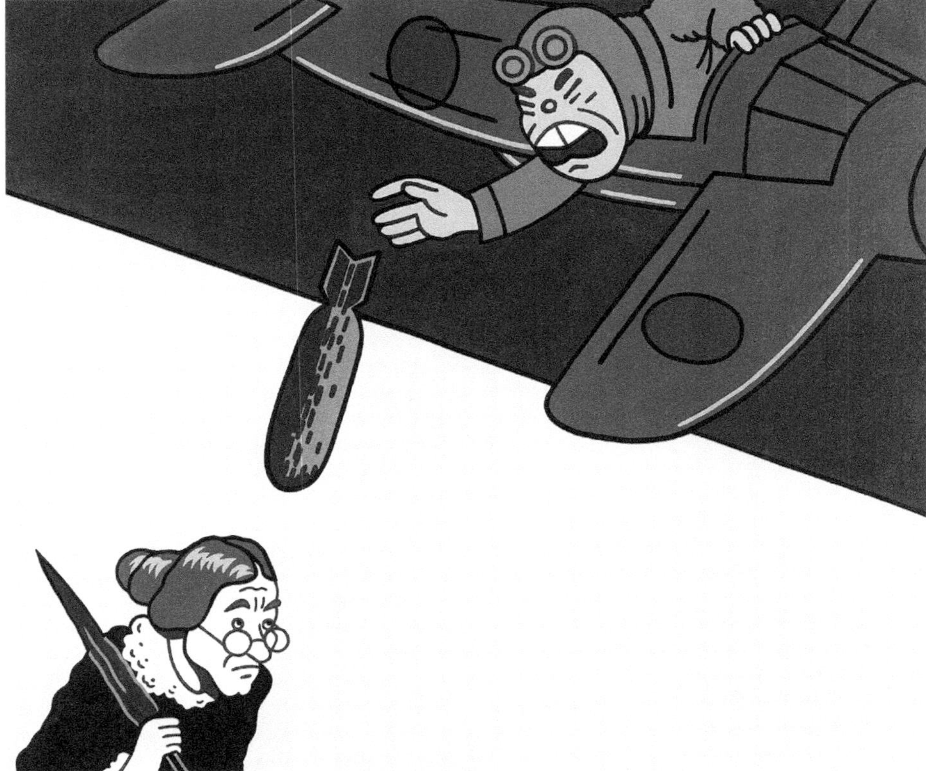

FIGURE 1.1. Roger Shimomura, *Remember Pearl Harbor*, 2002, acrylic on canvas, 20 × 24 in. Collection of the artist. Photograph courtesy of the artist.

on Convergence, a 2017 arts festival organized by the Smithsonian Asian Pacific American Center in Washington, DC.[5]

An artist of mixed Japanese and Mexican heritage, Saldamando has relatives who were interned. To pay homage to all interned Japanese Americans, she solicited visitors' participation in fabricating a large lei—a Polynesian garland of flowers—from shredded paper replicas of federal documents authorizing proscriptive policies for groups historically deemed to threaten national interests.

Used in Hawai'i as a symbol of remembrance among other things, the lei is entwined with black ribbons to recall the paper wreaths crafted by

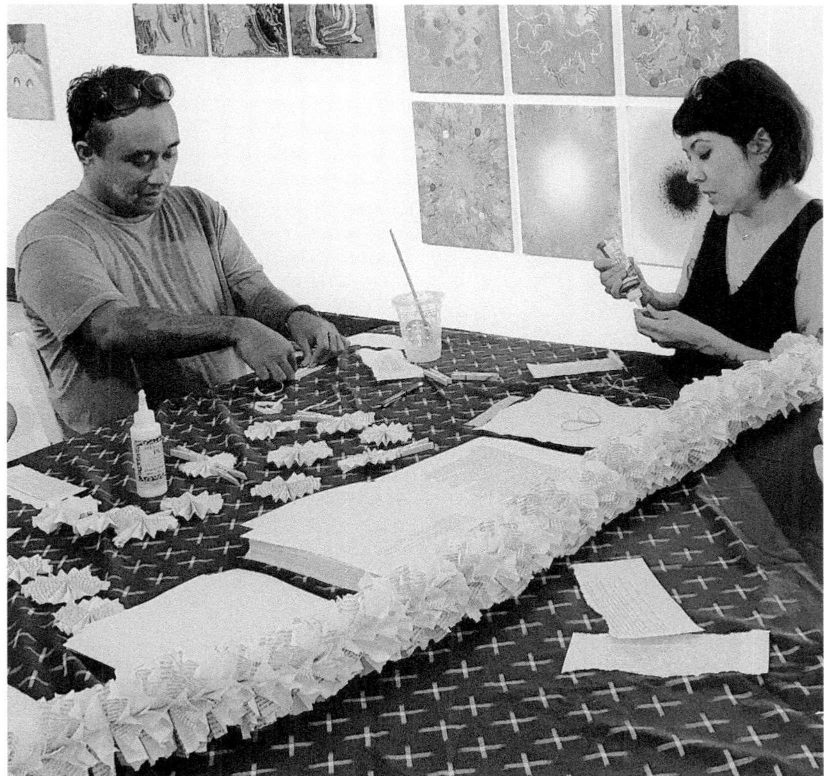

FIGURE 1.2. Shizu Saldamando, *Farewell to Honouliuli: Reflections on Manzanar, Rohwer, and the Japanese Incarceration in Hawai'i*, communal workshop in progress, 2017, mixed media installation, *'Ae Kai: A Culture Lab on Convergence*, July 7–9, 2017, Honolulu, Hawai'i. Photograph by Len Higa. Photograph courtesy of the artist.

internees to honor fellow Japanese Americans who perished during the war.[6] As a corresponding commentary on the Trump administration's anti-immigrant policies, Saldamando includes the 2017 edict banning entrants from many Muslim nations. The hands-on act of ripping apart and repurposing these "politically loaded" texts allows visitors to share in the artist's "symbolic gesture of resistance" against the federal government's recurrent demonization of entire categories of people.[7]

In 2005, Hawai'i-born Mona Higuchi (b. 1942), an Arizona-based artist of mixed Japanese and Korean heritage, addressed the internment of Aleutian natives after learning that they were included in federal reparations

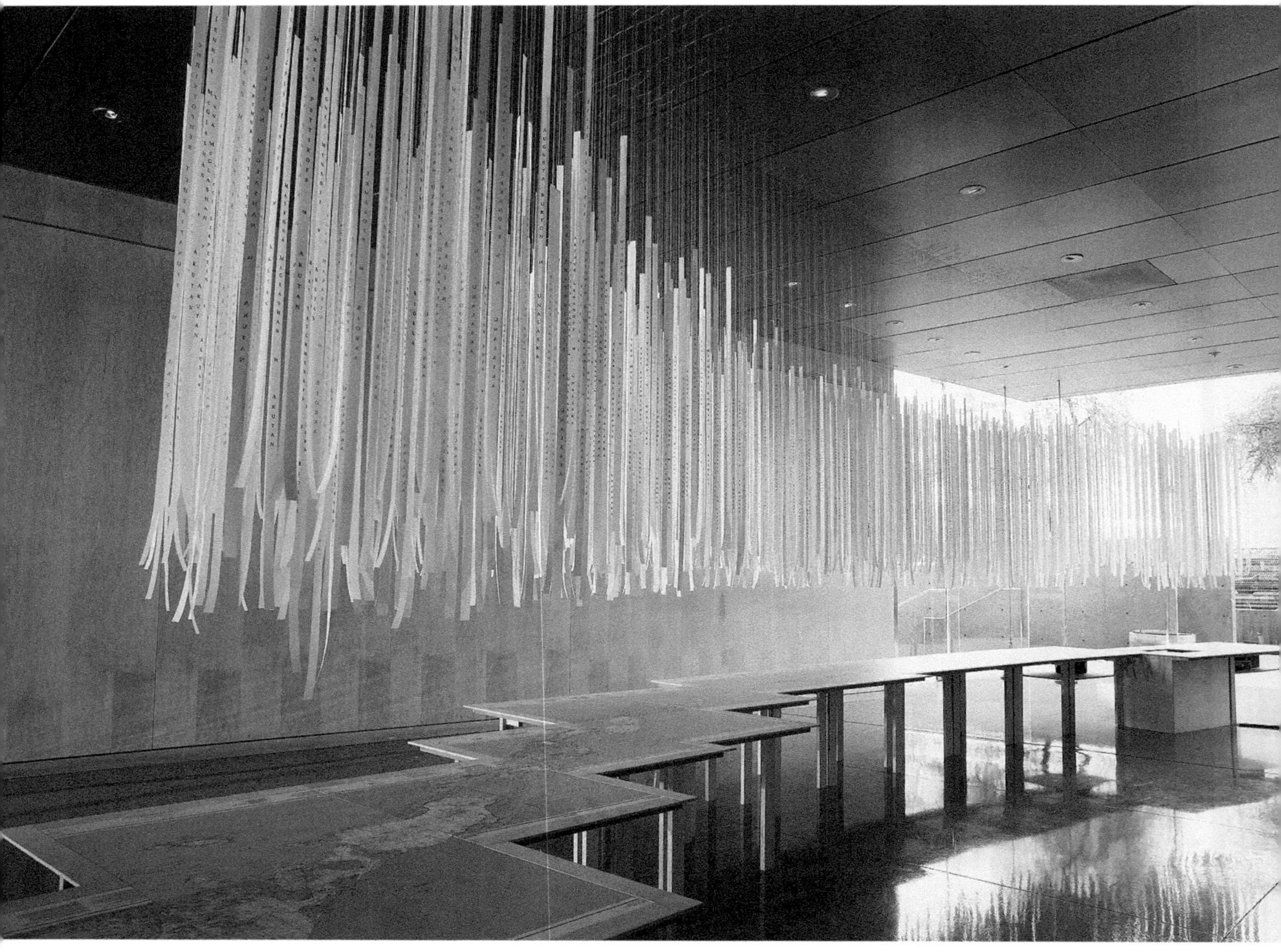

FIGURE 1.3. Mona Higuchi, detail from *Relocation: Alaska 1942–45*, 2005, multimedia installation in collaboration with Richard Lerman, sound and video artist, Central Gallery, Burton Barr Central Library, Phoenix, Arizona. Photograph by Brandon Sullivan. Photograph courtesy of the artist.

provided to former internees in 1988.[8] The multimedia installation *Relocation: Alaska 1942* commemorates a largely forgotten event, when in early 1942 Japanese forces occupied the southernmost islands of the Aleutian chain.

The United States forcibly relocated the Indigenous Unangan inhabitants from neighboring islands to set up military bases, profoundly disrupting their communities.[9] The central component of the installation suggests the elongated shape of the Aleutian chain by presenting US Geological Survey maps of the region on a series of tables grouped together to form a twenty-four-foot-long arc. Suspended above, a cloud-like cluster of nine hundred white vellum strips memorializes each evacuee by name, age, and place of origin. On an adjacent birch platform, a stand of willow branches evokes the Alaskan woodlands of the distant mainland, where the natives were compelled to move, while video monitors play images and sounds recorded at the relocation sites.

The US Pacific War: Signs of Presence and Absence

Though born in New York City, Indiana-based artist Osamu James Nakagawa (b. 1962) views himself as having acquired another culture through marriage to an Okinawan woman. Since the early 2000s Nakagawa has repeatedly visited Okinawa to photograph sites of the final major battle of the Pacific War. Trapped between Japanese and American forces, nearly a quarter of the civilian population died in the onslaught. Okinawa's numerous caves—traditional sacred sites—provided shelter for Japan's soldiers and desperate locals alike. Many noncombatants committed suicide by jumping from the island's sheer seaside cliffs.

Testifying to the fullness of their history, the mute legacy of the battle-blackened limestone caves and lofty cliff faces fostered the artist's long engagement with these natural features of the Okinawan landscape. The stark rugged beauty depicted in the digitally altered composite photographs of the interrelated 2008 *Banta (Cliffs)* and 2009–11 *Gama (Caves)* series belies the fierce combat witnessed by this coastal landscape. Citing the "act of searching for something that you cannot see" as a leitmotif, in the *Gama (Caves)* series Nakagawa employs powerful flashlights to scrutinize the contours of these pitch-dark caverns and uncover traces of their former occupants.[10] The resulting shadowy images register a sense of historical vertigo. By conjuring these ambiguous "interstitial space[s]," the artist—who spent his formative years in Japan and maintains active affiliations with America, Okinawa, and Japan—seeks to "critique all three sides of the story" surrounding this tragic history.[11]

Nakagawa later traveled to island battlegrounds seized earlier in the American advance. The 1944 campaign for Saipan and Tinian in the Northern Mariana Islands, now a US territory, placed Japanese cities within range of the new American bomber, the B-29. In forty images of the *Remains* series (2001–9) the artist draws on photographs he shot in Saipan, Tinian, and Okinawa to foreground the capacity of absence to educe shared haunted histories. To trigger associations with how visible "elements of the past quietly remain today," the images are individually paired with letterpress captions in Japanese and English.[12]

In *Tank* (2006), a US Sherman tank, rusting and semisubmerged in a lagoon, soundlessly attests to the ferocious assault on Saipan. Images from nearby Tinian depict a traditional torii gate and stone lantern, artifacts of prewar Japanese colonization. Saipan had the largest civilian Japanese population, with many inhabitants—anticipating the mass suicide in Okinawa—throwing themselves off cliffs at the battle's conclusion.[13]

Tinian has singular significance as the site where the atomic strikes on Japan were launched. Much larger than standard bombs, these weapons were hoisted into the B-29s from specially built loading pits. One of these recessed structures, marked with a commemorative plaque and encapsulated by a protective glass structure, is the subject of the drily acerbic image titled *A-Bomb Loading Pit*, Tinian Island, 2006. Another photograph, emblematic of how a fifth of Okinawa remains occupied by the US military, captures an American plane flying over its home base to signify how that presence provides locals with a "constant reminder of WWII."[14]

The sculptures and installations of Kaili Chun (b. 1962), a Native Hawaiian with Chinese and European ancestry, confront the "challenge [of] continu[ing] to exist as a Hawaiian."[15] Having grown up in an island environment shaped by US interests, the artist recognizes that the present-day lives of the Hawaiian people are necessarily envisioned beside and against the dominant non-Indigenous presence. Invoking this tension, Chun

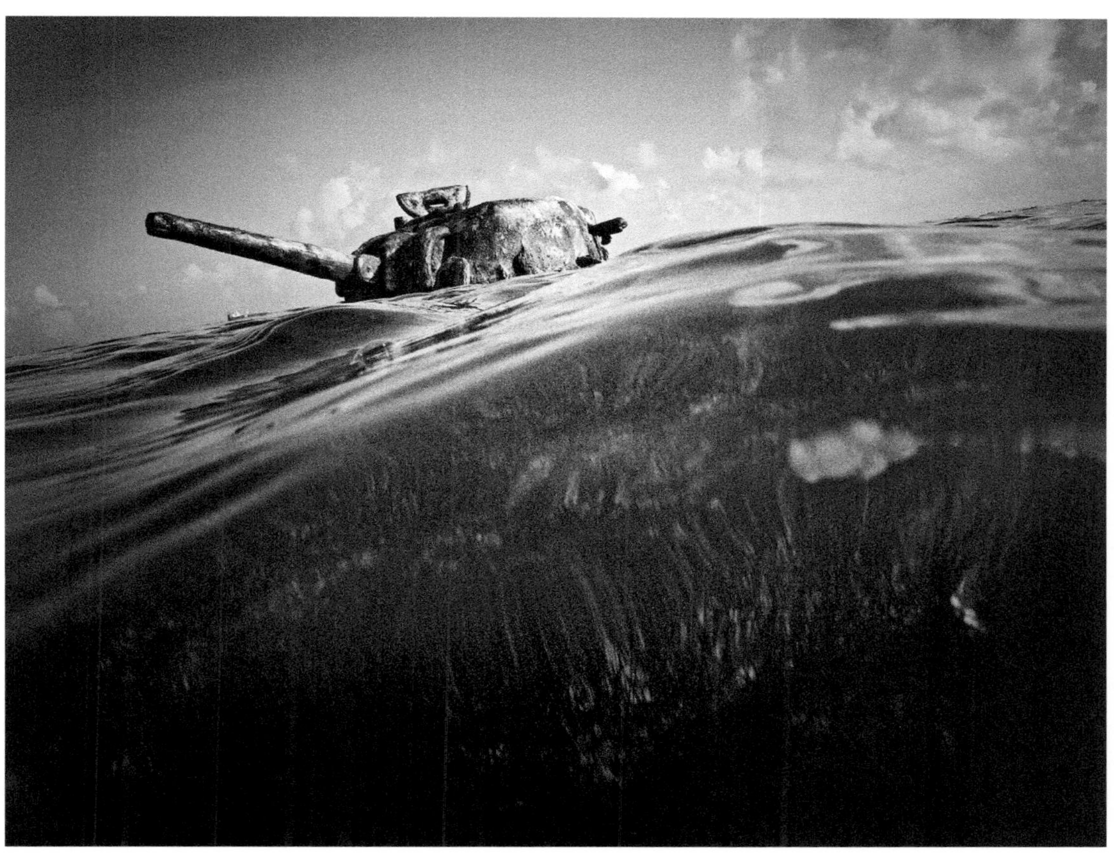

FIGURE 1.4. Osamu James Nakagawa, *Tank*, Saipan, 2006, from the *Remains* series (2001–9), archival pigment print on Epson Ultrasmooth paper with letterpress text, dimensions 15.5 × 22 in., image size 8 × 10 in. Photograph courtesy of the artist.

probes points of mutual contact by which Indigenous positions are constituted in response to this inescapable state of affairs.

The 2006 sculptural installation *The Irony of Trust* brings forward this mixed legacy via the US scramble to survey and assert sovereignty over uninhabited Pacific islands at a time when Japanese expansionism was increasingly viewed as a rising threat. Mounted at the University of Hawai'i Art Gallery in the 2006 group exhibition *Reconstructing Memories* (November 5—December 13), *The Irony of Trust* references the covert settlement operation using young Native Hawaiian volunteers to extend US dominion in the Pacific region.[16] Deployed over the seven-year span between 1935 and 1942, the mission established de facto control over remote, uninhabited islands located along strategic air routes in the Equatorial Pacific.

The Native Hawaiians, presumed to be better suited to "stand the rigors" of harsh tropical environments, lived and worked in temporary encampments under challenging conditions.[17] Two of the volunteers died when Japanese aircraft bombed the islands a day after the attack on Pearl Harbor. By early 1942 the remainder were evacuated and "instructed to remain silent" about their involvement.[18] As the title indicates, Chun finds it deeply ironic that a "colonized people" should be called upon "to colonize another land in the name of the colonizer," even as she concurrently recognizes that the selection of these men to serve their country is a source of deep pride for her parents' generation.[19]

Standing six feet tall, the stelae-like group composing *The Irony of Trust* acts as an unofficial memorial to Native Hawaiian support of US prewar preparations in the Pacific. Chun erected five closely clustered roughhewn rectangular concrete pillars, corresponding to the occupied sites, embedded with dark Hawaiian basalt rocks to honor the Native Hawaiians' "amazing accomplishments, and the grace in which they served.[20] An artist with an architectural background, Chun chose forms and building materials associated with Europe—the Greco-Roman column and concrete—to embody the dominance of "Western culture and expansionism" in Hawai'i. By contrast, the artist's use of local stone signals the animate presence of the Indigenous people who trace their spiritual and genealogical relationships to the land and denotes how the *'āina*, the land itself, has been annexed for externally imposed structures, both physical and social.

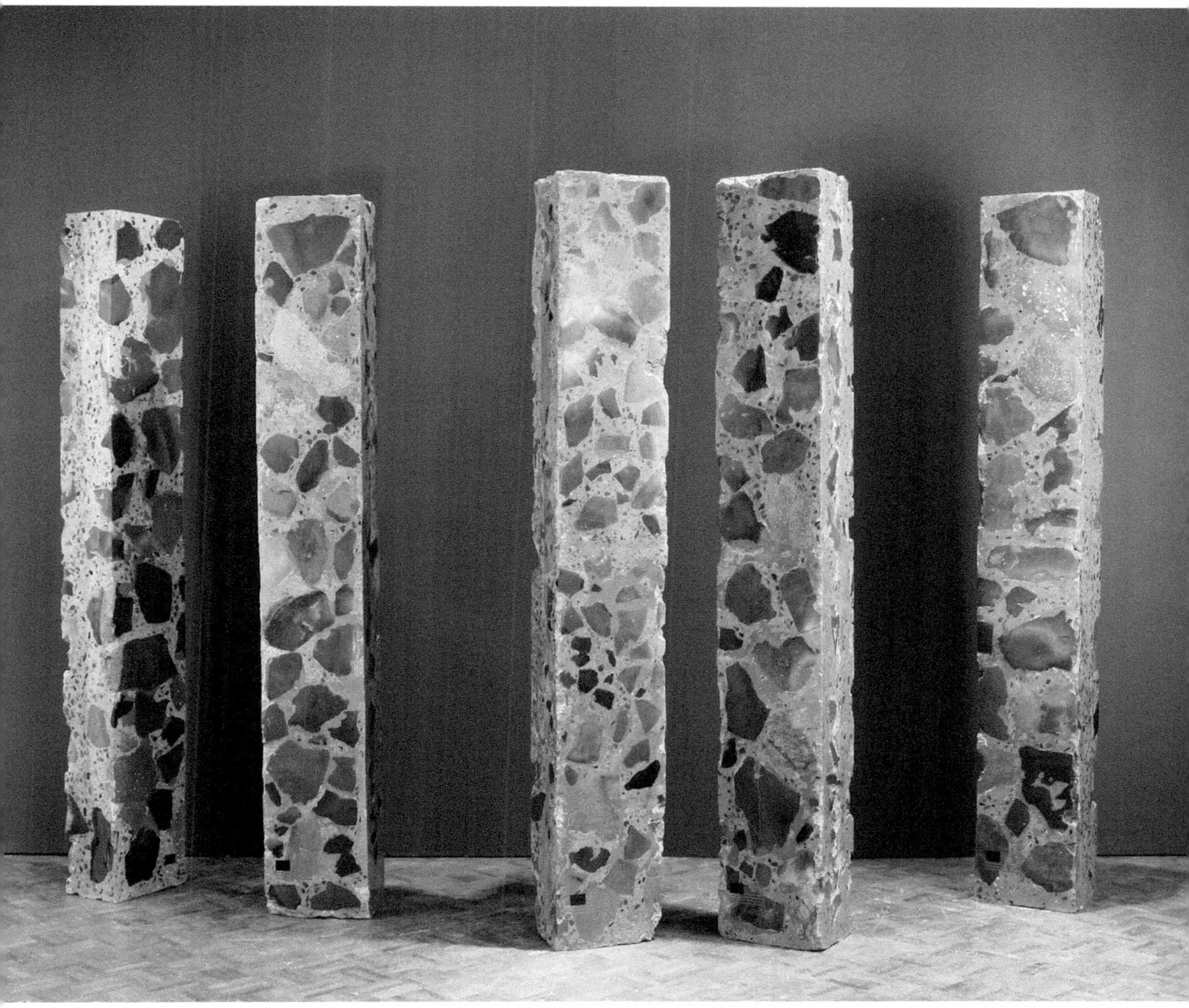

FIGURE 1.5. Kaili Chun, *The Irony of Trust*, 2006, steel-reinforced concrete, basalt, 72 × 11 × 11 in. each. Installation view, *Reconstructing Memories*, University of Hawai'i at Mānoa Art Gallery, Honolulu, November 5–December 13, 2006. Photograph by Hal Lum. Photograph courtesy of University of Hawai'i at Mānoa Art Gallery.

Much as crushed volcanic basalt provides an additive for concrete used to construct the local infrastructure, the artist's incorporation of this material likewise manifests the indispensable role of Hawaiians in "build[ing] the very system that positions us at the lowest end of society."[21]

Often centered on connections among the Philippines, maritime Asia, and the Americas, Michael Arcega's (b. 1973) projects invoke centuries-old transpacific encounters. As American goods have been incorporated in Filipinos' daily lives, food provides the Philippine-born, San Francisco–based artist with a visceral medium to register cultural hybridity via the impact of US domination. Growing up in Manila in the 1970s before moving to California, the artist nostalgically recollects eating Spam. Curious about the pervasive acceptance of this widely sold canned American processed pork product in the Philippines, Arcega realized that Spam is an artifact of the US military presence, having made its way to civilian populations across the Asian Pacific region during World War II.

SPAM/MAPS (1999–2007), crafted as a series of low-relief wall sculptures in which all landmasses are carved from slabs of Spam, draws on the processed meat itself as a sculptural medium. With the Philippines, Guam, Japan, Okinawa, South Korea, China, and Hawai'i constituting the largest present-day markets for Spam, Arcega uses this simulated cartographic device in the form of world, regional, and country "maps" to offer a farcically apt emblem for "America's ongoing influence on many nations."[22]

(de)fence (2017) is a participatory installation that combines images and texts with off-the-shelf objects and industrial hardware to draw attention to historic commonalities between Guam (Guåhan in the local language) and Hawai'i. A collaboration between Craig Santos Perez (b. 1980), a native Chamoru/Chamorro poet, scholar, and activist from Guam, and his wife, Brandy Nālani McDougall, a Kānaka Maoli / Native Hawaiian poet from Hawai'i, this mixed media piece was exhibited in Honolulu as part of *'Ae Kai: A Culture Lab on Convergence.* An accompanying publication affirmed connections and solidarity among Pacific islands by recognizing the active part Indigenous artists and writers play in regional demilitarization movements.[23]

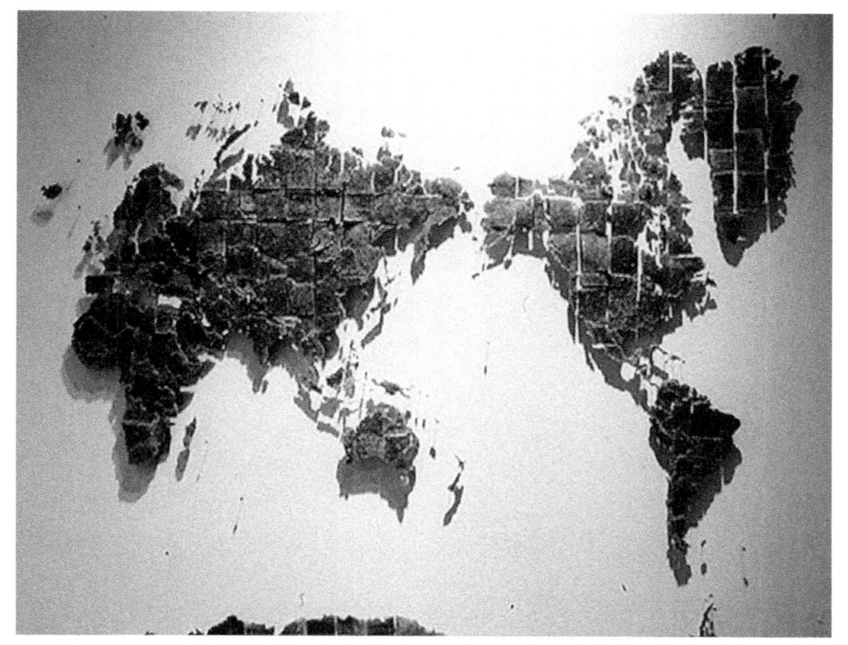

FIGURE 1.6. Michael Arcega, *SPAM/MAPS: Oceania*, 2007, Spam luncheon meat, 4 ft. × 3 ft. × 2 in. Collection of the artist.Photograph courtesy of the artist. See also plate 2.

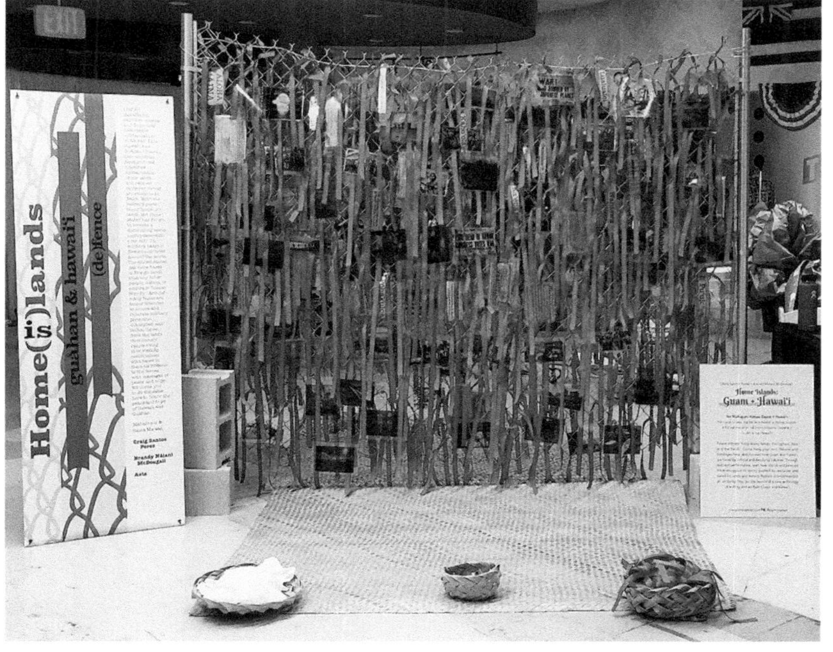

FIGURE 1.7. Craig Santos Perez and Brandy Nālani McDougall, *(de)fence*, 2017. Mixed media installation with steel mesh fence (8 × 10 ft.). *'Ae Kai: A Culture Lab on Convergence*, July 7–9, 2017, Honolulu, Hawai'i. Photograph by Craig Santos Perez courtesy of the artists. See also plate 3.

The central component and symbol of *(de)fence*, to which its punning title alludes, is a section of chain-link fence made from steel wires interlocked in a distinctive diamond-shaped grid pattern. Visible throughout present-day Guam and Hawai'i as metallic barriers snaking their way across the landscape, Perez underscores how this "very prevalent" feature sharply demarcates "inside and outside, what's occupied military land and what's civilian land."[24] Stretched upright between six-foot-tall steel posts, the wire mesh fence is densely festooned with bright red and white ribbons and fabric strips hung back-to-back with texts and archival images. To give equal weight to each island, the front face is dedicated to Hawai'i and the obverse to Guam, the open latticework configuration enabling visitors to literally see through the links these islands have with one another.[25] Imprinted on transparent plastic sheets, key wartime and postwar photographs, newspaper headlines, and statistics document the shared history that "haunts our present moment": the bombing of Pearl Harbor, the Japanese military occupation and US "reinvasion" of Guam, Spam labels, nuclear testing, and island-based protest movements.[26]

Nestled within the thicket of material are inspirational handwritten messages affirming visions of "hope, peace, and demilitarization," informed by ribbons tied by protestors to barriers that demarcate the demilitarized zone in Korea and US air bases in Okinawa.[27] Since visitor involvement was integral to the agitprop-like project's realization, the artist-collaborators provided viewers with writing implements and fabric materials set out in baskets on mats woven from leaves of the pandanus tree, found throughout the tropical Pacific.

Wartime Japan: Memories and Legacies

Centered on the Japanese fighter plane that gained notoriety for its devastating assault on Pearl Harbor and for kamikaze suicide attacks against US naval vessels, Japanese artist Katsushige Nakahashi's (b. 1955) series *Zero Projects* (1999–2016) provides a catalyst to engage in supranational dialogue. From a generation without personal experience of the Pacific War, Nakahashi is acutely aware of the postwar Japanese public's disconnection from wartime events. Although the war deeply marks earlier Japanese generations, most rarely speak of those difficult times. Indeed, it was only after his work was shown publicly that the artist's father disclosed his own World War II role as a mechanic for the Zero fighter plane. Prompted to address the rupture between generations and the lacunae in his homeland's historical memory through the immediacy of face-to-face interaction, to date the artist's mnemonically focused project has been staged in nineteen venues connected to Japanese aerial warfare in Japan, Australia, and America.

Commercially available Japanese models of the Zero act as haptic conduits to these historic events. Their use stems from the artist's childhood fascination with assembling plastic toy military aircraft that ironically represented his only immediate means of relating to the war.[28] For these photo-sculptural projects, Nakahashi shoots thousands of microphotographs of the miniature's external details. These images are greatly enlarged and systematically taped together in patchwork sections around locally scavenged wood and plastic frameworks to form highly scaled-up impermanent versions of the model plane, reminiscent of unique, single-use parade floats.

Public participation and dialogue are crucial to the *Zero Project*'s realization, as local volunteers are solicited to construct each replica onsite. By including military veterans and wartime eyewitnesses in this open-ended, socially driven process, space is created for past enemies to come to terms with their memories of the period and to share in one another's reflections on the violent nature of warfare and its traumatic aftereffects. Such encounters underscore the artist's pivotal aim, to "work toward a true reconciliation" via respectful mutual interaction.[29] To provide a sense of finality, the project's contributors form a procession at each staging to carry the assembled Zero effigies outdoors for immolation in a ceremony equated with the Japanese ritual of "lighting fires to send off the souls of the dead."[30]

Zero Project #BII-120, Hawaii, mounted in Honolulu at the University of Hawai'i Art Gallery for the 2006 group exhibition *Reconstructing Memories,* invokes the crash landing on the Hawaiian island of Ni'ihau of a Zero that earlier participated in the attack on Pearl Harbor.[31] Some of the remote island's Japanese American residents rendered assistance to the injured pilot prior to his violent death in a confrontation with Indigenous Hawaiians.[32] This seemingly minor incident holds significance for the artist because it is cited in some accounts as contributing to federal calls for internment by fueling suspicions about Japanese American loyalty.[33] The project in Honolulu included war veterans who served with the celebrated

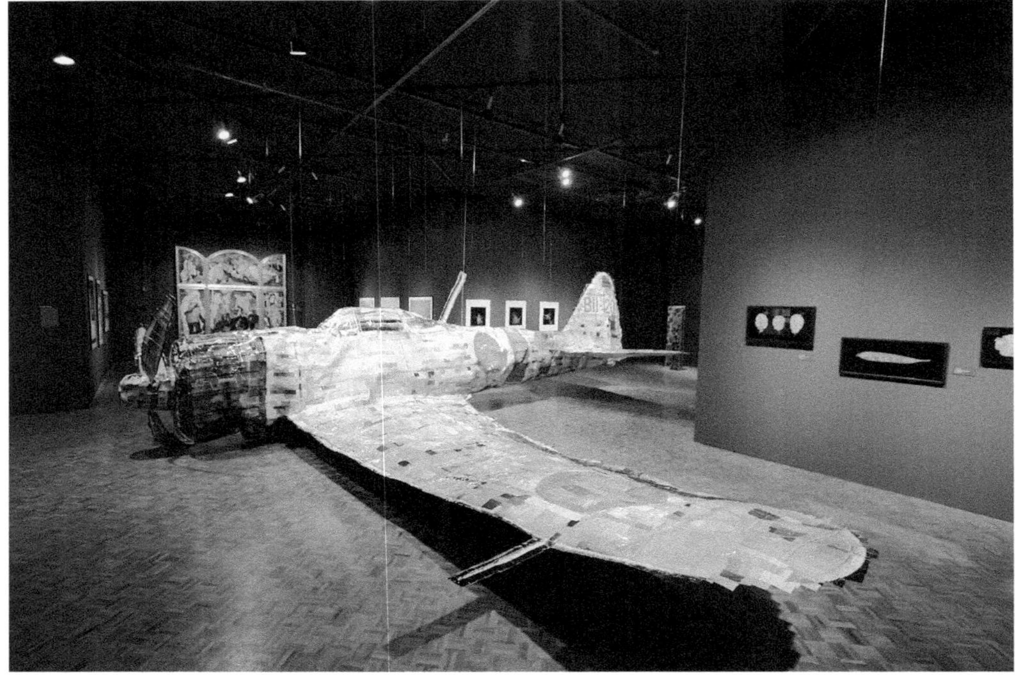

FIGURE 1.8. Katsushige Nakahashi, *Zero Project #BII-120, Hawaii*, 2006, mixed media sculpture, approximately 25,000 photographs, paper, tape, 39 × 30 ft. *Reconstructing Memories*, University of Hawai'i at Mānoa Art Gallery, Honolulu, November 5–December 13, 2006. Photograph courtesy of University of Hawai'i at Mānoa Art Gallery. See also plate 4.

Japanese American 442nd Regimental Combat Team and 100th Infantry Battalion.

For the final gathering to burn the replica, held on the sixty-fifth anniversary of the Ni'ihau Incident, a group of volunteers carried the "plane" to a site on campus that once served as a wartime bunker. Nakahashi's aged father also participated in the event, having flown in from Japan to recount his memories of the war.

Intrigued by the "complexities of wartime memory in Japan," in *Resplendent*, first mounted at the P.P.O.W. Gallery in New York (2001), Hawai'i-born Japanese American sculptor and installation artist Lynne Yamamoto (b. 1961) assays the "ambivalent symbolism" of the cherry blossom as a celebrated cultural icon suborned in support of Japanese militarism and imperialism under the guise of faith via State Shintō.[34] *Resplendent* is a

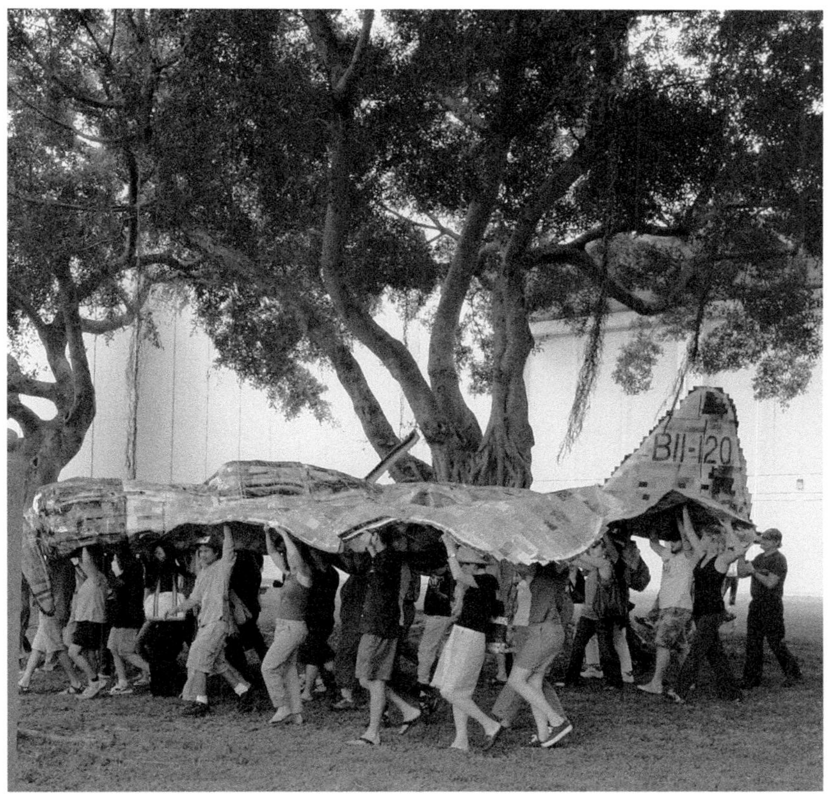

FIGURE 1.9. Katsushige Nakahashi, *Zero Project #BII-120, Hawaii*, 2006. Group carrying *Zero* sculpture to be burned, December 13, 2006. Photograph courtesy of University of Hawai'i at Mānoa Art Gallery.

visual meditation on the emotive power "behind the use of a . . . Japanese trope associated with notions of identity and soul [*yamato damashii*]," a venerated motif that was recast to stoke nationalism by glorifying and aestheticizing death in battle, in tandem with the warrior values of Bushido. During World War II soldiers were told to "die like beautiful falling cherry petals for the emperor," and kamikaze pilots on suicide sorties wore cherry blossoms on their flight suits.[35] Whereas Japanese regard the blossom's rapid demise after blooming as emblematic of life's beauty and inherent ephemerality, during the war, as Yamamoto stresses, "this traditional conception was manipulated to grant a sublime beauty to the act of falling from the sky . . . to safeguard the Emperor and one's country."[36]

Resplendent follows from Yamamoto's first trip to Japan in 1999, during which she visited Yasukuni Shrine (Yasukuni Jinja) in Tokyo, a Shintō religious complex founded in the nineteenth century that honors over 2.4 million Japanese war dead, most killed during the Second World War. Yet, because those revered in the shrine include Class-A war criminals, the site remains a political flashpoint. Public demonstrations of patriotism at the sanctuary by high government officials regularly ignite vocal condemnation outside Japan, especially in Korea and China.[37]

Reappropriating Japan's wartime aesthetic to the artist's own use, the walls of the room-size mixed media installation echo the traditional form of *byobu,* large freestanding folding screens that typically display nature-themed designs and calligraphy.[38] Covered with pearlescent paint to confer an elegantly luminous effect, three contiguous wall surfaces in *Resplendent* are adorned with hand-cut digital prints of cherry blossoms sporting miniature portraits of servicemen killed in the conflict—giving a real human face to elegiac wartime propaganda that likened kamikaze pilots to cherry petals falling from the sky.

Grouped in a continuous pattern, the raised blossoms, meticulously affixed in place with straight pins to cast elongated low-relief shadows, appear to leisurely drift downward as if borne by a gentle wind. The serene and orderly setting achieves the artist's aim, according to one commentator, of invoking an "ethereal realm" akin to "the paradisical afterlife imagined by the Japanese soldiers."[39]

Principally concerned with how ordinary people—combatants and civilians alike—experienced the era, the artist selected commonplace portraits of servicemen from a commemorative photographic volume prepared by a Japanese town that lost one hundred and eighty inhabitants.[40] Since the number nine, pronounced "ku," refers to suffering and pain in Japanese numerological tradition, in the installation each facial likeness is replicated nine times, to total 1,620 paper blossoms. Yamamoto's research also revealed a range of vernacular postwar opinion that offers a counterweight to official memorialization of the war, which scrupulously avoided commentary critical of the role of the Japanese emperor. Among these accounts, she recalls how a mayor of Nagasaki risked career and even life to suggest, during a 1988 session of the local city assembly, that the emperor bore some responsibility for the conflict, unexpectedly resulting in thousands of Japanese publicly expressing ardent agreement.[41]

FIGURE 1.10. Lynne Yamamoto, *Resplendent* (detail), P.P.O.W. Gallery, New York, 2001, room size 20 ft. w. × 40 ft. l. × 13 ft. h. Glass, paper, pearlescent paint, historical photographs. Photograph by Lucretia Knapp and Lynne Yamamoto courtesy of the artist. See also plate 5.

In contrast to the artist's use of portraiture to signal an abiding human presence, a line of nine large glass bell jars, arrayed in stately single-file procession, form the installation's central corridor, their shapes reminiscent of the elongated conical nose sections of piloted, jet-powered flying bombs likewise dubbed cherry blossoms (Ōka). Each jar bears the distinctive cherry blossom insignia emblazoned on these unique kamikaze aircraft, purpose-built for suicide missions in the last desperate year of the war (1944–45). Again summoning the wartime subversion of mythos-laden cultural conventions, under dramatic overhead lighting the cherry blossom emblems appear as a parade of ghostly shadows, each encircled within the glowing floor space of its transparent bell jar.

The installation and performance-based works of Yong Soon Min, a Los Angeles–based Korean American artist, curator, and activist, tie Korea's

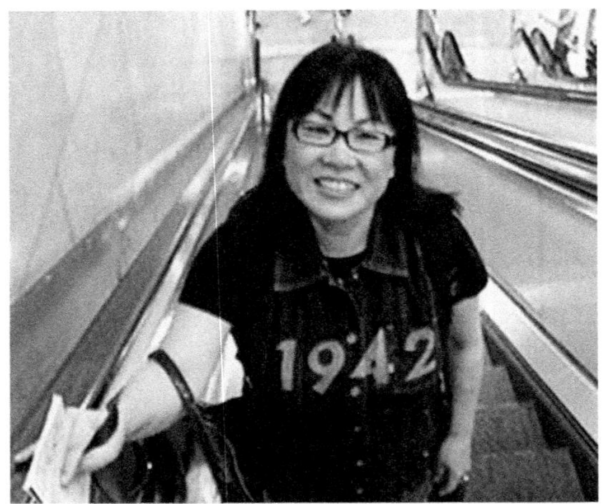

FIGURE 1.11. Yong Soon Min, *Wearing History*, 2007, photograph of the artist, Münster, Germany. Photograph courtesy of the artist.

strife-filled history to her personal situation. That difficult heritage is marked by successive foreign invasions, Japan's decades-long colonization, the subsequent Korean War, postwar hardships, and episodic outbreaks of violence against the Korean diaspora in the United States. Born in 1953, the year fighting ended in Korea, Min describes herself as a "Cold War baby."[42] Arriving in the United States as a child from a nation laid waste and divided through alliances with outside forces, Min's highly politicized sensibility extends to other peoples and nations gripped by the worldwide struggle between competing superpowers that arose in the aftermath of World War II.

Since 1993 a prominent theme in Min's work has been the mass exploitation of Koreans and other Asians as "comfort women"—the euphemistic term for women and girls forced to provide sexual services for the Japanese military. By the early 1990s, growing numbers of these women were publicly testifying to their horrific ordeal. In tandem with corroborating documentation from South Korean, Chinese, and Japanese scholars, the actions of the Japanese military and state in establishing this institutional system of sexual enslavement were brought to international attention.[43] Concurrent efforts to honor, to bear witness, and to document the stories of the elderly survivors ignited an outpouring of expressive production. Live performance—often incorporating the comfort women's own narratives—conjured the experiences of the victims to invoke this sexual violence as a corporeal reality, underscoring the potential of "embodied practice" to "alter the ways we imagine and practice a more expansive view of redress."[44]

Wearing History was initiated for *Trauma, Interrupted,* a 2007 international group exhibition held in Manila at the Cultural Center of the Philippines that featured eighteen women artists from six countries whose work "present[ed] their bodies as the very site of remembrance."[45] With the thematic focus on all forms of suffering encountered by women in Asia, these artists assayed matters of traumatic memory, healing, and spiritual regeneration that extended from overarching historical traumas precipitated by war and conflict—including the plight of "comfort women" from the Philippines, South Korea, China, and Japan—to natural and human-made disasters and personal maladies.[46]

In *Wearing History,* a quotidian vestimentary approach and performativity are combined with installation to embody the artist's sense of connection to an ordeal whose memory "must be kept alive."[47] For the piece, Min reconfigured a portion of her everyday wardrobe to enumerate the seventy-five years that had elapsed between the artist's 2007 project and 1932, the year Japan's military established the first "comfort station" in Shanghai, China. Corresponding to this chronotopic sequence, seventy-five articles of clothing were stenciled with eye-catching numerals, each individually inscribed with a calendric year across the artist's chest. During the exhibition, selected garments were installed for display on a clothing rack, accompanied by Min's 2004 video work, *Strangers to Ourselves.* To manifest the "immediacy and everyday presence" of this troubling history, the artist donned the altered apparel daily, beginning the moment she boarded the plane for the Philippines, during her entire stay, and for some time after returning to Los Angeles.[48] The schema was later reconstituted with updated elements for new projects presented in Korea and Germany.[49]

Since Min conceived of *Wearing History* as an intervention to further demands that the Japanese government "accept unequivocal official responsibility" following decades of denials and ambivalence, a related performative action involved the distribution of postcard-size "calling cards" to anyone she encountered who inquired about the significance of the dates on the artist's clothing.[50] The cards were imprinted with information

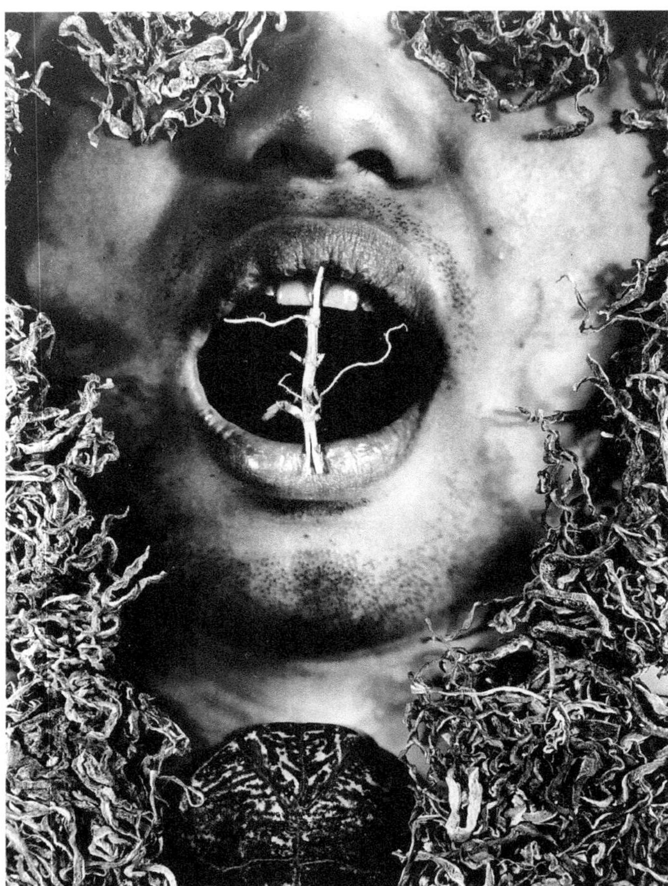

FIGURE 1.12. Marlon Fuentes, *Stick in Mouth*, 1987, from *Circle of Fear* series (1981–91), gelatin silver print, 8 × 10 in. Photograph courtesy of the artist.

on the "comfort women" and how Japan hasn't accepted full culpability for this "war crime."[51]

The 1942–45 Japanese wartime occupation of the Philippines is strikingly invoked in *Stick in Mouth* (1987), part of the 1981–91 *Circle of Fear* series by Manila-born California photographer and filmmaker Marlon Fuentes (b. 1954). In these manipulated black and white photographs, the artist melds elements of Catholic religious paraphernalia, disarticulated animal parts, and human faces in arresting pseudo-ritualistic tableaux to incarnate a tormented transgenerational vision of a homeland that has witnessed three centuries of foreign domination and cultural overlay by Spain, the United States, and Japan.

Comparing the image to a "death mask of sorts," in *Stick in Mouth* Fuentes presents a close-up view of a Filipino, his gaping mouth jammed open by a twisted twig.[52] Echoing the placement of coins on the eyelids of the deceased in funerary rituals, the man's eyes and forehead are concealed beneath a tangled mass of encircling Japanese seaweed. Obsessed by his mother's graphic accounts of violence inflicted on Filipinos who resisted the occupation, the artist highlights the severity of interrogation techniques employed by the Japanese occupiers and their local collaborators. Akin to waterboarding, this form of torture involves a rubber hose being forced down the prisoner's throat to compel rapid ingestion of large quantities of water. To inflict maximal agony, the captors would vigorously jump on the prone victim's greatly distended stomach.

Beyond evoking the collective pain suffered by "countless victims of torture during the Japanese occupation," the image offers a means for the artist to revisit the family story of his father's survival of the infamous Bataan Death March.[53] During the 1942 Japanese invasion, over sixty thousand defeated Filipino and American combatants suffered continual beatings and executions on a forced trek to distant prisoner of war camps, leading to the deaths of an estimated five thousand to eighteen thousand Filipino captives alone.

The Atomic Bomb and Beyond

The family history of Clement Hanami (b. 1961), an artist from Los Angeles, California, equally blends transpacific and Japanese American perspectives. World War II affected Hanami's parents quite differently: his Hiroshima-born mother, a *hibakusha* (atomic bomb survivor), immigrated to the United States after the war, and his Idaho-born father fortuitously managed to avoid internment. Although a resident of California when the conflict began, the artist's father was allowed to return to his home state of Idaho, where he spent the war years as a "voluntary evacuee."

Hanami long remained ignorant of the physical ordeal his mother endured, since during the artist's youth she never mentioned being a hibakusha. It was only in college that the artist learned of the long-term effects of nuclear exposure and how survivors were afflicted with radiation-induced keloid scars. The images Hanami saw reminded him of similar scars glimpsed on his mother's disfigured legs. Prompted to question his mother about these injuries, Hanami was deeply troubled by his ignorance of this absent yet critically important aspect of her life and how that lack implicitly ruptured the close bond they shared. Yet in hindsight, the artist saw his mother as having been thrust, like others from Hiroshima and Nagasaki, into an appalling situation that collectively marks them as the only civilians ever "exposed to an atomic bomb en masse."[54]

The multimedia video installation *Camera Obscura or Fat Man / Little Boy*, first exhibited in 1998 at the Los Angeles Center for Photographic Studies, emerged from the artist's need to grapple with the immeasurable "chasm between my mother's experience and my own."[55]

To represent the bombings on August 6 and 9, 1945, the installation's focal point is a plastic model of the B-29—the aircraft that dropped the atomic weapons—accompanied by the recorded rumbling sounds of these bombers in flight.[56] Suspended overhead and theatrically backlit, the replica B-29 bomber's elongated ground shadow portentously appears as if cast to scale by the approaching aircraft soaring high over Japan. Since the ensuing death and destruction defy routine comprehension, the use of a model stresses Hanami's incapacity to have more than a "simple toy-like understanding" of these unprecedented events, whereas the airplane's ominous dark shadow serves to incarnate the experience of his mother, "visible and real yet ephemeral . . . unimaginable beyond any possible description."[57]

From this highly affective perspective, Hanami conceives of the repercussions of the bomb as analogous to being made part of a vast and terrible involuntary experiment, in which survivors were subjected to US and Japanese studies monitoring the long-term health and genetic effects of radiation exposure. Comparing the challenge of "trying to discover my mother's . . . atomic experience" to biological research conducted on "the genes of Drosophila melanogaster" (fruit flies), the installation also incorporates displays and images of scientific apparatus, preserved insects, and genetic testing.[58]

Through deeply personal sculptural installations and site-specific performances, Yukiyo Kawano, an artist based in Portland, Oregon, grapples with the legacy of the atomic bomb from the vantage point of an artist

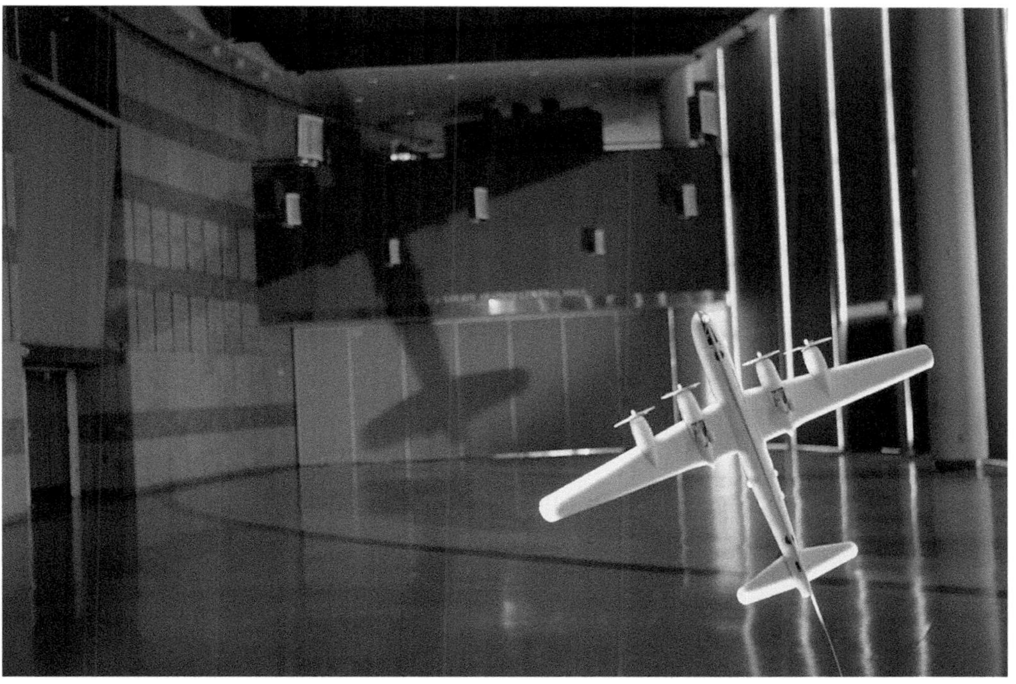

FIGURE 1.13. Clement Hanami, *Camera Obscura or Fat Man / Little Boy* (installation view), August 9, 2005, mixed media installation, Japanese American National Museum, Los Angeles. Photograph courtesy of the artist.

from Hiroshima who now makes her home in the United States. Born in 1974, Kawano terms herself a "third-generation hibakusha" whose understanding of the destruction draws on her multigenerational family legacy.[59] Despite the immediate death of eighty thousand inhabitants, her maternal grandfather miraculously survived being near the atomic explosion's hypocenter. Kawano's mother, born two years after the war ended, attended Honkawa, the closest elementary school to ground zero, where more than four hundred students perished.

As a child, Kawano accompanied her mother to community events in memory of Hiroshima, including a slideshow where distressing images of women with epilated scalps left an indelible impression.[60] Such profoundly disturbing formative experiences induced an aura of lingering disquietude that infuses Kawano's art, through which she seeks to "retell" this tragic history and ensure that the sufferings of the hibakusha will never be forgotten.[61] Consequently Kawano is critical of the local government's concerted effort, since the 1970s, to "brighten" Hiroshima's image as an international "City of Peace"—a rebranding that largely excluded hibakusha voices.[62]

Citing their well-known US code names, the mixed media sculptures *Little Boy (folded)* (2011) and *Fat Man (folded)* (2012) are full-scale sculptural replicas of the atomic bombs dropped on Hiroshima and Nagasaki constructed from kimono fabric wrapped around paper lantern–like armatures. To suggest hair loss from radiation exposure and insert her own "DNA" into the project, strands of the artist's hair are interwoven throughout both effigies. Often displayed as a pair, these objects' handcrafted artisanal quality and pieced together fabrication from reprocessed traditional Japanese garments contrast markedly with the ominous metallic bulk of the weapons of mass destruction to which they allude.

To provide a material and bodily conduit to the gendered history of her female forebears, *Little Boy*, the first of these works, incorporates a silk kimono the artist inherited from her maternal grandmother, a hibakusha who was a professional kimono maker. Describing *Little Boy* as a "prayer to deal with the death and fear," for Kawano the time-consuming, quasi-ritualistic activity of meticulously dismantling the handmade garment stitch by stitch became a meditative act of communion with a departed ancestor that elicited the sensation of *mono no aware*.[63] This Japanese concept of impermanence denotes a "gentle sadness, a wistfulness, [a way of] reflecting on the ephemera of things," which allows the artist to better apprehend and interrogate her relationship to historic events of overwhelming magnitude. [64]

A visual and performance artist, filmmaker, and photojournalist, Shinpei Takeda is presently based in both Tijuana, México, and Düsseldorf, Germany. (Takeda and some of his collaborators write about his work in chapters 5 and 6 of this volume.) The concerns and projects of the artist, who regularly travels between Latin America, the United States, Japan, and Germany as an itinerant resident, reflect a multicentered cosmopolitan perspective. A member of the postwar generation born in Osaka, Japan, in 1978, Takeda's active interest in the atomic legacy of World War II began in 2004, when he was employed as a translator for an American documentary profiling a female bomb victim.[65] Deeply moved by the experience, the artist began to seek out and record the stories of hibakusha living near the

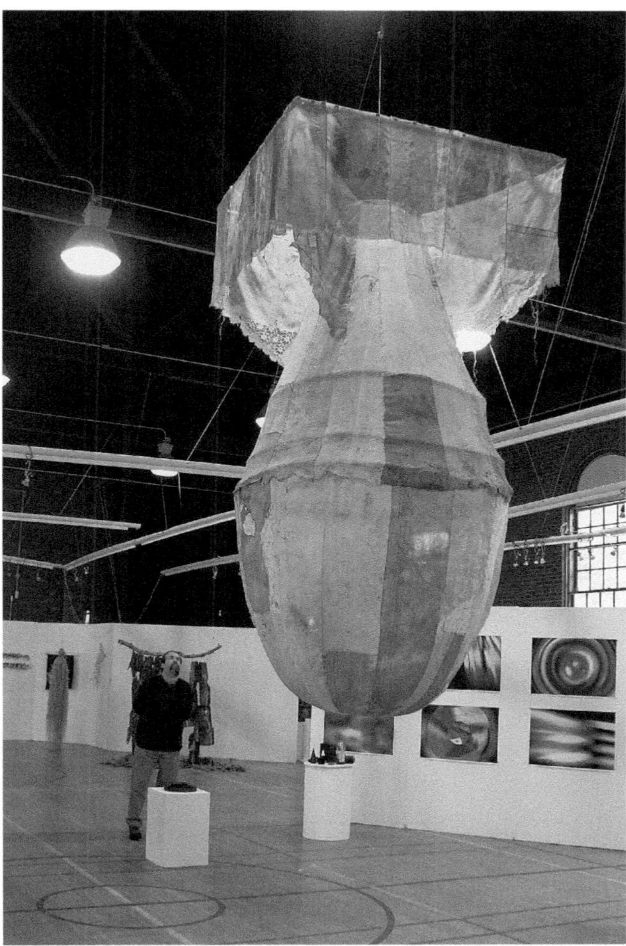

FIGURE 1.14. Yukiyo Kawano, *Fat Man (folded)*, 2012, kimono, foam, wood, hair, ink, baisen mordant dye, 5 × 5 × 10 ft. Collection of the artist. Photograph courtesy of the artist.

US-Mexican border and subsequently initiated interviews with survivors across the Americas and Hawai'i.[66]

Three interrelated works from 2010 draw on hibakusha oral testimonies: a documentary film, a self-documented video performance, and an architectonic multimedia installation: *Hiroshima Nagasaki Download: Memories from the Americas*, *Self-Seismography (Autoseismografía)*, and *Alpha Decay / Decaimiento Alfa*. The film, *Hiroshima Nagasaki Download* (released 2011), chronicles a 2009 road trip with a Japanese collaborator to record hibakusha living along the Pacific coast from Canada to México.[67] In a series of intimate vignettes, the magnitude of each survivor's anguish is made palpable as they struggle to articulate what was witnessed during and after the bombing and how these traumatic memories still haunt them. As an interviewer with no immediate connection to anybody with experience of the war, the artist intercuts the victim's testimonials with ruminations on his own process, motives, and ethical concerns in pursuing the project.

The digital editing of *Hiroshima Nagasaki Download*, a repetitive process requiring the artist's obsessive concentration on the audio component of the film, prompted the approach he followed in the later video. To "vibrate in contact with their stories," in *Self-Seismography* spectrographic voiceprint patterns derived from the filmed oral testimonies act as visual templates for Takeda to generate analogous drawings.[68] As he solemnly presents himself in a seated pose with his face veiled in white makeup, the video focuses on the artist's recurrent act of inscribing elongated cardboard boxes with an unbroken pencil stroke to visually echo the continuous zigzag wave form pattern of each survivor's distinctive voiceprint. For Takeda, this repetitive freehand process emulates the function of a scientific instrument, the tracing of the interviewees' voiceprints being comparable to "a seismometer measuring the trembling of the earth."[69]

The numerous boxes accumulated during the making of the video provide the tunnel-like walls of the next piece, *Alpha Decay / Decaimiento Alfa*. Built to human scale, this cavernous multimedia installation, mounted in México at Centro Cultural Tijuana, comprises a circuitous dimly lit passageway Takeda associates with the tubular shape of the gastrointestinal tract. The project expands on the artist's impulse to palpably interface with traumatic memory by internalizing the survivors' emotionally charged accounts via an equivalent bodily response, summoning the medium of art to figuratively ingest and convert their enduring pain into positive expressive energy.

Since 2005, New York–based sculptor and filmmaker Hiroshi Sunairi (b. 1972) has pursued the *Tree Project*, a transnational initiative to perpetuate public memory of the devastating World War II atomic bombing of Hiroshima and its globe-spanning reverberations. The Hiroshima-born artist disseminated irradiated seeds donated by a collaborating Japanese arborist from *hibaku jumoku*—trees that survived the bombing—to individuals

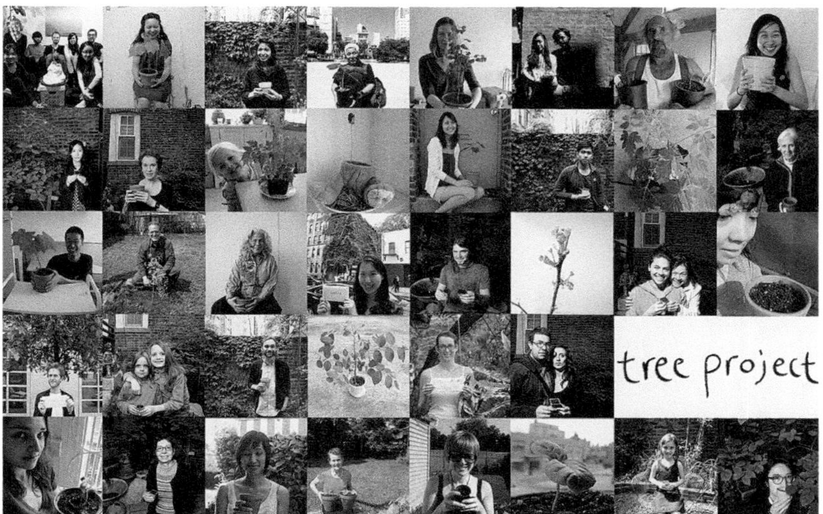

FIGURE 1.15. Hiroshi Sunairi, *Tree Project*, 2006–9, poster showing Hiroshi Sunairi with *Tree Project* participants, archival inkjet print, 44 × 35 in., edition of fifteen. Photographs by Hiroshi Sunairi and Tree Project participants courtesy of the artist.

around the world who agreed to plant and share documentation of the seedlings' progress.

Hundreds of people from twenty-three countries have since taken part in this socially engaged, group-sourced project, initiated in 2006 along with Sunairi's dedicated website.[70] Beyond a literal means of sustaining the existence of these trees through collaborative micro-interventions, for the artist these shared acts of cultivation underline the pressing need for humankind to provide stewardship to actively ensure the continued propagation and regeneration of life, given increasing challenges to survival on a planetary scale.

Sunairi's 2005 *A Night of Elephants*, commissioned by the Hiroshima City Museum of Contemporary Art to mark the sixtieth anniversary of the atomic bombing, provided the catalyst for the ongoing *Tree Project*. Inspired by the adage "an elephant never forgets," the central element of his installation is a steel-framed sculpture in the form of a recumbent, life-size elephant packed with branches and fragrant dried leaves from *hibaku*

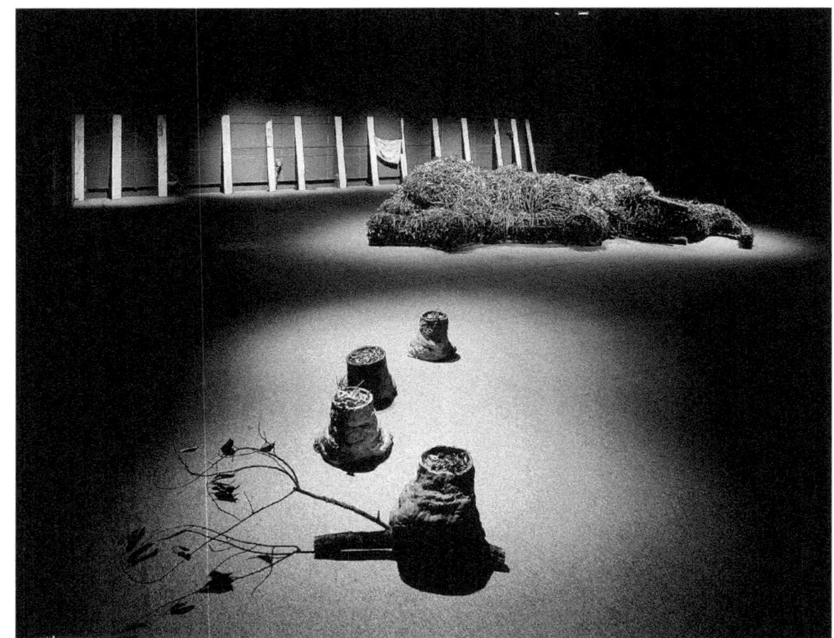

FIGURE 1.16. Hiroshi Sunairi, *A Night of Elephants*, 2005, tree branches and leaves, metal, metal sheet, ceramic and found objects, 12 × 12 × 3 ft. Installation at Hiroshima City Museum of Contemporary Art. Photograph by Hiroshi Sunairi. Photograph courtesy of the artist. See also plate 6.

trees. Through his incorporation of these cuttings the artist provides a "silent expression of survival . . . resonat[ing] through the past, present, and future."[71]

The use of the Pacific for nuclear weapons testing provides a compelling subject for Alexander Lee (b. 1974). The California-born sculptor, painter, and mixed media artist is the descendant of nineteenth-century Chinese agricultural workers in French Polynesia. The artist, who holds dual American and French citizenship, is currently based in Tahiti and maintains close identification with the island's Polynesian culture.

Concerned with the toxic effects of nuclear testing on local inhabitants, ecosystems, and surrounding seas, Lee's work references US and French detonations conducted in the Marshall Islands and French Polynesia. With an uneven base resembling dense volcanic rock littered with disarticulated plant and animal forms, Lee's distinctive large-scale sculpture, *Recitations from the Great Fish Changing Skies* (2008), resembles the ominous mushroom cloud of a nuclear blast. Yet the design equally alludes to the epic volcanic eruptions billowing high over the ocean that brought many Pacific islands into being. Since the piece is specific to Tahiti, the artist's

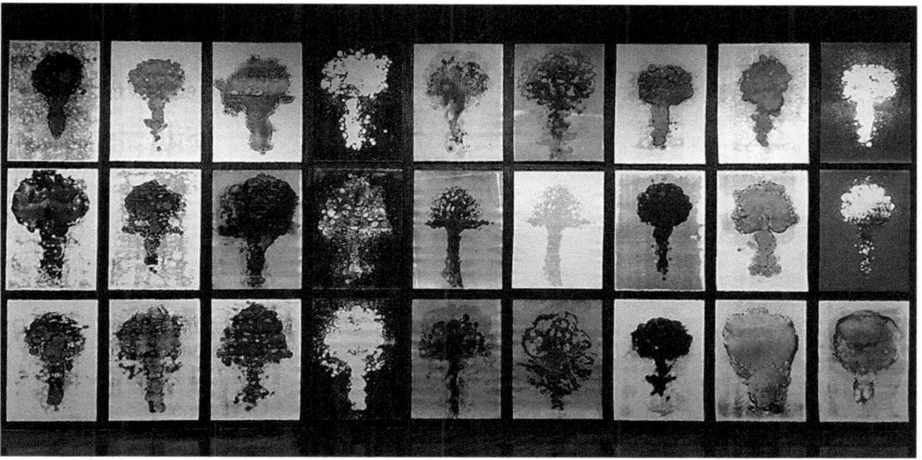

FIGURE 1.17. Alexander Lee, *Te atua vahine mana ra o Pere* (*The Great Goddess Pere*)—*L'Aube où les Fauves viennent se désaltérer*, 2017. Installation detail from the 1st Honolulu Biennial *Middle of Now | Here*, Honolulu, Hawai'i, March 8–May 8, 2017. Photograph courtesy of the artist. See also plate 7.

expansive schema vividly fuses disparate historic moments to epitomize the entire epic saga of the island to date: its explosive volcanic genesis, its indigenous creation story and first peopling, its Western colonization, and its role in France's emergence as a nuclear power.[72]

Participation in the transoceanic 2017 Honolulu Biennial *Middle of Now | Here*[73] provided a platform to bring forward affinities between Lee's Asian heritage and Polynesian cultures, or, as he states, to be "Asian in both of my Polynesias —French Polynesia / Tahiti and American Polynesia / Hawai'i."[74] *Te atua vahine mana ra o Pere* (*The Great Goddess Pere*), a sprawling multiroom installation, foregrounds symmetries between the two island groups' cultural, colonial, and militarized histories.[75] The centerpiece features floor-to-ceiling rows of monotype prints of nuclear explosions. Titled "starbursts," these deceptively attractive images graphically reference the irony behind the quasi-poetic French use of astronomical designations for stars as the operational code names of their nuclear tests.

Coda

Art practice, as a source of empathic connection to social memory and geographies of absence, brings affectivity to historical knowledge via tangible material, sensory, bodily, and face-to-face engagement. For artists from around the Pacific, the past often remains unresolved, charged by deep-rooted issues arising from traumas of war, displacement, loss, and societal rupture. Gathered together, such artistic interventions contribute to the continually expanding visual archive that registers strategies and positions by which to grapple with and bestow coherence on understandings of the lasting impact of momentous events like the Second World War and its perilous nuclear legacy. In this elastic use of the term, an archive is conceived not simply as collected images, objects, documents, and so on, but rather as a coextensive "set of traces of actions" grounded in dynamic dialog with cultural producers about the range of multifaceted ideas, animating beliefs, cultural affinities, lived conditions, and processes of engagement that bring their projects into being.[76]

Notes

1. Roger Shimomura and Stacey Uradomo-Barre, *Yellow Terror: The Collections and Paintings of Roger Shimomura* (Seattle: Wing Luke Asian Museum, 2009).
2. "How to Tell Japs from the Chinese," *Life* 11, no. 25 (December 22, 1941): 81–82, http://digitalexhibits.wsulibs.wsu.edu/files/original/cf2dcf0cbabc74b6359e319276d5091a.jpg
3. Lucy R. Lippard and Roger Shimomura, *Roger Shimomura: Stereotypes and Admonitions* (Seattle: Greg Kucera Gallery, 2004).
4. Incident related in Lippard and Shimomura, *Roger Shimomura.*
5. See *'Ae Kai: A Culture Lab on Convergence*, July 7–9, 2017, Honolulu, Hawai'i, accessed August 1, 2018, http://smithsonianapa.org/aekai/.
6. Jane E. Dusselier, *Artifacts of Loss: Crafting Survival in Japanese American Concentration Camps* (New Brunswick, NJ: Rutgers University Press, 2008), 135–38.
7. Shizu Saldamando, interview with author, Honolulu, Hawai'i, July 7, 2017.
8. Mona Higuchi, telephone interview with author, November 23, 2014.
9. See "World War II Aleut Relocation Camps in Southeast Alaska—Introduction," National Park Service, accessed August 17, 2018, https://www.nps.gov/articles/aleu-mobley-intro.htm.
10. Natalie Zelt, "Osamu James Nakagawa, Banta Cliffs + Gama Caves," *Spot*, Houston Center for Photography, Fall 2012, https://hcponline.org/spot/osamu-james-nakagawa-banta-cliffs-gama-caves/.

11. Osamu James Nakagawa, email message to author, May 22, 2015.
12. Osamu James Nakagawa, artist statement, *Remains 2001–2009*, https://www.lensculture.com/projects/7788-remains.
13. Jeff Kingston, "Battle of Saipan: A Brutal Invasion That Claimed 55,000 Lives," *Japan Times*, July 5, 2014, https://www.japantimes.co.jp/news/2014/07/05/national/history/battle-saipan-brutal-invasion-claimed-55000-lives/#.W3iMe34nZ7Y.
14. Osamu James Nakagawa, email message to author, April 1, 2016.
15. Kaili Chun, interview with author, September 20, 2007.
16. See Aaron Kerner, *Reconstructing Memories* (Honolulu: University of Hawai'i at Mānoa Art Gallery, 2006), 12–15.
17. Noelle M. K. Y. Kahanu, "Enduring Legacies of the Panalā'au Expeditions," in *Hui Panalā'au: Hawaiian Colonists in the Pacific, 1935–1942* (Honolulu: Center for Oral History, University of Hawai'i at Mānoa and Bernice Pauahi Bishop Museum, 2006), xxix–xxxii, https://scholarspace.manoa.hawaii.edu/bitstream/10125/27420/4/huipanalaau_1_frontmatter_introduction.pdf
18. Danielle Lampe, *A Story of the Hui Panalā'au of the Equatorial Pacific Islands* (Honolulu: US Fish and Wildlife Service, 2013), 2.
19. Kaili Chun, email message to author, July 3, 2018.
20. Kaili Chun, email message to author, July 3, 2018.
21. Kaili Chun, email message to author, July 3, 2018.
22. Michael Arcega, *SPAM/MAPS: World*, accessed August 19, 2018, https://arcega.us/artwork/2062376-SPAM-MAPS-World.html.
23. Brandy Nālani McDougall and Craig Santos Perez, eds., *Home(is)lands: New Art and Writing from Guåhan and Hawai'i* (Honolulu: Ala Press Offering, 2017).
24. Craig Perez, interview with author, Honolulu, Hawai'i, July 8, 2017.
25. Craig Perez, email message to author, May 24, 2018.
26. Perez, email message to author, May 24, 2018.
27. Perez, interview with author, July 8, 2017.
28. See Yoichi Uozumi, "ZERO Journey: NAKAHASHI Katsushige and the ZERO PROJECT," accessed December 28, 2017, http://www.academia.edu/4539849/ZERO_Journey.
29. Katsushige Nakahashi, email message to author, February 11, 2018, trans. Yan Yang.
30. Kodama Gallery, *ZERO Project #601-1XX*, Tokyo, 2003, n.p.
31. See "Katsushige Nakahashi," accessed August 18, 2018, http://online.sfsu.edu/amkerner/memory/nakahashi.htm.
32. See Allan Beekman, *The Niihau Incident* (Honolulu: Heritage Press of Pacific, 1982). Also see Geoffrey M. White, *Memorializing Pearl Harbor: Unfinished Histories and the Work of Remembrance* (Durham: Duke University Press, 2016), 186–200.
33. Katsushige Nakahashi in Aaron Kerner, "The Depth of Memory: An Interview with Katsushige Nakahashi," trans. Shoko Okuda, *Camerawork: A Journal of Photographic Arts* 34, no. 2 (Fall/Winter 2007): 20–27.

34. Lynne Yamamoto, email message to author, June 25, 2018; Lynne Yamamoto, artist's statement, *Resplendent (2001–03)*, accessed May 26, 2018, http://www.lynneyamamoto.net/resplendent/respltext.html. This installation was also mounted at the Munson Williams Proctor Arts Institute, Utica, New York (2003) and the University of Hawai'i Art Gallery (2006).
35. Emiko Ohnuki-Tierney, *Kamikaze, Cherry Blossoms, and Nationalisms: The Militarization of Aesthetics in Japanese History* (Chicago: University of Chicago Press, 2002), 107, 3.
36. Artist's statement, *Resplendent*, Lynne Yamamoto website, accessed March 25, 2023, http://www.lynneyamamoto.net/resplendent/respltext.html.
37. See Akiko Takenaka, *Yasukuni Shrine: History, Memory, and Japan's Unending Postwar* (Honolulu: University of Hawai'i Press, 2015).
38. Yamamoto, email message to the author, June 25, 2018.
39. Kerri Sakamoto, "Unbroken Blossoms: Ambivalence and Beauty in the Work of Lynne Yamamoto," in *Resplendent* (Utica, NY: Munson Williams Proctor Arts Institute, 2003), 5.
40. Lynne Yamamoto, email message to author, May 27, 2018; Heiwa e no Ashiato Henshū Iinkai, *Heiwa e no ashiato* (Mizunami-shi: Hiyoshi Gōyūkai, 1972).
41. Norma Field, *In the Realm of a Dying Emperor* (New York: Vintage Books, 1993).
42. Biography, Yong Soon Min website, accessed July 1, 2018, http://www.yongsoonmin.com/biography/.
43. Elizabeth W. Son, *Embodied Reckonings: "Comfort Women," Performance, and Transpacific Redress* (Ann Arbor: University of Michigan Press, 2018), xviii.
44. Son, *Embodied Reckonings*, xix.
45. Flaudette May V. Datuin, "Uncommon Sense: On Trauma Interrupted," *n.paradoxa international feminist art journal* 21 (2008): 5–15.
46. Datuin, "Uncommon Sense."
47. Yong Soon Min, email message to author, June 30, 2018.
48. Yong Soon Min, email message to author, June 30, 2018; Datuin, "Uncommon Sense."
49. Yong Soon Min, group exhibition, *Nobody*, Seoul Museum of Art, Seoul, Korea, 2014.
50. *Wearing History*, Yong Soon Min website, accessed July 4, 2018, http://www.yongsoonmin.com/art/wearing-history/.
51. Yong Soon Min, email message to author, July 8, 2018.
52. Marlon Fuentes, email message to author, July 26, 2018.
53. Marlon Fuentes, email message to author, July 26, 2018.
54. Clement Hanami, interview with author, Los Angeles, California, February 25, 2018. See also Clement Hanami, *Fat Man / Little Boy* (Los Angeles: Los Angeles Center for Photographic Studies, 1998).
55. Clement Hanami, email message to author, February 4, 2018. The installation was later restaged at the Japanese American National Museum in Los Angeles in 2005.
56. Hanami, email message to author, August 18, 2018.

57. Hanami, email message to author, February 4, 2018.
58. Hanami, interview with author, February 25, 2018.
59. Yukiyo Kawano website, accessed May 21, 2018, http://yukiyokawano.com/about/
60. Yukiyo Kawano, email message to author, May 31, 2018.
61. Yukiyo Kawano, "Active Intransitive: Memories, Histories, Places, Bodies," MFA thesis, Vermont College of Fine Arts, 2012.
62. Kawano, "Active Intransitive."
63. Yukiyo Kawano, telephone interview with author, May 26, 2018.
64. Kawano, "Active Intransitive," 2012.
65. Shinpei Takeda, interview with author, Evanston, IL, April 25, 2015. The documentary was *The Last Atomic Bomb*, 2006, dir. Robert Richter .
66. See Shinpei Takeda and Naoko Wake, *Hiroshima Nagasaki beyond the Ocean* (Nagasaki: Yururi Books, 2014).
67. *Hiroshima Nagasaki Download*, Shinpei Takeda website, accessed August 20, 2018, http://www.shinpeitakeda.com/my-product/hiroshima-nagasaki-download/.
68. Takeda, interview with author, April 25, 2015.
69. Shinpei Takeda, *Alpha Decay: How Can Contemporary Art Express the Memory of A-Bomb*, trans. Mio Higgins (Tokyo: Gendai Shokan, 2014), unpublished English language translation, 16.
70. Julia Bryan-Wilson, "Aftermath: Two Queer Artists Respond to Nuclear Spaces," in *Critical Landscapes: Art, Space, Politics*, ed. Eliza Scott and Kirsten Swenson (Oakland: University of California Press, 2015), 77–81. See also Hiroshi Sunairi website, https://sunairi.wordpress.com/2014/12/10/tree/; http://treeproject.blogspot .com/.
71. Hiroshi Sunairi, "A Night of Elephants," in *A Night of Elephants*, exhibition catalog (Hiroshima: Hiroshima City Museum of Contemporary Art, 2005), n.p. See Hiroshi Sunairi website, https://sunairi.wordpress.com/category/sculpture-2005-a-night-of -elephants/.
72. Alexander Lee, email message to author, May 23, 2014.
73. See Honolulu Biennial, *Middle of Now | Here*, accessed August 20, 2018, https://www .honolulubiennial.org/hb17/.
74. Alexander Lee, email message to author, September 3, 2017.
75. The full title of Lee's 2017 installation is *Te atua vahine mana ra o Pere* (*The Great Goddess Pere*)—*L'Aube où les Fauves viennent se désaltérer.*
76. Sue Breakell, "Perspectives: Negotiating the Archive," *Tate Papers*, no. 9 (Spring 2018), https://www.tate.org.uk/research/tate-papers/09/perspectives-negotiating-the -archive.

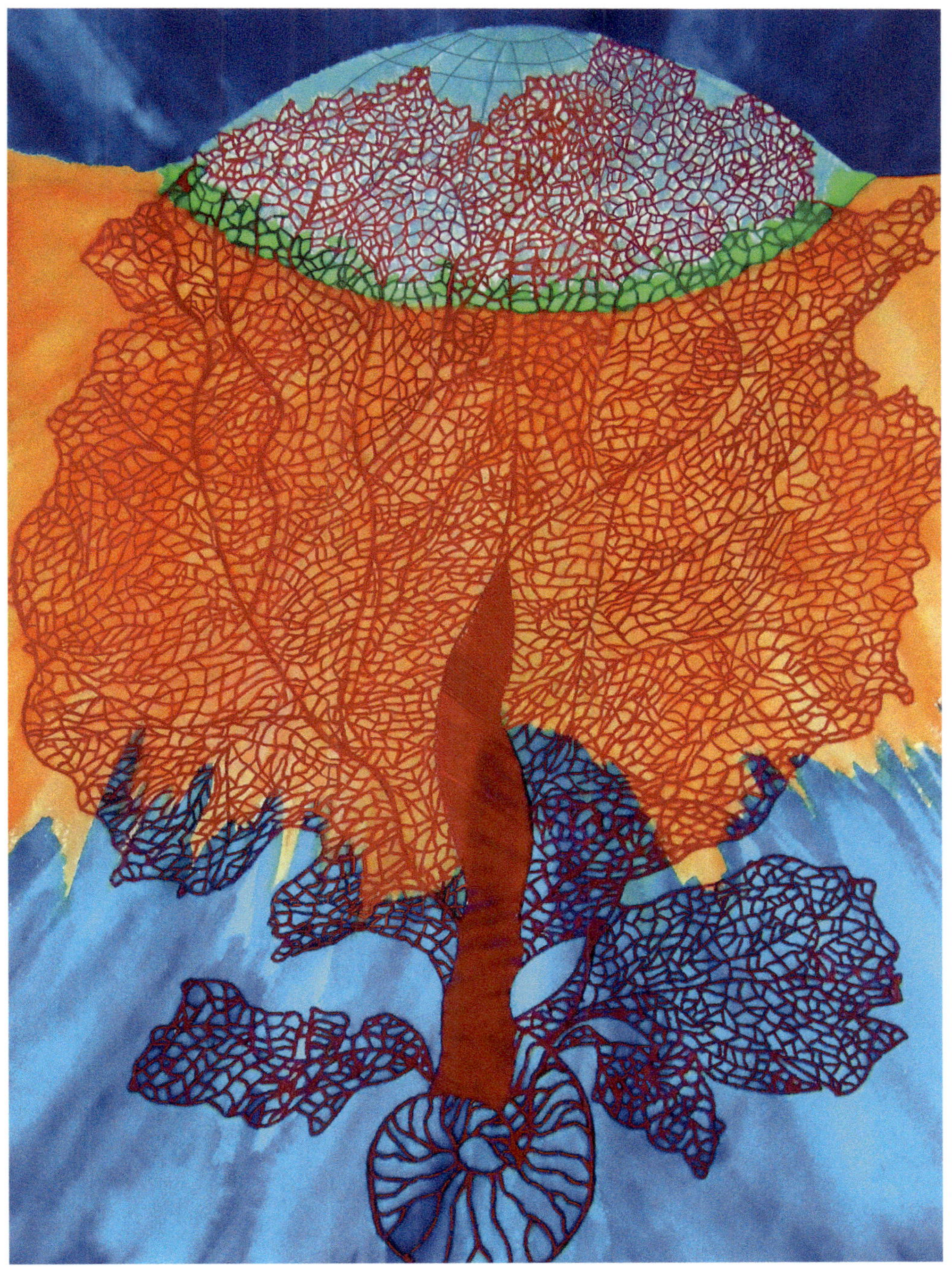

PLATE 1. Joy Enomoto (Kanaka Maoli), *Nuclear Hemorrhage: Enewetak Does Not Forget*, 2017, watercolor and thread, 16 × 12 in. (unframed). Collection of Brandy Nālani McDougall. Image courtesy of Joy Lehuanani Enomoto.

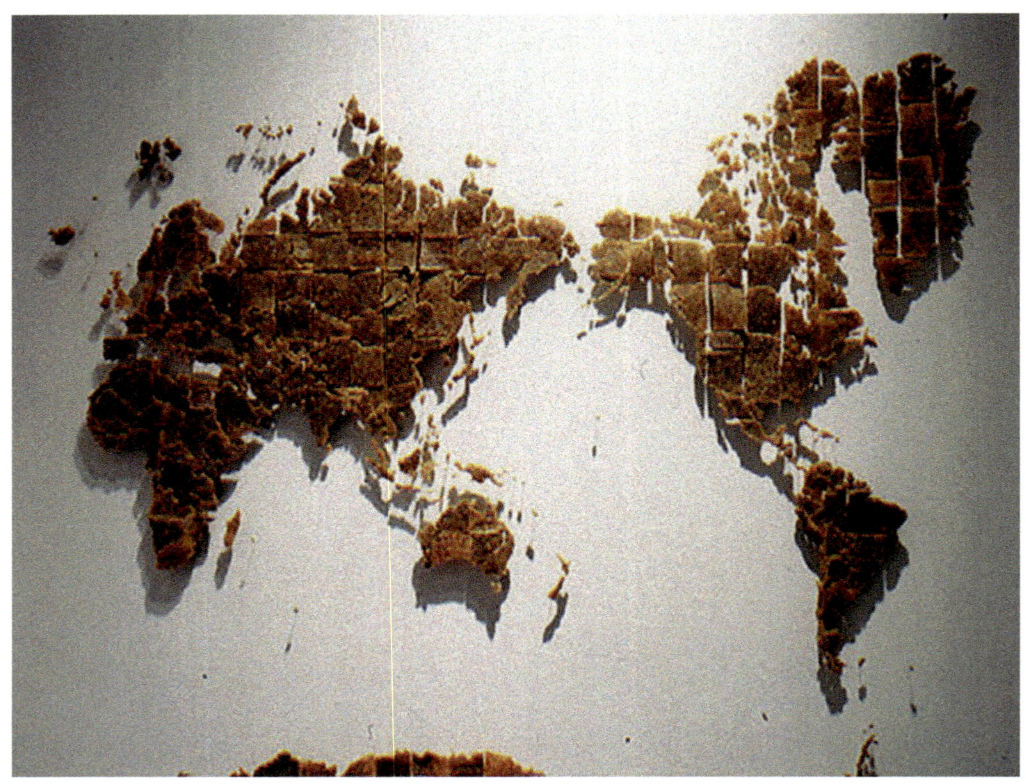

PLATE 2. Michael Arcega, *SPAM/MAPS: Oceania*, 2007, Spam luncheon meat, 4 ft. × 3 ft. × 2 in. Collection of the artist. Photograph courtesy of the artist.

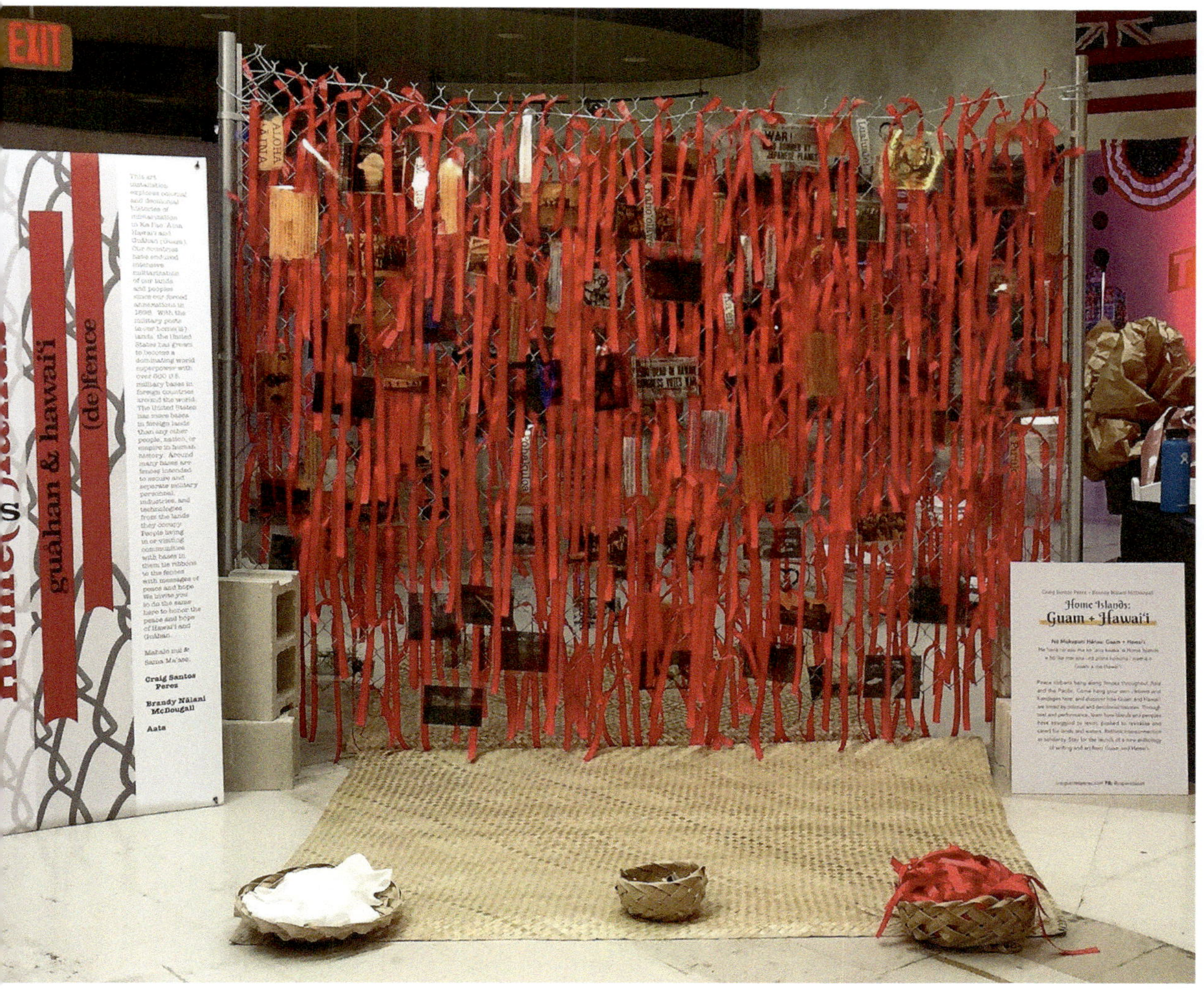

PLATE 3. Craig Santos Perez and Brandy Nālani McDougall, *(de)fence*, 2017. Mixed media installation with steel mesh fence (8 × 10 ft.). *'Ae Kai: A Culture Lab on Convergence*, July 7–9, 2017, Honolulu, Hawai'i. Photograph by Craig Santos Perez courtesy of the artists.

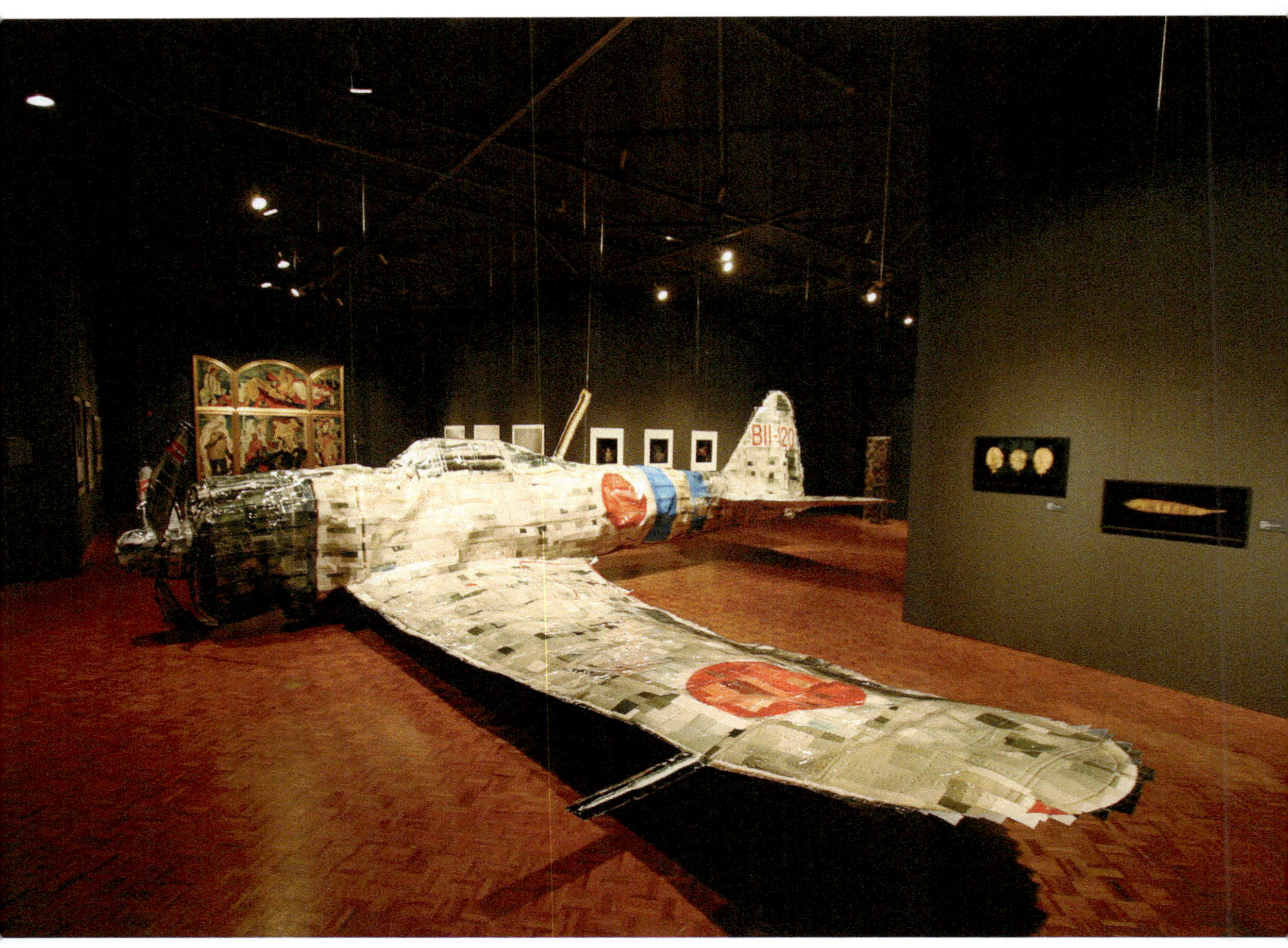

PLATE 4. Katsushige Nakahashi, *Zero Project #BII-120, Hawaii*, 2006, mixed media sculpture, approximately 25,000 photographs, paper, tape, 39 × 30 ft. *Reconstructing Memories*, University of Hawai'i at Mānoa Art Gallery, Honolulu, November 5–December 13, 2006. Photograph courtesy of University of Hawai'i at Mānoa Art Gallery.

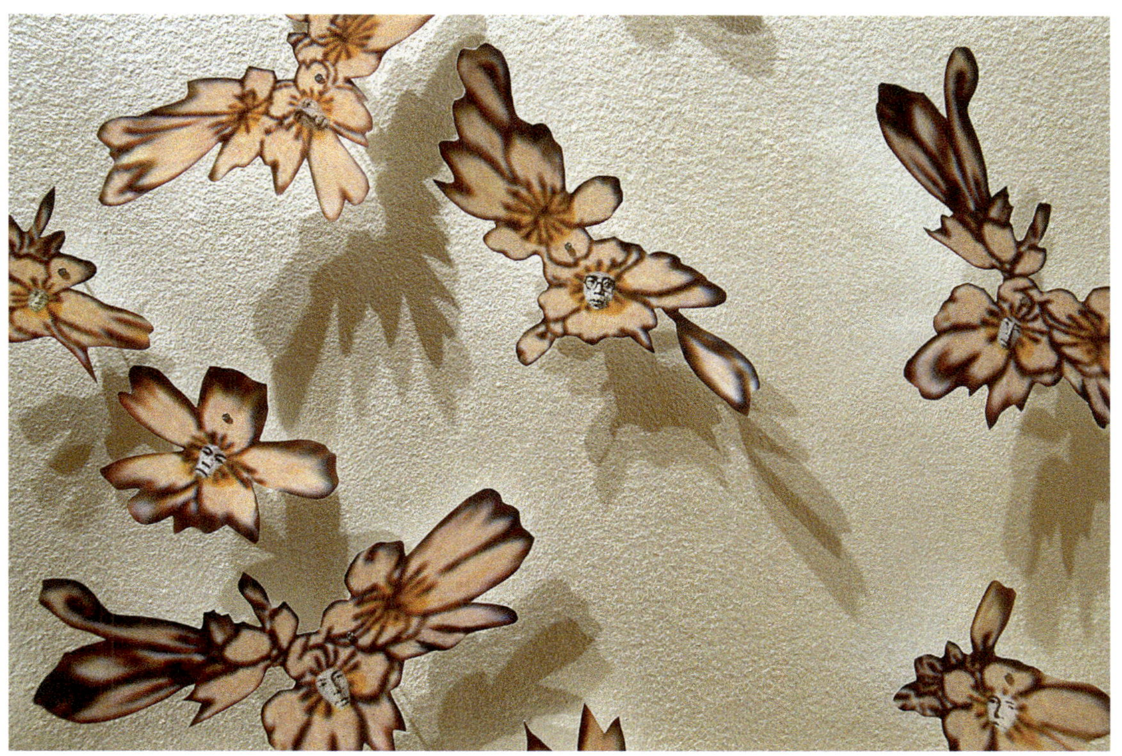

PLATE 5. Lynne Yamamoto, *Resplendent* (detail), P.P.O.W. Gallery, New York, 2001, room size 20 ft. w. × 40 ft. l. × 13 ft. h. Glass, paper, pearlescent paint, historical photographs. Photograph by Lucretia Knapp and Lynne Yamamoto courtesy of the artist.

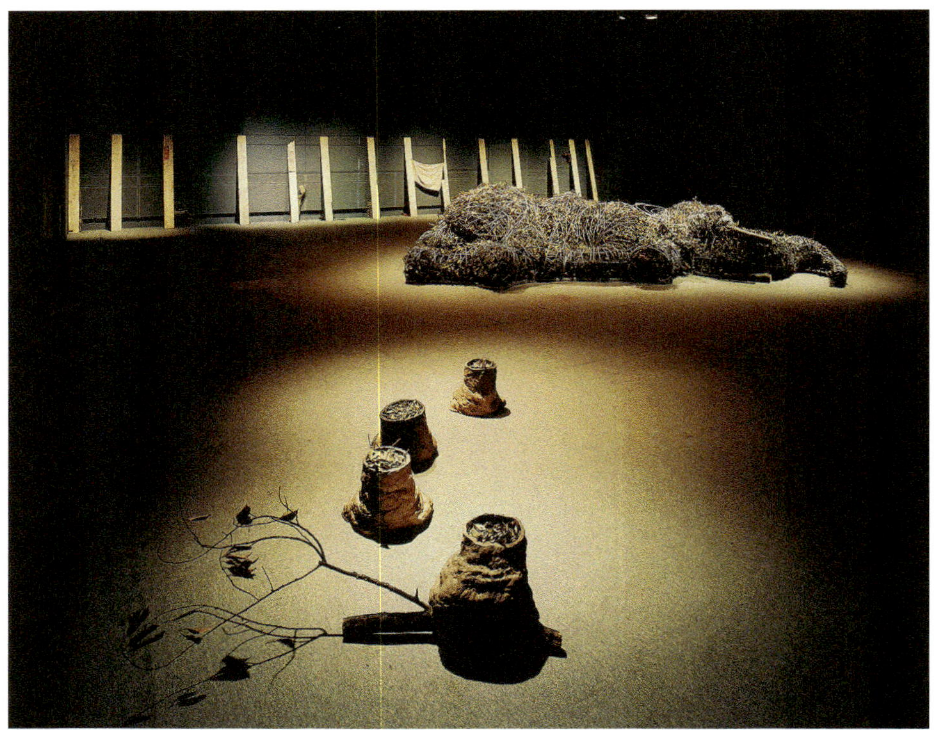

PLATE 6. Hiroshi Sunairi, *A Night of Elephants*, 2005, tree branches and leaves, metal, metal sheet, ceramic and found objects, 12 × 12 × 3 ft. Installation at Hiroshima City Museum of Contemporary Art. Photograph by Hiroshi Sunairi. Photograph courtesy of the artist.

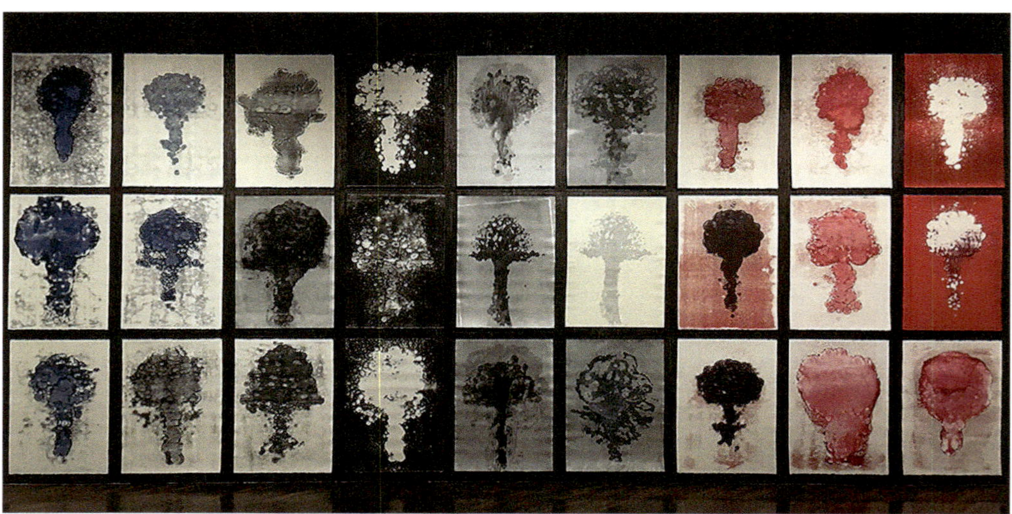

PLATE 7. Alexander Lee, *Te atua vahine mana ra o Pere* (*The Great Goddess Pere*)—*L'Aube où les Fauves viennent se désaltérer*, 2017. Installation detail from the 1st Honolulu Biennial *Middle of Now | Here*, Honolulu, Hawai'i, March 8–May 8, 2017. Photograph courtesy of the artist.

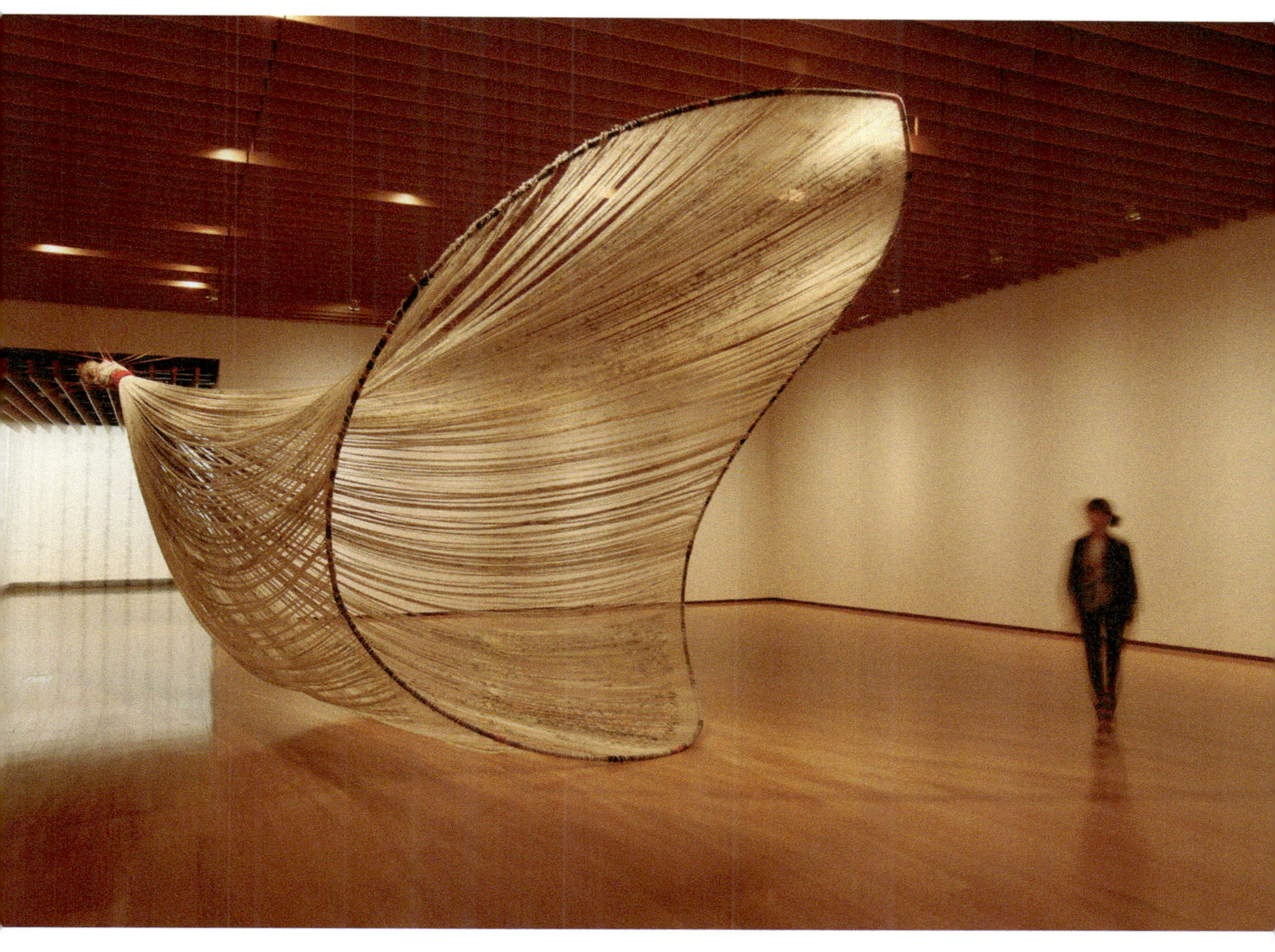

PLATE 8. *Beta Decay 5 (Antimonument)*, Nagasaki Prefectural Art Museum, August 1, 2015. Photograph courtesy of Shinpei Takeda.

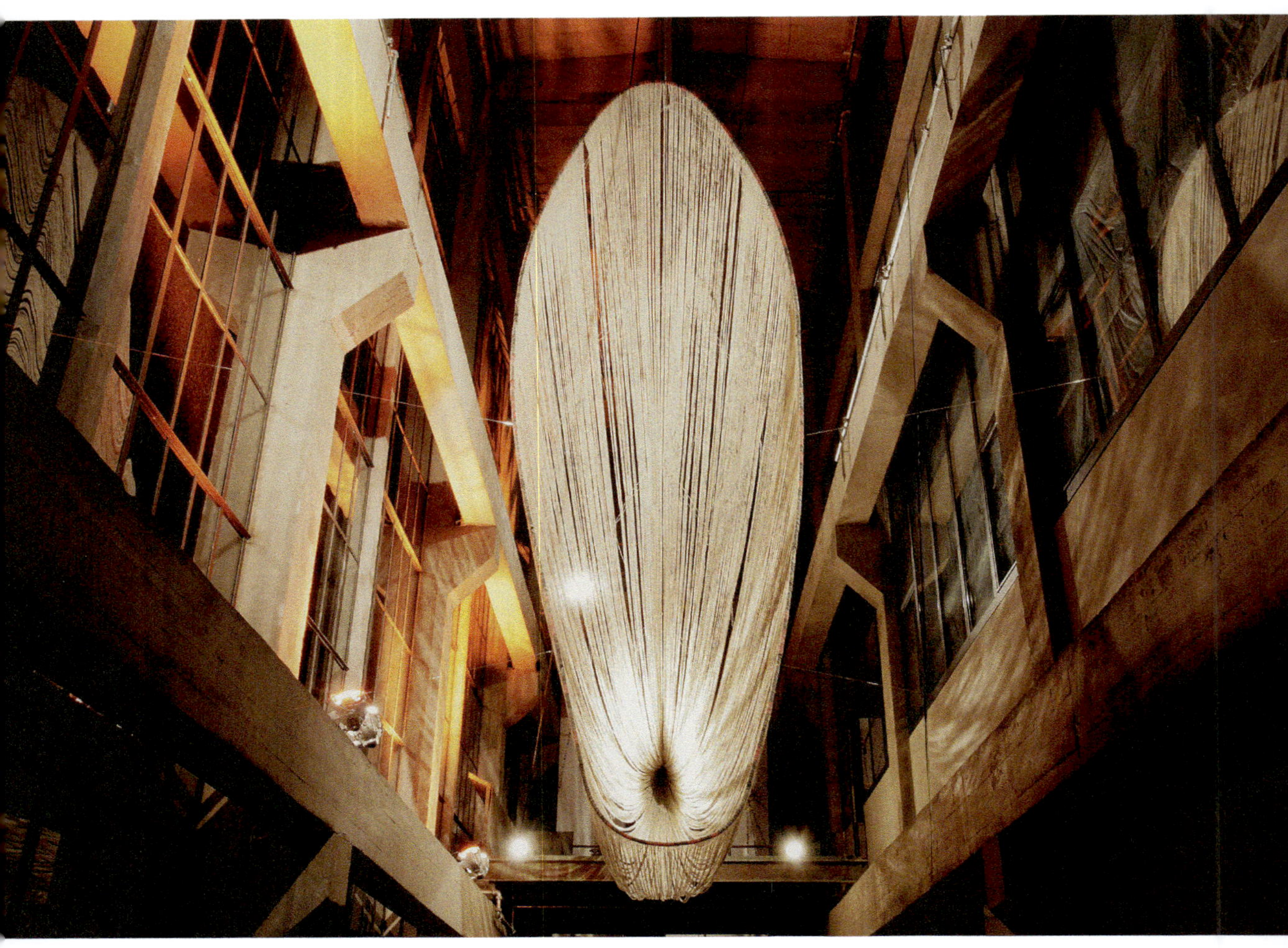

PLATE 9. *Beta Decay 5 (Antimonument)*, Kraftwerk Mitte-Dresden, September 26, 2016. Photograph by Kosuke Okahara courtesy of Shinpei Takeda.

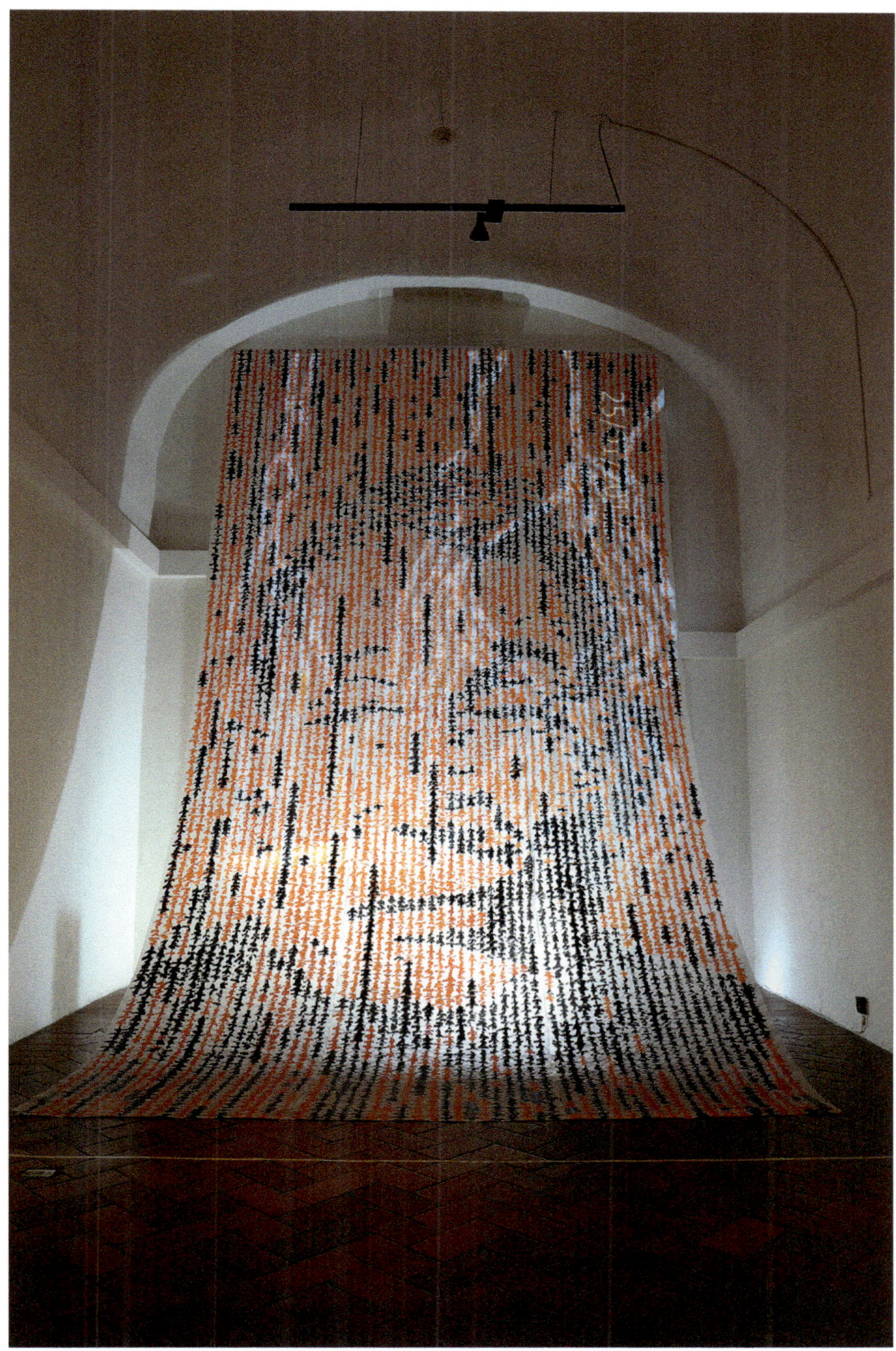

PLATE 10. *Alpha Decay*, Museo de Arte de Querétaro, January 26, 2017. Photograph courtesy of Shinpei Takeda.

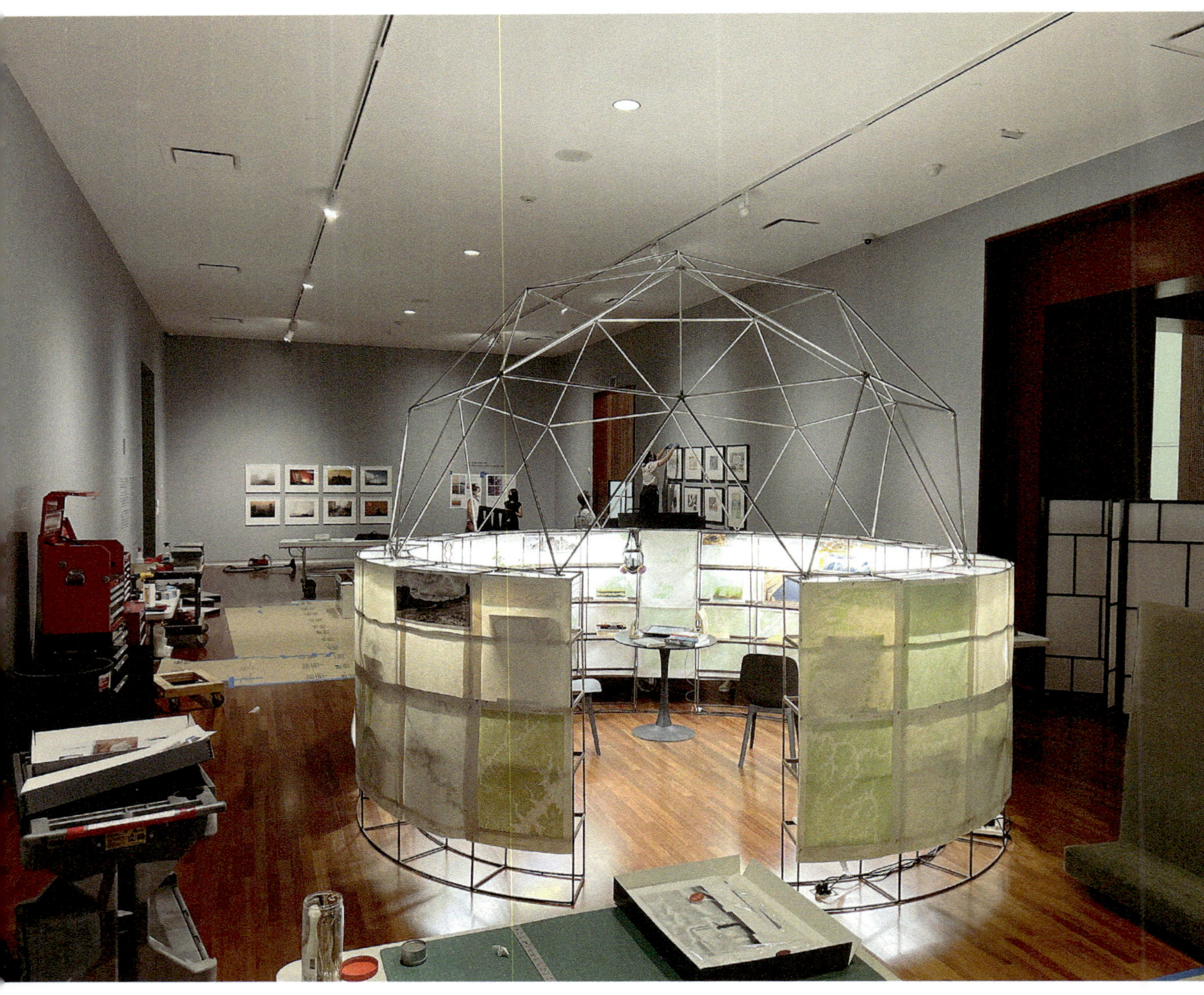

PLATE 11. Will Wilson, *Auto Immune Response Laboratory*, installation view, Utah Museum of Fine Arts, 2022. Courtesy of the artist.

PART ONE

REMEMBERING ORIGINARY MOMENTS

TRINITY, HIROSHIMA, NAGASAKI

Security and Sacrifice

Nuclear Tourism in New Mexico

MELANIE ARMSTRONG

CHAPTER 2

The sun had not yet risen when a hundred tourists boarded two luxury coaches idling in an Albuquerque Walmart parking lot. It was the first Saturday in April, one of the two days per year when the White Sands Missile Range opens its gates to allow visitors to see the Trinity Site, where the first nuclear device exploded in 1945. As we pulled onto the interstate and the suburban lights gave way to starry desert skies, a subdued chatter took over the bus. The travelers were nuclear hobbyists of many varieties, including employees of Los Alamos and Sandia National Laboratories and descendants of Manhattan Project workers. Though docents from the National Museum of Nuclear Science and History were running our tour, these family members and their firsthand accounts of life in nuclear New Mexico were the showpiece of the event. Lured by history and recreation, commemoration and curiosity, we came together as fellow pilgrims and participants in a small tourism industry built around visiting the landscapes sacrificed to the US nuclear project.

The buses sped down the highway for two hours and then sat for two more in a mile-long line of cars waiting to access the missile range. While soldiers inspected the underside of the bus with mirrors, a docent walked down the aisle collecting photo IDs from passengers for the military guard to scan. Cleared to enter, we drove farther onto the missile range on a lonely road where periodic yellow signs warned drivers to watch for exotic oryx antelope, until we saw a cloud of smoke rising in the distance. As we turned toward it, our senses suggested that the wafting smoke came not from explosives but from an industrial barbecue grill set up by one of several vendors to feed the biannual influx of tourists. The jumble of cars and people milling about the dirt field testified to a strong desire to see how the A-bomb had fused desert sand into a new American landscape. More than commemorating an event, this semiannual pilgrimage renews the contracts of national security written between citizens and governments for the nuclear age. The tourists permitted to enter that day bore an additional burden of witnessing to the rest of the world the stories embodied in that landscape.

I visited the site with curiosity, seeking to understand how this place connected to ongoing work to transform the desert Southwest into a testing ground for the national security project. The violence of the Trinity explosion has been repeated time and again in the deserts of the American West, and these forms of state-sanctioned violence against citizens continue to be remade for the modern age. Throughout New Mexico, monuments to the nuclear age stand as both art and tourist destination, while museums manage national narratives of nuclearism. Meanwhile, the health and vitality of local residents and landscapes have been continually and involuntarily sacrificed. This chapter tours sites that illustrate how the national security project continues in New Mexico today through nuclear tourism, sustaining power relations that are the "continuation of war by other means."[1]

The "disequilibrium of forces manifested in war," as Michel Foucault describes peacetime politics, inscribes relationships of power in social institutions and creates inequalities.[2] Cultural practices of tourism transform spaces into destinations, imbuing innumerable texts (e.g., photos, guidebooks, advertisements) and kitsch (postcards, mugs, keychains) with politics that create social difference and affirm authority.[3] How, then, does the observer's remembrance of violence through monuments and tourism fix power relations, and with what consequences upon people's lives? The analysis of New Mexico's nuclear tourism industry presented here explores four key perspectives about how the national nuclear narrative and its accompanying landscapes are made through ongoing politics of sacrifice and secrecy.

First, the experiences of war ingrained during the rise of the nuclear age have been remade for today's banal acts of everyday warfare. The Manhattan Project crafted new narratives about governance and the role of the nation-state in securing its citizens, while simultaneously shrouding governing systems in secrecy. After 9/11, the United States engaged in a new, globalized, totalizing, and potentially unending war against terrorism, ushering in a state of hypersecurity that was to be the "new normal."[4] Hypersecurity revived Cold War narratives of secrecy that allowed political systems to operate outside public view and required citizens to trust in government to secure their lives. When power relations remain skewed, the government is able to make national security demands of citizens as a patriotic duty, without further explanation or discussion of social effects. Tourism operates as a national security device by which modern subjects navigate these new cultural politics. As Marita Sturken says, "The mode of the tourist, with its innocent pose and distanced position, evokes the American citizen who participates uncritically in a culture in which notions of good and evil are used to define complex conflicts and tensions."[5] Further, tourists enter a place with an expectation to learn, seeking new understandings of place, ready to study and absorb the rituals of modern citizenship.[6]

Second, tourism confounds boundaries between insiders and outsiders, past and present, which sustains the disequilibrium of politics. Tourists take a detached stance, assuming the role of outsider while seeking an insider experience. Nuclear scholar Hugh Gusterson describes nuclear tourism in New Mexico as "the promise of a glimpse into the sublime and the forbidden," a positioning that infuses technological awe and Cold War secrecy into the tourist experience.[7] Joseph Masco and others demonstrate how the governance of the Cold War required poor, ethnically diverse residents of New Mexico to bear the health effects of the cradle-to-grave nuclear economy, a sacrifice that could only be seen through the breakdown of secrecy.[8] "This tension between national security and national sacrifice is what secrecy works to repress," maintaining a fiction that legitimate threats exist only outside the nation's borders.[9] When secrecy breaks, conversations about sacrifice are made possible. The cases presented here further propose that by gating certain zones to tourists and limiting, though not completely eliminating, entry, the state gathers public support for secrecy, building trust in security practices that further enable the suspension of individual human rights for the sake of the public good.

Next, these cases illustrate how the nuclear project operates on a cycle in which one sacrifice begets another. The production of the desert as a wasteland and the erasure of its inhabitants were used to rationalize the bombing of our own nation from 1945 to 1992, and now those narratives of

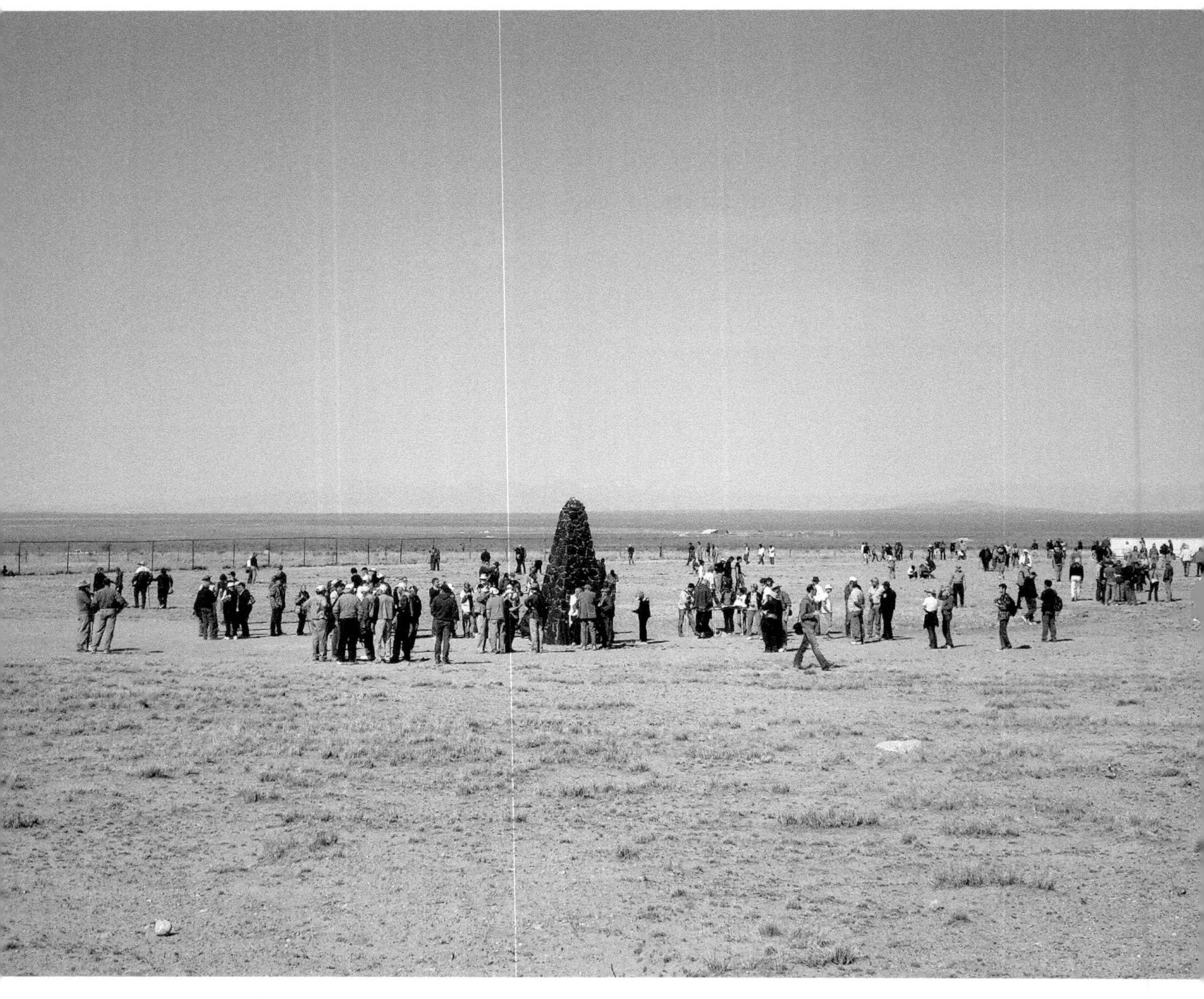

FIGURE 2.1. Trinity Site Open House, April 2010.
Photograph courtesy of Melanie Armstrong.

sacrifice reverberate in a new cultural landscape. Power relations inscribed in the place generations ago manifest again as rural communities invest their economic future in military industries, binding their individual and collective lives to a perpetual state of war. A pattern in which sacrifice is deemed necessary, work is done to justify the communal sacrifice, and then the sacrifice is ultimately memorialized communicates a national ideal of patriotism to citizens who come to witness at the memorial site.

Finally, can opportunities to resist nuclear legacies emerge through the tourism state? Looking closely at the creation and planning of nuclear tourism sites shows how the power regimes that sustain the national security state pervade the tourist experience, reinforcing the ongoing lived experience of security through a national storytelling of war, secrecy, and science. Monuments come into being through social systems and work in support of cultural narratives that sustain power relations. Richard Peet calls such monuments the "spatial surfaces of regulatory regimes, intended to frame social imaginaries often in definite, system-supportive ways" that articulate with "regional and national systems of power."[10] This is a symbolic landscape, but also a physical one where tourism is expected to be a safe experience. Nuclear tourism communicates that the toxic legacy has been remediated. By bringing their bodies to those places, tourists communicate an acceptance of that message, making it difficult to be both tourist and activist simultaneously. Still, by playing with the forms of tourism and memorialization, citizens satirically present alternative, grassroots, multiperspective counternarratives about an ongoing and extant nuclear legacy.

Trinity Test Site: White Sands Missile Range, New Mexico

A squat brown obelisk with a dull brass plaque, the Trinity Monument itself is unremarkable. The memorial sits at the exact center of four pilings, the remnants of scaffolding erected to suspend the world's first nuclear bomb above the ground before exploding it in midair. Erected twenty years after the explosion, the simple plaque reads, "Trinity Site where the world's first nuclear device was exploded on July 16, 1945." A smaller plate below designates the site a National Historic Landmark "possess(ing) national significance in commemorating the history of the United States of America." The site is not dedicated as a landmark of science or memorialized as a site of war and loss but categorized as a place integral to the formation of a nation.

At the Trinity Site, the land surrounding the obelisk tells the story of military might and scientific capability more than the messaging at the site itself. A mile of chain-link fence draws a circle in the desert, seeming to define a distinct perimeter of the blast; woody shrubs push on the fence from the outside, but within the circle the land is flat and bare, as if irrevocably damaged and barren. If one kicks at the sand, it glimmers with glassy green fragments of Trinitite, the material created as force from the fireball drew up sand from the earth and fused it with shattered fragments of the bomb and the tower that supported it. The bomb physically transformed the land here, penetrating the earth with pieces of the bomb itself and creating a landscape materially distinct from any other on the planet at the time. In a place where even the cacti seem to be withering in the sun, the dehumanized view of nature perpetuates the ongoing narrative of a wasteland that would be minimally harmed by the atomic blast.

Materially, monuments convey social ideals and reinforce power relations, meanings that can be discovered in the physical and cultural landscapes that surround the site.[11] From a Marxist perspective, memorials empower elites to perpetuate preferred narratives and "establish continuity with a suitable historical past."[12] Eric Hobsbawm argues that societies respond to new situations by referencing old situations to create a social continuity that is unchanging. The fact that an obelisk stands in the desert behind guarded gates indicates a social need to commemorate this new form of warfare using rituals similar to those employed during previous conflicts, such as the monoliths erected at Civil War battlefields. The message here is complexly that "everything has changed" yet "nothing has changed." The power relations are intact, and citizens are helpless to advocate for their own rights to not be sacrificed.

Today, the tourists' view of the site captures a moment eerily quiet after that initial act of violence, not frozen in time but gradually receding into the desert. The iron casing called Jumbo, which was brought to the site to contain the valuable plutonium in the event that the device did not ignite, sits outside the chain link near the souvenir tents and improvised parking area. Jumbo survived the 1945 test intact, but the top and bottom were lopped off in later military tests, and the rusty, broken shell now suggests that it was a victim of the nuclear explosion it originally withstood. The homestead where the bomb was assembled two miles from the test site has fallen into disrepair, and the collapsed ceilings and crumbling walls of the outbuildings, flagged with red tape warning visitors to keep out, weave the image of abandoned buildings decaying over time into the narrative of sacrifice to the nuclear project.

The dominant message of a visit to Trinity is one of remoteness and isolation. Standing near that commemorative stone, one can look over hundreds of miles of land and see few signs of human use or occupation, evoking perhaps some of the sentiment that located New Mexico as a site for the Manhattan Project and Trinity test. The sparseness of the monument along with the remoteness of the site work to affirm the wasteland myth, masking any harm to local residents, downwinders, or the land itself.

Scholarly conversations about monuments and memorials attempt to understand the different work of war monuments and war memorials in order to acknowledge the cultural effect of each. Art critic Arthur Danto points to a distinction in purpose, where monuments are about remembering and memorials are created to ensure that we never forget. Further, he argues, "monuments commemorate the memorable and embody the myths of beginnings. . . . With monuments we honor ourselves."[13] Ultimately, the Trinity Site acts as a monument to mark the dawn of the nuclear age and remember achievements of scientists and technology, rather than a memorial for the lives sacrificed to the nuclear industry.

Hugh Gusterson described a visit to the monument on the fiftieth anniversary of the Trinity test. He witnessed kitsch selling and photo taking similar to what I saw at the semiannual opening, but also watched a person splatter the monument with fake blood precisely at the 5:29 a.m. anniversary moment. Another group surrounded the monument, held hands, and hummed, while soldiers managed visitor complaints that the group was interfering with their opportunity to photograph the obelisk. Gusterson questions whether these were acts of protest, conceding that the complaining tourists, like nearly all of the thousands of visitors that day, were seeking the chance to look, observe, and "make real" through photographs, "rather than to make a point." The landscape offers little opportunity for counternarratives, and when the humming group moved to place feathers and trinkets near the remnants of the tower where the bomb had hung, "soldiers closed in on the obelisk, ready to defend it against further incursions." With military weaponry, the soldiers secured the normal operations of tourism.[14]

The semiannual opportunity to tour the closed site seems to signal a willingness on behalf of government to open the chapter on the nuclear industry of the past, even as its location on a missile range affirms that secrecy is still the "organizing principle in American society."[15] Remembering the secrecy of the Manhattan Project creates an opportunity for tourists to frame the work of current governments in a social history of secrecy and security. The tension between sacrifice and security continues in the post-9/11 world, where governments require citizens to sacrifice privacy on telephone calls or time waiting in airport lines as everyday acts of national security. The tourist experience at Trinity affirms the continuity of the regimes of power that created the nuclear bomb in modern systems of governance.

Energetic Materials Research and Testing Center: Socorro, New Mexico

Our tour group from the nuclear museum spent the morning at the monolith and then gathered for a lecture and picnic lunch on the golf course at the New Mexico Institute of Mining and Technology. After lunch, we traveled to the school's Energetic Materials Research and Testing Center (EMRTC), where we further commemorated New Mexico's explosive past by watching people blow things up. The EMRTC range lies on a gated road that leads from campus into the foothills west of town. As we entered our second restricted area of the day, the buses navigated hairpin turns through a landscape littered with the shells of bombed-out cars and exploded bunkers, remnants of earlier exercises. At a high point overlooking Socorro to the east and a firing range to the west, we gathered around a muscled EMRTC guide standing in the back of a pickup truck, who described the demonstration we would see, using bits of tubing and detonators to explain why C4 worked well for certain types of explosions and what exactly constitutes a fertilizer bomb.

After the lesson, we huddled behind a cement and plexiglass barrier, gazing up into mirrors to watch while the crew blasted a grapefruit, a wooden stand, and a steel plate with increasing quantities of explosives.

Before each round, the guide slowly counted down from five, and the audience inhaled in anticipation. Following each snap, bang, or boom, the group collectively exhaled and then chattered eagerly about the detonation, trying to put into words what they had just seen and heard. The last and largest explosion drew a collective "ooooo" from the audience as it pulsed the ground beneath our feet and shattered one of the mirrors above our heads. Crouching behind that wall, we were reenacting in a small way the experiences of July 16, 1945, when scientists and spectators gathered at a distance to watch the blast that rang in the atomic age. We tourists participated firsthand in the sensory experience of a bomb, reenacting the rituals of the nuclear tests, if on a much smaller scale. We could feel the shaking of the ground, see the flashes of light, hear the delayed echoes of sound, and share the collective experience of hunkering down behind a wall to anticipate the blast.

People's raw and reflexive reactions to the explosives demonstration at the EMRTC paralleled the group's general excitement to commemorate the Trinity blast, raising the question of why a powerful explosion in the past can be so readily accessed in the present. Scholars have theorized that people learn about violence by witnessing acts of trauma, a form of spectator citizenship made possible through media forms.[16] Demonstrating technologies of violence in the mountains outside Socorro makes the experience of a bomb accessible to a live audience. Such commemorations promise to make known some part of the local experience of place along with a firsthand knowledge of how a bomb—whether a nuclear device or a wad of C4—can change a place.

The secrecy that shrouds these sites in the present also creates continuity with the past. From the Manhattan Project to the present, the practices that inscribe the New Mexican landscape with the marks of war and terror persist alongside a devotion to secrecy. Masco contends that the secrecy of the Cold War set the stage for present-day counterrorism measures.[17] At the EMRTC, the attraction to explosives is put to work for civil defense purposes or homeland security. The center markets its expertise in the explosives field to the public and private sectors and has been federally designated a regional center for homeland security.

The Materials Research and Testing Center also markets research, specifically information about the behaviors of war. The security state is sustained by the continual input of information and the quest to calculate human behavior in order to govern more effectively. The national security project that began before Trinity emerges in contemporary form in New Mexico, with new impacts upon the lives of citizens. Residents of this economically poor and geographically rural state seek out ways to make the landscape viable. Building upon the nuclear science work that brought the state into the center of US military might, New Mexicans continue to work in military development, as well as in the broad domestic preparedness projects, and the desert landscape continues to fulfill a specific role in providing landscapes for secrecy and testing. The security practices instituted in the region inscribe New Mexico's desert "wasteland" with national purpose, continuing to render the state a national sacrifice zone. In a landscape that has been mined, built, and blasted for the nation's nuclear project, and where citizens' bodies have been harmed by the work they did for the nuclear industry, the sacrifice zone is a place where destruction is writ upon the surface, perpetuating a belief that this is indeed a land of waste. Thus, a land bombed once becomes the best site to bomb again; moreover, people harmed by the militarization of their homeland are also unable to make a living outside the security economy and therefore embrace military industries as the only option for their own survival. The involuntary sacrifice of communities to the military complex presents a complicated case of justice and equality, where an original sacrifice makes way for an economy that depends upon ventures that further the sacrifice demanded of residents.

Manhattan Project National Historic Park: Los Alamos, New Mexico

On November 10, 2015, the US secretaries of interior and energy signed an agreement defining how their two agencies would work together to manage the newly created Manhattan Project National Historic Park. For more than a decade, public and private entities across multiple states, including New Mexico, Tennessee, and Washington, had advocated for the creation of a national park unit to protect historical resources associated with the Manhattan Project, a secretive mobilization of scientists, engineers, and technicians to create an atomic weapon during World War II. The new park included sites in Los Alamos, Oak Ridge, and Hanford, and gave management responsibility jointly to the Department of Energy (DOE) and the National Park Service (NPS). Thus, the agency driven by the mission to "ensure America's security and prosperity by addressing its energy, environmental and nuclear challenges" linked arms with the agency that "preserves unimpaired the natural and cultural resources and values of the national park system for the education, enjoyment, and inspiration of this and future generations" to create an organization, a story, and a tourism industry around the United States' nuclear legacy.

Creating a national park is a powerful act of nationalism. Parks translate "geographical space into canonical landscapes," an act deemed of high political importance to creating and maintaining a cohesive nation.[18] The NPS role in producing a national narrative can be seen in the remarks of Interior Secretary Sally Jewell about the Manhattan Project Park: "Visitors will *soon be able to see* the contributions of more than 600,000 Americans who played a role in this significant chapter in history" (italics added).[19] Though people would have limited access to high-security DOE sites at the parks, Jewell's remarks indicate the perceived role a national park has in crafting a story: making visible something formerly unseen, including citizen sacrifice.

Notably, from the earliest conversations about the potential for a nuclear park, the content of that story has been questioned and scrutinized, whether by antinuclear groups or by disempowered communities whose narratives have been and continue to be muted or distorted to promote a powerful nationalism.[20] In his statement on the new park, NPS director Jonathan Jarvis described the agency's work "to tell the complete and complex story," reinforcing the idea that NPS narratives can be "complete," even in their complexity.[21] Such beliefs don't strictly emerge from within the agency, however. Press coverage of the site creation affirmed the power the NPS would have over the national nuclear narrative through its interpretation of the Manhattan Project. One reporter wrote that until the park was fully funded, the "final story of Las Alamos remains unwritten."[22] Given the cultural and political authority of the NPS to manage national narratives, it is essential to evaluating tourism's potential to resist nuclear regimes to consider the state's power to define its own nuclear legacy through the management and promotion of tourism.

Creating a new national park requires a combination of executive and administrative acts, as well as countless planning activities. One of the earliest exercises of the new Manhattan Project site was the creation of a foundation document, an assessment that gives direction to park planning by articulating a narrative describing what is "important" about the park, as defined by a team of agency officials with some public input.[23] The foundation document does not prescribe management actions, but resources identified as important stand poised to receive attention as funding becomes available.

The foundation document also presents a set of interpretive themes, or narrative of the place, that "help explain why a park story is relevant to people who may otherwise be unaware of connections they have to an event, time, or place associated with the park."[24] Themes are crafted with the intent to guide park employees in creating opportunities (through signs, public programs, and individual interactions) for visitors to learn to care about a place.

What, then, does the Manhattan Project Foundation Document say to inform the national narrative of secrecy and sacrifice around the US nuclear regime? The park's first interpretive theme reads, "The 'secret cities' created for the Manhattan Project, and the sacrifice and displacement connected to them, exemplified this massive wartime effort and demonstrate remarkable opportunities to reflect on the extraordinary lengths to which people and nations go to protect their futures."[25] The narrative recognizes the displacement of tribes and other settlements and the sacrifice of "homes lands and waters, sacred sites, and the access to sacred sites" as part of the national nuclear project, and its inclusion as an interpretive theme suggests an expectation that people will ideologically connect to the need for such displacement during times of exception.[26] The document elaborates on how the Manhattan Project led to violation of tribal treaties, segregation of minority workers, and harm to Japanese people, but also crafts a narrative that rationalizes such actions as necessities of war. Other statements recognize the harmful human and environmental legacy of nuclear war but step away from assigning responsibility or illuminating a pathway to resistance.[27] Tourists who travel through the site are encouraged to focus on the "many complex decisions," "profound choices and consequences," and "severe human costs and environmental consequences" of the Manhattan Project, however excruciating, as a necessity of war.[28]

Finally, the physical spaces of the new national park work similarly to the Trinity Site on the White Sands Missile Range in using tourism to affirm the work of the national security state. The foundation document delineates a purpose to "provide access to these sites consistent with the mission of the Department of Energy." Some sites included in the park have been restricted due to visitor safety concerns and ongoing cleanup activities. In public hearings about the park, people expressed concern about "how visitors might move around when 'behind the fence.'"[29] Still, access was prioritized in the park's enabling legislation, directing managers to promote visitation through guided activities and virtual experiences. This type of visitation aligns with nuclear tourism patterns established in other locations, where access through controlled circumstances affirms the need for secrecy and citizen control. Opening a site to visitors also recruits them as cocreators in the site's narratives. Visitors sacrifice freedom to move through the space, embodying a prominent narrative of national security—the sacrifice of individual rights for the good of the nation—through the tourist experience. It works in these places because it fits.

Such tourist endeavors do little to create opportunities for individuals to resist nuclear legacies. Opponents of the park expressed concern that the site would serve as propaganda for the ongoing weapons work of Los Alamos National Laboratory or that the physical displacement of the past would be repeated by excluding from the narrative stories of the community or those who were harmed. When the first NPS director described national parks as an "antidote for national restlessness," he likely envisioned the soothing health effects of fresh air and forests in places like Yosemite, but the agency's cultural work of delineating history similarly offers to calm social unrest.[30] By providing a cohesive historical narrative, connected to the present, with opportunities for tourists to gaze at what is otherwise unseen and enter into remediated spaces, the state assuages fears of nuclearism and celebrates it as an experience of the past.

From park creation and planning to the daily visitor experience, national parks also centralize the authority of the state to tell the nation's history. Not only is America's ongoing nuclear legacy a site for resistance in national parks, but the form of the park itself is subject to reconsideration.

In what ways might the practices through which a national park, trail, or historic site functions be used to shift power systems in ways that transform parks into "social processes [or] participatory, decolonial spaces"?[31] Two examples of speculative national parks show how telling the nuclear story using the trope of a national park creates landscapes of activism and resistance.

National Park: Form and Resistance

In 1990, artist Robert Misrach proposed the Bravo 20 National Park for the site of the Nevada bombing range used by the US Navy since 1952. Along with a photographic exhibition and written account of the site's military history, Misrach proposed the park as a "permanent reminder of how military, government, corporate, and individual practices can harm the earth . . . [and] a national acknowledgment of a complex and disturbing period in our history."[32] The Bravo 20 National Park proposal included commissioned architectural renderings of a visitor center and grounds, along with site maps, interpretive programs, museum, cafe, campgrounds, and a viewing tower. While the exhibit was criticized as having no "radical edge" as a political statement, Catrin Gersdorf proposes that by employing the mechanism of park creation, Bravo 20 National Park had a reformative effect.[33] By using the national park form, Misrach taps into the logics of remediation that characterize the daily work of the National Park Service, not only on ecological landscapes but through memorialization of the past. Here, the remediation of a militarized "wasteland" is accomplished through beautiful photographs: "It is meant to improve the landscape but also somehow to remediate our practices of military testing or our militaristic posture towards nature in the twentieth century."[34] The form of the park proposal, complete with architectural renderings, underscores the reality of parks as cultural constructs, created through practices like those that formed the Manhattan Project National Historic Park.

Parks and monuments also work to make visible that which might not otherwise be seen, such as ecological processes, stories, pasts, and people. As a primary object of the tourist gaze, parks are designed to be seen, inviting those who come near to engage with the place. Still, as illustrated in the formation of the Manhattan Project site, government agencies manage what people see and how. Two decades after Bravo 20, a second speculative production plays with the invisibility of America's toxic nuclear legacy, not only of the radiation itself but the remote, inaccessible, and hidden sites that form the physical spaces of the nuclear story.

Artist Sarah Kanouse and geographer Shiloh Krupar established the National Toxic Land/Labor Conservation (TLC) Service to memorialize the ongoing nuclear project in a way that enables a critique while also "sincerely commemorating" the bodies and landscapes sacrificed to the nation's nuclear project. Beginning with its charter in 2011, this "wishful government agency" set about attending "to the domestic issues of environmental justice, labor, and human rights related to US military activities."[35] Through its website, uniforms, logo, brochures, badges, and PowerPoint presentations, the TLC "takes hold of authority without having it."[36] This "aesthetic of bureaucratic camp," in Kanouse's characterization, imitates the techniques the government uses to build authority, right down to the adoption of the bald eagle mascot.[37] Part satire, part sincere, the National TLC Service uses its assumed bureaucratic authority to characterize the nuclear state as in need of an institutional response and establishes itself as the institution responsible for providing such. It then sets about the work of creating the National Cold War Monuments and Environmental Heritage Trail, "a collection of speculative, grassroots markers, actions, and routes to mark atomic geographies on a regional basis."[38] It is notable that the institution chosen for this mission imitates most closely the National Park Service, the government's storytelling and authority-building apparatus.

Recognizing that the dominant story of the Cold War has marginalized numerous counternarratives, the National TLC Service proposes to draw public attention to left-out stories. The service hosts "design charrettes," a form of public engagement popularized in agency processes where stakeholders collaborate in designing structural responses to an issue. Charettes both sustain authority and offer a venue for participatory processes. In making the Heritage Trail, the charette plays with power systems by redistributing the assumed power of the National TLC service to citizens through an invitation to design their own monuments and memorials.

During the all-day charrettes, participants first critique a map of their local atomic geography, noting inevitable omissions. Next, groups sketch "experimental routes" to draw attention to how the atomic story is told

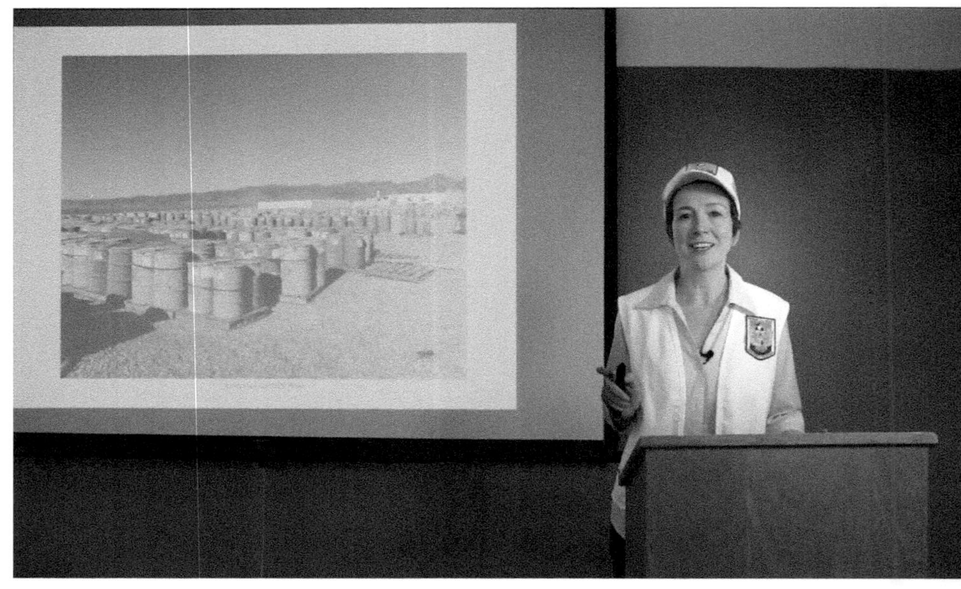

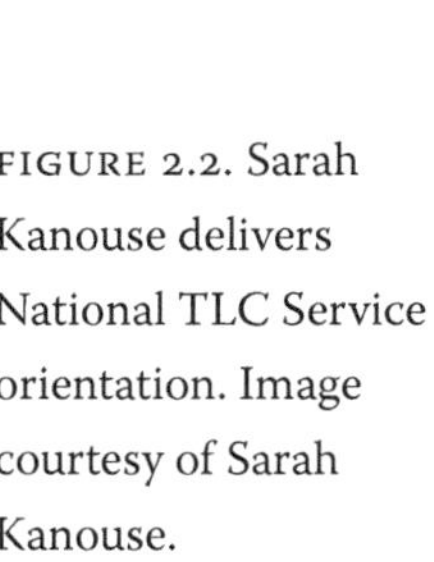

FIGURE 2.2. Sarah Kanouse delivers National TLC Service orientation. Image courtesy of Sarah Kanouse.

through movement and to propose particular ways of moving through space. One group in Illinois designed a railroad tour, following tracks that once carried nuclear material. Another group imagined a "self-directed tour, completely interconnected, yet with no beginning or end spot."[39] At each stop, visitors would hear a spoken narrative, see a direction pole pointing toward other sites, and take a rubbing of a site marker as a "take-away" component. A third group proposed a bus tour where the driver provides general narration but when asked questions responds, "I'm not authorized to disclose that," underscoring the secrecy of nuclear sites.[40]

The charrette concludes around monuments and the question "How can a monument make present and collective our knowledge of the persistence of the atomic in our lives, lands, and bodies?"[41] Proposed monuments ranged from the collection of passport-stamp-like rubbings to a memorial where visitors walk through elements of the water cycle to commemorate those victimized by rainwater fallout. One group designed a Mobile Radiation Lab, "an ultra-government project" that collects both personal stories and statistical data. Visitors would have their hair tested for heavy metals while recording personal histories. Participant Amber Ginsburg explained, "This project comes out of the frustration of insufficient documentation

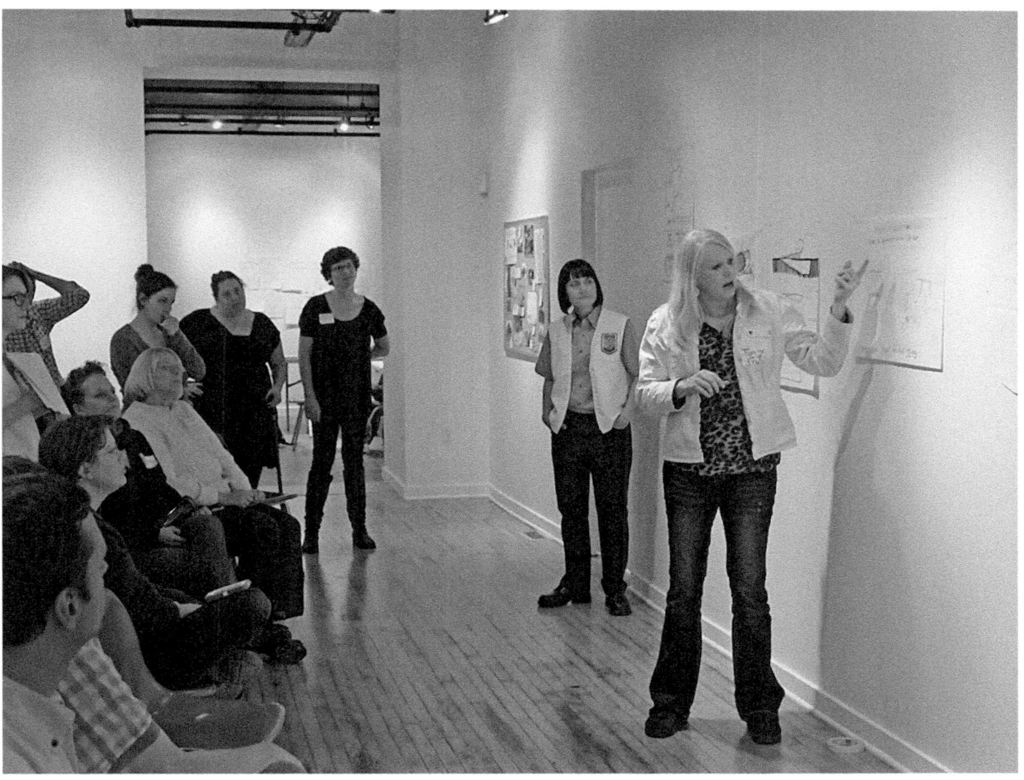

FIGURE 2.3. Jennifer Smith of the Saint Louis Radioactive Waste Action Coalition explaining the Mobile Radiation Lab proposal to the group during the final session of the 2013 National TLC Illinois charrette. Photograph by Sara Alsum Wasenaar. Image courtesy of Sarah Kanouse.

on toxins stored in our bodies and with disease classification . . . recognizing that disease, environment and storytelling are enmeshed."[42] The charettes produce historical information and current circumstances that are situated, individual, and subject to interpretation, and the trail takes shape through acts of imaginative memorializing, for landscapes do not preexist their construction. Individual citizens use the tools of state memorialization to share perspectives not just on the Cold War of the past but on its present and future.

Though speculative, the National TLC Service performs fiction as fact, a technique for contesting the accuracy of the historical narrative.[43] Significantly, the performance also "prefigures a different world" where "the change[s] we desire from our governments and institutions are feasible, actual realities."[44] By using the trope of a national park to imagine and materialize the practices to create such landscapes, artistic endeavors like Bravo 20 National Park and the National TLC Service resist a singular Cold War narrative as told through memorials and monuments like the Trinity Site or the Manhattan Project National Historic Park.

The material landscapes of New Mexico have long been a laboratory for new forms of violence. The US government transformed the desert ecosystems, including human populations, to pursue knowledge and weapons of war. The sensory experience of war pervades these landscapes. Sacrifice zones endure due to the belief that the growth of the nation's military strength will require sacrifice and compromise from its citizens. New Mexico's sacrifice to the nuclear industry has been ecological, biological, and cultural, but the sacrifice has also involved binding up freedoms and futures with a singular economic purpose. Nuclear tourism seeks to open a door to a new economy but does little to upset power strata or create narratives outside the nuclear past. From one site to another, citizens experience themselves as part of history and rehearse a pro-nuclear point of view as part of their national learning.[45]

If national security depends upon a focus on the future, sites like Trinity drop out of the security narrative through the loss of its future. Tourism also gives a historical site a future: "What truly effects the re-signification of the landscape is the visit itself. Your body at the site, the family being-there, acts as a witness of the transubstantiation—the touristic ritual enacting a transformation of land and event from dangerous and secret, to safe and touristed."[46] By integrating bodily experiences of remediation and secrecy, tourism greenwashes toxic legacies while vitalizing the ongoing national security project and its nuclear regimes. Through rituals of commemoration and the work of tourists like our group from the National Nuclear Museum, tourism keeps the narrative of sacrifice vibrant in the national security project. Each sneak peek into the inner workings of the nation's war laboratory in New Mexico retells stories of power and military might, sustaining the security apparatus that today reverberates through the nation's borderlands.

Notes

1. Michel Foucault, *Society Must Be Defended: Lectures at the College de France, 1975–1976* (New York: Picador, 1997), 15.
2. Foucault, *Society Must Be Defended*, 16.
3. Marita Sturken, *Tourists of History: Memory, Kitsch, and Consumerism from Oklahoma City to Ground Zero* (Durham: Duke University Press, 2007); Miriam Kahn, "Tahiti Intertwined: Ancestral Land, Tourist Postcard, and Nuclear Test Site," *American Anthropologist* 102, no. 1 (March 2000): 7–26.
4. Joseph Masco, *Nuclear Borderlands: The Manhattan Project in Post–Cold War New Mexico* (Princeton, NJ: Princeton University Press, 2006), 285.
5. Sturken, *Tourists of History*, 10.
6. Sarah Kanouse, "Critical Daytrips," in *Critical Landscapes*, ed. Emily Eliza Scott and Kirsten J. Swenson (Berkeley: University of California Press, 2015), 43–56.
7. Hugh Gusterson, "Nuclear Tourism," *Journal for Cultural Research* 8, no. 1 (January 2004): 24.
8. Masco, *Nuclear Borderlands*; Ward Churchill, *A Little Matter of Genocide: Holocaust and Denial in the Americas 1492 to the Present* (San Francisco: City Lights Books, 1997); Valerie Kuletz, *The Tainted Desert: Environmental Ruin in the American West* (New York: Routledge, 1998); Traci Brynne Voyles, *Wastelanding: Legacies of Uranium Mining in Navajo Country* (Minneapolis: University of Minnesota Press, 2015).
9. Masco, *Nuclear Borderlands*, 277.
10. Richard Peet, "A Sign Taken for History: Daniel Shays' Memorial in Petersham, Massachusetts," *Annals of the Association of American Geographers* 86, no. 1 (March 1996): 37.
11. Peet, "A Sign Taken for History."
12. Eric Hobsbawm, "Introduction: Inventing Traditions," in *The Invention of Tradition*, ed. Eric Hobsbawm and Terence Ranger (Cambridge: Cambridge University Press, 1983), 11.
13. Arthur C. Danto, "The Vietnam Veterans Memorial," *The Nation*, August 31, 1985, 152.
14. Gusterson, "Nuclear Tourism," 27–28.
15. Masco, *Nuclear Borderlands*, 284.
16. Carrie A. Rentschler, "Witnessing: US Citizenship and the Vicarious Experience of Suffering," *Media, Culture and Society* 26, no. 2 (2004): 296–304; Susan Sontag, *Regarding the Pain of Others* (New York: Farrar, Straus and Giroux, 2003).
17. Masco, *Nuclear Borderlands*, 284.
18. Catrin Gersdorf, *The Poetics and Politics of the Desert: Landscape and the Construction of America* (Amsterdam: Rodopi, 2009), 301.
19. Department of Interior, "Interior and Energy Departments Formally Establish the Manhattan Project National Historical Park," news release, November 10, 2015, https://www.doi.gov/pressreleases/interior-and-energy-departments-formally-establish-manhattan-project-national.

20. Ellen McGehee and John Isaacson, "Interpreting the Bomb: Contested History and the Proposed Manhattan Project National Historical Park at Los Alamos," *Journal of the West* 50, no. 3 (2011): 51. For alternative points of view, see Los Alamos Study Group, "DOE, Park Service to Create New National Park for Old Nuclear Weapons—the Ones Dropped on Cities: Group Warns of Cultural Consequences," news release, November 9, 2015, https://www.lasg.org/press/2015/press_release_09Nov2015.html; Raffi Edward Andonia, "Nuclear History: Debating the Meanings of the Manhattan Project National Historical Park" (MA thesis, University of Georgia, 2013), 41–55.
21. Department of Interior. "Interior and Energy Departments Formally Establish."
22. Megan Kamerick, "Passions Flare over Memory of the Manhattan Project," National Public Radio, January 14, 2017, https://www.npr.org/2017/01/14/508743747/passions-flare-over-memory-of-the-manhattan-project.
23. National Park Service, *Foundation Document: Manhattan Project National Historic Park. Tennessee, New Mexico, Washington,* January 2017, https://www.nps.gov/mapr/upload/MAPR_FD_PRINT.pdf, 3.
24. National Park Service, *Foundation Document,* 26.
25. National Park Service, *Foundation Document,* 26.
26. National Park Service, *Foundation Document,* 17.
27. National Park Service, *Foundation Document,* 17.
28. National Park Service, *Foundation Document,* 26.
29. "Summary of Open House Comments," Manhattan Project, National Park Service, May 26, 2016, https://www.nps.gov/mapr/learn/management/summary-of-public-open-house-comments.htm.
30. National Park Service, *Report of the Director of the National Park Service to the Secretary of the Interior,* 1923, 7.
31. "Prefigurative Park Services," Nicholas Brown website, accessed March 25, 2023, https://www.nicholasanthonybrown.net/prefigurative-park-services.
32. Richard Misrach, *Bravo 20: The Bombing of the American West* (Baltimore: Johns Hopkins University Press, 1990), 95.
33. Richard Grusin, *Culture, Technology and the Creation of America's National Parks* (Cambridge: Cambridge University Press, 2004), 166; Gersdorf, *The Poetics and Politics of the Desert,* 305.
34. Grusin, *Culture, Technology and the Creation,* 168.
35. "Welcome," National Toxic Land/Labor Conservation Service, accessed March 25, 2023, https://www.nationaltlcservice.us/.
36. Joseph M. Sussi, "Living with Our Toxic Legacy," *Hemispheres: Visual Cultures of the Americas* 11, no. 1 (2018): 62.
37. Sarah Kanouse, "National Toxic Land/Labor Conservation Service," May 15, 2016, https://readysubjects.org/portfolio/national-toxic-landlabor-conservation-service/.
38. "Our Programs," National Toxic Land/Labor Conservation Service, https://www.nationaltlcservice.us/.

39. National Toxic Land / Labor Conservation Service, *Charrette Report Illinois*, 2014, 8.
40. National TLC Service, *Charrette Report Illinois*, 12.
41. National TLC Service, *Charrette Report Illinois*, 14.
42. National TLC Service, *Charrette Report Illinois*, 24.
43. Sussi writes about the National TLC Service as "parafictional practice," the intentional act of portraying fiction as fact, in "Living with Our Toxic Legacy," 57.
44. Brown, "Prefigurative Park Services"; Sussi, "Living with Our Toxic Legacy," 72.
45. Sturken, *Tourists of History*, 9.
46. Sean Simon, "A Visitor Centre for the Next Nuclear Disaster," *Performance Research* 24, no. 5 (2019): 64.

CHAPTER 3

A People's Atlas of Nuclear Colorado

Art and Activism in the Digital Space

MELANIE ARMSTRONG, SARAH KANOUSE
AND SHILOH R. KRUPAR

A People's Atlas of Nuclear Colorado (www.coloradonuclearatlas.org) is a digital public humanities project that documents and interprets nuclear geographies and legacies of the Cold War. The essays, issue briefs, artworks, and interpretive works that compose the *Atlas* engage with nuclear materials and ecologies through different approaches, engagements, and scales of operation in relationship to nuclear geographies. Creators Shiloh R. Krupar and Sarah Kanouse use the atlas format to provide context to thousands of nuclear sites that dot the map of Colorado, showing how the landscape and its maps were created over time.

Sarah Kanouse is an interdisciplinary artist and writer examining the politics of landscape and space. She is associate professor of Media Arts in the Department of Art + Design at Northeastern University. Shiloh Krupar is a geographer and Provost's Distinguished Associate Professor at Georgetown University, where she directs the Culture and Politics Program in the School of Foreign Service. This interview took place on September 10, 2021, via Zoom.

MELANIE ARMSTRONG: **How did *A People's Atlas of Nuclear Colorado* build upon your earlier work in art and activism, such as the National TLC service?**

SARAH KANOUSE: I'm primarily an artist—an unusual kind of scholarly artist but definitely not a scholar by training. I love the capaciousness of art and its methodological heterogeneity—characteristics shared to a certain degree by the discipline of geography. Shiloh and I met during a moment in the 2000s when artists and geographers were finding each other, and I found in Shiloh a very artistic scholar. We came up with the idea of the

National Toxic Land and Labor Conservation Service, which employed sincere satire to talk about the inadequacies of the existing governmental response—but also the profound impossibility of any kind of adequate response—to the toxic domestic legacies of the Cold War. We created an alternate government agency operating, wishfully, within the Department of the Interior and offered tours and public programming around nuclear legacies.

SHILOH R. KRUPAR: I also had been thinking about critique as an organizing tool and different forms of geographical practice. As an educator located in an international relations school in Washington, DC, I continually confront a kind of privileged thoughtlessness—perpetuated by American exceptionalism—about everyday nuclear conditions and colonialism in the United States and elsewhere. I thought, how might performance-based practice in environmental education take into account Cold War legacies of violence?

Through a series of public workshops, the National Toxic Land and Labor Conservation Service brought together different parts of communities impacted by Cold War work, including folks positioned antagonistically within the nuclear complex, such as nuclear weapons workers and environmentalists. Through role playing, we collaborated on the design of a national memorial trail—the National Cold War Monuments and Environmental Heritage Trail—using art as a speculative kind of knowledge sharing and social organizing device. I really appreciated the agency's emphasis on everyday experience as a site of play and experimentation—as the grounds for making connections across different sites and struggles. The parodic inhabiting of a government agency can work to make the fear and uncertainness of the nuclear into something more livable and actionable.

KANOUSE: Then in 2016, Donald Trump was elected president, and suddenly this space of wishful, sincere satire didn't feel like the right register to be operating in. At the beginning of his administration, web pages were being taken down, scientific information on the EPA [Environmental Protection Agency] website was disappearing, and there was great rejoicing on the part of polluters everywhere that regulation was going to just disappear. Government employees were at great personal risk, salvaging research and making it available. The space of sincere satire did not seem like it was honoring the efforts of the people who were working in the existing government. We conceived of the *Atlas* around this time as a way of making what is often fairly impenetrable in federal law a little bit more accessible and integrative. We also wanted to include interpretive essays, personal narratives, artworks, and other elements that would make an affectively rich space that was habitable by human beings, not just the often bloodless language of policy.

ARMSTRONG: What opportunities do you see in the digital form to create that depth you seek in the *Atlas*?

KANOUSE: It is much cheaper to include rich visual materials than in a printed book, so the *Atlas* is very, very richly illustrated with photographs, documents, historical maps, and contemporary digital "dots on a map" maps. Juxtaposing engineering and technical reports from the 1950s or 1960s and EPA documents from the 1990s and 2000s with a photograph of the site as it exists in the present day reinforces that nuclear sites are layered places shaped by a variety of forces.

KRUPAR: As somebody who has not worked extensively in the digital space, one of the concerns I had early on emerged from my preconceived notion of materiality and the digital. I was concerned about what would happen in digital space, possibly not being able to think in depth or get at the different registers of materiality going on within the nuclear complex from the scale of political economy to someone having a piece of uranium in their home as a keepsake. In the process of working on that, I realized that the binary was already problematic, of course. The digital platform and different materials composing the *Atlas* allow for productive dissensus. The *Atlas* holds together sometimes antagonistic perspectives that can function as an antifilter bubble instead of the echo chambers on social media. It acknowledges and invites different users and uses. It doesn't force a consensus but holds the stuff in a conceptual framework. It is not arguing that an official account, like the Manhattan Project National Historical Park, is wrong; rather, the *Atlas* organizes layers and adds nuance and complexity to it.

ARMSTRONG: The *Atlas* is structured around the nuclear fuel cycle. This forms a spine for the collection and brings the abstract notion of the cycle into those places where nuclear products and effects move through the environment.

KANOUSE: The nuclear fuel cycle is an organizing principle that is always pushing against its own limits. There are three primary ways of navigating the *Atlas*: there's a map view, a search function, and a more linear narrative that loosely follows the fuel cycle. This third approach is privileged in terms of the user interface. If users were to go through everything in a linear fashion, they would actually see the same material more than once and some materials two or three times. The organizing principle of the discrete phases of the fuel cycle quickly breaks down, and you realize that material of the *Atlas*—like nuclear by-products themselves—cannot be so easily contained or classified.

We also have paired each stage of the nuclear fuel cycle with its shadow, which we understand as the consequences and products that are disavowed by the official, positivist version. Wherever there is refining, there is also exposure. Wherever there is nuclear production, there is also friction or resistance, whether that presented by activists or the uncontainable materials themselves. At the end of each chapter, the user may either jump to the next official or positivist part of the fuel cycle or explore the shadow side.

KRUPAR: More recently I have realized that a value of the project is its conceptual use of the fuel cycle as a counterpractice against *governance through separation*. Drawings of the nuclear fuel cycle are pristine. Often, they have a clear, developmental, unilinear end point, delineating "earth" and "waste," or a tidy circle with waste containment feeding back into the cycle. This is profoundly disturbing and just not true, given how much waste there is along every step of the process. Essentially the formal ways that the *Atlas* refutes this tidy fuel cycle architecture *is* the argument.

ARMSTRONG: You also use the shadows to represent irreconcilable dualisms.

KANOUSE: In early conversation with our designers, we emphasized avoiding the idea that the shadow side was simply the negative or just the inverse of the positivist side. A shadow is not the negative of the thing that is casting it; it is the effect of that thing in the world. By blocking light, an object produces a shadow. So, visually, this grittier, earthy gradient is overlaid on a lot of the same material, because entries can exist both in the positivist path and in the shadow. Although the content is the same, it may appear differently because you are looking at it through a different lens. This is not the familiar "pros and cons" of these technologies but rather what is avowed and disavowed when we look at the nuclear fuel cycle through that technocratic positivist vision. The shadow side draws attention to the necessary disavowals that support the technocratic worldview.

KRUPAR: One of the things I like about the integration of the so-called shadow side of the *Atlas* is that what is uncertain or unintelligible or unclear is actually material and empirical. Integrating these shadow effects into the *Atlas* is not about revealing the truth or dispelling them; it is making those shadows intelligible. It is about recognizing that the indeterminacies, impurities, and embodied effects of the nuclear age are here with us—that is the norm and the status quo. Working through modes of material critique that acknowledge and promulgate different subjective interpretive analyses is an important counterpractice to the resilient militarized life and environmental security that is sought after amid widespread, mounting conditions of insecurity and risk. There is such a range of remainders created by the nuclear fuel cycle, like subjugated knowledges, impure bodies, illnesses, contaminated land, nuclear waste. We can bring them together and think about their relationship to the positivist technocratic, techno-utopian, heroic narrative at work. The *Atlas* shows that the material toxic legacies of warmaking do not protect citizens or secure the territorial integrity of the country.

ARMSTRONG: The introduction to the *Atlas* says it is designed to help people "better understand the consequences of our nuclear past, the condition of the nuclear present, and the shape of the nuclear future." How does the *Atlas*'s emphasis on artistic approaches and ongoing community authorship further that goal?

KANOUSE: Art is one of the only socially sanctioned places for experimenting with the contours of perception and with propositions for a different way of seeing and inhabiting and feeling the world. Some artworks in the *Atlas* envision mechanisms for caring for nuclear waste. Others are monuments to toxic sites, commenting through visual means on the legacies of absence, abandonment, and amnesia. They operate at the register less of argument and evidence and more in terms of affect and aesthetic. If we understand the aesthetic as less what is subjectively pleasing and more as what we—culturally—allow ourselves to perceive, expanding that is extraordinarily important for our collective ability to apprehend what is invisible, like the nuclear itself.

KRUPAR: Another big question for this project was how can we build a civic infrastructure that invites different knowledges and forms of meaning making to coexist in the same geospatial, historical, first-person, art-based space—as a living resource and platform that people working on policy and regulation or local activism can mobilize or be mobilized by? Putting art in proximity to policy is an important potential effect of engaging with the *Atlas*. A lot of policy does not engage with the idea that it has a subjectivity at work or a perspective or an ideology.

KANOUSE: The other part of placing art in proximity to policy is placing policy in proximity to art. A number of pieces in the *Atlas* I first encountered in exhibitions about the nuclear. Coming out of the gallery, I might have an intense experience of my nuclear subjectivity and a deeper ethics of care but no idea about the policies that support regulation, governance, or expansion of the nuclear. There is a lot to be learned from both sides by placing them in mutual dialogue.

One of the more difficult things about the *Atlas* was deciding when we had "enough" material to put out there in the world. Several thousand uranium mine holes have been drilled in Colorado; we have ten key mines in the *Atlas*. We have been forced by reality and our own capabilities to impose artificial boundaries on this project—starting with its geographical boundary. The project will be forever incomplete because the nuclear has a global racialized order. Mining has declined in Colorado over the last fifty years as it has increased in Africa and central Asia. Colonial extraction on Indigenous lands is both a US and global phenomenon. In terms of additional content, we are maintaining the *Atlas* as an open invitation to build out this sense of global entanglement, to *unsettle* settler understandings of territory. We also plan to work in partnership with institutions in Colorado so that students and scholars can offer an on-the-ground experience of some of these sites. This constant placing into relation of a more global vision and an awareness of how experiences on the ground are shaped by these global machinations is what we hope the *Atlas* can do moving forward.

Atoms for Life and for Death

Nuclear Energy and Hiroshima Activism in the 1950s

RAN ZWIGENBERG

CHAPTER 4

Until recently, the entrance to the town of Futaba, abandoned after the March 11, 2011, tsunami and nuclear disasters, had a sign bearing the town's motto, "Nuclear Energy for a Bright Future," greeting those who entered its deserted streets.[1] This uncanny reminder of Japan's disastrous engagement with nuclear power encapsulates the idea of nuclear power with its utopian promise and nightmarish failure. In the 1950s, merely a decade after the bombing of Hiroshima and Nagasaki, the dream of safe nuclear power was widely promoted and enthusiastically accepted in Japan. Even the city of Hiroshima was part of the campaign. In 1956 hundreds of thousands of Hiroshima citizens lined up to see a *Nuclear Power for Peaceful Purposes* exhibit, which remained a major part of the Hiroshima Peace Museum up to 1967. In the mid-fifties not only top politicians but also most Japanese, including leading figures of the antinuclear and *hibakusha* (A-bomb survivors) movement, supported the Atoms for Peace campaign promoted by President Eisenhower. That campaign, initiated following widescale protests over US H-bomb tests in the Pacific, was a public relations and technology transfer initiative that aimed to present the atom as a positive force for progress. In sharp contrast to the widespread antinuclear protests that swept Japan following the Bikini tests, criticism of Atoms for Peace was muted. Only in the late sixties and seventies did a serious movement to oppose nuclear energy develop in Japan. With the exception of one faction of the broader antinuclear movement (Gensuikin, which split from the larger Gensuikyō antinuclear coalition and only came out against nuclear power in 1971), the antinuclear movement that emerged in Hiroshima, as well as the larger hibakusha movement, did not oppose nuclear power until after Chernobyl or, in some cases, Fukushima.[2] The main task of this chapter is to ask why so many in Hiroshima and the antinuclear movement supported nuclear power, and how this came about.

The Atoms for Peace importation into Japan was very much a product of the unequal power relations between Japan and the United States during the early Cold War. At least until 1960, if not later, politically, militarily, and culturally, Japan was embedded in a hierarchical relationship with its former occupying power. But the atom was not just forced on the Japanese; many accepted it wholeheartedly. The Atoms for Peace campaign was successful in Japan exactly because it was promoted in terms the Japanese were intimately familiar with. The Atoms for Peace campaign in Japan was part of a wider project of modernization, the model for which was the United States with its consumer glamour and technological advancement. The campaign connected the atom to everyday life improvement and the then-ongoing consumerization and modernization of Japanese society. It was about the Japanese desire to be modern and affluent so they could, in the words of one promoter of the Hiroshima atom exhibit, "live the dream of tomorrow."[3]

Antinuclear activists' willingness to accept the atom was also connected to their understanding of postwar democracy and science. As historian Jennifer Miller has demonstrated, in the first decade after the war American and Japanese elites shared a concept of democracy that was predicated on the creation of a rational and psychologically healthy Japanese citizenry.[4] Using the rise of fascism as a cautionary tale, many Americans and Japanese concluded that the militarists had been able to manipulate the Japanese people because they were weak and fundamentally susceptible to simplistic, emotional appeals. Thus, given this weakness of the average Japanese, "it was the task of the elites to defend freedom."[5] This racialized understanding of Japanese psychology, which had its roots in wartime psychological warfare research, was shared even by many of America's critics. Advocates of Cold War democracy extolled the benefits of "reason," loathed "extremism," and called for a trust in expertise. Science had an important role to play in the creation of the new Japanese subject and society. The United States promoted science and scientific reason as objective and free from political and ideological constraints.[6] To come out against scientific expertise in the mid-1950s in Japan was a highly contentious move. Both ideas, science and the democratic subject, were promoted to set postwar

Japan apart from totalitarian, communist regimes. In this early Cold War conceptual ecosystem, science and reason were connected to democracy and peace. These notions came together in the Atoms for Peace campaign, as ideas about science, democracy, and prosperity underlined the presentation of the atom as a force for progress. It was hard for critics of the campaign to come out against such consensus. And significantly, only when the underlying assumptions fueling Japanese dreams of consumerism and prosperity, and the attendant ideas connecting democracy and scientific reason, were challenged by the Anti-US-Japan Mutual Security Treaty (ANPO) movement, the environmental movement, and the counterculture of the late 1960s, did portions of the antinuclear movement start to oppose nuclear power in earnest.

Atoms for Life / Atoms for Death

The antinuclear movement in Japan became a nationwide grassroots movement following the 1954 *Lucky Dragon* incident (discussed further in part 2) and the radiation scares following America's aggressive nuclear testing on Bikini Atoll.[7] The suffering of the hibakusha of Hiroshima and Nagasaki was very much a regional issue up to the mid-1950s. Most Japanese had to contend with their own suffering and hardship following the defeat and showed little interest in the antinuclear cause per se. Even in the stricken cities, hibakusha were fast becoming a minority and were facing discrimination in marriage and employment opportunities. Most hibakusha (a term that did not come into full use until 1955–56) did not identify as survivors for fear of discrimination and chose to blend in as much as they could. Hiroshima City did champion the survivors' cause and became active politically in nuclear disarmament, as well as in commemoration activities, but there was a disconnect between the lofty ideals of peace and the day-to-day caring for and communication with the survivor community.

The sense of rejection and suspicion felt by hibakusha activists was captured by poet Ōta Yōko, who recalled, "After the [Bikini] hydrogen bomb incident, radioactive fallout arrived in Tokyo. [Then] I thought to myself 'it serves [them] right.' Covered with the lethal radiation . . . [they] could now truly comprehend how the human soul is tormented by modernity's angst;

[now] their heart will be truly shaken."[8] Many survivors, indeed, truly felt "modernity's angst" and were suspicious of atomic energy and even, as with Ōta, modernization in general. But Hiroshima city government and most of the peace movement embraced postwar modernity.[9] Most of the early commemoration and preservation activities of A-bomb sites and objects was done as part of a campaign by the city and tourism officials who sought to capitalize on Hiroshima's newfound status as a symbol of modernity. In early postwar peace discourse, Hiroshima was presented as a transformed city of peace—a symbol for reconciliation, which looked to the future.

Such ideological emphasis on optimism and renewal was the result of both occupation era dictate and genuine Japanese pacifism and hope for the future. Living under severe censorship that precluded any open discussion of the atomic bomb and its horrors until 1952, many Japanese sought to talk of the bomb in terms of its transformative power and as a lesson that would prevent the horrors of another global war, this time with atomic weapons.[10] Such optimism was inscribed in the very shape of the city by the 1949 "Hiroshima Peace City Law," which equated building a city of peace with building a rational modern metropolis. Hiroshima's wide avenues (some as wide as one hundred meters) and rational city plan, along with the peace museum's modernist design of exposed concrete, were an expression of the ideals of high modernism.[11]

Such an embrace of modernity extended to an acceptance of the Atoms for Peace agenda. This dynamic was clearly on display in 1955, when a proposal by US congressman Sidney Yates to give Hiroshima a nuclear reactor as "a symbol of peace and cooperation" split the antibomb movement in the city.[12] Yates explicitly connected the bomb and nuclear energy, calling for "using atomic energy for life rather than death."[13] He proposed "giving preference to Hiroshima, which was the first victim of the atomic bomb, in access to the resources of the peaceful atom."[14] In congressional debates over the proposal he stated, "A nuclear reactor in the land of the rising sun, built by Americans and out of America's resources, would be a lasting monument to our technology and good will."[15] Yates also planned to construct a special hospital for the thousands of citizens of Hiroshima who had been exposed to the bomb and had medical issues as a result.[16]

Yates was not the first to make this connection between the A-bomb and atomic energy. In October 1954 the Atomic Energy Commission's

(AEC) Thomas E. Murray, in almost identical terms, called on the United States to give a reactor to Hiroshima as "a dramatic and Christian gesture . . . a lasting monument to our technology and our good will."[17] A number of other proposals were also floated later as part of the Atoms for Peace campaign.[18] Such proposals had a Cold War context, which was made abundantly clear by the proposal of John Jay Hopkins, CEO of General Dynamics, for an "Atomic Marshall plan" in December 1954, which he saw as "the only effective means of stopping the spread of communism."[19]

The political context of Yates's proposal was immediately picked up by Hiroshima newspapers. A January 1955 editorial in the *Chūgoku Shinbun*, a leading liberal newspaper in Hiroshima, was largely supportive of the proposal but also cautious. "There has been widespread opposition to nuclear military uses," the editorial argued, "but no one is against the harnessing of this great energy for peaceful purposes." However, it continued, "installing a nuclear power plant in Hiroshima is extremely political. In other words, it would seem that [the United States] wants to erase the bad image of nuclear energy, which Hiroshima represents." Many residents, argued the editorial, are rightly skeptical of nuclear power, but if the plant will "promote the recovery of Hiroshima City and contribute to the enhancement of Hiroshima citizens' [lives]," the editorial writers saw this as generally positive. Those who are still critical "need to deepen their knowledge of nuclear power and at the same time develop the right understanding [of the issue]."[20]

The editorial's generally positive, yet somewhat mixed, reception of the prospect of building a nuclear plant in Hiroshima reflected wider attitudes in the city. On the day the *Chūgoku Shinbun* came out in favor of the proposal, it held a roundtable with Moritaki Ichirō, the head of the local Gensuikyō antinuclear coalition, Mayor Hamai Shinzō, and other politicians, activists, and business interests. Moritaki was one of the founders of the antinuclear movement, a professor of ethics, and a hibakusha. He was a symbol of Japanese resistance to the A-bomb, particularly in Hiroshima. Though skeptical at first, Moritaki declared his support for nuclear power in 1956. In 1955, however, Moritaki still seemed to be on the fence about the issue. Moritaki opened the roundtable with a cautious rejection of the proposal. Significantly, from the outset, he resorted to scientific expertise to back his position, stating, "I am not an expert on the topic but according to Dr. Tsuzuki [Masao] and others it is still not possible to dispose of radiation completely, and, thus, peaceful use is not possible at this stage." Moritaki expressed his and other hibakusha's anxiety over the proposal and added, "The country should listen to the worries of the citizens who were the first to suffer from the baptism of the nuclear age."[21] The rest of the roundtable participants were much more positive than Moritaki. Indeed, Moritaki and the local branch of Gensuikyō were opposed to the Yates offer from the beginning. But at no point did the activists reject nuclear power in toto, and generally speaking, they sought to portray the movement's position as broadly supportive of science.

The atomic power plant was opposed primarily because it could be a target for Soviet attack, putting Hiroshima at risk yet again. It also provoked anxiety over radiation danger. While the Hiroshima branch of Gensuikyō, including Moritaki, supported nuclear energy generally, they opposed the nuclear plant because of these reservations. In their statement of opposition to the proposal they cautioned, "[We] hope that this immense energy source of the future will supply us with boundless sources of power. This is especially important for our resource-poor country. But [we must remember] this great source of energy was also used in Hiroshima as a tool of slaughter, so we must ensure that it will be used [now] for the welfare of mankind."[22] Gensuikyō's opposition angered Mayor Hamai, who told the press, "I have been calling on the United States to spearhead the peaceful use of nuclear energy for the past two years. . . . Starting the peaceful use of nuclear energy in the first city victimized by atomic energy would serve as our tribute to the deceased victims. Our citizens, I am sure, will welcome it. . . . I want to believe that this [nuclear plant] is intended as a life-affirming gift of goodwill."[23]

Hamai's assurances of popular support met with opposition in the Hiroshima assembly and in the press. Assembly member Tsuchioka Kiyokazu challenged Hamai's assertion that "Hiroshima residents will be pleased" with having "a large scale [nuclear] power plant . . . inside the city." Tsuchioka argued that the problem of "the [proper] methods to dispose of radiation is far from being resolved." He also wondered where exactly the power plant would be located and took issue with Hamai's connections to Mike Masaoka, a Japanese American politician who was the national secretary and field executive of the Japanese American Citizens League.

Masaoka, according to Hamai, was crucial in connecting Hiroshima City and the various American actors seeking to build the nuclear power plant. Tsuchioka asked about donations that supposedly had gone missing. Hamai brushed off Tsuchioka's questions about Masaoka and doubled down on the power plant issue. "I have a rather poor grasp of chemistry," Hamai answered, "and I do know there are a couple of problems left to be solved with radiation disposal, but I was told these would be solved before the construction of the plant."[24]

Radiation waste disposal was the most prominent issue raised by opponents of the nuclear plant proposal. Supporters of nuclear energy usually sidestepped the issue and instead talked in grand statements about peace and the welfare of mankind. Mike Masaoka, in an opinion piece defending the proposal, connected it to his effort "to call on people all over the world to come together and make Hiroshima a 'bridge for peace.'" Masaoka also detailed his campaign, claiming support from the Rockefeller Foundation and other organizations, as well as noted American politicians, to establish a medical nuclear research center in addition to the reactor in Hiroshima.[25] An advocate of Japanese Americans cooperating with the wartime US government, Masaoka was active during the war in negotiations with the Roosevelt administration on the creation of a regiment of Japanese Americans in the US army.[26] His rhetoric of Hiroshima being a "bridge for peace" was built on notions of Japanese Americans as "bridges across the Pacific."[27] As historian Eiichiro Azuma has argued, Japanese Americans in Japan often were presented as role models for Japanese regarding how to be modern, rational Japanese subjects, becoming a "poster child for postwar liberal discourse."[28] By accepting the atom, Hiroshima would perform the same role for the rest of Japan.

As the debate continued, it became clear that Hiroshima city was losing the argument to the antinuclear activists. Radiation, again, was the main source of contention. In another roundtable discussion in February, Sakuma Kyōshi, a physics professor and activist, challenged Hamai on his "difference of opinion" with Gensuikyō, to which Hamai replied defensively that he "respects the movement's position . . . but [still] thinks the proposal is mostly beneficial" and suggested everyone wait for more details before making any judgments. Sako Chiyoko, a reporter for *Fujin Shinbun*, pointed out the continued impact of radiation on the city, saying,

"There is much fear of the effects of radioactivity [in this city]. . . . Just recently, Mr. Mitani, a student at Hiroshima University, died of A-bomb disease." Hamai agreed with Sako that radiation was still an unresolved issue and was unsettling, especially in Hiroshima, but added, "It seems that in America they do a lot of research [to solve] this." Hamai's remarks were dismissed by Sakuma, who pointed to the military, economic, and diplomatic interests behind the Atoms for Peace campaign, and Tanabe Kōichiro, a cultural commentator who chaired the panel, who pointed out the pressure put on scientists to paint nuclear power positively. Tanabe referred to the encounter of Tsuzuki Masao (to whom many of the participants also referred) with "Diet member N. [probably Nakasone Yasuhiro] who asked the doctor whether he will be willing to give a positive medical evaluation of nuclear power," which Tsuzuki refused to do.[29]

Hamai, who saw himself as part of the peace movement, again brought up the tropes of peace and reconciliation. Yet he urged his fellow activists to be rational and pragmatic. "Americans," he argued, "feel very sympathetic to Hiroshima's sacrifice and want to compensate [Hiroshima for what happened]. However, it is different from the feeling of having done a bad thing. . . . [Thus,] we [he and Masaoka] felt we shouldn't appeal to Americans for compensation or reparation for the atomic bombing of Hiroshima. But there are so many Americans who are thinking about doing something positive for Hiroshima, because initially nuclear power [which was discovered by the United States] was not used peacefully and Hiroshima was made a victim [by it]." Hamai's pragmatism was affirmed by Watanabe Kanae, the dean of liberal arts at Hiroshima University, who faced the issue of radiation head on: "Even if the radioactive material that is generated in many nuclear power sites is harmful to the human body, chemistry is steadily progressing, so even if it is harmful at this stage, [the issue] will be resolved sooner or later." Addressing the issue of the power plant becoming a target for Soviet attack, he continued, "Also politically there is no need to be all too anxious; yes, there is conflict between the powers [over Atoms for Peace] now but this will probably be solved soon through the UN."[30]

The moderates' stance was dismissed by Moritaki, who, throughout the long debate, only gave short, pointed replies: "If the Americans think so highly of Hiroshima's sacrifice, they should provide medical assistance to the hibakusha who are suffering." He then compared a nuclear reactor to a "gunpowder magazine" (*kayakuko*) and said he would not want one in a civilian area.[31] Indeed, the issue of Hiroshima becoming a victim of nuclear power again, through an accident or through the plant becoming a target, was raised repeatedly by activists. Moderates' calls for reason were met with skepticism. Tanabe, citing Nakaizumi Masanori of the University of Tokyo, prophetically raised the issue of an earthquake "damaging the reactor's core." This should worry Japanese, he added, "especially in a country like our own, which is prone to earthquakes." Women activists seemed to be particularly averse to the proposal. As I have discussed elsewhere, the tropes of motherhood and the threat posed to the mother and child bond by the alien force of radiation were repeated motifs in women's activism in Hiroshima.[32] As Sako stated, "We [in Hiroshima] have an understanding of and [rightly] fear radiation because of our experience of the bomb. Furthermore, after Bikini . . . we are more aware of the genetic impact on humanity. From the standpoint of a woman [who] is connected with motherhood, I am instinctively concerned by the genetic impact on our offspring."[33]

Yet even Sako and Nakaizumi expressed their confidence in science and scientific expertise. Sako concluded by saying she was sure that with the progress of science the issue would be resolved soon. Moritaki and Tanabe as well based their rejection of the reactor on concerns voiced by Tsuzuki and other scientists. The trust vested in science was, ironically, the result of the A-bomb itself. During the war Japanese propaganda challenged American material superiority and, indeed, modernization itself, with claims of a superior Japanese spirit. But, as John Dower has argued, the bomb was Janus-faced; it was both a reminder of the folly of the war waged by the Japanese and also a symbol of the new power of science.[34] Thus, even fierce opponents of the proposals, such as Tsuchioka, were prepared to accept Yates's proposal if they were assured of the safety of the reactor by competent scientific authorities. In July 1955, with the debates over the reactor still continuing in Hiroshima, Tsuchioka sent a letter to Yates via the Methodist minister Tanimoto Kiyoshi. Tanimoto and Tsuchioka assured Yates that "the people of Hiroshima are opposed to the building of a reactor unless certain conditions are met," but "if we are [assured] that there is no danger of radiation [leaks] we will accept the offer."[35] Tanimoto's brief involvement with the issue was quite apt. Tanimoto traveled to the United States as part of his Hiroshima Maidens project, a symbol of reconciliation and the peace movement.[36] The Hiroshima Maidens were a group of young female victims chosen by Norman Cousins and Tanimoto to undergo plastic surgery in the United States to remove keloids and other scars caused by the bomb. Just like with nuclear power, the humanitarian gesture of giving those female victims a chance to live a normal life again was part of a larger project of transforming the image of science. As David Serlin has pointed out, the project organizers sought not only to normalize the maidens' lives but also to normalize the terms under which "modern science could absorb its capacity for recklessness and turn trauma into opportunity."[37]

Such connections were playing on a powerful narrative in Japan's modern history. Tying atomic power with science and progress was a natural extension of the Japanese discourse of modernization, which held sway across the ideological spectrum in Japan. Itty Abraham, in his work on the Indian atomic power program, observed that in the non-Western, postcolonial world the atom was entangled with the discourse of development and state power.[38] This is certainly how figures like the Liberal Democratic Party's Nakasone Yasuhiro and Shōriki Matsutarō, owner of the major daily newspaper *Yomiuri Shinbun*, the main power brokers who promoted the atom in Japan, saw it. [39] Such anxiety led those men into cooperation with the United States and support for the Atoms for Peace program. As Abraham notes, "postcolonial" elites (and one can arguably include many post-occupation Japanese elites in this category) demonstrated deep anxiety not only toward the West but also toward their own populations.[40] "Post-colonial time is always time in waiting," Abraham writes, "in being able to see the future in the present through conditions prevalent in advanced states yet always being behind them."[41] This anxiety created a sense of urgency that translated into a strong desire to modernize and rationalize: a desire to transform not only the economy but also the psychological makeup of the citizens. That was an Enlightenment-derived project, which the Japanese were quite familiar with. Japanese elites from Meiji on tried to modernize and educate their citizens. Atomic power exhibits like the many other industrial exhibits popular throughout post-Meiji Japan were a way to inform, to educate, but also to awe the populace with the power of science.[42] Faced with enormous models of reactors, spaceships, and complex scientific jargon, the populace (went the thinking) could not resist. In many ways this was, again to turn to Abraham, "science as modern fetish." Atomic energy was treated as a triumph of science. To stand against it was to stand against science and rationality, to be caught in the past and "against progress."[43]

Yet, even for some Americans, the idea of building Hiroshima as a center of nuclear science was a bridge too far. When Lewis L. Strauss raised the issue with Eisenhower, the president thought it indicated "a sense of guilt which he felt was misplaced."[44] The embassy in Tokyo was also against the scheme. In a June 1955 letter, the director of the Atomic Bomb Casualty Commission (ABCC, an American medical research center in Hiroshima), Robert Holmes, proposed to the embassy, in conjunction with Yates's proposal, "that Hiroshima should be the atomic center of Japan with ABCC as a natural center of activities of this nature." Holmes planned to assist the campaign by promoting treatment in the ABCC for sick hibakusha, encouraging cooperation with the Hiroshima Medical University, and donating materials to the planned Hiroshima Peace Museum. The exhibits were to counter the current ideological line of the museum, which emphasized Hiroshima's victimization. As his interlocutor in the embassy commented, "Dr. Holmes believes that there will be anti-US material [at the museum] possibly including skeletons, etc., but thinks it better to join the exhibition and refute anti-US propaganda with material pointing up the beneficial uses of atomic energy and the function of the ABCC rather than leave the anti-US propaganda unrefuted."[45]

Holmes apparently saw the reactor proposition as a welcome addition to his plan but was surprised when the embassy did not follow through and felt "that the embassy erred in not recommending Hiroshima as the site for the first atomic reactor." Holmes also "took strong exception to the views of the PAO [Public Affairs Officer] in Hiroshima [Abol Fazl Fotouhi] who has apparently not been overly enthusiastic."[46] Abol Fazl Fotouhi, an Iranian-born American diplomat in Hiroshima, played a crucial role in the later *Atoms for Peace* exhibit that followed the reactor proposal. His rejection of it demonstrates how divided official circles were over the proposal. His displeasure and that of others led to the proposal eventually being discarded. The precise reasons for this are not clear. After mid-1955 the proposal disappears from the archival records. Shimamoto Mayako speculated that it was Eisenhower's disapproval that led to the end of the campaign.[47] This author found no definite proof for this in the archives. Regardless of the eventual fate of the reactor proposal, the State Department, significantly, did accept the second part of Holmes's proposal and planned for a massive *Atoms for Peace* exhibit in Hiroshima, which, unlike the reactor proposal, did eventually get Hiroshima activists on the nuclear power bandwagon.

Atoms for Peace / Atoms for War

The *Atoms for Peace* exhibit was part of a larger all-Japan campaign launched jointly by US and Japanese political and media interests. Getting Hiroshima on board was of obvious importance for the organizers. The *Atoms for Peace* exhibit in Hiroshima, however, had a very rocky start, as the city decided to remove over two thousand artifacts from the atomic bomb museum to make room for the exhibit. Local residents and the Hiroshima Gensuikyō expressed alarm and went into action. Just as with the Yates proposal, the *Atoms for Peace* exhibit was not opposed in principle, but primarily because of the removal of the artifacts. Gensuikyō stated, "We are not against the exhibit as such [but against the use of the museum for that purpose]. Behind these a-bomb artifacts there are the 200,000 victims. . . . These are more important than the exhibit and should not be moved."[48] Radiation was again an issue, as one resident voiced the concern widespread at the time that the exhibit would contain active radioactive material and would thus "contaminate our city again." The most prevalent complaint, however, voiced by Moritaki and others, was "If the city and prefecture have funds for this, they should pay for *hibakusha* welfare."[49]

Responding to critics, the exhibit sponsors organized a public symposium in March where the issue was debated. The editor of the *Chūgoku Shinbun* spoke first, saying, "Hundreds of thousands of people have seen the exhibition which depicts the miraculous use of the destructive atom in many peaceful ways," and urging Hiroshima residents not to lag behind. Fotouhi then similarly told the meeting that "as a friend of the Hiroshima people and as a member of the community I felt that the Hiroshima people should not be deprived of the opportunity to see the many benefits that the atomic energy is now providing the mankind [*sic*]. My government therefore agreed to include Hiroshima in the scheduled showings."[50] The editor pressed Fotouhi about the complete absence of the bomb from the exhibit. He answered that the exhibit was "indeed, only about nuclear power. The dark side [of atomic power], the bomb, is spoken of incessantly, thus, I would like the exhibit to inform people more about the side of peaceful use."[51] The hibakusha representatives protested this attitude but only mildly. Yamaguchi Yūko from the Hiroshima Society for the Protection of Children was worried that the Atoms for Peace connection might dilute the message of the antibomb movement.[52] Fujii Heiichi of the local Gensuikyō branch repeated the organization's position on the issue but also said that one could not ignore "the dark side" of nuclear power and that it should also be incorporated. Both also voiced concerns over radiation.[53]

These objections were met by Fujiwara Takeo from Hiroshima University, who told the meeting, unaware of the historical irony of his words, "It is absurd to think that an advanced nation like America would knowingly bring unprotected fissionable material to any country."[54] When another resident spoke of the items in the museum as relics, Fujiwara protested, demonstrating exactly the kind of elite anxiety discussed above: "What is the museum? Is it a shrine? Is it a place like our Miyajima? If that is so, why then don't you have the marking of a shrine? Why should our ancestors object to anything if it means the future welfare of mankind? . . . We need to understand the basic principles of peaceful living. We must see what the future promises."[55] What Watanabe meant by the "basic principles of peaceful living" was the commonsense understanding of a democratic subject that is guided by science and rationality rather than superstition. Japanese supposedly lacked this understanding, as "they remained mired in the wilds of 'tradition' . . . 'inward looking, inert, [and] superstitious.'"[56] Given the early postwar view of wartime Shintō as "irrational mythology," accusing activists of an irrational attachment to the relics of the dead (*ihin*) associated them with resistance to science.[57]

Science and peace were indeed the watchwords of the exhibit. American and Japanese officials and scientists stressed the importance of a "correct" (i.e., rational and scientific) understanding of the atom. A Japanese scientist from the ABCC commented, "The region of Hiroshima has an inseparable relationship with nuclear power and thus should have a correct understanding [of it]." Former (and future) mayor Hamai took a similar approach. "I heard much about this. It is good to see it firsthand. . . . [I]t is the first step that people should talk of deepening our understanding of nuclear power."[58] The equation of American science and ideas of progress with neutral or positive values was ever-present. A few, however, had serious doubts. Chief among their concerns was radiation. Tanabe Koichirō, Moritaki, and others repeated many of the arguments they had made in connection with Yates's proposal. [59] Unlike with the reactor issue, however, critics were the minority when it came to concerns about radiation. And as the exhibit continued, they were heard less and less. The *Atoms for Peace* exhibit was a celebration of modernity. In the mid-fifties, when most Japanese still lived in poverty, the sleek exhibits assembled in the museum represented a promise of prosperity many in Hiroshima could only dream of. As I examined elsewhere, the organizers sought to actively use the exhibit to educate and transform the attitudes of both hibakusha and Hiroshima residents.[60] The arguments, again, were quite similar to these advanced during the reactor debates, but now they were demonstrated through a space-age exhibit with life-size models of reactors and atomic planes, electronic exhibits, and a PR blitz that included some of Japan's most notable scientific names.[61]

Thus, the Atoms for Peace campaign embedded the atom within an intimately familiar narrative of progress. This was quite successful. Following the exhibit, many hibakusha showed their support for using the atom for peace. In Nagasaki in August 1956 Moritaki proclaimed as part of Hidankyō's founding statement, "Atomic power . . . must absolutely be converted to a servant for the happiness and prosperity of humankind. This is the only desire we hold as long as we live."[62] It was not until the 1970s that Moritaki backtracked and completely rejected the ideas of Atoms for Peace. This change, significantly, came about through his deep concern with the problem of radiation, which brought him into contact with leading international activists who, likewise, also started to come out against nuclear power. The sixties saw the first stirrings against the project of fast-paced modernization and economic growth that Japan had undergone since the war. It was the coming together of these different strands and the greater challenge to the course of Japanese modernization that brought this change. Moritaki and others came to recognize the many connections among unbridled consumerism, developmental capitalism, environmental degradation, and radiation hazards.

In 1971, Moritaki, as head of Gensuikin (Japan Congress against A- and H-Bombs), which had split from Gensuikyō, declared, "Humanity and the atom cannot co-exist." Moritaki's and Gensuikin's rejection of nuclear power was tied to the deep cultural and ideological change that swept Japan and the world in the 1960s. Following the ANPO protests (against the US-Japan Security Treaty) activists lionized popular mobilization and distanced themselves from the paternalist attitudes of the 1950s.[63] If in the first decade after the war Japanese and American elites sought to guide the masses, after 1960, the people, activists argued, no longer needed the advice of experts to shepherd them into democracy. Gensuikin's change of position came at the same time that environmental issues became important, with the emergence of Minamata disease and other incidents disturbing the Japanese "dream of tomorrow." In 1972 Gensuikin adopted a resolution that stated, "Let us oppose the introduction of nuclear power . . . which will cause major environmental disruption and radioactive pollution." Moritaki recalled that the change "resulted largely from our deepening understanding of nuclear issues; its backdrop lay in escalating environmental destruction and pollution occurring in Japan due to high-speed economic growth."[64] Thus, it was only with the reintroduction of doubts over modernity and its cost that nuclear power could be resisted.

The Atoms for Peace confluence of progress, science, and affluence was a powerful tool. It built on the desire of the Japanese for a "bright future" and a "bright peace," equating both with consumer desire and capitalist visions of the "dream of tomorrow." This project was construed as a natural continuation of the Meiji slogans of culture and enlightenment and as part of a road toward modernization that Japanese shared with many around the world. Moritaki and others' resistance to nuclear power revolved mostly around fears of radiation and skepticism regarding American intentions. This caused multiple crises and difficulties for promoters of nuclear power in Hiroshima. Such resistance by peace organizations derailed the reactor idea, but it could not withstand the media blitz of the *Atoms for Peace* exhibit. Very few in 1950s Japan could stand "against science," and science, at the time, was still on the side of the United States and its nuclear power agenda. Such was the power of the Atoms for Peace campaign. Disastrously for Japan, its grip on the Japanese imagination lasted well into the twenty-first century.

Notes

1. *Asahi Shinbun*, March 11, 2019.
2. Both Gensuikyō (Gensuibaku Kinshi Nihon Kyōgikai) and Hidankyō (Nihon Gensuibaku Higaisha Dantai Kyōgikai) officially supported "nuclear power for peaceful purposes." Gensuikin, which was left of the mainstream, split from the larger coalition following the 1960 protests against the US-Japan Mutual Security Treaty.
3. *Chūgoku Shinbun*, May 29, 1956.
4. Jennifer M. Miller, *Cold War Democracy: The United States and Japan* (Cambridge, MA: Harvard University Press, 2019), 9.
5. Miller, *Cold War Democracy*, 11.
6. Audra Wolfe, *Freedom's Laboratory: The Cold War Struggle for the Soul of Science* (Baltimore: Johns Hopkins University Press, 2018), 2.
7. Ran Zwigenberg, *Hiroshima: The Origins of Global Memory Culture* (Cambridge: Cambridge University Press, 2014), 68.
8. Quoted in Zwigenberg, *Hiroshima*, 69.
9. For Kanai, see http://www.hiroshimapeacemedia.jp/peacemuseum_d/jp/text/voice018.html (accessed September 9, 2019).
10. Zwigenberg, *Hiroshima*, 23–64.
11. Zwigenberg, *Hiroshima*, 23–64.
12. Ran Zwigenberg, "The Coming of a Second Sun: The 1956 Atoms for Peace Exhibit in Hiroshima and Japan's Embrace of Nuclear Power," *Asia-Pacific Journal* 10, issue 6, no. 1 (February 6, 2012), https://apjjf.org/2012/10/6/Ran-Zwigenberg/3685/article.html.
13. Zwigenberg, "The Coming of a Second Sun"; Hiroshima-shi, hen, *Hiroshima shinshi: Rekishi hen* (Hiroshima: Hiroshima-shi, 1984), 208.
14. Hiroshima-shi, *Hiroshima shinshi*, 208.
15. Cited in Mayako Shimamoto, "Abolition of Japan's Nuclear Power Plants? Analysis from a Historical Perspective on Early Cold War," in *Japan Viewed from Interdisciplinary Perspectives: History and Prospects*, ed. Yoneyuki Sugita (Lanham, MD: Lexington Books, 2015), 265.
16. *Chūgoku Shinbun*, February 5, 1955.
17. Quoted in Zwigenberg, "The Coming of a Second Sun."
18. See Zwigenberg, "The Coming of a Second Sun."
19. Quoted in Shimamoto, "Abolition of Japan's Nuclear Power Plants?," 266.
20. *Chūgoku Shinbun*, January 29, 1955.
21. *Chūgoku Shinbun*, January 29, 1955.

22. Hiroshima-shi, *Hiroshima shinshi*, 208–9.
23. Quoted in Hiroshima-shi, *Hiroshima shinshi*, 208.
24. *Chūgoku Shinbun*, January 30, 1955.
25. *Chūgoku Shinbun*, February 5, 1955.
26. "Mike Masaoka," in *Densho Encyclopedia*, accessed June 2, 2020, https://encyclopedia.densho.org/Mike%20Masaoka/.
27. Eiichirō Azuma, *In Search of Our Frontier: Japanese America and Settler Colonialism in the Construction of Japan's Borderless Empire* (Oakland: University of California Press, 2019), 244.
28. Eiichiro Azuma, "Brokering Race, Culture, and Citizenship: Japanese Americans in Occupied Japan and Postwar National Inclusion," *Journal of American-East Asian Relations* 16, no. 3 (2009): 185.
29. *Chūgoku Shinbun*, February 7, 1955.
30. *Chūgoku Shinbun*, February 8, 1955.
31. *Chūgoku Shinbun*, February 8, 1955.
32. Zwigenberg, *Hiroshima*, 84.
33. *Chūgoku Shinbun*, February 8, 1955.
34. John W. Dower, "The Bombed: Hiroshima and Nagasaki in Japanese Memory," in *Hiroshima in History and Memory*, ed. Michael J. Hogan (Cambridge: Cambridge University Press, 1996), 123.
35. *Chūgoku Shinbun*, July 26, 1955.
36. On the maidens, see Rodney Barker, *The Hiroshima Maidens: A Story of Courage, Compassion, and Survival* (New York: Viking, 1985).
37. David Serlin, *Replaceable You: Engineering the Body in Postwar America* (Chicago: University of Chicago Press, 2004), 182.
38. Itty Abraham, *The Making of the Indian Atomic Bomb: Science, Secrecy and the Postcolonial State* (New Delhi: Orient Longman, 1999), 2.
39. Zwigenberg, "The Coming of a Second Sun."
40. Abraham, *The Making of the Indian Atomic Bomb*, 11.
41. Abraham, *The Making of the Indian Atomic Bomb*, 19.
42. Yoshimi Shunya, *Yume no genshiryoku* (Tokyo: Chikuma Shobō, 2012), 187.
43. Abraham, *The Making of the Indian Atomic Bomb*, 29.
44. Quoted in Shimamoto, "Abolition of Japan's Nuclear Power Plants?," 268.
45. C. Segwick to Mr. Morgan and Mr. Hackle, "Dr. Holmes (20 June 1955)," RG 84, Box 187, Folder 3, National Archives and Research Administration, College Park, MD.
46. C. Segwick to Mr. Morgan and Mr. Hackle, "Dr. Holmes (20 June 1955)," RG 84, Box 187, Folder 3, National Archives and Research Administration, College Park, MD.
47. Shimamoto, "Abolition of Japan's Nuclear Power Plants?," 268.
48. Abol Fazi Fotouhi papers, 200. I thank Farida Fotouhi for giving me access to her fathers' unpublished papers. See the *Chūgoku Shinbun*, March 22, 1956 for an edited text of the meeting.

49. Fotouhi papers, 198. See also *Chūgoku Shinbun*, February 14, 1956; Hiroshima-shi, *Hiroshim shinshi*, 209.
50. *Chūgoku Shinbun*, March 22, 1956.
51. Moritaki diary entries at http://www.gensuikin.org/data/mori1.html (accessed May 28, 2019).
52. *Chūgoku Shinbun*, March 22, 1956.
53. *Chūgoku Shinbun*, March 22, 1956.
54. Fotouhi papers.
55. *Chūgoku Shinbun*, March 22, 1956.
56. Jennifer M. Miller, *Cold War Democracy: The United States and Japan* (Cambridge, MA: Harvard University Press, 2019), 241.
57. Jolyon Baraka Thomas, *Faking Liberties: Religious Freedom in American-Occupied Japan* (Chicago: University of Chicago Press, 2019), 208.
58. Zwigenberg, "The Coming of a Second Sun."
59. Zwigenberg, "The Coming of a Second Sun."
60. Zwigenberg, "The Coming of a Second Sun."
61. Zwigenberg, "The Coming of a Second Sun."
62. Zwigenberg, "The Coming of a Second Sun."
63. Nick Kapur, *Japan at the Crossroads: Conflict and Compromise after Anpo* (Cambridge, MA: Harvard University Press, 2018), 6–7.
64. Moritaki Ichirō, *Kaku to jinrui wa kyōson dekinai: Kaku zettai hitei e no ayumi* (Tokyo: Kabushiki Kaisha Nanatsumori Shokan, 2015), 234.

The Politics of Antimonumentalism

An Exhibit in Five Cities

SHINPEI TAKEDA

CHAPTER 5

Antimonumentalism is a conceptual framework that I initially created and developed as I traveled with the exhibition *Antimonument.* In this exhibition, the marginal, recuperated, and reappropriated memories of Hiroshima and Nagasaki, as well as the very act of reappropriation, were highlighted as an art exhibition with its parallel programs. Initially conceived as a title of my individual exhibition in Nagasaki Prefectural Art Museum in 2015 as a part of the seventieth anniversary of the Nagasaki atomic bombing, the exhibition later traveled to Dresden, Germany, and to three other locations in Mexico (Querétaro, San Miguel de Allende, and Mexico City). The sites of the exhibition varied from a seventeenth-century convent for nuns to a nineteenth-century former power plant, while each city provided its own context to the ongoing issues of violence, radiation, and nuclear threats. At each stop, Hiroshima and Nagasaki touched on different themes, emotions, and issues. Meanwhile, as an artist, I had to work with the history of the local context so that the exhibition somehow wove into local sentiments against violence. At each stop, Nagasaki survivors accompanied the exhibition as a parallel program, creating another experiential dimension to the exhibition. Meanwhile during the three and half years of the exhibition's itinerary, various frictions emerged. The frictions became questions constantly changing based on physical distance from the hypocenter and distance in time since doomsday. They include problems of objectivity within the subjective context of art, as well as the coexistence of abstract forms presented together with concrete historical facts filtered via public institutions. In navigating between the loaded symbols of Hiroshima and Nagasaki and a sensitive and abstract reinterpretation of the personal narratives behind these symbols, I had to come up with my proper guiding principle of antimonumentalism.

Prequel, Maruki Gallery for Hiroshima Panels, July 2014

Opening: July 26, 2014
Distance: 300 km from hypocenter
Time: 68 years and 351 days

Located in the countryside of Saitama Prefecture, about an hour and a half from the center of Tokyo, Maruki Gallery for the Hiroshima Panels is the former studio of Maruki Iri and Maruki Toshi that has become a museum. In some ways, this is as close as one gets to the heat of the hypocenter within driving distance from the megalopolis capital of Japan. Known for their *Genbaku no zu*, a series of nine painted folding panels that depicted the aftermath of atomic bombings, the artist duo's aesthetics have been monumental in their size, their urgency, and their intensity. The two artists are also monumental in that they have made their way into the public consciousness. They appear in elementary school history textbooks and have created an "image" of the horrors of the aftermath of atomic bombings.

However, what is most impressive in this museum is the largest hall, at the end of the building, where the artist duo created large murals depicting horrors they didn't witness. The horrors of Auschwitz, Nanjing, Minamata, and Sanrizuka were depicted with at least the same level of intensity, if not more, as the sites of the atomic bombings. These large paintings gave me great insight into how artists can break through shells of a charged political narrative to reach human emotions. This requires courage and commitment when the artists are depicting horrific events from which they are distanced in both time and space. Like Maruki Iri and Maruki Toshi depicting the horrors of Auschwitz without having been there and without having any personal relationship to those events, I, too, am depicting the horrors of Nagasaki and Hiroshima without having been there at ground zero and without having any family relationship to the bombings. I thought through questions about my positionality in depicting the pain of others. As I thought about issues of authenticity, the commitment, sincerity, and honesty expressed in their brushstrokes somehow gave me the assurance that it is okay to continue to explore the metaphorical epicenter of Hiroshima and Nagasaki's legacy.

Perhaps it was no coincidence that my exhibition, titled *Beta Decay 2: How to Unwind the Time of Violence*, was installed next to the hall containing the

Marukis' *Genbaku no zu* panels in July 2014. As I worked on mounting the exhibition, many questions still roamed in my head. Do I have the freedom to express my subjective perspective on a tragedy of such scale? After all, am I not making art out of the suffering of millions of others? Is it possible to transcend the limitations of subjectivity and objectivity? Many difficult questions arose as I felt the scorching heat of summer in Japan. Somehow my body associated this heat with a story I heard about the intense heat of the atomic bomb. Another anniversary of the atomic bombing was around the corner.

Chapter 1

Antimonument #1—Nagasaki, Japan
Opening: August 1, 2015
Distance: 4 km from hypocenter
Time: 70 years and 351 days

On August 1, 2015, my exhibition *Antimonument* opened at the Nagasaki Prefectural Art Museum. It was the result of weeks of research and investigation of a new curatorial concept for my exhibition. The intention was to create a clear and different set of expectations as people approached the exhibition, but I was fully aware that the "anti-" platform indicated in its title was also a marketing strategy deployed by popular culture platforms. Coincidentally the American pop singer Rihanna debuted her album and tour titled *ANTI*, while a movie, *Antisocial*, was being released theatrically, both in the same year. In addition, "antiestablishment" populists were sweeping across the political landscapes of the Western Hemisphere. With a popular desire for all things "anti-" in evidence, I had to put forth a serious commitment to the notion of an "anti-" platform and needed to examine this notion beyond its superficial appeal.

The initial idea of "anti-" came from one thing I knew clearly: I didn't want my exhibition to be another monument. I didn't want another ceremony to cherish the anniversary of the atomic bombing and become another decoration to the official discourse on the memory and remembrance. In fact, my idea for this title was initially met with questions from the Nagasaki Prefectural Art Museum, another public institution that is mostly funded by Nagasaki Prefecture.

One essential factor was the museum's distance from the hypocenter. Even though it was only 2.5 miles from the hypocenter, the Nagasaki Prefectural Art Museum is located near Dejima, on the other side of Nagasaki. Dejima is a man-made island originally located in Nagasaki Bay (though now surrounded by land), and it was the only place westerners had been allowed to stay in Japan during the Tokugawa period (1600–1868). Today it is considered a cultural district, giving tourists glimpses of the complex layers of history even before the atomic bomb was dropped. At the time of the atomic bombing, this part of Nagasaki was not damaged as severely as other neighborhoods because of the city's topography. The hills around the hypocenter prevented the explosive blast and fire from reaching Dejima. What is not to be underestimated is the way this relatively short distance of 2.5 miles—between Urakami district, which bore the brunt of the blast, and the nearby but protected Dejima district —created enormously different discourses and public sentiments around the remembrance of the atomic bombing.

The exhibition consisted of three different halls. The first hall had a "beta decay" thread sculpture, a horn-shaped, fishnet-like thread sculpture almost floating in the middle of the room.

The second hall's walls were all covered with the voice patterns of survivors' interviews that I had copied by hand. The third hall was a projection room for my movie *Hiroshima Nagasaki Download* in a pitch-black setting. It was designed so that visitors would enter the exhibition starting with the most abstract representations and exit with the least abstract representations.

The exhibition opened smoothly and had strong attendance. It was considered one of the bigger events leading up to the anniversary of the bombing on August 9th. As I expected, there was no critical feedback. In the city of Nagasaki, the political power of survivors' groups has kept self-critical discourse mostly out of discussions of the bombing. However, I believe that the title of the exhibition, with its hint of criticality, as well as the fact that these were radically different representations from what people were accustomed to, allowed people to look at this exhibition with a different mindset.

A few days after the opening I asked Shimohira Sakue to visit the exhibition. I wanted to see her reaction and ask her to promote the exhibition

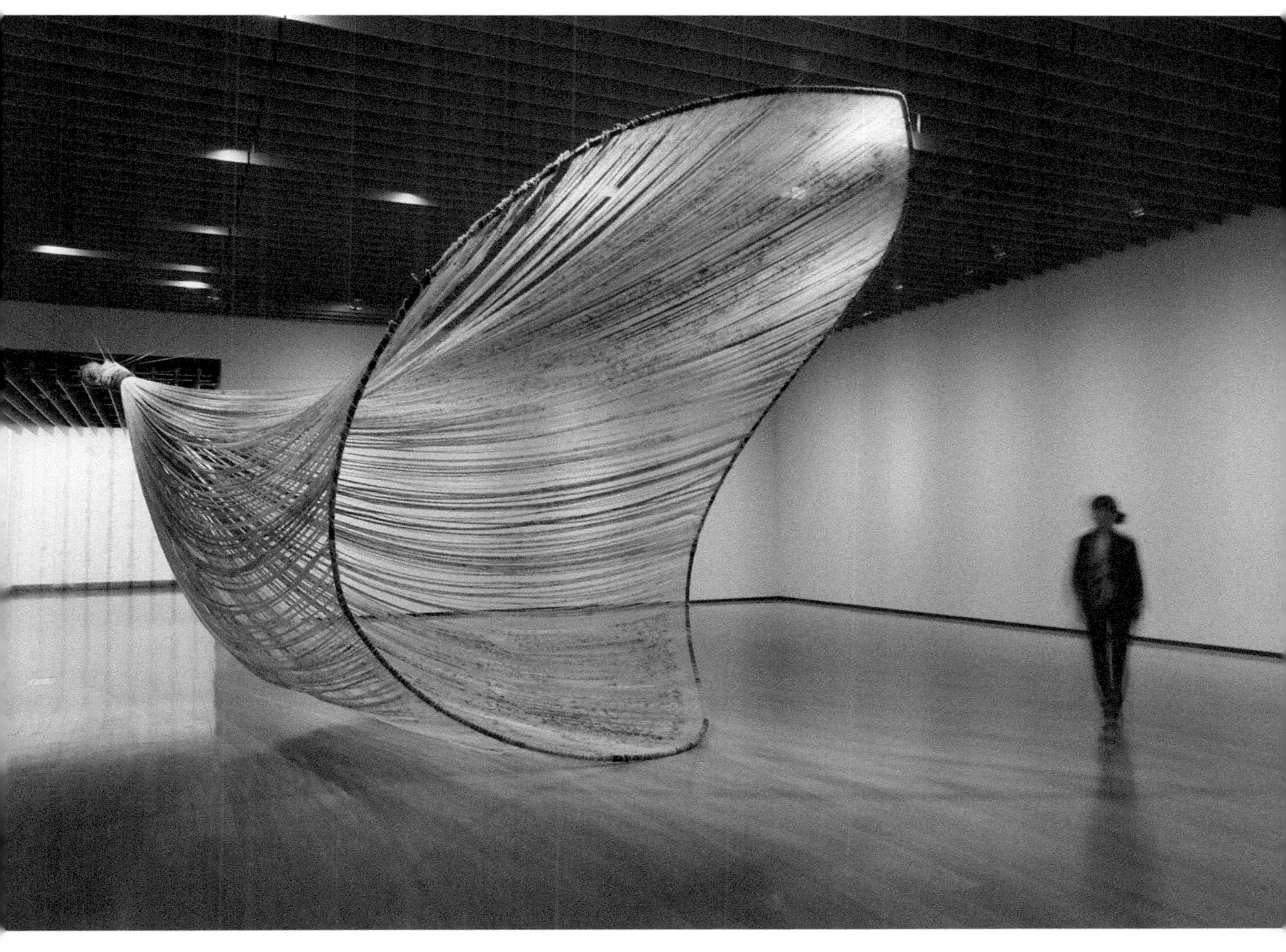

FIGURE 5.1. *Beta Decay 5 (Antimonument)*, Nagasaki Prefectural Art Museum, August 1, 2015. Photograph courtesy of Shinpei Takeda. See also plate 8.

to other survivors. I had personally known her since 2005, and she was an important figure among the various groups of survivors. When she arrived in the lobby of the museum, she asked where she was supposed to give a talk about her experience. Having been active for many decades as a storyteller, that role is deeply ingrained in her. It was difficult to ask her to change her role to that of a viewer for an art exhibition. Upon seeing my work, she told me that it reminded her of the dark mushroom cloud and the black rain that came afterward. However, at that point I realized that the question of how my artwork could do justice to such a deeply personal and life-changing moment was unanswerable. As a gesture of respect, I asked her to tell her stories with my works in the background. I then recorded it. I have heard her stories many times, but it was her work and her years of commitment that I felt the need to acknowledge.

Even within the small city of Nagasaki, which still contained survivors and many monuments, the meaning of *Antimonument* took a very different shape than I initially expected. I was starting to recognize that it was important to be contextual in speaking about *Antimonument* and that this notion was constantly shifting and must be fine-tuned to both micro and macro contexts.

Chapter 2

Antimonument #2—Dresden, Germany
Opening: September 26, 2016
Distance: 9,061 km from hypocenter
Time: 71 years and 48 days

The abandoned power station from the early 1900s located behind the historical part of the city of Dresden was being renovated as a new cultural campus called Kraftwerk Mitte. A building that had just been renovated with a bare concrete floor was the location for the exhibition *Erinnerungshorizonte Dresden Hiroshima Nagasaki,* literally translated as "memory horizon."

The exhibition included an intricate negotiation with the National Nagasaki Memorial Hall for the Victims of Atomic Bombings in Nagasaki. I was able to include the *Antimonument* exhibition as part of their official 2016 overseas atomic bomb exhibition. I secured two large exhibition halls in this building. One hall with a lower ceiling was dedicated to the official atomic bomb exhibition from the Nagasaki Memorial Hall, while the other hall, an elongated space with a sixty-foot-high ceiling, was used to install my work *Beta Decay*.

The idea was to create a space for the didactic information and a separate space for contemplation. Technically, it became a complicated challenge for me as simultaneously producer, curator, organizer, and artist. Furthermore, creating an exhibition about the atomic bomb in a city known for suffering massive air-raid attacks during World War II presented a unique opportunity to contextualize the narrative of atomic bombing.

The official overseas atomic bomb exhibition is a set of outdated panels accompanied by testimonial videos as well as several artifacts. The panels start with official greetings from the mayors of Hiroshima and Nagasaki, then go through the events of the atomic bombings chronologically. After thirty panels or so that read more like a short textbook, the exhibition ends with a plea for a world without nuclear weapons. As much as I was critical of some of the text as well as its use of some extremely graphic images, I was not allowed to make any major changes to the exhibition. I also knew that putting my work next to the official atomic bomb exhibition was experimental enough, so I was careful about trying to edit too much of the official content of the exhibition.

My installation *Beta Decay* was in some ways an abstraction of this historical event. The main question was whether such a work could coexist with an exhibition based on a very didactic presentation of historical information. Would this juxtaposition add to or subtract from what each exhibit was trying to communicate to its audience? These were the questions I wanted to pose in this exhibition. The overseas atomic bomb exhibition panels were made with the intention of communicating the real threat of nuclear weapons, but they did not actively offer an opportunity for the viewer to feel close to this historical event. In short, they were there to monumentalize these historical events rather than humanize them.

The citizens of Dresden had lived with the ruins of Frauenkirche, a Lutheran church, right in the middle of the city until 1994, when the destroyed church was rebuilt after the reunification of Germany. Upon seeing photographs of the ruins, I was immediately reminded of the Urakami Cathedral of Nagasaki, badly damaged by the atomic bomb. Dresden approached the reconstruction of this church in a very different manner from how Nagasaki rebuilt Urakami Cathedral. The Frauenkirche was rebuilt faithfully to its original form, using as much material as possible from the ruins. To this day the walls of the church summarize the mixture of future and past—a mosaic of blackened old bricks among the new fresh cream-colored bricks tells of the process of reconstruction. In comparison, the Urakami Cathedral was completely rebuilt with only a column of the church and the top roof of the original chapel tower remaining as a relic in the same compound.

Perhaps this notion of history hybridizing with the present is best summarized in the German word *Erinnerungskultur*, literally translated as "memory culture," a field of culture that includes different forms and methodologies of relating to the past. The expansiveness of remembrance culture allowed me to consider situating my work next to the official atomic bomb exhibition panels. Moreover, it permitted me to actively draw parallels between the bombings and contemporary events in Germany at the time. This was particularly important, as Germany was transforming itself by welcoming millions of refugees while also witnessing a sharp rise in ethnic nationalism, with nationalist riots often centered in Dresden. These developments also affected our activities in that the city of Dresden was not able to support our exhibition financially after the culture budget was cut in half to support housing for newly arriving refugees.

This was the context in which the exhibition opened. The exhibition was realized with the support of the mayor's office in Dresden and an official delegation from Nagasaki. It opened with official remarks by the mayor of Dresden, as well as remarks by a representative from the Japanese embassy in Berlin. I had to carefully navigate my antimonument stance in this official setting with politicians and bureaucrats. The mayor himself congratulated me on my work, and surprisingly many others were quite satisfied with the juxtaposition of my work next to the official atomic bomb panel exhibition.

Upon talking to some visitors, I was surprised to discover how many of them were uninformed about the atomic bombings and how many were left speechless by the official overseas atomic bomb exhibition. I noticed that some were so overwhelmed by what they saw that they did not even notice my work hanging in the second exhibition hall.

The high point of the exhibition was one of its parallel programs. A Nagasaki survivor of the atomic bomb, Kazumi Yamada, who had traveled from Nagasaki for the exhibition opening, spoke with a survivor of the Dresden air-raid bombings, Nora Lang, about their experiences and exchanged stories, which had striking similarities. The darkness and the sound and vibrations of the blasts as physical sensations were deeply ingrained in their memories. Both of them emphasized that they had been young children not fully comprehending what was happening. Nora Lang brought a black charred spoon she had found in the aftermath of the bombing as a gift for Mr. Yamada. Recognizing that he was part of the official delegation, he respectfully passed the spoon to the Nagasaki officials. While the official delegation from Japan was initially against accepting the gift as a governmental institution, the spoon was ultimately brought to Japan and put on display in their exhibition hall. It was frustrating to see what I already knew: the officials from the Nagasaki delegations were not as invested in creating a critical discourse with their exhibitions as following proper protocol.

After the Japanese delegation had left, the local organizers and I took more of an antimonumental approach by inviting Dresdner Sinfoniker, one of the more progressive orchestra groups in Dresden. We contacted this group, known for engaging in socially inclined themes, because they had premiered a piece called *Barefoot Gen* in the city several years earlier. This event brought in much wider audiences. They projected slides from the *Barefoot Gen* comic books, authored by Japanese atomic bomb survivor Keiji Nakazawa, with German subtitles on the screen while the musicians made electronic and saxophone sound interventions to the visuals. The free concert was packed and brought a new audience to the exhibition. I noticed in people's faces that they understood what I was trying to accomplish. Perhaps it was because of the inclusive concept of *Erinnerungskultur* and the distance from Hiroshima and Nagasaki, or perhaps it was because of the local history of Dresden having gone through a massive air raid. Or maybe it was the physical distance from Hiroshima and Nagasaki, as this type of experimental event would never have been possible close to ground zero.

Although intertwined with the official exhibition, the "antimonument" stance of my contribution became much clearer as I opened the exhibition.

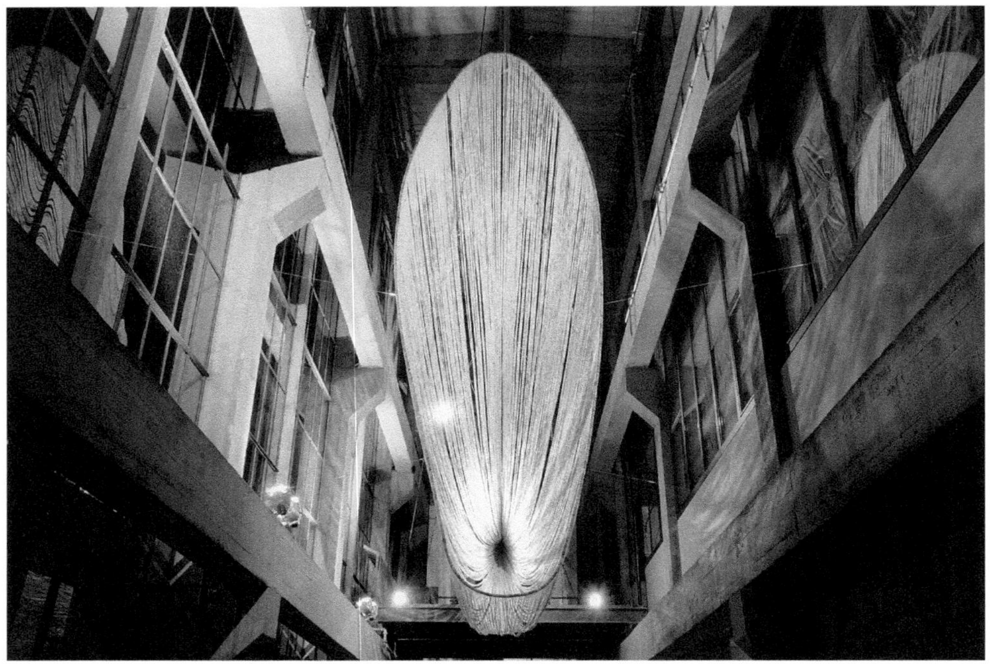

FIGURE 5.2. *Beta Decay 5 (Antimonument)*, Kraftwerk Mitte-Dresden, September 26, 2016. Photograph by Kosuke Okahara courtesy of Shinpei Takeda. See also plate 9.

It slowly wove itself with local memories as I invited different collaborators to participate. While I might have focused too much on the "anti-" aspect in Nagasaki, I also realized that it was crucial that *Antimonument* remain open, flexible, and inviting to different, sometimes unexpected, interpretations.

Chapter 3

Antimonument #3—Querétaro, Mexico
Opening: January 26, 2017
Distance: 11,967 km from hypocenter
Time: 71 years and 170 days

Having lived in Mexico for over ten years, I was aware that the discourse on the atomic bomb reverberates strongly among the public in Mexico. Needless to say, it is fueled by an anti-imperial stance against the United

States. Many writers, poets and artists in Mexico have long pondered and discussed this event, which changed the fate of humanity. Most often, upon hearing the words *bomba atomica* people respond by thinking about its moral implications.

Upon bringing the *Antimonument* exhibit to the Museo de Arte de Querétaro in the city of Querétaro, one of the main capitals of the rapidly growing industrial region of Bajío, I had to change my thinking in terms of how to exhibit the works in a way that would make sense for this context. It was not the first time for me to do an exhibition related to the atomic bombing in Mexico. In 2010, I had done a large installation called *Alpha Decay* in Tijuana. However, Querétaro was a radically different context.

The Museo de Arte de Querétaro is located in an eighteenth-century convent that was converted into a museum in 1988. Situated in the historic center of the city, the museum had several large, elongated halls with high, rounded ceilings surrounding a courtyard. I was given three large halls to exhibit the works from the *Antimonument* traveling exhibition.

What made this exhibition special was the guest of honor, Yamashita Yasuaki, a survivor of the Nagasaki atomic bombing. He lived only about one hour from the city and was able to speak at the opening. Among the many survivors of the atomic bombings I have met, he was very special. He was one of my first interviewees, marking the beginning of what was to become a ten-year-long journey during which I interviewed over seventy people across North and South America.

In 2012, when I worked with the United Nations Disarmament Office to launch a multilingual website of survivors living in North and South America (www.hiroshima-nagasaki.com), I invited Yamashita Yasuaki and Setsuko Thurlow in a parallel launch event to the First Committee of the UN General Assembly. Upon hearing my presentation, in which I explained the need to involve the arts in understanding the horrors of the atomic bombings, Setsuko Thurlow cried and expressed her disappointment with my work, upset that she didn't feel a call to action as she had felt from viewing the works of other young activists. She had assumed that I would have a different type of proposal. However, Yamashita understood what I was trying to do, and he even encouraged others to accept that we needed new language for discussing this matter. Because he was a survivor of the atomic bombing and a fellow artist active in Mexico, as well as a Japanese expatriate in Mexico, I felt a strange sense of solidarity with him.

He was himself a monument. He was a witness. His life had completely changed because of the atomic bomb. He came to Mexico initially as a translator for a Japanese Olympic delegation in 1968 and ended up pursuing art to express his experiences through different mediums. What is my role as an artist in front of someone like Yamashita Yasuaki? What is my antimonument stance in this scenario? I created a new work at the site. I painted an abstract portrait of his face on a piece of paper 20 × 40 feet. I stayed up until three in the morning for three nights in a row to create this painting. This huge mural was hung in one hall that was not yet filled, and I projected a moving animation on top of this mural. In the video one can see the words of the testimonials floating over his face. Whether it was consciously or subconsciously done, and whether it is antimonumental or not, it was my tribute to Mr. Yamashita.

In the entrance of the first exhibition hall, I had written directly on a wall this phrase from my "Antimonument Manifesto," which I had previously authored as part of my first exhibition in Nagasaki:

> *Una vez vuelta a la vida, la memoria nos guiara dándonos hilos con los que podamos, una vez mas, tejer nuestro futuro aun desconocido.*
>
> (The memory, once again alive, will provide us with a guiding thread to once again weave our unknown future.)[1]

In this exhibition, I needed a poem to weave through the entire exhibition so that the antimonument stance became something that was not static but had a flow with sensitivity. After all, I had included Mr. Yamashita in the exhibition. He was a monument to which I had to pay proper respect, and I had to show that my antimonument stance was not in opposition to him and his history but rather meant to embrace the marginalized stories of survivors like him with sensitivity and compassion. The use of thread in my works not only coincided with this idea but also augmented this sensitivity in the exhibition.

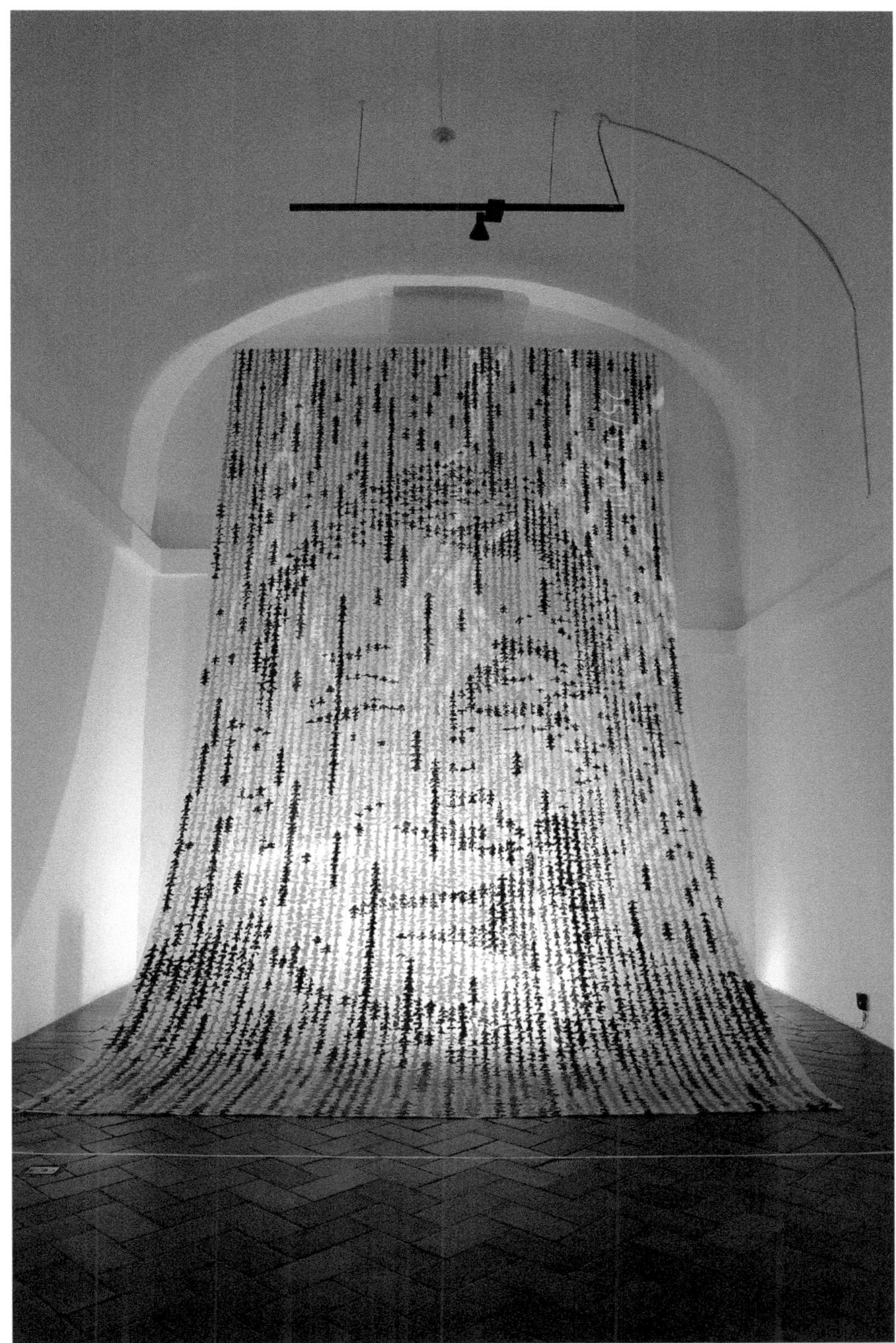

FIGURE 5.3. *Alpha Decay*, Museo de Arte de Querétaro, January 26, 2017. Photograph courtesy of Shinpei Takeda. See also plate 10.

Chapter 4

Antimonument #4—San Miguel de Allende, Guanajuato, Mexico
Opening: February 2, 2018
Distance: 11,940 km from hypocenter
Time: 72 years and 177 days

Centro Cultural Ignacio Ramírez "El Nigromante" is located in the center of the colonial town of San Miguel de Allende, in the state of Guanajuato. Known for a long tradition of welcoming expatriates and as a getaway for tourists from Mexico City and abroad, the colonial center of the city features several cultural institutions and museums. Like the museum in Querétaro, Centro Cultural Ignacio Ramírez "El Nigromante" is a former convent from the eighteenth century. Coincidentally the museum was very near the home of Mr. Yamashita Yasuaki. Fate somehow made it such that the curator from this museum saw the exhibition in the neighboring city of Querétaro and wanted to bring it to her museum. This then became the site of the fourth iteration of the *Antimonument* exhibition.

Mr. Yamashita is an established artist well known in the city. As in the case of the first exhibition in Nagasaki, *Antimonument* had to work alongside another monument. This time, the monument was Mr. Yamashita Yasuaki; the exhibition was a short fifteen-minute walk from his home.

I realized at that point that I was particularly aware of his presence. I knew part of this was because I saw myself in him as a fellow expatriate Japanese artist in Mexico. Another part that was important was that I wanted this exhibition to be rooted in the reality of the atomic bomb. Somehow, I had been concerned that my exhibition was romanticizing the tragedy of Hiroshima and Nagasaki. People died, and people are still suffering, and we are faced with thousands more of these weapons. In this context, there is nothing more real than a person who has witnessed an actual atomic bombing, and the fact that the person happens to be living in the same city as you only furthers this sense of reality.

I knew that this would not be the same in 2030, when the majority of the people who witnessed the actual event will be gone. I knew that in 2030 this exhibition itself would have a completely different dimension of abstraction, and I also knew that the whole discourse would be open to much wider interpretations and politicization. I knew because over ten years of

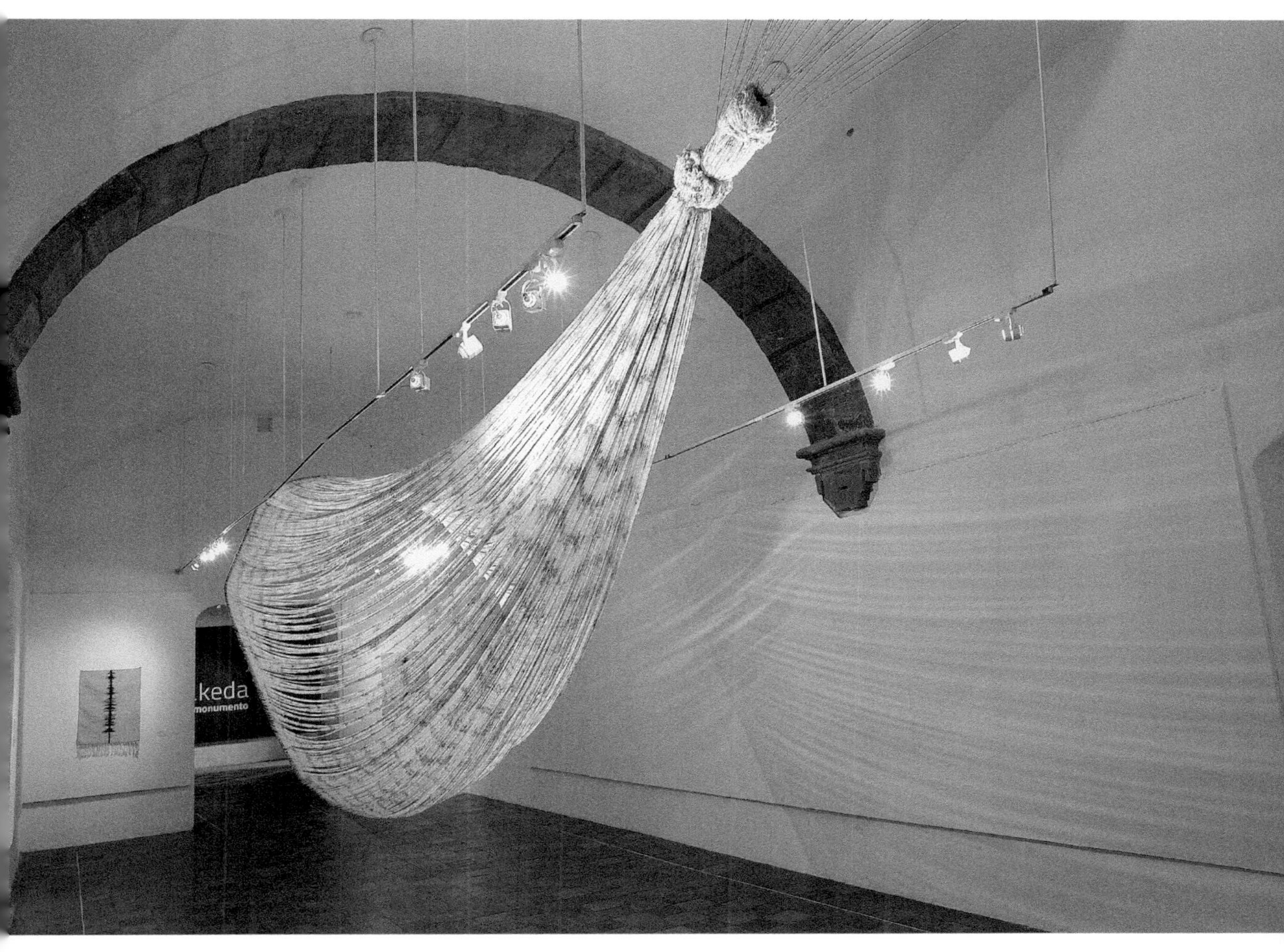

FIGURE 5.4. *Timeline of Our Memory (Beta Decay 3)*, Centro Cultural Ignacio Ramírez "El Nigromante," San Miguel de Allende, September 20, 2018. Photograph courtesy of Shinpei Takeda.

hearing the interviews of atomic bomb survivors, I myself have forgotten and have interpreted things differently. I knew that this is the nature of our memory and that its evolution cannot be stopped.

Next to the exhibition hall was another hall with a large mural by David Alfaro Siqueiros. His unfinished murals, made in the 1940s, cover the sides and the curved ceiling of a large hall. In the middle of the ceiling is a drawing of an obelisk with an orange triangular tip like a modern destructive rocket firing burning explosive beams. On the walls are geometric lines that hint at something scientific. Given that the work was not completed because the building changed owners in 1948, it would not be a wild speculation that he used the atomic bomb as an inspiration for his large murals. If one follows this thought, one can feel the artist's concern regarding the possibility of human annihilation that we humans have brought on ourselves. Similar to how I felt exhibiting my works next to those of Maruki Iri and Maruki Toshi, I somehow understood what Siqueiros was trying to do as an artist.

The exhibition opened to a large audience and a warm welcome. Unfortunately, Mr. Yamashita was away, but toward the end of the exhibition he came and gave a speech as part of the screening of my film from 2010, *Hiroshima Nagasaki Download*. Although he had already spoken of his experience in San Miguel de Allende a long time ago, my exhibition put his story in a different light and again provided a forum for him to share his life stories with new audiences in his city.

Chapter 5

Antimonument #5: Mexico City, México
Opening: September 20, 2018
Distance: 12,225 km from hypocenter
Time: 73 years and 42 days

The arrival of the exhibition in the capital, Mexico City, was symbolic in many ways. At the fifth stop of the tour, I was beginning to reflect on the fact that perhaps my antimonument approach was also a strategy to better understand monuments. After all, the antimonument exhibition required proximity to monuments, whether that was another artist's works, an actual survivor, or another tragedy.

My work was to be exhibited at the Museo de la Cancillería, a museum within the Instituto Matías Romeros, the Foreign Ministry's diplomatic academy. As I was installing the work, a series of events surrounding Mexican Independence Day was taking place. The Grito, literally translated as "shout," is a major ceremony of the Mexican Independence Day celebration that takes place in the Zócalo, the central square in the middle of the city, only a few blocks from the museum. The president comes out on the balcony of the presidential palace facing the square and shouts the name of the founder with a famous phrase, "Viva México!" The day of the Grito, I was working until late evening installing the work. As constant fireworks echoed in the sky, I was overwhelmed with a strange feeling. I was all by myself in a governmental building in the historical center of Mexico City. I had to ask myself: for whom am I making this exhibition, and whose agenda am I fulfilling with it?

I am only an artist, and my work can only be a medium for a wider dialogue. Nevertheless, I needed to be aware of these factors. The exhibition was part of the agenda of the Foreign Ministry of the Mexican government. The intention was clear. The Mexican government had invested heavily in nuclear disarmament, most notably through the Treaty of Tlatelolco, signed in 1967, which prohibited nuclear weapons in Latin America and the Caribbean. As the director of the institute mentioned in her opening remarks, it was important for them to show the government's commitment to the disarmament negotiations, and hence it was important for them to once again highlight the horrors of the Hiroshima and Nagasaki atomic bombings.

I did know the only thing I could do was to continue my antimonument stance and create works that spoke to its philosophy. Quite similar to the exhibition space in San Miguel de Allende, in this eighteenth-century former convent building there was a courtyard with a fountain in the middle. I created a new work at the site called *Cuatro gritos para Antimonumentalismo* (Four shouts for antimonumentalism). The work was hung with four "horns" facing outward in the middle of the courtyard.

Four outward-facing openings were all connected at the center. However, they were not tied; rather, they wove into each other in a way that left an empty space in the middle. There was a sense that whatever came in from these four openings would go through to the other openings. I knew that

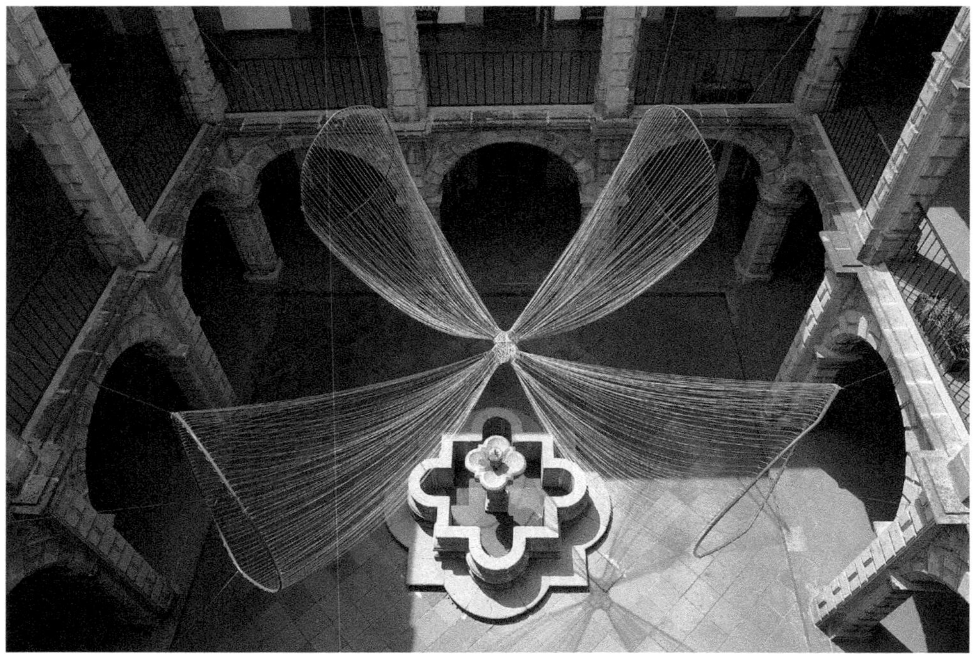

FIGURE 5.5. *Cuatro gritos para Antimonumentalismo*, Museo de la Cancillería, Mexico City, September 20, 2018. Photograph courtesy of Shinpei Takeda.

this was going to be the last iteration of the traveling exhibition *Antimonument*. Hence this work, in one way or another, summarized the complexities, flexibilities as well as sensitivities, of antimonument philosophy.

The exhibition opened successfully and continued throughout the fall, ending with a screening of my film and the speech by Mr. Yamashita Yasuaki, who graciously traveled five hours by bus to Mexico City to share his story. The first time I met him in 2005, he was sixty-six years old. Now he was seventy-nine. Seventy-three years had already passed since the last atomic bomb was dropped in wartime.

The entire traveling exhibition at five different sites over the three and a half years started with the "Antimonument Manifesto" at the Nagasaki Museum. This manifesto developed over the course of the exhibitions into a set of guiding principles. These principles helped me make various aesthetic and philosophical decisions as an artist.

Different sites created different contexts and required different senses of urgency. Physical distance from ground zero, as well as distance from the events in terms of time were very important factors in determining how to frame the exhibition. Also, it was important to consider the local context in terms of both its history and contemporary issues. I had to work with history and sentiments within the local context, be it the existence of a decommissioned power plant or an eighteenth-century convent. Meanwhile it was also important to consider the specific framework of each institution and its political agenda. Each place had a slightly different perception of Hiroshima and Nagasaki, and hence I was required to think about different methodologies and strategies for showing works. The physical distance of these sites to the ground zero of Hiroshima and Nagasaki played a significant role in these perceptions. The distance in terms of time played another interesting role—how long it had been since the moment of the ground zero, and how close it was to the anniversary days in August. I needed to be strategic and yet flexible with these local parameters while being creative in finding threads to contextualize the stories of this massive tragedy in the everyday life of the local and present-day context.

However, most important of all was the constant process of self-awareness and self-criticism. The discourse of the atomic bombing is extremely complicated and multidimensional in that it touches politics, health, science, and environment. Therefore, it was important for me to always focus on the human story and the human perspective. I had to be very careful to not abuse its symbolic meanings. I was also constantly open to criticism and attempted in every way possible to include a self-critique. I was able to accomplish this with by being aware and being inclusive of the monuments—for example, the survivors of the atomic bombings, other artists' works, and other tragedies of massive scale—at every exhibition.

Traveling with the *Antimonument* exhibition was an act of sharing the human perspective under the mushroom cloud. To retain as much control as possible, I had to create, curate, and produce the exhibition. As much as it was a daunting task not only to put on this traveling exhibition but also to highlight this massive issue in a sensitive yet critical way, I had to always remember that it was the same act of humanity that continues to threaten us with nuclear wars and nuclear waste to this day.

Note

1. Takeda Shinpei, *Takeda Shinpei Anchimonumyumento tenrankai zuroku = Shinpei Takeda Antimonument Exhibition Catalogue* (Nagasaki: Nagasaki Prefectural Museum of Art, 2015).

The Antimonument Research Collective

SHUHEI MATSUKUBO, MARIKO MIKAMI,
MAIKA NAKAO, AND SHINPEI TAKEDA

The Antimonument Research Collective formed in 2020 to explore the concept of antimonumentality originally put forth by artist Shinpei Takeda in his 2015 manifesto.[1] Antimonumentality demands continuous critical inquiry and rejects the static, fixed representation of monuments. The group was organized by Takeda and is composed of artists, producers, curators, and researchers. In addition to Takeda, the collective includes Shuhei Matsukubo, a curator at the Nagasaki Prefectural Art Museum whose main focus is modern and contemporary Japanese art; Maika Nakao, an associate professor at Hiroshima University who specializes in the history and culture of the nuclear age; and Mariko Mikami, an independent curator, project manager and producer of contemporary art and interdisciplinary projects currently based in Düsseldorf, Germany, and Tokyo, Japan.

Shinpei Takeda, Artist and Filmmaker

Tijuana, Mexico, and Düsseldorf, Germany

After traveling with the exhibition *Antimonument* from 2015 to 2018 from Nagasaki to Mexico, my project took me back to Nagasaki in the summer of 2020. I was to make a public art intervention at Hypocenter Park, right at the foot of the monuments. The ambitious project met with positive reviews. Nevertheless, I felt the need to address the contradictory nature of locating my projects at the site of monuments even though I have been advocating an antimonument stance. I felt a particular sense of apprehension because there was not a single public criticism of my project. Instead, it received only superficial media coverage that lacked any critique or insight. There must have been mixed feelings and reactions regarding an experimental art project in such an emotionally and politically loaded site. But either I was not allowed into those conversations or perhaps no such dialogue is allowed in Nagasaki.

So, in my desire to not let the project end up becoming monumental and to create space for critical dialogue, I decided to ask other scholars, curators, and producers from different disciplines to participate in this continuous inquiry by forming a group called Antimonument Research Collective. Throughout the year, monthly discussions were held with guests, with whom we discussed the concept of antimonument from multiple perspectives. We inquired what *antimonument* means—from figurative to abstract, physical to metaphysical, and contextual to philosophical. I believe that the essential thing is to continue these conversations.

Below are both personal and critical reflections by members of the collective that highlight our diverse perspectives.

Shuhei Matsukubo, Curator

Nagasaki Prefectural Art Museum

August 9, 2020, 6 p.m., Nagasaki. The rain had just ended, and countless candles flickered in Hypocenter Park. This was *Memor(y/i)al: Voice and Light Performance*, part of *Memory Undertow* (*Seimon Genba* in Japanese) orchestrated by artist Shinpei Takeda.[2] The night was filled with the voices of the volunteer recital group Towa No Kai reciting the experiences of the atomic bomb survivors (*hibakusha*) living abroad and the sound of snare drums played by percussionist Nagasawa Satoshi. All over the ground below was *Memory Undertow*, the voiceprint of the hibakusha transcribed by Takeda.

Overlooking the monument literally at ground zero—the center of the atomic bomb explosions—the voiceprints of A-bomb survivors covered the area of over eight hundred square meters, more than half the surface of Hypocenter Park. These voiceprints, transcribed by Takeda's hand, are computer-generated visualizations of the voices of twelve Nagasaki natives exiled in North and South America, whose stories Takeda collected over the years. Naturally, it is not possible to trace back to the content of the stories from the voiceprints. Therefore, they are only traces of the amplitude of the voices and emotions of hibakusha who recount their very specific experiences.

In this project, an augmented reality application developed in collaboration with the University of Applied Sciences in Düsseldorf complemented the use of the voiceprint sequences. By scanning the markers placed at various spots on the ground covered with voiceprints using a specially designed app installed on a smartphone, a flag-like motif appears in the augmented reality, and one can hear the voices of the hibakusha, the source of the voiceprints, through the app.[3]

As viewers, we physically enter into the work, wandering over the voiceprint and listening to the actual voices of the hibakusha. When the voice and the voiceprints mix on the surface of the hypocenter, we feel as if the voices of the hibakusha are echoing through the voiceprint at our feet from a deeper layer of the hypocenter.

It should be noted, however, that these white voiceprints were transcribed by Takeda's hand. In a sense, this anachronistic, analog use of the hand has been persistently repeated in Takeda's previous works. Takeda's works, starting with the *Alpha Decay* series of installations using voiceprint motifs, began with his "daring attempt to somehow try to understand and to touch," based on his acceptance of the inherent impossibility of understanding the essence of the A-bomb experience.[4]

When Takeda spent an enormous amount of time under the blazing sun, perhaps foolishly yet sincerely transcribing voiceprints, the amplitude of the voiceprints was not only the fluctuation of the emotions of the hibakusha and their recounting of their horrifying experiences, but also an expression of the fluctuation of Takeda's own body and mind at that moment.[5] Through this ritualistic process, Takeda makes an attempt to understand the hibakusha. However, at the same time he embodies the memory of the atomic bombing as an issue of his own individuality in the present. In parallel with creating works using voiceprints, Takeda has been working to archive the stories of atomic bombing survivors that he has collected. The two seemingly different approaches of expression and preservation are the two wheels that define Takeda's positions.[6] Takeda continues to weave a thread that connects 1945 to the present and to the future as a matter of his own individual existence within a single axis of time.[7]

Initially, *Memory Undertow* was to be erased by Takeda and his volunteers without waiting for the anniversary of the bombing on August 9, as if to suggest that the memories of all disasters, including Nagasaki, would fade with the passage of time. However, due to the wishes of the Nagasaki citizens, the exhibition was extended through August 9 and a performance held on the final night. Although this was contrary to Takeda's original intention, the performance was a successful conclusion to the monthlong project.

On the night of the event, the stories of Nagasaki and the hibakusha were summoned to the hypocenter through the bodies of reciters functioning as devices. The sound of the drums resonated with their voices, echoing like a call. At the end of the performance, they formed a circle, and all the reciters read at the same time. Each voice mingled with the others, and the waves of sound spread out like an ocean. When I immersed my body in this sea of sound, a swell of vibration, my body resonated as if it was being drawn to the vibration of the hibakusha, the reciters, and Takeda.

Takeda, standing beside the reciters, uses a small projector to project their voice patterns from their feet to their hearts. It is as if the voices of the hibakusha, called in from the deeper strata of the hypocenter, are downloaded through their feet touching the earth, into their bodies, and released through their throats into the air of Nagasaki.

Maika Nakao, Historian

Hiroshima University

Nagasaki is a place where one can feel and connect with the dead. One of the things that fascinated me while I lived in Nagasaki was the relationship of the living and the dead. During the Obon festival in mid-August, when the dead are supposed to return, fireworks are set off, and families eat and drink at graves. On the last day of Obon, Shōrō Nagashi is held, in which the spirits of the dead are sent off.[8] Countless firecrackers are set off, and the dead are carried off on spirit boats in a lively atmosphere. By investigating more about the history and culture of Nagasaki and the connection between the living and the dead, I began to relate much more personally to tombstones and became attracted to stone monuments.

In this context, I believe that a monument is something that connects, or at least was built to connect, the dead and the living. As a historian of the atomic bombing, I am interested in the monuments representing the victims of the atomic bombing. The most famous in Nagasaki are the monuments in Hypocenter Park and Peace Park. Art critics like Odawara Nodoka and others have argued that these monuments are inappropriate for the place.[9] Rather than these well-known monuments, I would like to think about the myriad monuments that are not well known.

There is a book, *The Monument Appeals* (Ishibumi wa uttaeru), which lists many memorial monuments, both known and unknown, to the victims of the atomic bombing in Nagasaki.[10] With this book in hand, I walked through the streets and mountains of Nagasaki. These monuments were erected out of mourning for the victims by the people left behind. However, they have faded with time and often stand in secluded places without much attention. It became important for me to trace the fading monuments one by one and ponder upon the context in which these monuments were built.

Therefore, when I first heard the term *antimonument* and the ideas associated with it, it seemed to me to belittle history. But through monthly discussions with Takeda and others I have gained a lot of inspiration. Monuments are created by the politics of their time, as a result of negotiations among people living at the time. The meaning of a monument changes depending on where it is placed and who sees it. If the meaning of a monument is something that changes, what is the point of protecting it? A monument leaves behind an intention, and that can trigger violence just by its continued existence. After talking with Shirakawa Yoshio, it somehow became clear to me that monuments themselves have no meaning.[11]

Monuments don't tell us anything by themselves. There are those who create monuments, those who try to preserve them, those who question them, and those who try to dismantle them. It is a negotiation—a negotiation over history and story. Monuments thus serve as a mode of negotiation. If they were not left in some form or shape, we would not even have a chance to think about what this something means. Therefore, I see monuments as facilitating thinking.

To think about monuments is also to think about how we deal with the people and events that we do not have direct memories of. The memory of the atomic bombing will fade away. But I would like to keep the memories and records of those who left them behind and those who are trying to leave them behind in the hope that they, along with the monuments, will inspire and invite the people of the future to further negotiations.

Mariko Mikami, Curator

Düsseldorf, Germany, and Tokyo, Japan

Antimonument is about the dynamism of erecting and destroying monuments; a wake-up call to our collective numbness, which prevents us from thinking beyond the surface; and a critical attitude that seeks to update the narratives of monuments that have been recorded and remembered. Shinpei Takeda points out a paradox in his "Antimonument Manifesto" of 2015: the concept of antimonument becomes monumental when it becomes static. I believe that this state of suspension is its essence.

Public monuments have been erected, maintained, and even removed as communal memory devices to govern people in the name of establishing a community or a nation-state.[12] The history of monuments reveals who is/was in power at the time and who is/was excluded. It is also true that history has been written by those who were privileged enough to evaluate and distinguish between you and me, here and there. A dualistic approach, however, is incapable of grasping those who exist between categories or those who are directly on the boundaries. The attitude of antimonument, which questions the static nature of what is classified in front of our eyes, encourages us to imagine what has become invisible as a result of dualistic historical judgment. This transboundary approach is where art and literature, or their interdisciplinary expression, come into play as powerful tools.

The works of Kobayashi Erika, which depict human nature as enthralled by light, radiant materials, and invisible entities that transcend reason, provide a clue to considering the attitude of antimonument.[13] In her literary installation *She Waited* (2019), the monumental symbols and events under fascist regimes in the West and in the East reverberate as an underlying tone. Those symbols include, for example, the "sacred" torch relay of the 1936 Berlin Olympics as well as the relay planned for the cancelled 1940 Tokyo Olympics, the discovery of uranium, and the development of nuclear weapons. The protagonists of the story/work, on the other hand, are unnamed girls called "her," who have been waiting for the sacred fire of the

Olympic torch to arrive. Unlike the imperialist powers that be, who prefer massive, macho monuments, the works that compose the installation are small and made of subtle materials such as paper, mirrors, and projection. Expanding literature into installation, Kobayashi slips these fragile, fluxing voices of anonymous girls into a dark space with blanks that correspond to spaces between the lines.

The anonymous girls from Kobayashi's installation demonstrate how what is out of frame or between the lines can serve as an invisible monument even in the absence of names and entities. It is their destiny to permanently evade becoming static because their existence is dependent on the reception, interpretation, and imagination of each reader and viewer. This suspended state—namely, their ephemeral and intangible beings—resists dualistic judgment. This is the point at which the attitude of antimonument resonates, prompting us to defrost our static viewpoint of history and providing us with a third eye to reflect on our stories.

Notes

1. Takeda Shinpei, *Takeda Shinpei Anchimonumyumento tenrankai zuroku = Shinpei Takeda Antimonument Exhibition Catalogue* (Nagasaki: Nagasaki Prefectural Museum of Art, 2015).
2. This performance was held as part of the Nagasaki Evening of Prayer and Pledge for the 75th Anniversary of the Bombing.
3. An application named "Ground-0" is used. The flag-like motifs that appear after scanning the markers are composed of titles assigned by Takeda and photographs of Nagasaki after the bombing.
4. "Conversation: Shinpei Takeda and Yukinori Okamura," in Takeda, *Takeda Shinpei Anchimonumyumento tenrankai zuroku.*
5. For more on Takeda's transcriptions of voiceprints, see also Ryuta Imafuku, "For the Second Witnessing of the Atomic Bomb," and Akira Nonaka, "Anti-Monument: To Remember the 'Two Times,'" in *Shinpei Takeda Antimonument Exhibition Catalogue.*
6. In the project *Memory Undertow*, "Memory Undertow Web Dialogue" was conducted as a parallel event. The themes of the four dialogue sessions are as follows: "#1 Inheritance (Guests: Asanaga Masao and Osera Ryo)," "#2 Stories of the Public and the Individual (Aorai Yuichi and Nakao Maika)," "#3 Disarmament (Yoshida Fumihiko, Ageo Haruka)," "#4: Atomic Bomb and Art (Hasegawa Arata, Nonaka Akira)." The implementation of these side events expresses Takeda's attempt to not let this project remain static or be forgotten as transitory, but rather to open up a path to the next phase of development.

7. Following *Alpha Decay*, Takeda presented *Beta Decay*, a series of installations using countless threads.
8. Editor's note: This is the "spirit boat procession," part of the Obon festival that is specific to Nagasaki and surrounding areas.
9. Odawara Nodoka, a sculptor and art critic born in 1985, criticizes Peace Park for being a "sculpture yard" with no connection to the atomic bombing and points to it as a problem for modern Japanese art and sculpture. Odawara joined our monthly discussion on June 9, 2021.
10. *Ishibumi wa uttaeru: Genbaku monyumento, ikou shū* (The monument appeals: Collection of A-bomb monuments and remains) (Nagasaki: Nagasaki Kokusai Bunka Kaikan, 1986).
11. Born in 1948, Shirakawa Yoshio has continued his expressive activities based on local history and culture, rooted in his Dadaist stance. He was invited to the collective's monthly discussion on May 9, 2021.
12. The number of Confederate monuments removed in the United States has increased since the latter half of the 2010s in response to the Black Lives Matter movement. Changes in or removal of monuments may be decided primarily by local authorities and governments. To this end, Shirakawa Yoshio has criticized the conservative Japanese government's revisionist approach through his mobile fabric life-size sculptures of the hypocenter in Nagasaki and the Memorial Monument of Forced Displacement of Koreans in Gunma Prefecture.
13. Kobayashi Erika is a novelist, manga artist, and visual artist living in Tokyo. Radiation is one of the leitmotifs in her work.

Creating the Atomic Sublime

The Perpetual Production of Nuclear In/Security

JENNIFER RICHTER AND SHERRI WASSERMAN

CHAPTER 7

The atomic bombs detonated by the United States over the Japanese cities of Hiroshima on August 6 and Nagasaki on August 9, 1945, thrust the world into a new geopolitical order. In response to public fear and uncertainty, the US government reframed the atom as a globally beneficial yet American-controlled technology that would expand the American economy as well as its sphere of political influence. However, nuclear weapons continue to create a persistent threat to the existence of humanity, even as nuclear proponents continue to call for the expansion of nuclear energy to address climate change. The legacies of the dichotomous and paradoxical ends of atomic technologies stem from the initial decade of nuclear development, as evidenced in the atomic imagery produced by the US federal government.[1] These images reflect an attempt to reconcile the destructive and productive atom in the first decade of nuclear development in the United States.

The initial stages of the era are defined by the destructive power of atomic weaponry, creating a deep insecurity on the part of humans anxious to survive the nuclear age. Images of nuclear tests were distributed widely through American society, providing the public with evidence of the massive power of atomic bombs to destroy society and nature.[2] Yet the federal government also used images to quell and suppress fears of mass annihilation and to secure public support for nuclear development. This chapter argues that the production of "in/security" is central, not incidental, to the development of nuclear technologies and that insecurity is inherently a product of nuclear technologies, even as they are positioned as technologies that contribute to securing the growth of the nation's people and economy. The roots of this cycle are evident in the first decade of the atomic era, when the US government had to constantly demonstrate the power of the atom while reiterating its control over that power. The enemy, post–World War II, was not just the threat of other nations gaining control of the bomb to destabilize and destroy the United States, but also the possibility that public fear would undermine support for innovations in nuclear technologies.[3] The development of nuclear technologies was publicly rationalized through discourses of progress and control, to create the illusion that the US government had complete control over atomic innovation. The US government sought to position itself to the American public (as well as international audiences) as the only supplier of both risk and security.

This fostering of perpetual nuclear in/security is evident in atomic images produced by the US government, where nuclear weapons and energy serve as evidence of both "power as resource and power as discourse," as Andrew Blowers notes. These interconnected discourses "set the frame of reference or possibilities within which power relations interact."[4] Blowers's framing of technocratic nuclear discourses describes the coproduction of contradictory ideas about nuclear technologies as both destroyer and savior, established through the creation and reiteration of a "discourse of trust in technology."[5] In each iteration of the atom produced over this decade, US government agencies sought to assure the American public that the destructive power of the atom was controllable and even beneficial, even as the images produced and transmitted implied the opposite. By attempting to produce the securitization of the nation through nuclear technologies, the systemic insecurity engendered by atomic bombs had to be constantly demonstrated, explained, contained, and attenuated. To impress upon the public the complete destructive power of, yet complete control over, the atom, the US government sought to create a myth of the atomic sublime.

Crafting the Atomic Sublime

While the end of World War II produced an initial outpouring of celebration from the American public, that celebration was tempered by uncertainty about how these new technologies would and should be received.[6] To quell those fears and silence any resistance to nuclear technologies, the federal government created the myth of what historian Peter Bacon Hales calls the "atomic sublime, whose signal importance lies in the very fact that it is manmade, and whose beauty is partly a product of its sources in that American triad of science, capital and military government."[7] Elements of the discourse of the atomic sublime are found in the images and narratives of elites closest to this national project. In these discourses, the mushroom cloud stands in for the previously unimaginable power of the atom, meant to overwhelm the viewer with the force and magnitude of destructive capability; meanwhile, American military and political leaders trumpet their mastery over this power by their governance, aided by the sophistication and prowess of scientists and engineers.[8]

The atomic sublime is an evolution of the Romantic sublime, which saw poets and writers articulating their awe at the devastating power of nature as evidenced in raging rivers and earthquakes, and the technological sublime, where human control over nature through huge dams and earthworks is the source of wonder and fear.[9] Melding these two together, the atomic sublime seemed to mark a new age of American exceptionalism, where "the atomic explosion became not a purely human circumstance (for which we must accept responsibility), but rather a part of that benign collaboration among man, nature and divinity that had defined American destiny, a predetermined, even foreordained event."[10] In discourses of the atomic sublime, the United States was the only nation that could responsibly harness these new nuclear technologies, as both inventors of the atomic bomb and stewards of democracy, both domestically and abroad.[11]

Historian John Dower describes the contradictory allure of devastation from atomic bombs, as well as control over this new technology: "Mass destruction itself was mesmerizing—horrific from the victim's perspective, but attractive to the point of being beautiful, even rapturous, if one was the victimizer instead."[12] Atomic weapons are a source of fear and awe, as well as pride and wonder, as articulated by witnesses of the Trinity detonation in New Mexico in 1945: "It was like a grand finale of a mighty symphony of the elements, fascinating and terrifying, uplifting and crushing, ominous, devastating, full of great promise and great foreboding."[13] The discourses surrounding the paradox of the atomic sublime, as both a novel and beneficial use of knowledge of atomic particles as well as a devastatingly destructive weapon, haunts the sanitized images produced to garner public support.

Selling the Atomic Sublime

To control not only the science and technology of atomic technologies but also public attitudes toward them, Congress passed the Atomic Energy Act in 1946, which created the Atomic Energy Commission (AEC). The AEC was charged with developing nuclear technologies, while also safeguarding public and environmental health, by continuing and expanding on existing corporate partnerships created during the war, in places like Hanford, Washington, where General Electric continued work started by the DuPont Company on processing plutonium for weapons.[14] The Federal Civil Defense Administration (FCDA) was created by Congress in 1951 to deal more explicitly with the public side of the atom, including preparing Americans for public evacuation and survival in the event of a nuclear attack. Civil defense also included producing materials and images to shape public attitudes toward living daily with the threat of nuclear war.[15] Joseph Masco has noted, "A map of the institutions involved in the production of any US nuclear device is a map of the significant political, industrial, academic and scientific relationships in American society."[16] A critical part of the constellation of nuclear institutions included the private sector. The FCDA used private contractors' knowledge of atomic science to promote films like *Hanford Science Forum*, a 1957 television program created by General Electric that disputed the effects of radiation on life in the Columbia River.[17] Using these relationships, the American government used the atomic sublime to create positive publicity for atomic technologies in American society, including schools and libraries, while also trying to position nuclear weapons as the ultimate safeguard for democracy.[18] A technocratic discourse of control and containment also served to foreclose public doubt, resistance, and opposition to developing more powerful bombs and other nuclear technologies, by producing a cyclical narrative around the atomic sublime that showed the danger of atomic technologies but also their necessity to promote American values, while assuring the public of mastery over the atom.[19] Controlling this "atom for peace" would situate the US government as a "responsible regulator" for the world while also forcing open markets for nuclear-nascent nations.[20] The enlistment, mobilization, and integration of the civilian sector into the production of the atom is an integral part of the production of national in/security, and the concept of the atomic sublime was used to situate atomic technologies as simultaneously terrifying and benign, yet under complete control, in the visual culture produced by commercial and national interests.

Containing Chaos in an Image

Images and films from early atomic visual culture are emblematic of government attempts to produce order out of chaos, creation out of destruction, security out of insecurity. Even as these images impart horror and amazement, they also attempt to foreclose resistance or dissent on the part of the individual or community.[21] Photographic documentation of the power of the atom was critical in creating the ideal of the atomic sublime to explain and quantify claims of control and security. The power of these images lies in bringing atomic technologies to a human scale, where individuals coexist with nuclear technologies, and the atom becomes a part of daily life, even as it threatens the continuation of life itself. As documentarian Errol Morris states, "Photography allows us to uncritically think. We *imagine* that photographs provide a magic path to the truth."[22] In the atomic age, photographers were critical for creating proxy witnesses to the formation of the atomic sublime: "They are there not only to record what happens, but also to assist in the production of what happens."[23] Photography, and eventually cinematography, were essential tools for creating a visual narrative of progress weaving nuclear technologies into national visions of never-ending economic growth and political stability, secured through complete control over the both peaceful and destructive atom. In the atomic sublime, human labor, natural resources, and scientific and technological innovations were brought together in a unified scale for one purpose: to cement the United States' economic and military might.[24]

Four sets of images, produced between 1945 and 1954, demonstrate how a discourse on the atomic sublime originated and how the atomic sublime evolved during subsequent bomb tests and the creation of nuclear power, in order to shape public sentiment toward nuclear technologies. Each set of images presented here demonstrates a different stage of the atomic sublime, from chaos and destruction to a tightly woven narrative of power and control. We describe these stages as: (1) the "destructive" atom, demonstrating the power of atomic bombs; (2) the "collaborative" atom, used to enlist and mobilize myriad social and political groups in the creation of atomic materials and technologies; (3) the "playful" atom, used to convince the public of the federal government's complete control over the atom; and (4) the "productive" atom, epitomized by the invention of nuclear energy. These aspects of atomic visual culture demonstrate the tenuous claims of control and orderliness, as nuclear in/security bleeds over the borders of even the most sanitized image, challenging the reality of these scenes. In *Camera Lucida*, Roland Barthes challenges this temptation to see the image as "real" and evidentiary: "The important thing is that the photograph possesses an evidential force, and that its testimony bears not on the object but on time."[25] No matter what objects actually appear in the photo, the subject of these photos is a "shared hallucination" of the atomic sublime: that despite their destructive power, all risks to the American public are safely contained.[26]

Phase One: The Destructive Atom

The US Strategic Bombing Survey (USSBS) mission of 1945–47 evaluated the military effects of World War II, materially and economically, to assist in planning future military investments, specifically aerial offenses.[27] The USSBS photographers were tasked with trying to document the effects of this new weapon. Some of the images from the USSBS are familiar ones: the aftermath of the attacks on Hiroshima and Nagasaki, empty cities whose charred, twisted spires of former buildings and houses reach from the ground to the sky, a completely razed urban center left as a smoking shell, suddenly silenced of life. Photos such as a medical facility in Hiroshima are evidence of the complete carnage wrought by atomic bombs, where humans are engulfed by the massive scale of destruction but still exist at the margins, moving through the wreckage. To capture and account for the extent of destruction, civilians were selected by the military to head each of the USSBS divisions, creating "impartial" documentation to inform military experts on the power of this newly unleashed weapon.[28] The USSBS ranks were made up of engineers, architects, and photographers recruited from the US Army, Navy, and civilian life.[29]

If the images are stark, the language used in the reports is dry and descriptive in its accounting of the known strengths and weaknesses of

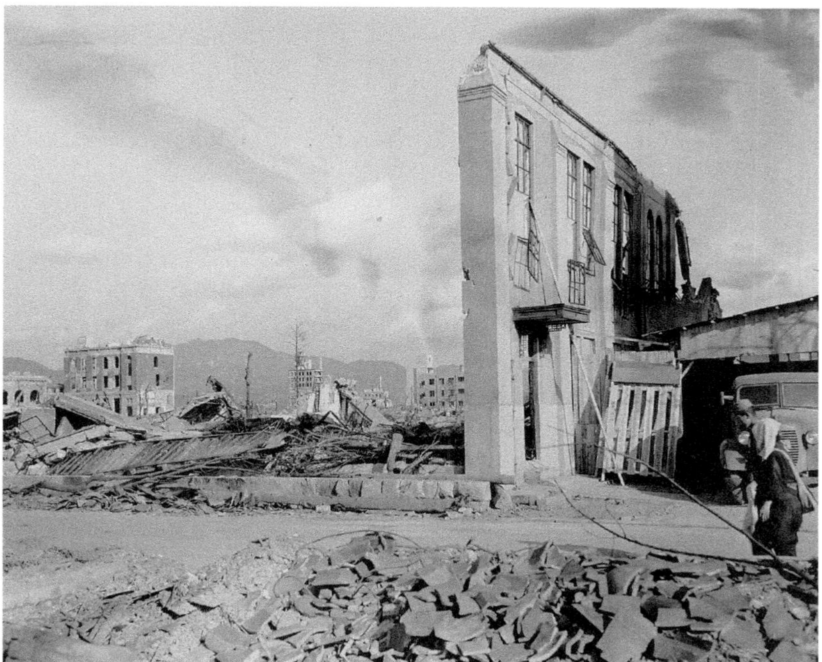

FIGURE 7.1. Unidentified photographer, Looking E./Looking E. general view building 42, October 29, 1945. International Center of Photography, purchase, with funds provided by the ICP Acquisitions Committee, 2006 (2006.1.152).

Japanese infrastructure, such as the large number of highly flammable wooden buildings that housed the Japanese workforce.[30] The USSBS describes atomic bombs as an "ideal weapon" that is, "by its nature, an area weapon capable of producing heavy casualties and a high degree of housing destruction throughout the entire area of its primary effectiveness."[31] In the euphemisms of war, the atomic bombs were simply another tool to annihilate human societies; the residents of Japan were reduced to an abstract "labor force" for "enemy industrial potential" that was rationalized as imminently expendable.[32] The images captured by the USSBS demonstrated the immense insecurity and destabilization that the United States could inflict on any country at any time.

The military used the USSBS images to account for the destructive power of this new weapon; however, there is no accountability in these images and narratives by the US government. Historian Gian Gentile has noted that the USSBS reports are "a loose amalgam of studies, sometimes prepared more to shape the future than to assess the past," used internally by the military to justify the use of atomic weapons, to advocate for the creation of an independent air force, and to aid in designing infrastructures that could withstand atomic blasts.[33] Externally, the photos would be used to craft and control public narratives about atomic weapons and America's military and technological supremacy.[34] The redemption of the destructive atom would set the stage for the next phase of crafting the discourses of the atomic sublime.

Phase Two: The Collaborative Atom

The USSBS photos were used internally to inform decision-making for the US military and government, including how different branches of the military would be organized around the deployment of atomic bombs.[35] Under the collaborative atom, the production of the atomic sublime required the involvement of private industry and popular media. John O'Brian refers to this collaboration as central to the "economy of fear" that began in 1949 when the USSR tested its first thermonuclear weapon.[36] The atomic sublime, therefore, was not only about impressing upon the American public the power of the atom, but also about convincing foreign nations to respect and fear the United States as a nuclear-armed nation.

As the Cold War began, a key challenge for the AEC was managing public expectations and fears, impressing upon the public the power of the atom but also the unique beneficent control over the atom possessed by the American government, military, and scientific community.[37] In convincing the public that atomic weapons could be used for the benefit of American life and the growth of the American economy, the AEC took advantage of new innovations to capture and promote images of the atomic sublime.[38] Cameras were deployed "as instruments of war" that "frame and form the human and non-human target along with a field of collateral damage."[39] As the USSBS reports showed, atomic weapons threaten the existence of all life and underscore the precarity of human existence in the new atomic era. The AEC subsequently harnessed photos and films to enlist an uneasy public into the myth of the atomic sublime and to gain and maintain the public's cooperation in a national nuclear project of building atomic bombs.[40]

In this second set of images, the atomic sublime emerges in the collaborations between photographers and cinematographers working on crafting a pronuclear narrative for atomic technologies. The development of nuclear weapons reshaped geopolitical relationships around the world, and bomb "tests were means of establishing the credibility of the overwhelming nuclear threat before the adversary and of communicating before the same adversary American competence and control."[41] The photographers became credible witnesses who would support discourses emerging around the atomic sublime, while the AEC curated what the public would see.[42]

Photographers became experts in capturing the scale and scope of destruction in this new atomic era, as new methods and innovations in aerial and ground photography compensated for fallout from radiation that previously ruined film. For instance, Dr. Harold E. Edgerton, who worked on timing systems for the atomic bombs, also developed sophisticated new camera, film, and equipment housing technologies capable of documenting atomic blasts.[43] Edgerton and his colleagues founded EG&G, an industrial partnership that contracted with the AEC to photograph bomb tests throughout the 1950s.[44] Photographers, as a main conduit for capturing images of the atomic arsenal for both the American public and foreign audiences, were afforded federally sanctioned spaces to film bomb tests, a critical element in crafting the sublime. Bomb tests in the deserts of the American Southwest and the Pacific islands were a means of demonstrating the destructive power of increasingly more powerful weapons, always contained in remote places and the edges of the photo, further creating a sense of containment and control over the production and use of atomic bombs.

The federal government also employed cinematographers, as military production studios and private industry were used to create visual narratives that would give a sense of logic and control to atomic developments. For instance, in 1947, the 4881st Motion Picture Squadron established a production facility, Lookout Mountain Studios, to produce movies and photos that would contribute to classified military efforts to test the power of new kinds of atomic weapons.[45] Peter Kuran notes that the proximity of Lookout Studios to testing sites allowed access to emerging film technologies, as well as Hollywood power players such as actor and veteran Jimmy Stewart and director John Ford, thus creating a symbiosis between

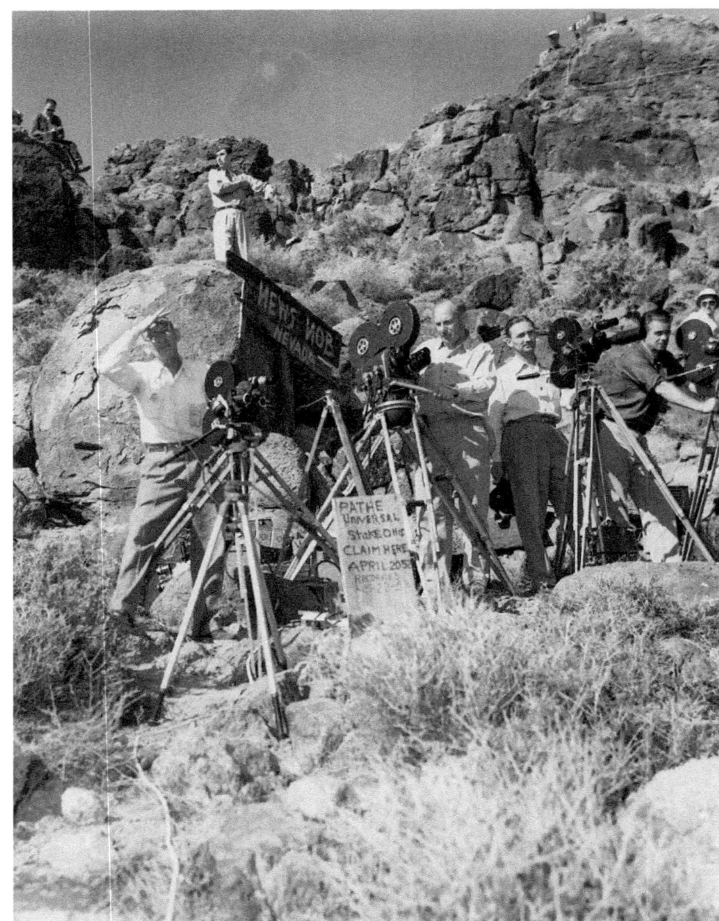

FIGURE 7.2. Unidentified photographer (cameramen on News Nob, Nevada, televising the atomic bomb test at Yucca Flat, Nevada), April 21–22, 1952. International Center of Photography, purchase, with funds provided by the ICP Acquisitions Committee, 2006 (2006.1714).

the goals of the AEC and access to military funding for production studios.[46] Additionally, both Universal Pictures and Paramount Pictures were key producers of newsreels that contributed to a discourse of containment and trust in atomic technology using Hollywood production values and actors.[47] In 1946, Time Life produced *Atomic Power,* a film that linked the power of the bomb to the commercial power of energy.[48] As the "secret cities" of Los Alamos, Hanford, and Oak Ridge became better known, telling the story of the creation of the bomb through film was one way to create a streamlined and seamless narrative depicting both the technological prowess and inevitability of the creation of the bomb through the marriage of science and the military. Scientists and military personnel, including Dr. J. Robert Oppenheimer, General Leslie Groves, and Dr. Albert Einstein, were asked to re-create the important moments of the planning and testing of the Trinity device. In outtakes from the film, Einstein rewrites his letter to President Roosevelt requesting federal support for research, over and over again. Oppenheimer's stand-in walks purposefully across the desert to the test facility in Los Alamos, over and over again. In the bunker, Oppenheimer expresses staged uncertainty over the success of the test, while Groves dictates notes to his secretary at his desk, over and over again. These famous men are used as evidence of the scientific and engineering innovations that led to the atomic bombs, reducing them to actors in a mythology of inevitable progress and control. Einstein's apparent boredom and Oppenheimer's woodenness speak to their discomfort in this new role, even as scientists Vannevar Bush and James Conant re-create their experience at Trinity by hunkering down, using protective eye shades, and shaking hands in a "desert" crafted in a warehouse in Massachusetts.

The repetition of these actions creates critical moments that contribute to the discourse of the atomic sublime by creating a larger narrative of purpose, control, and the inevitability of the American success story of developing and controlling the bomb. In this film, the uncertainty that underscored the actual Trinity test gives way to a narrative supported by images where any risks are contained by science and technology under the guiding hand of the military and government joined in the AEC. The advent of publicly oriented atomic images through film and photos was pivotal for creating a discourse of the atomic sublime by demonstrating the power of larger and more powerful bombs, while simultaneously trying to create a narrative of uniquely American control over that power through scientific and technological innovations.

Phase Three: The Playful Atom

In the next stage of establishing the atomic sublime, the civilian and the military join together to create a story of an American public coexisting peacefully with the bomb. In these images, the people depicted stand in for the public, instructing viewers on how to live peacefully with and react appropriately to the threat of nuclear annihilation. In these images, fear is a

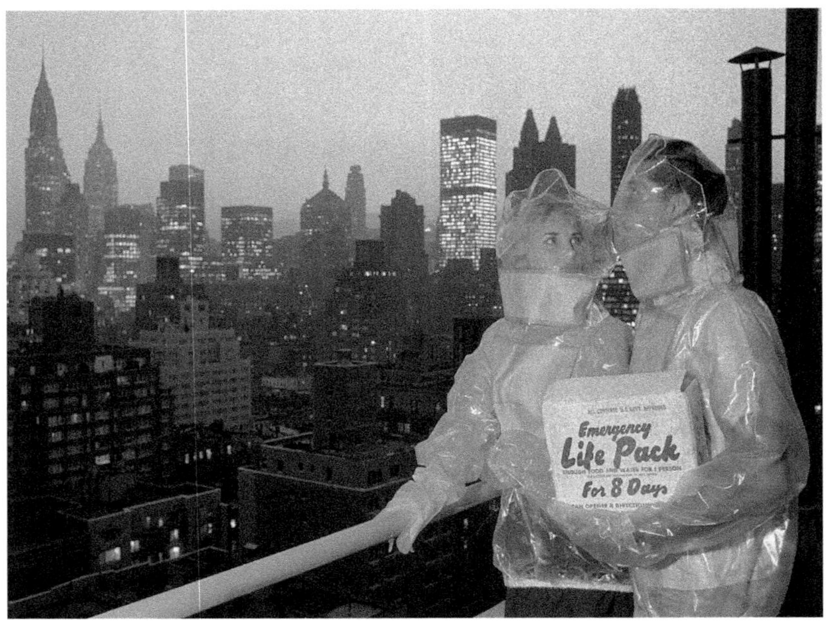

FIGURE 7.3. Max Scheler, *The Fallout Suit for $21*, New York City, 1961. Copyright Max Scheler Estate, Hamburg, Germany.

rational response, but nuclear threats are containable as long as the public trusts in the power of not only the federal government but also their own preparation. The contained risks are a "shared hallucination" among the public, where the danger is now knowable, understandable, predictable, and controllable.[49] In the playful atom phase, America is no longer laboring to win the war, but rather enjoying the fruits of victory while preparing responsibly for potential destruction. In one image that encapsulates the concept of the atomic sublime, a young couple wearing protective suits enjoys an evening view of their thriving, fully operational city from a balcony while they plan their future and enjoy the skyline. Unlike the residents of Hiroshima and Nagasaki, this couple is prepared for nuclear warfare, with their two-day life pack and protective suits, a precursor to underground bunkers and radiation measurement devices for the public.

In the playful atom phase, the population was disciplined to take control of their own protection in case of nuclear attack, demonstrating how the advent of nuclear technologies had created systemic and pervasive

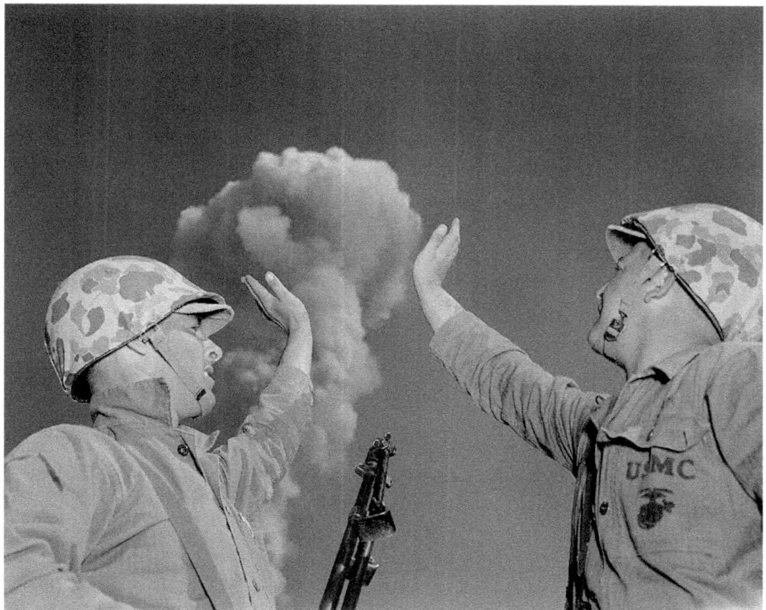

FIGURE 7.4. Unidentified photographer, soldiers pose below an atomic cloud at the Nevada Proving Ground, 1952. Image used under license from Shutterstock.com.

insecurity around the ability of life to continue after nuclear war.[50] This ideal of individual responsibility ran counter to reality, where confidence relied on the stability of the local, state, and federal governments to warn the public of an attack and to address the systemic insecurity, uncertainty, and precarity of daily life in the wake of an attack. These images enlisted the viewer in the myth of the atomic sublime and shifted responsibility from the government and military to the individual, whose onus was to be prepared at all times.

The atomic blast was also depicted as a source of entertainment, in opposition to photographs of the bomb that were meant to evoke awe and terror, including the model cities and homes populated by mannequins destroyed in test detonations in Nevada and the mushroom clouds over the Pacific.[51] But playful images brought the mushroom cloud down to earth, scaled to bring it fully in line with human interactions, where soldiers gently patted a mushroom cloud cupped in their hands. The atom here is rendered as benign; with this friendly object, fear was no longer necessary or appropriate, as the bomb had become a useful and productive companion to Americans, securing their bodily safety and preventing harm.

These images depict a shift in the discourse of the atomic sublime in the early years of the Cold War, from trusting in technocratic control to trusting in oneself to be prepared and not panic at the perpetual threat of atomic destruction. The risks engendered by the production of the bomb are now passed on to the individual, whose responsibility is to accept this risk and enjoy life even while living with perpetual nuclear in/security.

Phase Four: The Constructive Atom

By the early 1950s, large swaths of the United States contributed to the economy of the nuclear state, as military personnel, scientists and engineers, documentarians, downwinders, laborers, civilian organizations, and a public conditioned to fear appropriately and be prepared for disaster. To further temper the reputation of the destructive atom, the federal government posited nuclear energy as a novel and innovative solution for providing energy to the nascent post–World War II economic juggernaut. Nuclear energy would peacefully secure the economic and national future of the United States. Films, television shows, and advertisements created a seamless narrative of progress rooted in discourses of the atomic sublime that sought to indelibly link together new discoveries in science, inventions in technology, and the assumed and unified support of the American public. The risks from the atom were presented as fully contained and deployed safely and productively in the name of democracy. Government-contracted companies such as DuPont and General Electric worked with film companies to create company-sponsored materials promoting public education around nuclear technologies, hoping to reap additional benefits from producing electricity subsidized by the federal government.[52]

Atomic-themed films and shows continued to shape the appropriate role of the public in the discourse of the atomic sublime. In 1949, Time Life's *March of Time* series debuted "Report on the Atom," which focused on America's transition from a rural nation to a technoscientific global power. In this depiction, farmers gave up their land willingly and peacefully to uranium enrichment and plutonium processing facilities in places like the Savannah River site in Tennessee, Paducah in Kentucky, and Pike County in Ohio, so that the nation might achieve "maximum atomic strength." The constructive atom focused on developing civilian applications, including infrastructural investments that would transform the sleepy countryside into the modern industrial state, where "today's prospector is armed with a Geiger counter." Tools for agriculture are exchanged for tools of science to safeguard the public and democracy.

US president Dwight D. Eisenhower prioritized private sector development of nuclear energy, and companies like Westinghouse were incentivized to develop nuclear reactors, while places like Hanford were hopeful that the plutonium cycle could also contribute to nuclear energy production.[53] These companies also produced films, shows, and advertisements for nuclear energy, such as the educational cartoon *A Is for Atom*, produced in 1953 by General Electric. These contributions created a narrative of progress rooted in the inventiveness of science and technology, carried out with the unified support of a complicit American public that accepted the atomic sublime and Eisenhower's reassurances that the United States could contain the risks of the atom.[54]

On the international stage, Eisenhower delivered his famous "Atoms for Peace" speech in front of the United Nations in 1953, a speech remarkable for its implied threats against enemies of the United States and democracy, while offering explicit scientific and military support for allies (though leaving the knowledge of the production of weapons in hands of the United States).[55] In 1954, Eisenhower appeared on national television waving a "neutron wand" in Denver, Colorado, signaling the start of construction of the first American atomic energy plant, in Shippingport, Pennsylvania. However, in essence, nuclear energy was a fortuitous by-product of the weapons cycle due to the uranium enrichment process. The United States had many options to curtail proliferation of fissile material in the nuclear energy cycle through reactor design but chose a light water reactor (LWR) design specifically because of the plutonium that resulted from the LWR process for creating nuclear energy and its established use in the US naval program.[56] The decision to build LWRs as the main type of reactor in the United States would have repercussions for proliferation of fissile material for decades to come, but in this moment, the success of the bomb and the reactor were intertwined. Hence, Eisenhower's speech focused on the United States as the principal handler of fissile materials, creating a gulf

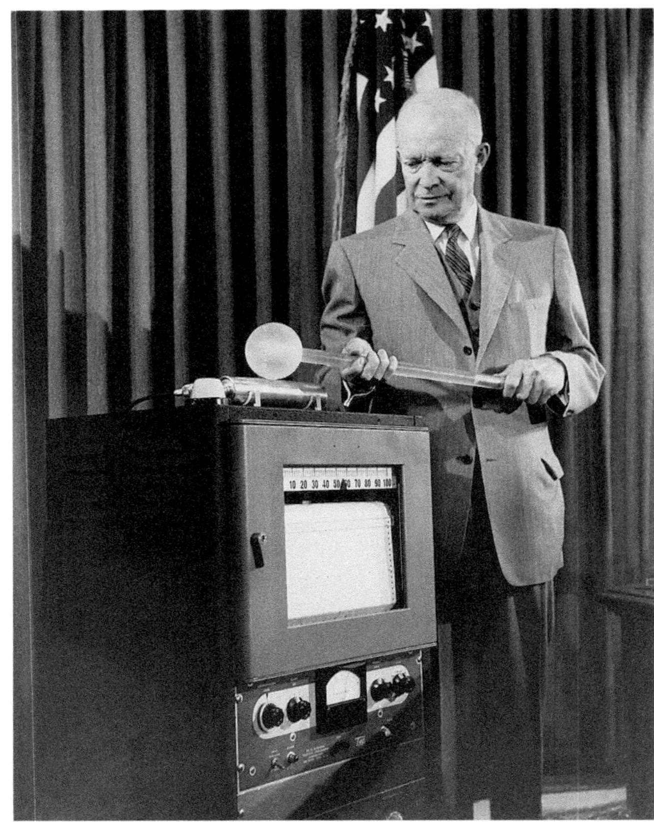

FIGURE 7.5. American president Dwight Eisenhower inaugurating the first atomic power plant, 1954, Keystone-France/Gamma-Keystone Collection via Getty Images.

between the supplier country and receiver countries in an effort to control global proliferation of enriched uranium and plutonium but encourage nuclear energy development.

The chaos engendered by atomic weapons is wholly tamed here into the constructive atom that will energize America and fuel economic and political progress, safely and cheaply. Yet this acceptance was predicated on the erasure of the right to information and the democratic process. The public was assumed to acquiesce to a nuclear future marked by technological developments in the name of security, yet had no recourse for challenging this discourse. The discourse of the atomic sublime never included political agency for the public, and nuclear technologies were fully in the power of a technocratic elite, harnessed by private industry in the service of the public to make energy that would be too cheap to meter.[57]

Legacies of the Atomic Sublime

In the first decade of modern nuclear technologies, images were used to establish the atomic sublime, which was used to create, stoke, and quell the fears of the American public toward atomic technologies, including weapons and energy production. Discourses of the atomic sublime were used to reassure the public that all was under control due to the firm hand of the federal government, the ingenuity of American scientists and engineers, and the willingness of the public to be constantly prepared; simultaneously, the function of the atomic sublime was to foreclose any resistance or counternarrative. The role of individuals, families, and communities was to support the development of nuclear technologies; to do otherwise would be unpatriotic, undermining national security. The negative environmental and human health legacies of atomic production were already felt across the nation but are nowhere to be found in the images produced to support the atomic sublime. Our analysis of these images from the first decade of nuclear production contribute to the continuing recognition that nuclear technologies are inherently political, embedded with human values. This recognition is critical for challenging discourses of technological determinism that frame nuclear weapons and energy as tools for power, control, and profit that are nonetheless beyond the scope of public concern. The collaborative, playful, and constructive atoms still infuse discourses that uncritically promote new nuclear technologies, but they are also sites of intervention that critique unproblematic visions of a peaceful future powered by nuclear technologies.

Notes

1. For arguments for the growth of nuclear energy, see Gwyneth Craven, *The Power to Save the World: The Truth about Nuclear Energy* (New York: Vintage, 2008); Robert C. Morris, *The Environmental Case for Nuclear Power: Economic, Medical, and Political Considerations* (St. Paul: Paragon House, 2000); *Pandora's Promise*, dir. Robert Stone, 2013. For recent reports on lapsed nuclear treaties, see Howard LaFranchi, "The Budding Nuclear Threat," *Christian Science Monitor Weekly*, March 19, 2019, 24–30.
2. Spencer R. Weart. *The Rise of Nuclear Fear* (Cambridge, MA: Harvard University Press, 2012).
3. Melvin E. Mathews Jr., *Duck and Cover: Civil Defense Images in Film and Television from the Cold War to 9/11* (Jefferson, NC: McFarland, 2011).

4. Andrew Blowers, *The Legacy of Nuclear Power* (New York: Routledge, 2017).
5. Blowers, *Legacy of Nuclear Power*, 14.
6. Paul S. Boyer, *By the Bomb's Early Light: American Thought and Culture at the Dawn of the Atomic Age* (Chapel Hill: University of North Carolina Press, 1994).
7. Peter Bacon Hales, *Atomic Spaces: Living on the Manhattan Project* (Urbana: University of Illinois, 1997), 351.
8. Peter Bacon Hales, *Outside the Gates of Eden: Dreams of America from Hiroshima to Now* (Chicago: University of Chicago Press, 2014).
9. David Nye, *American Technological Sublime* (Cambridge, MA: MIT Press, 1994); Thomas Hughes, *Human-Built World: How to Think about Technology and Culture* (Chicago: University of Chicago Press, 2004); Boyer, *By the Bomb's Early Light.*
10. Peter Bacon Hales, "The Atomic Sublime," *American Studies* 32, no. 1 (Spring 1991): 13.
11. Hales, "The Atomic Sublime"; Hales, *Atomic Spaces.*
12. John Dower, "Science, Technocracy, Beauty and Idealistic Annihilation," in *Hiroshima: Ground Zero 1945*, ed. Erin Barnett et al. (New York: International Center of Photography, 2011), 118.
13. Hales, *Atomic Spaces*, 324. See also Mark Fiege, *The Republic of Nature: An Environmental History of the United States* (Seattle: University of Washington Press, 2012).
14. John Findlay and Bruce Hevly, *Atomic Frontier Days: Hanford and the American West* (Seattle: University of Washington Press, 2011); Hales, *Atomic Spaces.*
15. Allan Winkler, "A 40-Year History of Civil Defense," *Bulletin of the Atomic Scientists* (July/August 1984): 16–22.
16. Joseph Masco, *The Nuclear Borderlands: The Manhattan Project in Post–Cold War New Mexico* (Princeton, NJ: Princeton University Press, 2006), 23.
17. *Hanford Science Forum*, produced by the Atomic Energy Commission and General Electric Company, 1957, available at https://archive.org/details/HanfordS1957.
18. Joanne Brown, "A Is for Atom, B Is for Bomb: Civil Defense in American Public Education, 1948–1963," *Journal of American History* 75, no. 1 (June 1, 1988): 68; Brett Spencer, "From Atomic Shelters to Arms Control: Libraries, Civil Defense, and American Militarism during the Cold War," *Information and Culture* 49, no. 3 (2014).
19. Hales, *Outside the Gates of Eden.*
20. Sheila Jasanoff and Sang-Hyun Kim, "Containing the Atom: Sociotechnical Imaginaries and Nuclear Power in the United States and South Korea," *Minerva* 47, no. 2 (June 2009): 121.
21. John O'Brian, *Camera Atomica* (London: Black Dog, 2015); Robert Del Tredici, *At Work in the Fields of the Bomb* (New York: Perennial Library, 1987); Carole Gallagher, *American Ground Zero: The Secret Nuclear War* (Cambridge, MA: MIT Press, 1993).
22. Errol Morris, *Believing Is Seeing: Observations on the Mysteries of Photography* (New York: Penguin, 2011), 92.

23. O'Brian, *Camera Atomica*, 11.
24. Merrit Roe Smith, "Technological Determinism in American Culture," in *Does Technology Drive History? The Dilemma of Technological Determinism*, ed. Merrit Roe Smith and Leo Marx (Cambridge, MA: MIT Press, 1994); Hales, *Atomic Spaces.*
25. Roland Barthes, *Camera Lucida: Reflections on Photography* (New York: Hill and Wang, 1981), 88–90.
26. Barthes, *Camera Lucida*, 115.
27. *United States Strategic Bombing Survey: The Effects of Atomic Bombs on Hiroshima and Nagasaki* (Washington, DC: Government Printing Office, 1946).
28. Gian Gentile, *How Effective Is Strategic Bombing: Lessons Learned from World War II to Kosovo* (New York: New York University Press, 2001).
29. Adam Harrison Levy, "Hiroshima: Lost and Found," in Barnett, *Hiroshima: Ground Zero 1945*, 40.
30. Gentile, *How Effective Is Strategic Bombing*, 82.
31. *United States Strategic Bombing Survey: The Effects of Strategic Bombing on Japanese Morale* (Washington, DC: Government Printing Office, 1947), 12.
32. John Dower, *Embracing Defeat: Japan in the Wake of World War II* (New York: W. W. Norton / New Press, 1999); Kristina Zarlengo, "Civilian Threat, the Suburban Citadel and Atomic Age American Women," *Signs* 24, no. 4 (July 1, 1999): 925–58.
33. Gentile, *How Effective Is Strategic Bombing*, 3–4.
34. For the backstory on *Hiroshima: Ground Zero 1945*, see Adam Harrison Levy, "Hiroshima: The Lost Photographs," *Design Observer*, May 23, 2011, https://designobserver.com/feature/hiroshima-the-lost-photographs/7517.
35. Gentile, *How Effective Is Strategic Bombing.*
36. O'Brian, *Camera Atomica*, 100.
37. Richard Burleson Stewart and Jane Bloom Stewart, *Fuel Cycle to Nowhere: US Law and Policy on Nuclear Waste* (Nashville, TN: Vanderbilt University Press, 2011).
38. Boyer, *By the Bomb's Early Light*; O'Brian, *Camera Atomica*; Peter Kuran, *How to Photograph an Atomic Bomb* (Petersburg, VA: VCE, 2006); Julia Bryan-Wilson, "Posing by the Cloud: US Nuclear Test Site Photography in Process," in O'Brian, *Camera Atomica*, 107–23.
39. Judith Butler, *Frames of War: When Is Life Grievable?* (London: Verso, 2010), 66.
40. Raymond Fielding, *The March of Time, 1935–1951* (New York: Oxford University Press, 1978), 291.
41. Kevin Hamilton and Ned O'Gorman, "Visualities of Strategic Vision: Lookout Mountain Laboratory and the Deterrent State from Nuclear Tests to Vietnam," in "Cold War Visual Alliances," ed. Sarah Bassnett, Andrea Noble, and Thy Phu, special issue, *Visual Studies* 30, no. 2 (May 4, 2015): 198.
42. Hamilton and O'Gorman, "Visualities of Strategic Vision."
43. Levy, "Hiroshima: Lost and Found."

44. Massachusetts Institute of Technology, "Visionary Engineer: Harold 'Doc' Edgerton," *Edgerton Digital Collections Project*, accessed June 16, 2020, http://edgerton-digital-collections.org/docs-life/egg-the-company.
45. Kuran, *How to Photograph an Atomic Bomb*, 37.
46. Kuran, *How to Photograph an Atomic Bomb.*
47. Hales, *Outside the Gates of Eden.*
48. Jack Glenn, *Atomic Power* (1946; New York City; March of Time), news reel.
49. Barthes, *Camera Lucida*, 115.
50. Majia Nadesen, *Governmentality, Biopower, and Everyday Life* (New York: Routledge, 2008).
51. Andrew Kirk, *Doom Towns: The People and Landscapes of Atomic Testing* (Oxford: Oxford University Press, 2017).
52. Findlay and Hevly, *Atomic Frontier Days*, 161.
53. Findley and Hevly, *Atomic Frontier Days.*
54. Marvin Miller, "Attempts to Reduce the Proliferation Risks of Nuclear Power: Past and Current Initiatives," in *Nuclear Power and the Spread of Nuclear Weapons: Can We Have One Without the Other?*, ed. Paul Levanthal, Sharon Tanzer, and Steven Dolley (Washington, DC: Brassey's, 2002).
55. Joseph Pilat, ed., *Atoms for Peace: A Future after 50 Years?* (Washington, DC: Woodrow Wilson Center Press, 2007); John Krige, "Atoms for Peace, Scientific Internationalism, and Scientific Intelligence," *Osiris* 21, no. 1 (2006): 161–81.
56. Robin Cowan, "Nuclear Power Reactors: A Study in Technological Lock-In," *Journal of Economic History* 50, no. 3 (September 1, 1990): 541–67.
57. Cowan, "Nuclear Power Reactors."

PART TWO

LEGACIES OF THE BIKINI TEST

Resisting US Nuclear Tests

The UN Petition from the Marshall Islands

SEIICHIRŌ TAKEMINE

CHAPTER 8

Within one year of the Hiroshima and Nagasaki bombings on August 6 and 9, 1945, the United States began nuclear testing on Bikini Atoll in July 1946. Enewetak Atoll, 190 miles west of Bikini, was also chosen as the site of the Pacific Proving Grounds in 1947. Nuclear weapons tests were conducted over the Marshall Islands a total of sixty-seven times between 1946 and 1958. The total yield was equivalent to over seven thousand Hiroshima-type bombs. The United States did not conduct its nuclear tests over a vast empty ocean; the nuclear tests were carried out on the homelands of Pacific Islanders.

On March 1, 1954, the United States conducted the nuclear test code-named Bravo on Bikini Atoll. The Bravo shot was the first test of Operation Castle, a series of six thermonuclear tests that ran from March to May 1954. It released large quantities of radioactive debris into the atmosphere. The explosion resulted in radioactive contamination of the inhabitants of the Pacific Islands. The ash and rain fell on the local people, American soldiers, and the crews of a number of vessels, including a Japanese tuna fishing boat, the *Daigo Fukuryūmaru* (*Lucky Dragon No. 5*).[1] This nuclear explosion triggered a worldwide public outcry against nuclear bombs in the mid-1950s.[2]

This chapter discusses the spread of the antinuclear movement globally after the nuclear test in 1954.[3] First, it examines how public opinion calling for a ban on atomic and hydrogen bombs spread internationally, focusing on the Japanese tuna fishing boat *Lucky Dragon No. 5*. Second, it highlights the actions of the people of the Marshall Islands in submitting a petition to the United Nations titled "Complaint regarding the Explosion of Lethal Weapons within Our Home Islands." Third, it examines how the US government took action against movements calling for a halt to nuclear testing.

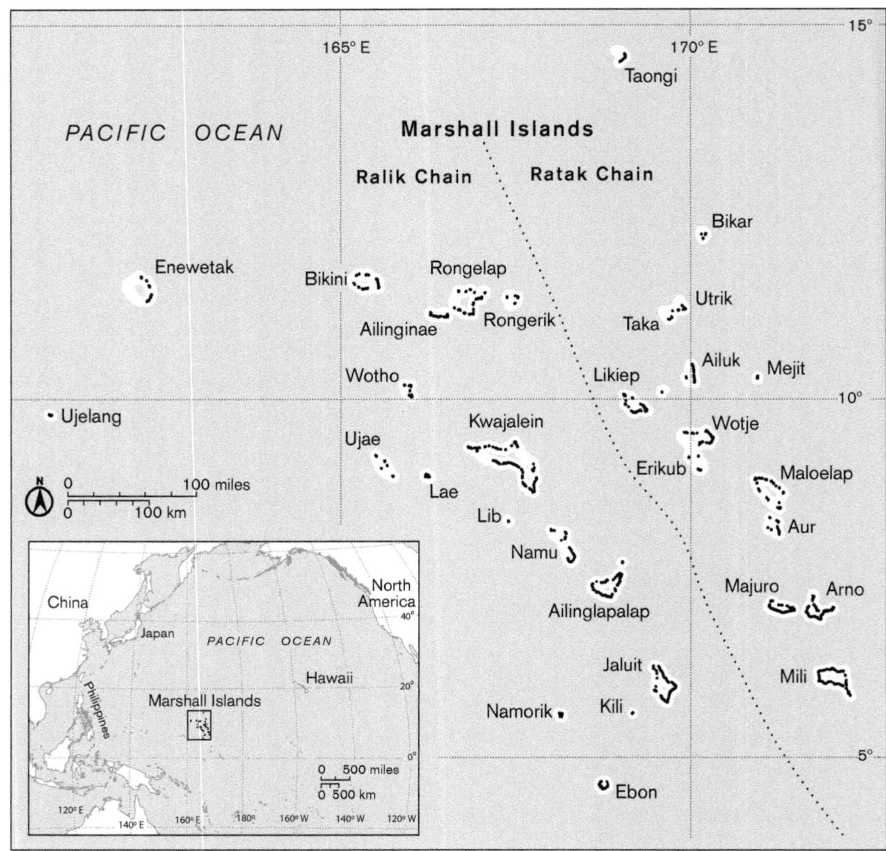

FIGURE 8.1. Map of the Marshall Islands. Map by Ben Pease, Pease Press Cartography, 2023.

Growing Calls for a Ban on Atomic and Hydrogen Bombs

The *Lucky Dragon No. 5* disaster alerted the general population to the dangers of nuclear testing. In Japan, petition drives calling for a ban on atomic and hydrogen bombs gathered large numbers of signatures.[4] However, the Japanese foreign minister at the time, Okazaki Katsuo, in consideration of Japan-US relations, stated to the national assembly, "We will cooperate with other free countries to ensure the success of these tests."[5] On the other hand, in the face of growing public opinion, the Japanese Fisheries Agency gathered experts in the fields of oceanography, atmospheric science, and radiation, and conducted a survey on the actual situation of radioactive contamination in the Pacific Ocean using the vessel *Shunkotsu Maru*.[6]

Lewis L. Strauss, chairman of the US Atomic Energy Commission (AEC), which was in charge of nuclear development, publicly stated that "the Atomic Energy Commission has conducted the tests of its larger weapons away from the mainland so that the fall-out would occur in the ocean where it would be quickly dissipated."[7] However, the *Shunkotsu Maru* survey found radioactive materials released by US nuclear tests in the seawater and various organisms. The results of that survey told the world for the first time that radioactive contamination of the ocean does not fade so easily and that radioactive materials can accumulate in the bodies of tuna through the food chain.

About six months after the Bravo test, the Japan Council against Atomic and Hydrogen Bombs (Gensuikyō) was formed in Japan to consolidate the signature drives that had taken place in various parts of Japan. The number of signatures calling for a ban on atomic and hydrogen bombs had reached approximately thirty-two million in Japan, and the petition drive had spread worldwide. In August 1955, the World Conference against Atomic and Hydrogen Bombs was held for the first time in Hiroshima, ten years after the atomic bombing. News of the *Lucky Dragon*'s exposure to radioactive fallout sent shockwaves around the world, especially after one crew member died from radiation exposure.[8]

According to testimony by David Bradley, a US Army medical officer who participated in Operation Crossroads in 1946, radioactive contamination from fallout had been occurring at Bikini Atoll since nuclear testing began.[9] At the start of the nuclear tests in 1946, US officials predicted that the fallout would spread beyond the Marshall Islands, and measurements were carried out all over the Pacific Ocean.[10] Merril Eisenbud, director of the AEC Health and Safety Laboratory in New York, reported at the AEC meeting that the radioactive fallout from Operation Ivy in 1952 had been monitored utilizing a worldwide network of 120 fixed stations, and the data indicated a low-order fallout detectable at all stations in the Northern Hemisphere.[11]

However, the public was not familiar with the radiation associated with nuclear testing and did not recognize fallout as an issue. Ōishi Matashichi, a crew member of the *Lucky Dragon No. 5*, recalled, "When I encountered the incident, all I knew about the atomic bombing was 'It seems a new bomb dropped on Hiroshima.'" He added, "I did not even know the word radiation."[12] Under such circumstances, the *Lucky Dragon No. 5* incident helped bring to light the problem of radioactive fallout from nuclear testing and the seriousness of the damage caused by radiation.

Professor Kimura Kenjirō of the Faculty of Science at the University of Tokyo and other scientists analyzed the ash brought back by the *Lucky Dragon No. 5*, and they detected uranium-237. This discovery led to an understanding of the mechanism of the hydrogen bomb, which had been classified by the United States.[13] The *Lucky Dragon No. 5* incident led to widespread public concern over the effects of nuclear radiation and became the starting point for a subsequent ban on atmospheric nuclear testing.

The *Lucky Dragon No. 5* incident served as the trigger for the first World Conference against Atomic and Hydrogen Bombs, held in Hiroshima in 1955. The testimonies of victims of the atomic bombings of Hiroshima and Nagasaki had a strong impact on participants at the conference, and victim assistance became one of the goals of the campaign against atomic and hydrogen bombs. The conference declaration stated, "Relief [for atomic and hydrogen bomb survivors] must be hastened through a worldwide movement. This is the true foundation of any movement against A- and H-bombs."[14]

The following year saw the creation of a national organization of A-bomb survivors of Hiroshima and Nagasaki, named the Confederation of A- and H-Bomb Sufferers Organizations (Nihon Gensuibaku Higaisha Dantai Kyōgikai: Nihon Hidankyō).[15] At the founding conference, the following "Message to the World" was issued:

> We have found this courage to stand up, thanks to the World Conference of last August. . . . We would like to express to the people of the world our sincere gratitude and our decision to rise with a firm resolve. . . .
>
> We appeal to the world for what we must. We demand of the nation what we must. We also stand on our own and help each other. . . . We pledge our determination to save ourselves and at the same time, through our experiences, to save all of humanity from this crisis. . . . Humankind must not repeat our sacrifice and suffering.

As the A-bomb victims united and gained support from the public, the Atomic Bomb Survivors Medical Care Law (Genbaku Iryōhō) was enacted, and the A-bomb Survivor Health Handbook system began in 1957. Eleven and a half years after the atomic bombing, relief measures for A-bomb victims, who had been sidelined by society, began, albeit inadequately.

The *Lucky Dragon* incident brought the plight of the victims of the atomic bombings of Hiroshima and Nagasaki to the attention of the public and made them a social problem in Japan. But ironically, the crew of the *Lucky Dragon No. 5* and others impacted by the Bikini incident were not recognized as victims of atomic and hydrogen bombs after the political settlement with the United States.

In 1955 the US government paid two million dollars to the Japanese government, and Japan waived its right to claim further compensation for damages. This was deemed a "full settlement." The two million dollars was in the form of an ex gratia payment, which did not acknowledge any US legal liability. Furthermore, as the US nuclear historian Takahashi Hiroko has discovered, the payment was not approved by the US Congress and instead was authorized by the US Office of Control and Coordination, which was responsible for psychological strategy and covert operations.[16] "We opposed the ashes, but we didn't do enough to save the crew," said Ikeyama Jurō, who was involved in the campaign to ban atomic and hydrogen bombs at that time. "The political settlement, that's what's going to ruin the whole Bikini issue."[17]

The Atomic Bomb Survivors Medical Care Law was limited in its application to the survivors of the atomic bombings of Hiroshima and Nagasaki. There was an initial proposal to include Bikini victims and, looking to the future, victims of nuclear power generation, but in the end the agreement excluded survivors of nuclear tests and victims of nuclear accidents.[18]

Petitions of the Marshallese to the United Nations

As the movement to ban atomic and hydrogen bombs gained momentum after the *Lucky Dragon No. 5* was exposed to radiation, what was happening in the Marshall Islands, where the United States conducted the nuclear tests? About three hours after the Bravo test, Rongelap Atoll was darkened by a thick fog, and white ash began to fall on a man named John, then serving as a district magistrate. He testified, "It was while I was picking a coconut out of the tree and eating it. Something raining down from the sky entered my mouth. It was like a powder. We took the coconuts and shared them with everyone at my home, but they were bitter."[19]

"Your hair is turning white," a friend told Jimako in Rongelap, so she washed her hair with seawater.[20] Hiroko, who was in elementary school at the time, reported, "I picked up the white powder and played with it."[21] The "white powder" was actually bits of irradiated coral reef particles that had been shattered by the hydrogen bomb test, carried by the wind, and eventually dropped on Rongelap Atoll, one hundred nautical miles from the hypocenter. The crew of the *Lucky Dragon No. 5* was exposed to what were called "ashes of death," but the residents of the Marshall Islands where the tests were conducted were not aware of this when ash began to fall on their atolls. Hiroko reported, "They complained of diarrhea, nausea, and pain, and all of them had no energy, so elementary school was canceled the next day. Some people were crying."[22] Etri testified, "After a day or two, to my surprise, when I combed through my hair, it started to fall out."[23]

Not only had Japanese fishermen been exposed to radiation, but also the people who lived on the islands. As a result of the contamination of their land, the people of Rongelap and Utrik Atolls were transported to Kwajalein, where a US military base was located.[24] The exposed residents were then the subject of a top-secret study called Project 4.1, officially named "Study of Response of Human Beings Accidentally Exposed to Significant Radiation Fallout.[25] These people argue that they were intentionally exposed to radiation and used as test subjects. In other cases, such as in Ailuk, Likiep, and other atolls in the Marshall Islands, Joint Task Force 7, which conducted the nuclear tests, confirmed the spread of significant radiation fallout.[26] However, the residents were never informed of this fact, were left without assistance, and were never evacuated.

Meanwhile, in Majuro, the capital of the Marshall Islands, a petition was addressed to the United Nations. The "Complaint regarding the Explosion of Lethal Weapons within Our Home" was drafted by two Marshallese schoolteachers, Dwight Heine and Atlan Anien.[27] Dwight Heine, who was thirty-five years old, had served as an intermediate school principal as well as a member of the Marshallese Congress Hold-Over Committee concerning the Trust Territory of the Pacific Islands.

As Heine told an Associated Press reporter, "We worked every day for nearly a month. We would meet with other Marshallese and put down their ideas. . . . We also read UN pamphlets and saw how petitions appearing in them were worded." "Some people think we are naive children of the tropics," he said. "We are not as naive as they think."[28]

On April 20, 1954, the Marshallese people submitted their petition to the Council of Trusteeship under Article 87 of the United Nations Charter with the signatures of all eleven members of the Marshallese Congressional Hold-Over Committee, representing all municipalities in the Marshalls, and one hundred other Marshallese citizens.[29] After stating that "the following should not be misconstrued as a repudiation of the United States as our governing agency for the United Nations under the trusteeship agreement," the petition claimed that nuclear tests caused bodily harm and threatened lives.

In addition, the petition addressed the danger that the land, which is "the very life of the people," could be taken away:

> The Marshallese people are not only fearful of the danger to their persons from these deadly weapons in case of another miscalculation, but they are also very concerned for the increasing number of people who are being removed from their land. Land means a great deal to the Marshallese. It means more than just a place you can plant your food crops and build your houses; or a place where you can bury your dead. It is the very life of the people. Take away their land and their spirits go also.

The petition requested that "all the experiments with lethal weapons within this area be immediately ceased," adding that "if the experiments with said weapons should be judged absolutely necessary for the eventual well-being of all the people of this world . . . all possible precautionary measures [should] be taken before such weapons are exploded." The petition further demanded that "all human beings and their valuable possessions be transported to safe distances first" and that "the people living in this area [should] be instructed in safety measures." The petition also included requests that islanders receive compensation for land, homes, and possessions in the event relocation should become necessary.

Marshallese leaders drafted the UN petition without the knowledge of US government officials, claiming according to an Associated Press news report that "we purposely did not let [the acting district administrator] or others [in the Trust Territory] know about it. We were afraid they would get into trouble."[30] The drafters were concerned that the petition"might give Russia some political ammunition in the June session of the United Nations, [and] that it might hurt close American friends in the Trust Territory, Civil Administration of the Island chain.[31]

Following the Pacific War, the Marshall Islands came under US control in 1944 after being ruled by the Empire of Japan. In 1947, the Marshall

Islands, along with what is today the Federated States of Micronesia, Palau, and the Northern Mariana Islands, were incorporated into the UN Trust Territory under the administration of the United States. The Trust Territory of the Pacific Islands was the only UN trust territory in the world to be designated a "strategic area" as defined in Article 82 of the UN Charter.

The Trusteeship Agreement was proposed by the United States and approved by the Security Council in April 1947.[32] Article V of the Trusteeship Agreement gave the United States the right to establish military installations, and Article XIII further provided that the United States could establish closed areas for security reasons. By establishing a "closed area," the United States could create an area that was under UN trusteeship but out of reach of the international community; the nuclear tests were carried out in this closed area.

Dwight Heine, who led the petition drive, worked for the US military government as an interpreter and guide shortly after US military occupation replaced the Japanese in the Marshall Islands.[33] His parents and grandparents had been killed by the Japanese, contributing to his position that "we Marshallese like the Americans."[34]

While under the control of the United States, the residents of the Marshall Islands openly objected to the US nuclear tests, which were conducted out of sight of the international community. It was not only in the framework of negotiations with the United States but also in the context of the UN trusteeship that people were driven off their land, their bodies were harmed, and their lives were threatened by nuclear tests. Dwight Heine said, "We are a small [number of] people—only 11,000 of us . . . and the only way to get people to pay attention is when we call loud [speak out] . . . .We have faith Americans will do something about it."[35]

Response to the Marshallese Petition

The UN Trusteeship Council formally accepted the petition filed by the residents of the Marshall Islands on May 6, 1954, placing it on the council agenda in July. In response to the petition, Mason Sears, the US representative to the Trusteeship Council, stated, "The fact that anyone was injured by the recent nuclear tests in the Pacific has caused the American people genuine and deep regret." He further expressed that "the United States

Government considers the resulting petition of the Marshall Islanders to be both reasonable and helpful." However, he also justified the US nuclear tests in the Marshall Islands: "The United States Government found that there is no other place in the world, over which the United States has jurisdiction, where experiments of this nature could be successfully conducted with less danger." Sears further insisted on the legality of conducting nuclear tests by referring to the Trusteeship Agreement of 1947. He rejected the Marshall Islanders' demand for a halt to nuclear testing with the argument that "no one could reasonably contend that the Soviets should be the only nation to conduct nuclear experiments." On the other hand, Sears pledged on behalf of the US government that future nuclear tests would not cause any problems for the Marshallese.[36]

In response to the petition submitted by Marshall Islanders, three types of resolutions were introduced at the UN Trusteeship Council.[37] First, the representative of the Soviet Union argued that "such tests were incompatible with the purposes and principles of the International Trusteeship System" and sponsored a draft resolution to request that the United States desist from such tests, compensate the population, and restore the land. Next, a joint resolution was introduced by Belgium, France, and the United Kingdom expressing "regret at the ill-effects and damage caused by the nuclear tests." Noting that "the health of those affected was reported to have been restored," it recommended that "any future tests be preceded by the precautionary measures." Finally, the Indian government representative, who also represented nonaligned countries, stated that "the use of a Trust Territory as a proving ground for thermonuclear or any other weapons of mass destruction [was] incompatible with the basic objectives of Trusteeship." The draft resolution said that "the legality of such use and the responsibility of the Administering Power in respect of the consequences should be determined by the International Court of Justice."

After much deliberation, the resolutions of the Soviet Union and India were each rejected by a small majority, and the joint resolution of Belgium, France, and the United Kingdom was adopted by the Trusteeship Council. The adopted resolution expressed "deep regret that a number of inhabitants of two atolls in the Marshall Islands suffered ill effects" but did not call for a halt to the testing.[38] Taking a positive view of the US response to the affected population, it recommended that "if the Administering

Authority considers it necessary in the interests of world peace and security to conduct further nuclear experiments in the territory, it take such precautions as will ensure that no inhabitants of the Territory are again endangered."

A little over one week after the council resolution on July 23, 1954, Mason Sears sent a confidential letter to Secretary of State John Foster Dulles. The classified document reported on the Marshallese petition and the joint resolution that "tacitly approved" the continuation of US nuclear testing in the region. However, at the same time, Sears warned that "the Trusteeship Council's action in no sense concludes the matter. . . . It is important . . . that the appropriate branches of the Government realize that this problem is a continuing one which will require careful consideration both immediately and in the future."

Sears proposed that the secretary of state ensure implementation of the following three measures:

> First of all, we cannot afford a recurrence of the accident which caused injury to a number of Marshallese as well as Americans and Japanese. We have formally and publicly undertaken to take every precaution against recurrence of this type of disaster.
>
> The second important matter relates to our undertakings to compensate adequately the people of the Trust Territory who as a result of nuclear tests have suffered. . . . Finally . . . [t]here is no doubt that attention will be focused in the Trusteeship Council next year whether just and prompt settlements have been made to these people. I urge that these settlements be worked out and made forthwith.[39]

Sears recommended to the secretary of state that all preventive measures be taken to prevent a recurrence, and that measures be taken to compensate the inhabitants and to bring back the people of Rongelap and Utrik, who were exposed to radiation as a result of the 1954 hydrogen bomb tests and had to be relocated to other areas. Sears expressed a sense of urgency, stating, "We might have difficulty in obtaining the support of even our closest Allies in the United Nations in our attempt to justify the continuation of nuclear experiments in the Trust Territory."[40] Despite the resolution's "tacit approval" of continued nuclear testing, the petition would become a new barrier to the US government's nuclear tests.

US Concern about the Public Reaction

The US officials continued nuclear testing despite the petition but were concerned about international opposition to the tests as well as the objections raised in the Marshall Islands. Two years after Operation Castle the United States planned Operation Redwing, a series of nuclear tests in the Marshall Islands. In March 1956, the United Nations Visiting Mission to the Trust Territories in the Pacific visited the Marshall Islands and met with members of the Marshallese Congressional Hold-Over Committee, including Dwight Heine, who drafted the 1954 UN petition. A variety of issues were discussed, but with the prospect of nuclear testing again in the not too distant future, the Marshall Islands reminded the UN Visiting Mission of the petition the Marshall Islands had submitted to the United Nations in 1954.[41] That petition stated that (a) nuclear testing in the Marshall Islands should be discontinued; and (b) if these experiments are absolutely necessary for the eventual well-being of all the people of the world and could not be conducted elsewhere, all the measures enumerated in the petition should be taken to reduce harm.

The Marshall Islands also wished to have the views expressed in the UN petition immediately recalled to the UN Trusteeship Council, and a new petition from the Marshallese Congress Hold-Over Committee was forwarded to the Trusteeship Council.[42] The UN Trusteeship Council, in consultation with the administering authority, the United States, acknowledged that the United States had declared that "further nuclear weapons tests are necessary for the maintenance of international peace and security."[43] Nonetheless, the Trusteeship Council adopted a resolution recommending the following three conditions for the conduct of nuclear tests: "(a) All necessary measures should be taken to guard against any possible dangers; (b) all necessary measures should be taken to settle forthwith all justified claims by the inhabitants of Bikini and Eniwetok relating to their temporary displacement from their lands; (c) all necessary measures should be taken to compensate the families which may have to be temporarily evacuated for any losses which may result from further nuclear weapons tests."[44]

The following year, in 1957, the people of the Marshall Islands tried again to petition the United Nations, after nuclear tests were repeated seventeen times in 1956 alone. However, William Lodge, the US ambassador to the

United Nations, moved to block the petition, according to Holly M. Barker, who served in the Marshall Islands embassy in the United States.[45]

The United States carried out a total of thirty-three nuclear tests between April and August 1958 as Operation Hardtack I. Prior to this series of tests, the AEC and the Department of Defense (DOD) worked together to develop a public information plan that would include announcements of only half the planned detonations.[46] To make it appear that the number of nuclear tests was small, "announcement should be made of detonations having yielded higher than 200 kilotons." In other words, it was decided not to make public any tests of two hundred kilotons or less. Also, in announcing a nuclear test of two hundred kilotons or more, US officials planned that "such statements will be limited to the nearest minute; and a general statement as to the place of detonation, e.g., on Eniwetok Atoll or Bikini Atoll." Information related to radiation exposure was omitted from the release.

Three days after Operation Hardtack began in 1958, the AEC and the DOD held a joint press conference in which they claimed that "protection of health and safety is a primary consideration in the conduct of the HARDTACK series of nuclear weapons tests."[47] They also claimed that the "test operation will be conducted in a manner designed to keep as low as possible the public exposure to radiation."[48] A campaign was undertaken to convince the public that all precautions were being taken.

With antinuclear public opinion in Japan in mind, a hurried change in the US nuclear test operation was made. A letter stamped "SECRET," dated May 16, 1958, from Lewis L. Strauss, chairman of the AEC, to Carl T. Durham, chairman of the Joint Committee on Atomic Energy, states that "I now wish to advise you that . . . the Commission has instructed the Commander of Joint Task Force Seven to defer all pending shots that might possibly yield more than 200 kilotons until after 11:00 p.m. Eniwetok time, May 22, 1958." Nuclear tests of less than two hundred kilotons would be conducted as planned, weather permitting. "You will recall," Strauss reminded the committee, "that the Commission has established criteria for the HARDTACK series where only detonations of more than 200 kilotons in yield are announced to the public."[49]

Why did they decide to postpone all large detonations until May 22, 1958? The chairman of the AEC explained in the confidential letter that the goal was "minimizing the possible adverse impact of the HARDTACK series on Japanese-American relations on the eve of the Japanese election which will be held on May 22, 1958."[50] The twenty-eighth general election for the House of Representatives, under the pro-American conservative government of Kishi Nobusuke, would be "the first-ever contest between conservatives and revolutionaries" in Japan, with the Liberal Democratic Party and the Democratic Party of Japan (both conservatives) merging to form the Liberal Democratic Party, while the Japan Socialist Party united the two wings.[51]

On the recommendation of the Department of State and with the concurrence of the DOD, the AEC instructed the commander of Joint Task Force Seven to postpone four nuclear tests in anticipation of Japan's general election. The goal was to ensure the continuation of a pro-American conservative government by not making nuclear testing an issue in the national election. Japan's general election resulted in the ruling Liberal Democratic Party losing some seats but largely maintaining the status quo as the pro-American Kishi government entered its second term.

After the general election, Walter S. Robertson, US assistant secretary of state for Far Eastern affairs, sent a confidential letter to Philip Farley, special assistant to Secretary of State Dulles, on June 4, 1958, in which he pointed out that "the Atomic Energy Commission's decision to defer certain 'Hardtack' shots until after the Japanese elections was entirely successful" in terms of the situation in the Far East.[52] It added that "nuclear weapons testing did not become an election issue despite the efforts of the socialists to make it so." Nuclear tests of more than two hundred kilotons resumed shortly after the election.

During the Hardtack tests, the UN Trusteeship Council held its twenty-second session from June 9 to August 1, 1958. In this session, Dwight Heine submitted the petition again on behalf of the Marshallese people and requested that the UN Trusteeship Council respond to the urgent request and take steps to improve the situation, recalling the 1954 petition.[53] In recognition of such a move, in November of 1958, Dulles and Farley expressed their feelings to the AEC that "further testing in the Marshalls would be most impolitic."[54]

On August 18, 1958, the sixty-seventh nuclear test, called Fig, was carried out on Enewetak. This was the last nuclear test conducted in the Marshall Islands. However, in November 1958, Alvin Luedecke, the commander of Joint Task Force 7, sent a confidential letter to the director of the Division of Military Application at the AEC stating that the nuclear test site at Enewetak Atoll in the Marshall Islands should be used more effectively by using it continuously as needed, without intervals, instead of using it every other year in the spring and summer.[55] The fact that more nuclear tests were planned has emerged from a US official document stamped "EYES ONLY." In a letter addressed to the chairman of the US Joint Committee on Atomic Energy, acting chairman of the AEC W. F. Libby revealed that "a nuclear detonation above the greater portion of the earth's atmosphere" was planned in the Marshall Islands.[56] However, the AEC had determined it could not guarantee the safety of the inhabitants of the Marshall Islands, particularly with regard to the potential for eye damage that could be caused by looking directly at the blast. For this reason, Libby recommended moving the larger test to Johnston Island, approximately eight hundred miles southwest of Hawai'i.

As international public opinion called for a ban on nuclear testing, the United States continued to conduct nuclear tests, keeping an eye on the Soviet Union. After October 1958, the United States announced a moratorium on nuclear testing. However, the conference to halt nuclear testing, which took place in Geneva in January 1961, stalled. The Soviet Union resumed its nuclear tests in September of that year, and President Kennedy ordered preparations for resumption of atmospheric nuclear tests on November 2, 1961.

In the midst of all this, there was a move to again conduct nuclear tests in the Marshall Islands. To take one example, on November 13, 1961, the AEC held a meeting in Albuquerque with A. W. Betts, director of military application at the AEC, and various laboratories on the subject of atmospheric test resumption. They decided that "the sites to be considered in order of desirability are first Eniwetok/Bikini," followed by "second Christmas Island and third Johnston Island and or Hilo."[57] In addition, Taongi Atoll, located in the northeast of the Marshall Islands, was considered as a new nuclear test site.[58] But nuclear tests never resumed in the Marshall Islands. The following year the US military chose Christmas Island and Johnston Island for the site of Operation Dominic. Why were further nuclear tests in the Marshall Islands avoided?

In a confidential letter to President Kennedy dated November 29, 1961, Glenn Seaborg, chairman of the AEC, stated that "technically the Eniwetok Proving Ground is the most desirable" but that "Eniwetok has political difficulties."[59] This was preceded by a letter to AEC chairman Glenn Seaborg from James Carr, acting secretary of the interior, who said he was "deeply concerned" over the possibility of Enewetak and Bikini Atolls again being used for the testing of atomic devices and recommended "against any further testing in the Trust Territory of the Pacific Islands."[60] Why the Department of the Interior objected was noted in the letter: "Atomic testing at Eniwetok and Bikini in the past has led to great concern in the United Nations with respect to the discharge of our obligations to the Micronesians, a concern which was greatly heightened by the accidental exposure of the people of Rongelap and Utrik to radio-active fallout in 1954."[61] A UN petition drive by the Marshallese triggered this debate and instigated growing concern at the United Nations.

The exposure of *Lucky Dragon No. 5* to radiation as a result of the 1954 Bravo H-bomb test brought the problem of radioactivity, especially radioactive fallout, to the surface. It is relatively well known in the history of nuclear resistance that, as a result, public support for a ban on atomic and hydrogen bombs spread not only in Japan but also in the world, leading to the Partial Test Ban Treaty in 1963.

At about the same time, Marshall Islanders submitted a petition to the United Nations to demand a halt to nuclear testing there. This chapter has examined how the US government recognized the objections of the local residents and international public opinion to the nuclear test and what kind of policy it adopted. The United States was engaged in an offensive with not only the Soviet Union but also public opinion, which was opposed to nuclear testing.

The UN petition from the Marshall Islands requested an immediate suspension of nuclear testing—a request that was not granted. However, this petition revealed to the international community the previously invisible fact that local people were suffering from the effects of the nuclear explosion, which was incompatible with the purpose of the UN trusteeship. The representative of the US government to the Trusteeship Council had conveyed to the secretary of state the fear that if the preventive measures and compensation requested in the petition were not enacted, and if the residents were to suffer again, the United States would lose the support of even Western nations.

In spite of this, the United States continued to conduct tests in the Marshall Islands after 1954. However, this chapter shows that US authorities could not ignore public opinion opposing the tests, especially in the Marshall Islands and Japan. In conducting the nuclear tests, the emphasis was on responding to world opinion. Just before the series of nuclear tests, the AEC and DOD, in a joint press conference, emphasized that protection of health and safety was a primary consideration. Further, to make the number of tests appear small, it was decided not to announce small and medium-size nuclear tests. In addition, just before the Japanese general election, a major nuclear test was postponed to keep US nuclear testing out of the view of Japanese voters. The people of the Marshall Islands did not give up, repeatedly expressing their opposition to the UN Trusteeship Council, based on the 1954 petition to the United Nations. In 1958, at a meeting of the UN Trusteeship Council, Marshallese people again submitted the petition, and the secretary of the interior finally told the AEC that "further testing in the Marshalls would be most impolitic."

After the sixty-seventh nuclear test in the Marshall Islands in August 1958, there were no other nuclear tests on the proving ground, even though there had been plans to conduct further tests. The US government judged that testing there was politically impossible.

The people of the Marshall Islands became increasingly marginalized in the world, burdened with the pain and suffering of exposure to radiation as a result of the US pursuit of nuclear security. However, the Marshallese cannot be viewed as weak and powerless. The UN petition drive from the Marshall Islands pushed the issue of nuclear testing in their lands onto the international agenda, made it visible, shook up the US government, and made it politically difficult to conduct nuclear testing.

Notes

1. Gurōbaru Hibakusha Kenkyūkai, ed., *Kakusareta hibakusha: Kenshō sabaki naki Bikini suibaku hisai* (Tokyo: Gaifūsha, 2005).
2. See Lawrence Wittner, *Resisting the Bomb: A History of the World Nuclear Disarmament Movement, 1954–1970* (Stanford, CA: Stanford University Press, 1997); Maruhama Eriko, *Gensuikin shomei undō no tanjō: Tōkyō, Suginami no jūmin pawā to suimyaku* (Tokyo: Gaifūsha, 2011). Earlier research on the anti–nuclear weapons movement triggered by the 1954 nuclear tests did not adequately consider the role played by the Marshall Islanders.
3. Parts of this chapter are translated from Takemine Seiichirō, *Māsharu Shotō: Owari naki kaku higai o ikiru* (Tokyo: Shinsensha, 2015), 227–62. The translation has been supplemented with additional material and analysis to reflect supplemental research.

4. For the birth of a signature movement in Japan, starting with the *Lucky Dragon No. 5* disaster, see, for example, Maruhama, *Gensuikin shomei undō no tanjō*; and Moriguchi's "Voices of Deep-Sea Tuna Fishermen" in this volume.
5. Miyake Yasuo et al., eds., *Bikini suibaku hisai shiryōshū* (Tokyo: Tokyo Daigaku Shuppankai, 1976), 417–18.
6. For the *Shunkotsu Maru* survey, see Komano Kamakichi and Taniguchi Toshio, *Warera suibaku no umi e: Shunkotsu Maru Bikini hōkoku* (Tokyo: Nihon Orimono Shuppansha, 1954); Okuaki Satoru, *Umi no hoshano ni tachimukatta Nihonjin: Bikini kara Fukushima e no dengon* (Tokyo: Junpōsha, 2017).
7. L. L. Strauss, press release, March 31, 1954, US Department of Energy OpenNet System (hereafter DOE OpenNet), NV0049192.
8. For the global movement against nuclear weapons in the wake of the 1954 nuclear tests, see Wittner, *Resisting the Bomb.*
9. David Bradley, *No Place to Hide* (Boston: Little, Brown, 1948).
10. Folder: Air Sampling, Operation Crossroads, Dec. 1945-Sept. 1946, Entry 4, Box 24, RG 77, National Archives at College Park, Maryland.
11. Advisory Committee for Biology and Medicine 34th Meeting on December 6, 1952, DOE OpenNet, NV0711867.
12. Ōishi Matashichi , *Koredake wa tsutaete okitai Bikini jiken no omote to ura: Daigo Fukuryūmaru norikumiin ga kataru* (Kyoto: Kamogawa Shuppan, 2007), 31.
13. Miyake Yasuo, *Shi no hai to tatakau kagakusha* (Tokyo: Iwanami Shoten, 1972), 38–47.
14. Nihon Gensuibaku Higaisha Dantai Kyōgikai, *Futatabi hibakusha o tsukuruna: Nihon Hidankyō 50-nenshi, 1956–2006* (Tokyo: Akebi sSobō, 2009), 73–74.
15. Nihon Gensuibaku Higaisha Dantai Kyōgikai, *Futatabi hibakusha o tsukuruna: Nihon Hidankyō 50-nenshi, 1956–2006* (Tokyo: Akebi Shobō, 2009), 86–90.
16. Takahashi Hiroko, *Fūinsareta Hiroshima, Nagasaki: Bei kakujikken to minkan bōei keikaku* (Tokyo: Gaifūsha, 2012), 161.
17. Ikeyama Jūrō, interview by author, Daigo Fukuryūmaru Exhibition Hall, Tokyo, March 11, 2005.
18. *Hoshō naki hanseiki: Kuni no hibakusha taisaku o tou*, Chūgoku hōsō, August 6, 1995.
19. John Anjain, interview by author, Ebeye, Marshall Islands, September 14–17, 2003.
20. Jimako Kobnij, interview by author, Ebeye, Marshall Islands, September 15, 2003.
21. Hiroko Langenbelik, interview by author, Majuro, Marshall Islands, September 26, 2003.
22. Hiroko Langenbelik, interview by author, Majuro, Marshall Islands, September 26, 2003.
23. Etri Enous, interview by author, Ebeye, Marshall Islands, September 13, 2006.
24. Takemine, *Māsharu Shotō*, 294–99.
25. Takemine, *Māsharu Shotō*, 300–302.
26. Seiichirō Takemine, "Invisible Nuclear Catastrophe Consequences of the US Atomic and Hydrogen Bomb Testings in the Marshall Islands: Focusing on the 'Overlooked' Ailuk Atoll," *Hiroshima Peace Science* 39 (March 2018): 43–68.
27. Associated Press Story on Marshallese Natives, Attach: Four Articles by Bill Waugh, DOE OpenNet, NV0400040, 11.

28. Memo to J. C. Bugher et al., Subject: Associated Press Story on Marshallese Natives, US Department of Energy, DOE OpenNet, NV0400040, 11, 2.
29. For the full text, see "Petition from the Marshallese People concerning the Pacific Islands," May 6, 1954, United Nations Digital Library, T/PET.10/28. Regarding the number of signatures, the petition states, "If more signatures are needed we will promptly supply them. The only reason we are not supplying more now is because to do so would mean a delay of some three months, the time necessary to make complete circuit of our far-flung atolls and islands by ship."
30. "Associated Press Story on Marshallese Natives, Attach: Four Articles by Bill Waugh," DOE OpenNet, NV0400040, 4.
31. "Associated Press Story on Marshallese Natives, Attach: Four Articles by Bill Waugh," 2.
32. For the full text, see "Trusteeship Agreement for the Former Japanese Mandated Islands," April 2, 1947.
33. "Associated Press Story on Marshallese Natives, Attach: Four Articles by Bill Waugh," 11.
34. "Associated Press Story on Marshallese Natives, Attach: Four Articles by Bill Waugh," 12.
35. "Associated Press Story on Marshallese Natives, Attach: Four Articles by Bill Waugh," 6.
36. For the statement by Mason Sears about the petition from the Marshallese, see "Press Release, Subject: Three Statements by Members of the United States Delegation to the Trusteeship Council in Connection with the Marshall Islanders' Petition to the Trusteeship Council," DOE OpenNet, NV0400107, 2.
37. UN Department of Public Information, *Yearbook of the United Nations 1954* (New York: United Nations, 1955), 360–63.
38. Resolution 1082 (XIV), see UN Department of Public Information, *Yearbook of the United Nations 1954* (New York: United Nations, 1955), 362–63.
39. "Letter to L.L. Strauss, Subject: Copies of Letters Received Recently by the Secretary from the US Representative to the UN Ambassador Henry Cabot Lodge, Jr., & Trusteeship Council, Mason Sears," DOE OpenNet, NV0408783, 3–4.
40. "Letter to L.L. Strauss, Subject: Copies of Letters Received Recently," 3.
41. Petition from the Marshallese Congress Hold-Over Committee concerning the Pacific Islands, see UN Digital Library, T/PET.10/29.
42. UN Digital Library, T/PET.10/29.
43. Resolution 1493 (XVII) Petitions from the Marshallese Congress Hold-Over Committee (T/PET.10/29), see UN Digital Library, T/RES/1493(XVII).
44. UN Digital Library, T/RES/1493(XVII).
45. Holly M. Barker, *Bravo for the Marshallese: Regaining Control in a Post-nuclear, Post-colonial World* (Belmont, CA: Wadsworth/ Thomson, 2004), 23–24.
46. For the public information plan drawn up for Operation Hardtack, see "Joint AEC-DOD Operation Hardtack Public Information Plan," Report to the General Manager by the Director of Division of Information Services, in Folder: Military Research & Application 7, Hardtack Vol. 3, Office of the Secretary General Correspondence 1951–58, Entry 67B, Box 208, RG 326, National Archives at College Park, Maryland.
47. "Press Release, Subject: Health and Safety Precautions for Enewetak Proving Ground Tests," DOE OpenNet, NV0408477, 1.

48. "Press Release, Subject: Health and Safety Precautions for Enewetak Proving Ground Tests."
49. See the letter from Lewis Strauss to Carl Durham on May 16, 1958, in Joint AEC-DOD Operation Hardtack Public Information Plan, Report to the General Manager by the Director of Division of Information Services, in Folder: Military Research & Application 7, Hardtack Vol. 3, Office of the Secretary General Correspondence 1951–58, Entry 67B, Box 208, RG 326, National Archives at College Park, Maryland.
50. Letter from Lewis Strauss to Carl Durham on May 16, 1958.
51. See "Shūgiin Kaisan," *Asahi Shinbun*, April 26, 1958, morning edition.
52. See the confidential letter from Walter S. Robertson to Philip Farley on June 4, 1958, in Joint AEC-DOD Operation Hardtack Public Information Plan, Report to the General Manager by the Director of Division of Information Services, in Folder: Military Research & Application 7, Hardtack Vol. 3, Office of the Secretary, General Correspondence, 1951–58, Entry 67B, Box 208, RG 326, National Archives at College Park, Maryland.
53. For the full text, see "Petition from the Marshallese Congress Hold-Over Committee concerning the Trust Territory of the Pacific Islands," March 26, 1956, United Nations Digital Library, T/OBS.10/5.
54. William E. Ogle, *An Account of the Return to Nuclear Weapons Testing by the United States after the Test Moratorium 1958–1961* (DOE Nevada Operations Office, 1985), DOE OpenNet, NV0092202, 140–41.
55. For the letter from Alvin Luedecke to the Director, Division of Military Application, see "Memo, Subject: Conduct of Future Overseas Nuclear Tests," DOE OpenNet, NV0404190, 1–2.
56. For the letter from W. Libby to the Chairman of the US Joint Committee on Atomic Energy, see "Note by the Secretary, Subject: Special Shots for Hardtack," DOE OpenNet, NV0072483, 2–3.
57. For the meeting held by the US AEC on November 13, 1961, see "Chron-12 Summaries of TWX's from Reeves to Gen. Betts, Details of the "Blue Straw' Operation, Highlights of 14 Nov 61 OFO Project Listings, LASL Report Library, from November 1961," DOE OpenNet, NV0411666, 24.
58. "An Account of the Return to Nuclear Weapons Testing by the United States after the Test Moratorium 1958–1961," DOE OpenNet, NV0092202, 345.
59. For the letter from Glenn Seaborg to President Kennedy, see "Letter to President, Subject: Study of Nuclear Weapons Test Shots Proposed by the Weapons Laboratories and DOD for Inclusion in an Atmospheric Test Program," DOE OpenNet, NV0073358, 5.
60. For the letter from James Carr to Glenn Seaborg, see "Note by the Secretary, Subject: Recommendation against Further Testing in Eniwetok and Bikini Atolls," DOE OpenNet, NV0075480, 2.
61. "Note by the Secretary, Subject: Recommendation against Further Testing in Eniwetok and Bikini Atolls," 2.

CHAPTER 9

Arts Education and the Nuclear Legacy in the Marshall Islands

JASMINE ALIK, HOLLY BARKER, KEYOKA KABUA, ARIANA TIBON, AND LEIMAMO WASE

On July 29, 2021, Ariana Tibon, current commissioner for the Republic of the Marshall Islands' National Nuclear Commission and director of education at the time of the interview, shared these ideas about the role of community and youth arts in response to the nuclear legacy with NNC commissioner Holly Barker.[1] As research assistants to the NNC at the time of this interview, Leimamo Wase and Jasmine Alik, MPH students at the time, participated in the interview to both learn from Ariana and cultivate their research and publishing skills as part of the NNC's emphasis on Marshallese capacity building. Keyoka Kabua, secretary for the NNC, participated in the Zoom discussion as well. Everyone involved in this chapter works together closely on a regular basis, but this interview provided an opportunity to reflect on the outcomes and goals emerging from recent activities spearheaded by Ariana. The participants engage in code-switching between English and Marshallese language throughout the interview. Translations of Marshallese words are provided where appropriate.

HOLLY BARKER: **Consider how art has played a role in Marshallese responses to the nuclear legacy. Could you describe the events that you were recently involved in related to young Marshallese and artistic responses to the nuclear legacy?**

ARIANA TIBON: *Inne*, yes, thank you. This event you are referring to took place on July 1, 2021, here in the Marshall Islands. July 1 was actually the seventy-fifth anniversary of the United States testing of the first bomb in the Marshall Islands, which was the Able shot under Operation Crossroads. We invited youth from the two colleges here as well as from the Upward Bound program, which is for high school students. It was hard to coordinate all the high schools because it's summer and school is out, but we did get the participation of about maybe fifty or sixty students. The workshop was formatted so that before the students got to the art portion, they received information about the nuclear legacy—not all the information but most of the main points, as it's hard to tell them everything about the nuclear legacy in just two hours. The students had a chance to learn about the nuclear legacy and the human rights violations associated with the legacy. We had a speaker (Katie Relang from the Pacific Community) present a breakdown of all the human rights that were violated because of the US nuclear weapons testing program. Students also had a chance to get together in teams and come up with solutions to issues they identified as caused by the nuclear testing. The students presented the solutions they came up with to the RMI's minister of foreign affairs, Honorable Casten Nemra.

After the presentation to RMI leadership, the students broke out into groups and worked in teams to begin painting. When they painted, it really showed what they were thinking in their heads about the nuclear legacy. It was really meaningful to have the students showcase their art through paintings; some students were getting disturbed and had goosebumps when they were even just thinking about what to draw.

HOLLY: Was this the first event you had been involved in that included the arts as a way to engage with the nuclear legacy?

ARIANA: It was the second one. The first one the NNC hosted last year when Johntos John painted his *jaki* [woven mat]. Last year the students from the College of the Marshall Islands' Nuclear Club participated in a painting workshop. It was actually a painting and poetry workshop, and some students wrote poems, and some students did paintings. This was a joint collaboration with Kathy Jetñil-Kijiner and [her NGO] Jo-Jikum, so Kathy was coaching the students about how to write poems and express their feelings through poems [the poem below was written by a former student and participant in a workshop in 2013]. We had a lot of good poetry that came out of that workshop, and it took place right after the March 1st event last year commemorating the Bravo test. The poetry and painting workshop was a way to keep the momentum going during the month of March after the commemoration ceremony.

I Am Who I Am

7 degrees north
171 degrees east
My approximate address
Where I live
Where loneliness is my only mate
Several years have gone by
Still people think I am unexciting
Not until a day
A disease struck me down
That I could barely move myself
Surprisingly, a man
Different in color and tongue
From the northwest block
Found me dying and ill
Took me to be one of his patients
He is known in every place
For he takes hold of different professions
This time, he prefers to be called doctor
Which he gave me sixty-seven shots
Or I would say horrible injections
Speaking of horrible
These shots often demoralize my spirit
As a result, having enough of them
Causes my four limbs to fall apart
But still, I am who I am

Jerry Anjolok
December 11, 2013

HOLLY: Do you have any general thoughts about the role of art in the nuclear legacy?

ARIANA: I feel like it's important because that's how people express their feelings. For example, one of my planning committee members is always quiet during the meetings and hardly ever says anything. When the workshop took place, he drew something that was so eerie, but he only shared this sentiment through his art. When he was mixing all the paint together and drawing, I was like, "What is that? A bullet?" and he said, "You'll see." When I saw it, I thought, "Oh, my goodness, that is so creepy," but with the painting he was able to express himself and his thoughts about the nuclear legacy. Had it not been for the workshop, I would have never known what he thinks of when he thinks about the nuclear legacy.

So I think art is important, especially for expressing feelings—expressing themselves.

It's also especially important to show what took place because some people learn by being able to see the legacy. Having artwork related to the nuclear testing means a lot, especially to the Marshallese youth who were the artists for this work.

It wasn't just the art program that was important but also the information session, since that is when they started coming up with ideas for their paintings. Their reactions to the nuclear legacy were shocking, and I kind of expect that a lot of them were not aware beforehand. When I do the information sessions, it feels like it really ignites some sort of flame within the students. They're angry, and they want to come up with solutions, so it was really good that the minister was there for the students to present their ideas. [Below is an example of a poem that illustrates Marshallese students' emotions. This piece was also written by a former student from the College of the Marshall Islands' Nuclear Institute]. When the youth become leaders, they are ready with our ideas or proposals for solutions for our people.

The Unforgotten Story

At the age of twelve
My grandfather told me a story
A story that never last
A story that truly broke my heart into pieces
A story that reminisced me of my beloved ancestors
And a story that has been carved in our hearts
That will never be vanished in our history
A story of my atoll being tested
That will never be vanished in our history
People got sick
Elders were mourning

And babies were crying endlessly
It was like a thunder after a storm
Hearing my atoll's story got me speechless
I was torn
I was in pain
I felt like my world was falling apart
There was nothing I could say
But just to say, "Everything is in God's hands."
I wished I was there to stand alongside my ancestors
To complain and maybe do something rather than just talk
If I were there at the times of nuclear testings,
I would've questioned the ones in charge of the nuclear testings,
"Why Bikini of all places?"
"What will become of our homes that we embrace?"
"Where will our kids/grandkids reside in the future?"
"Will we forever be refugees?"
"Aren't there any strategies?"
"Can't they do testings elsewhere?
A place with no inhabitants?"
I feel like a big part of who I am has gone astray
Questions keep crippling up in my head every day,
"Without my home, who am I?"
"Do I still have the right to call myself a Bikinian?"
To know that we won't be returning home,
It breaks my heart.
But I am happy to have alongside me my fellow Bikinians.
Though we may be away from our home,
I know for sure that in our hearts,
Bikini will forever be our home,
Memories of my ancestors' times in Bikini
Will be cherished and treasured in our hearts forever.

Ronnie Johnson
December 9, 2015

HOLLY: What's an example of something that the students don't know about before the information sessions that you wish they had learned beforehand?

ARIANA: So, one thing that I wish students knew was that there was more than one bomb. A lot of Marshallese young people believe that it was just one bomb. That's just the first basic fact about the nuclear testing program—it was more than just one, it was actually sixty-seven. I kind of also wish that they knew about Project 4.1 [an experiment to document the impacts of radiation exposure on human beings] and all the trauma associated with Project 4.1. Those are like my top two, but it's hard to prioritize what is more important. I wish they knew everything.

HOLLY: It is nice that you start them down that pathway to learning more and asking questions. You talked about the students feeling anger, wanting solutions. What do you hope Marshallese youth take away after participating in your programs and workshops?

ARIANA: I feel like their takeaway from the art workshop is that they have this knowledge now, and they're able to use it for their own social media platforms to talk about because *it's their history*, so I think that's the biggest takeaway—it's learning that piece of history that nobody really knows about. And I feel like the things that I know now about the nuclear testing, honestly, I feel like it's just like the tip of the iceberg. I feel like there's so much that hasn't been uncovered and hasn't been touched or seen by us. Yeah, but I feel like that's their takeaway—it's the knowledge that this is their history. I try to encourage them that they are the future leaders, lawyers, doctors, scientists. I tell them, "The knowledge is with you now, and it's up to you to use this knowledge to make change or make a difference."

HOLLY: I know exactly why we're interviewing you—that's so perfect! So, when you do art with the youth, do you find that there are aspects of Marshallese culture that can be expressed well through art?

ARIANA: Like handicraft making, it requires a lot of creativity to be able to weave those pieces together with those shells and those dried coconut leaves. It also takes patience. I feel like Marshallese people are really patient. They're patient and creative.

HOLLY: Are there strengths of the Marshallese culture that you think help people address the nuclear legacy? Does working on the nuclear legacy make you more aware of particular strengths in Marshallese culture?

ARIANA: Just to be honest, I don't see any strength because Marshallese *e lukun lap kautiej* [are very respectful]—we respect the Americans, respect each other, respect this piece of history by not talking about it. You know all the *manit* [cultural practices] that were broken, like being naked on the [US Navy] ship [during decontamination], they don't talk about it, so I'm sorry, but I can't really draw a link between the Marshallese cultural strength and nuclear legacy and efforts to advocate for justice. I sometimes feel like that's why nobody else is on the nuclear legacy boat, and everybody is focused on climate change. They all think, "Oh that's all in the past, and so what?" But then for climate change, it is the future. One thing I always tell the students is "It's good that you're fighting for climate change, but climate change doesn't cause cancer in families. It's the nuclear legacy that causes cancer. not climate change, not rising sea levels." I mean I'm not trying to bash the climate change folks, but everybody's like, "Oh, 1.5 to stay alive," but hello! we need a cancer care center to stay alive! If a wave comes in and washes up does that give you cancer? But do the chemicals that are still in the environment [from the testing] give you cancer? Yeah!

HOLLY: You were talking about the importance of *kautiej* in Marshallese culture and showing respect, including toward Americans. Do you see any intergenerational differences for youth compared to those who experienced the testing?

ARIANA: Yeah, I do see a difference, but it's through social media that people are more vocal, because they're behind the screen and they're posting on social media. To actually be vocal on the streets or to face somebody—I don't think the youth really do that. Social media provides a way for the youth to share their frustration not just with the leaders but with anybody. With all these grown-ups [in leadership positions], I just feel like the youth need a platform to share their frustration. Social media is there and it's free and the youth have accounts and they're able to just write paragraphs of their feelings and what they know about the nuclear testing, but then you wouldn't see a sixteen-year-old boy on the street talking on a megaphone about all the injustices.

HOLLY: What kinds of frustration about the nuclear realm do you see youth expressing on social media?

ARIANA: I see that a lot of them are frustrated that they didn't even know about the testing growing up because it wasn't integrated into the school curriculum for all these decades. And so that's one frustration. I also see that they're frustrated with what they see as nothing being done to help the nuclear survivors—helpless victims and survivors. The youth just feel frustrated that it seems like we're not going anywhere with this.

HOLLY: What would you want the world to know the most about the *RMI*'s nuclear legacy?

ARIANA: *Arrarr, ekwe inok* [ugh, I don't know]. I want them to know everything about the nuclear legacy. It's so hard, I cannot just pick one thing. I want them to know everything. Yeah. I want them to know about just everything. I cannot just say Project 4.1, because I also want them to know that the people of Enewetak were floating out on the sea for months while they did testing for Operation Hardtack and just *everything.*

HOLLY: Do you feel like there's a legacy of Marshallese protests that's part of the nuclear legacy?

ARIANA: *Inne.* Yeah. I feel like there's a lot of Marshallese protest. Just the other day I was shopping and a *Lerooj* [traditional female leader] told me, "You gotta' tell the Americans that *aolep, aolep, aolep, rimajol rebaam*" [every, every, every Marshallese is irradiated by the bombs]. So there is protest. There's this other lady whom I'm working with who was on leave for months because she had thyroid issues. She's young! She's really young, but she has thyroid issues, and I thought it was old people who had thyroid issues. Everybody I talk to about the nuclear testing, everybody says, "*Je bomb, je bomb, aolep rimajol rebaam*" [we're irradiated, we're irradiated, all Marshallese are irradiated]. They ask, "What are you guys [at the NNC] going to do about it *ke je lukun baam* [because we're all really irradiated by bombs]?" but there's nothing being done. There's no money, but I honestly feel like money cannot compensate people. It's not all about money. My *jimma* [grandfather] just passed away from cancer, and he has a claim at the Nuclear Claims Tribunal, but even if they give us his award, because he was eligible for $125,000—one of the highest claims—that wouldn't bring him back. They can give me the money, but it wouldn't fix the pain that's associated with the cancer and caring for a loved one with cancer. I know there is a legacy of Marshallese protests, but Marshallese are really humble, and they wouldn't really come out and rally outside the Nitijeḷā [Marshallese parliament] or the Cabinet—they just keep it to themselves and protest within themselves, I guess.

HOLLY: Are there aspects of working with the youth that inspire you?

ARIANA: Yeah, I like working with the youth because I know that they are the future, and working with them at such a young age we're able to kind of mold them. It's easier to work with the youth than to work with grown-ups who have already set their mind on what the facts are, but with the youth, we are able to share this knowledge and then they can express their ideas with adults.

HOLLY: Is there anything we didn't touch on that you want to talk about in terms of art and the nuclear legacy?

ARIANA: Only that they write songs, too. I didn't mention that they write songs. The College of the Marshall Islands' Nuclear Club has written three songs already that are just about the nuclear testing. And you—you heard the song they performed on March 1st, right?

HOLLY: Oh, my goodness, so good!

ARIANA: Yeah, we have some songwriters in the Nuclear Club learning about the nuclear testing.[2] They're motivated to keep writing more songs about it.

HOLLY: Jasmine and Mamo, do you have any questions for Ariana?

LEIMAMO WASE: No, just in awe—just in awe of everything she's saying. Oh, I have one more question about the curriculum. I know you're working with the teachers. How do you see this work progressing, and what is your vision for having it be part of the curriculum in the education system?

ARIANA: I just feel like integrating nuclear issues into the curriculum is *so* important because—Keyoka, did you learn about nuclear testing *ilo jikuul ko am* [during your schooling]?

KEYOKA KABUA: I learned most of my nuclear [history] from you, Ariana [*laughs*].

ARIANA: See, Keyoka didn't learn about it. My dad [a former senator] didn't learn about it. Keyoka worked at the MOFAT [Ministry for Foreign Affairs and Trade] for years, and she was always the emcee for Nuclear Victims Remembrance Day. She was at MOFAT for seventeen years, and she didn't know about nuclear testing.

Where did I learn all of this? Oh, my gosh, I did research. I would, like, read Holly's books, and I was so into it. I would just go to Google for nuclear testing in the Marshall Islands. Whenever I do research, like with the archives online—there's this archive website for the trust territory, and it's mostly photos—but then I would try to look for the source of those photos and then I don't know, I was just so into it for a few years.[3]

Going back to integrating nuclear legacy into the curriculum, I think it's so important because this is our history, people! And it's so funny that we don't know about it, and it would be even funnier, for example, if I knew nothing about the nuclear testing and then I went to Japan, and of course Japanese really know about Hiroshima and Nagasaki, and they also know about the Marshall Islands because they have a Peace Day, I think, on Bikini Day. March 1st is their Bikini Day. I would have been so embarrassed if I went there and had a young Japanese person tell me about my family's history, like, "Oh, you know your *jimma* [grandfather, Nelson Anjain] was the one who came to Japan and initiated all these conversations." I feel like we need to know this so that we're able to share it with people, and if it's not taught in schools, then I don't think it's going to be taught at home, because at home they don't talk about nuclear testing. When I asked my *bubu* and *jimma* [grandmother and grandfather] about the Compact stuff and how we came to a $150 million [nuclear] settlement with the US, Bubu didn't really like to go into detail. She would just answer my question and want me to ask Jimma. He would just answer the [precise] question that you're asking, then that's it—no elaborating. I feel like passing along knowledge is so important—really critical—because these survivors are passing away, and I don't think they're going to be alive when today's young students are learning the curriculum and becoming the leaders, but the youth are the ones who will be able to push for change.

When I talked to Jimma about jellyfish babies, I asked him if he knew my mother-in-law saw a jellyfish baby with no limbs and no legs and no head—it was a baby with just a slab of a body, and they could see the intestines and the heart beating. And then my grandfather told me, "I saw the files in the safe at the TT [trust territory] office." I had to ask, "What safe?" and then he said he was friends with somebody [in the government office], and they went through the pictures [in the safe], and he said there was a [picture of a] baby that had bones growing out of the head. He's like, "*Juon eo ninnin e lukun ainwot ke e* devil [a baby that was more like a devil]." The bones were sticking out of the baby's head, and then he said he saw pictures of those grape-looking babies [hydatidiform molar pregnancies], and then I'm just like, "*Etke kwoj jab ba?!* [okay, but why didn't you say something?!]." You know, I just get so angry that they know these things in life, and then they're like, "Well, you didn't ask," but now I'm asking. He only told me he saw the pictures and then they were burned [by the US government officials] and then that's it. I think they [the elders] think we already know, but I don't know. I don't know why people don't talk about it.

LEIMAMO: Do you think there are opportunities to connect the nuclear curriculum with the science curriculum?

ARIANA: I worked with the science teachers two years ago. We were trying to figure out how we should integrate the nuclear studies into the science part of it. But for the teachers, they thought this was going to be so hard. They said they could teach the students elements, like plutonium, and the difference between atomic and hydrogen, and fission and fusion. I just need to meet with the committee that organizes the science fair.

HOLLY: Thank you for talking with us, and for your leadership, Ariana. You inspire us all deeply so please always let us know if we can support your work. *Kommol* [thank you].

Notes

1. The NNC was established by the RMI government in 2017 to pursue nuclear justice on behalf of the Marshallese people. Alson Kelen is the current chair of the NNC and is the third commissioner, in addition to Ariana Tibon and Holly Barker.
2. O. Agrippa, C. Gideon, and T. Kabua [Voices Rising], *Enana | We Are Not Alone*, YouTube, February 28, 2021, https://www.youtube.com/watch?v=bX9OWVqluMs.
3. University of Hawai'i Image Archive, Trust Territory of the Pacific Islands, http://libweb.hawaii.edu/digicoll/ttp/photodescript3.html.

CHAPTER 10

Nuclear Temples

PETER GOIN

In 2017, the Bulletin of the Atomic Scientists moved the time of the Doomsday Clock a half minute closer to midnight. The prospect of human annihilation is less and less just a fictional narrative, as reckless actors on the global stage increase their provocative defiance of scientific truths. Nuclearized nations modernize their weaponry, and the taboo against the use of such weapons is awash in a disinformation campaign amplifying the increasing perils of a warming climate, provoked in part by a dizzying display of more than two thousand nuclear detonations since Trinity occurred at 5:29 a.m. on July 16, 1945. The nuclear age is our human legacy, and what we will leave behind us in the postcivilized world will be these nuclear sites. Plutonium, a radioactive chemical element (Pu), was first produced and isolated on December 14, 1940. Plutonium-239, the type used in nuclear tests worldwide, has a half-life of 24,100 years, a timescale beyond the ranges of cultural predictability.

After photographing at the Trinity Site, the Nevada Test Site, the Hanford Nuclear Reservation, and the Marshall Islands' Bikini and Enewetak Atolls, I produced a portfolio of color photographs detailing the legacy of atomic and thermonuclear detonations by the US government. However, I had preceded this nuclear sites fieldwork by conducting visual field studies at many Mesoamerican pyramids in Mexico, Guatemala, and Honduras.

During 1977–78, a good friend and I traveled extensively throughout Central America for more than seven months. This friend, Robert B. Cree, is a photographer and writer who earned his MFA at the Writers'

Workshop at the University of Iowa and today lives in Tempe, Arizona. He made the 35 mm black and white negatives and was kind enough, after all these years, to allow me to scan, prepare, and print them for this chapter. More than four decades have passed since then, and how times have changed. Although the internet was designed in 1974, it was not available well into the 1980s. Personal computers were on the verge of ubiquity but still in their infancy. In 1977 Jimmy Carter had been sworn in as president, the original *Star Wars* movie premiered, New York City suffered a massive blackout, Grace Jones was a disco queen, Elvis Presley died on August 16, and the space shuttle orbiter *Enterprise* completed its first manned flight.

To experience the diversity and character of the Latin American landscape, we decided to travel light, backpack, and camp in the rural regions near Mesoamerican archeological sites. Armed with survival Spanish and a few necessary idioms, we crossed *la frontera,* entering Mexico on our own self-guided tour, exploring the archeological identity of the Toltecs, Olmecs, Aztecs, Zapotecs, and the Maya, weaving photographs among adventures. The Mexican government prohibited 4×5 film and cameras, even tripods, as this equipment was perceived as evidence of potential commercial exploitation. Thirty-five-millimeter cameras were considered tools for artists and tourists, and were therefore not implicated in the list of restrictions.

We began the journey aiming toward one of the earliest known sites of Mesoamerican culture, the Olmecs. On our way to Veracruz on the Gulf of Mexico, we encountered other Mesoamerican sites, some identified and others disguised, overgrown, and only casually supervised. Rectangular and oval overgrown mounds, trees emerging, breaking free of stairs, wide, steep, and pervasive. Many of the sites had been loosely reconstructed by a variety of archeological teams. Others had been carefully rebuilt but without significant regard for the original role of each stone or rock in the facade of a structure. Upon close inspection, it was obvious that the carvings on the face of the rocks did not match and that they were placed according to their size and shape as elements in a grand puzzle but not as glyphs to be read. We visited the pyramids at Chichén Itzá, Tulum, Palenque, and Tikal in Guatemala, and Copán in Honduras, as well as other sites throughout Mexico and the rest of Central America. Many of the most interesting areas, however, were not identified or located on the map as archeological sites. A series of undefined mounds located near Palenque in Mexico appeared more suggestive, even mysterious because of sublimated architecture. The jungle overgrowth and the massive pyramids at Tikal presented a landscape neither natural nor urban. The landscape *was* architecture, artifacts of ancient cultures only partially understood. We visited these sites before they became canonized as national parks, with turnstiles, self-guided walking tours, personal guides, roped-off areas, and crowds of tourists.

After returning from Central America and pursing an alternative education running bookstores in San Francisco, in 1984 I joined the Department of Art faculty at the University of Nevada, Reno. Most of the land in Nevada, 84.9 percent, is federally owned, implying that there's plenty of territory open for camping, exploring, and photographing. However, one significant exception is the Nevada Test Site, a 1,350-square-mile government testing area, fenced with "off limits" and "no trespassing" signs. Underground nuclear detonations still occurred; the last US test, Divider, was conducted in September 1992. I had been told that it was impossible to gain access to photograph the site. The Department of Energy was not interested in providing access to photographers, especially considering the growing antinuclear movement. Many protesters were trying to escape detection by the Nevada Test Site security force so that they could arrive at ground zero and disrupt planned detonations. Announcements of nuclear tests had been delayed because of these tactics. A heightened veil of secrecy was draped over the test site. After a long and difficult negotiation, the Department of Energy finally granted permission for me to photograph within the Nevada Test Site. Crossing through the gates at Mercury, gateway to the test site, the landscape—at times recognizable due to the familiarity of historical and publicity films—provoked a feeling unlike the usual Nevada basin and range. Perhaps this feeling was created by a sense of exclusion and mystery. The physical threat at the Nevada Test Site, vague yet omnipresent, structures our collective response. Radioactivity is not visible, and it is potentially pervasive at the site. Subsidence craters are everywhere. Is a slight depression a potential subsidence crater, or is it a simple earthen depression that I am interpreting as dangerous?

Are the Mayan mounds an archeological site, or are they earthen mounds created by the forces of erosion?

The Marshall Islands sites of Bikini and Enewetak Atolls, significant testing areas for nuclear weapons, were next on the agenda. Gaining permission to photograph within these atolls involved a complicated process requiring coordination between the US Department of Energy and the US Department of State, the government of the Marshall Islands, the Bikini people, the Enewetak people, the airline of the Marshall Islands—with irregular schedules and subject to unscheduled stops, delays, and breakdown—and Holmes and Narver, the contractor maintaining the research stations. Bikini and Enewetak, soiled by sixty-seven nuclear detonations, had been subjected to a massive US government cleanup campaign. Although the bunkers survived numerous nuclear blasts, most of the debris and soil had been scraped and buried in crypts or craters. The islands have been seeded and planted with rows of coconut trees, and years of tropical growth have begun to overtake the remnants of the testing era. Each atoll is a collective of islands, and some of the islands no longer demonstrate surface radioactivity, but others, such as Runit Island in Enewetak Atoll, still suffer from hotspots. Signs in both Marshallese and English threaten trespassers with radioactive contamination. These landscapes of fear permeate the journey and are a constant characteristic of nuclear landscapes. Except for Enewetak Island, few of the islands are habitable due to the subsurface radioactivity. The food chain is contaminated; all the food for station workers and islanders is brought in by supply ship once a month or by the occasional airplane.

Photographing nuclear landscapes is an abject experience in the anxiety of the *real*, but what resonates is less the radioactivity than the consequence. These bunkers of the nuclear Pacific, with wooden ladders and vines inching their way over every crack and crevice, are not just reminiscent of an imaginary ancient civilization but evidence of our own legacy, measured in millennia. In the same way that Mesoamerican pyramids represent an era of conquest, militaristic societies, colorful deities, harsh realities, and cultural demise, so too do these nuclear temples symbolize the hubris of a global society at risk.

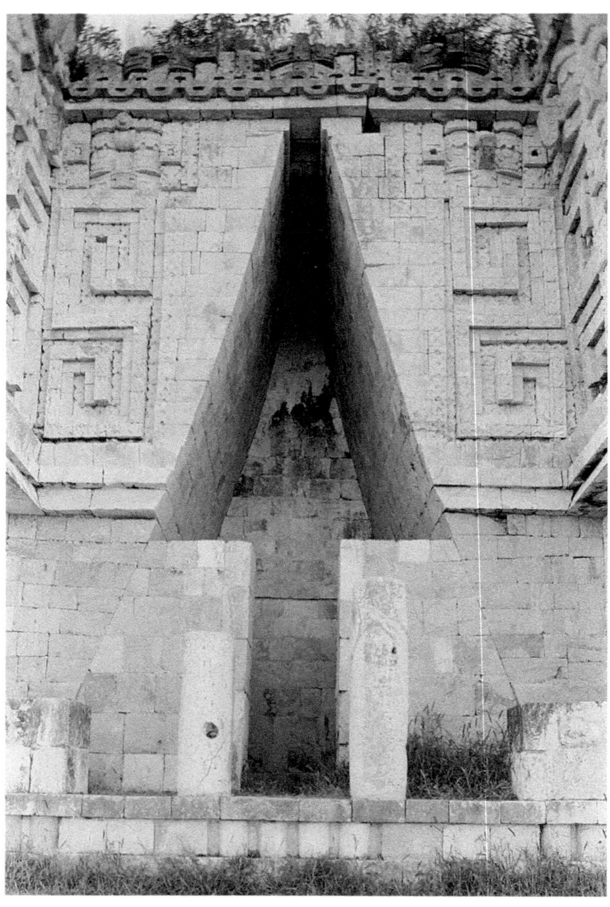

The façade of the Governor's Palace at Uxmal is one of the most celebrated examples of the Mayan Puuc style of architecture. The palace has an abundance of Venus glyphs, and combined with hieroglyphic throne inscriptions that depict Maya zodiacal constellations, it is no coincidence that Venus rising and setting coincides with specific architectural features. Uxmal, designated a UNESCO World Heritage Site, is an ancient Maya city of the classical period, located in the Puuc region of eastern Yucatán peninsula, approximately forty miles from Merida. Mayan architecture often included ornate friezes, columns, and trapezoidal shapes. The Maya lacked metal tools, pulleys, and the wheel, relying on abundant manpower. The large buildings were constructed of limestone that was quarried locally. Notable throughout Mayan architecture is the false arch, whose limitations required massive structural angles. Ancient roads called *sacbes*, which translates as "white roads," connect the buildings and lead to other cities in the area, especially Chichén Itzá. Uxmal was founded about 500 CE and was the most powerful site in western Yucatán. In alliance with Chichén Itzá, it dominated the northern Maya territory. After 1200 CE, no new major construction was added.

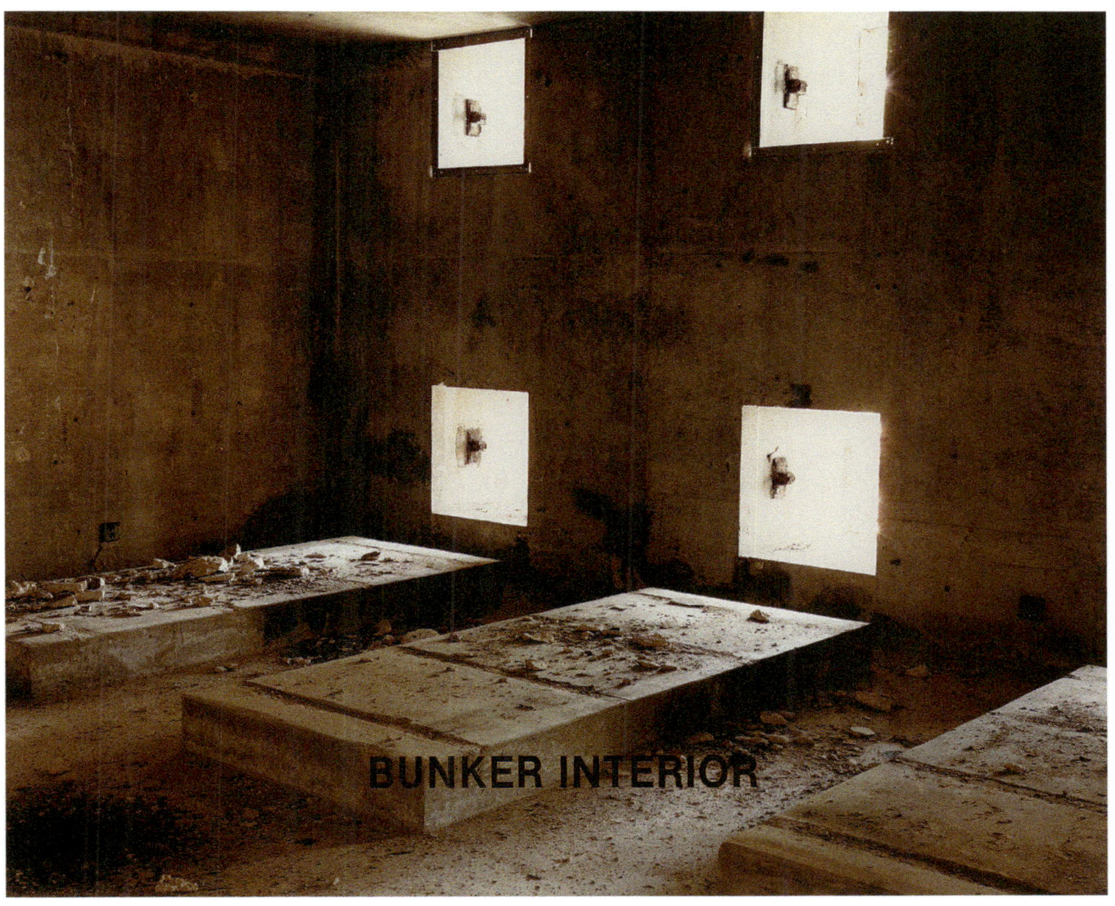

BUNKER INTERIOR

The nuclear bunkers throughout Bikini Atoll contain radioactive materials, essentially serving as postdetonation containment crypts. Bikini consisted of twenty-three islands surrounding a nearly 230-square-mile central lagoon, and the same number of nuclear detonations as islands—twenty-three—occurred either on the islands or in the lagoon, until testing terminated in 1958. The high levels of strontium-90 and caesium-137 detected in residents in 1970 required evacuation of the entire population that had been resettled on Bikini Island. The tests commenced with Operation Crossroads in July 1946, with the bomb code-named Able. Baker, the next test, was detonated underwater, generating a threatening radioactive mist. Able and Baker were the last nuclear tests conducted by the Manhattan Project. Although most of the nuclear bunkers were sealed during the 1970s, this bunker on Lele Island, Bikini Atoll, was left open. To withstand the extreme blast, winds, and debris cast out by a nuclear detonation, massive concrete bunkers were constructed. Bunkers such as this one were used to hold and protect testing equipment and were often very near ground zero. For this view, the color 4×5 film required an eight-hour exposure; normally, it would be quite dark inside, as light enters only through the small corridors to the outside.

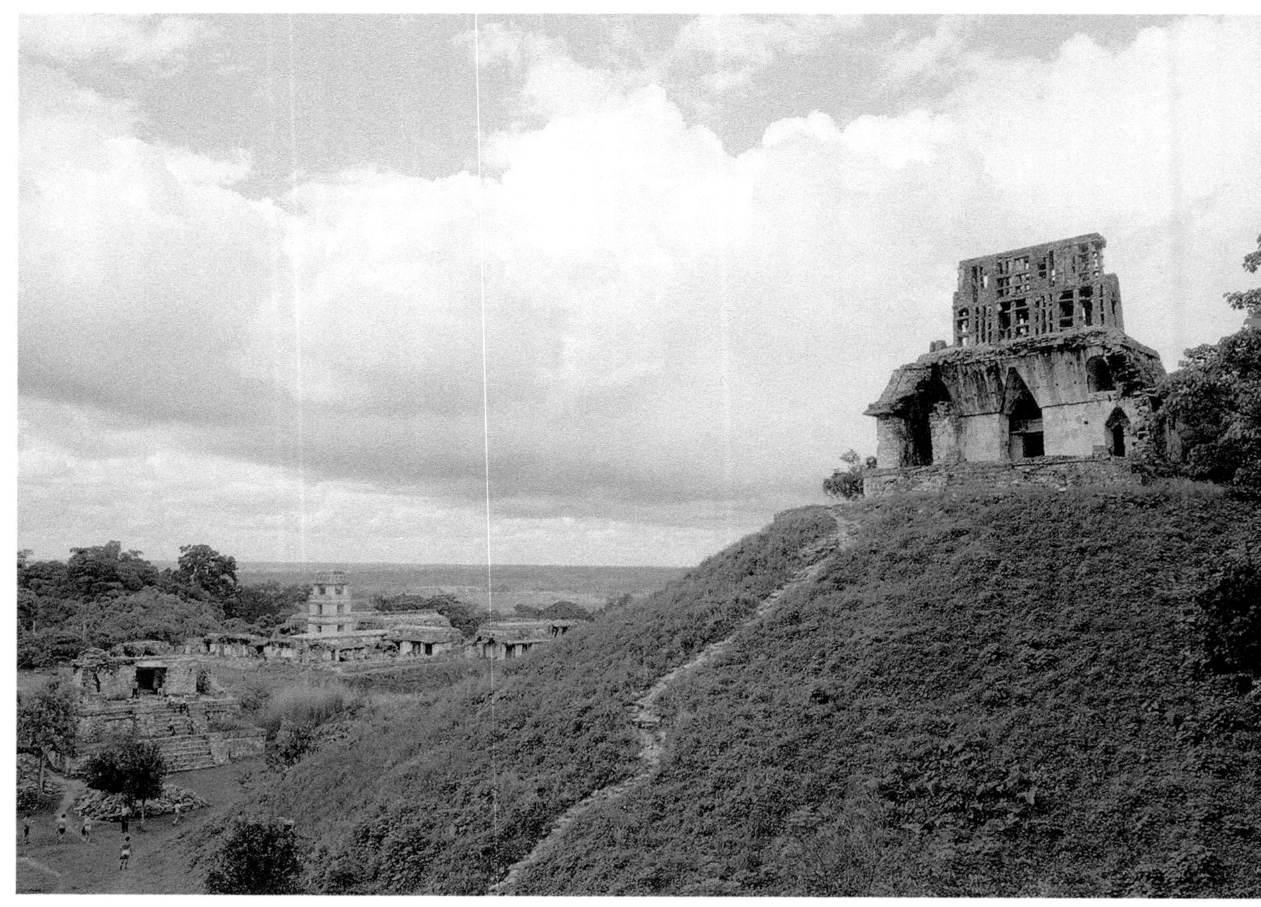

Palenque National Park, established in 1981 prior to the author's visit, is located in Chiapas. The settlement flourished approximately 400 CE to 850 CE, although these dates are contested. Its ancient name was Lakamha, translated as Big Water, and its modern name comes from the nearby Spanish colonial settlement of Santo Domingo de Palenque. The more significant buildings were evident circa 650 CE, when the palace and the Temple of the Inscriptions were constructed. The panels in the Temple of the Inscriptions include a text that is among the longest known from any Maya site, and it describes Palenque's dynastic history, referencing their patron gods, who were honored with three separate temples. Each temple was positioned on a step platform containing an outer and an inner room with a sanctuary, and a "comb" structure was built on the roof. Researchers have found evidence of sophisticated engineering techniques, including but not limited to a water pressure system for a large fountain.

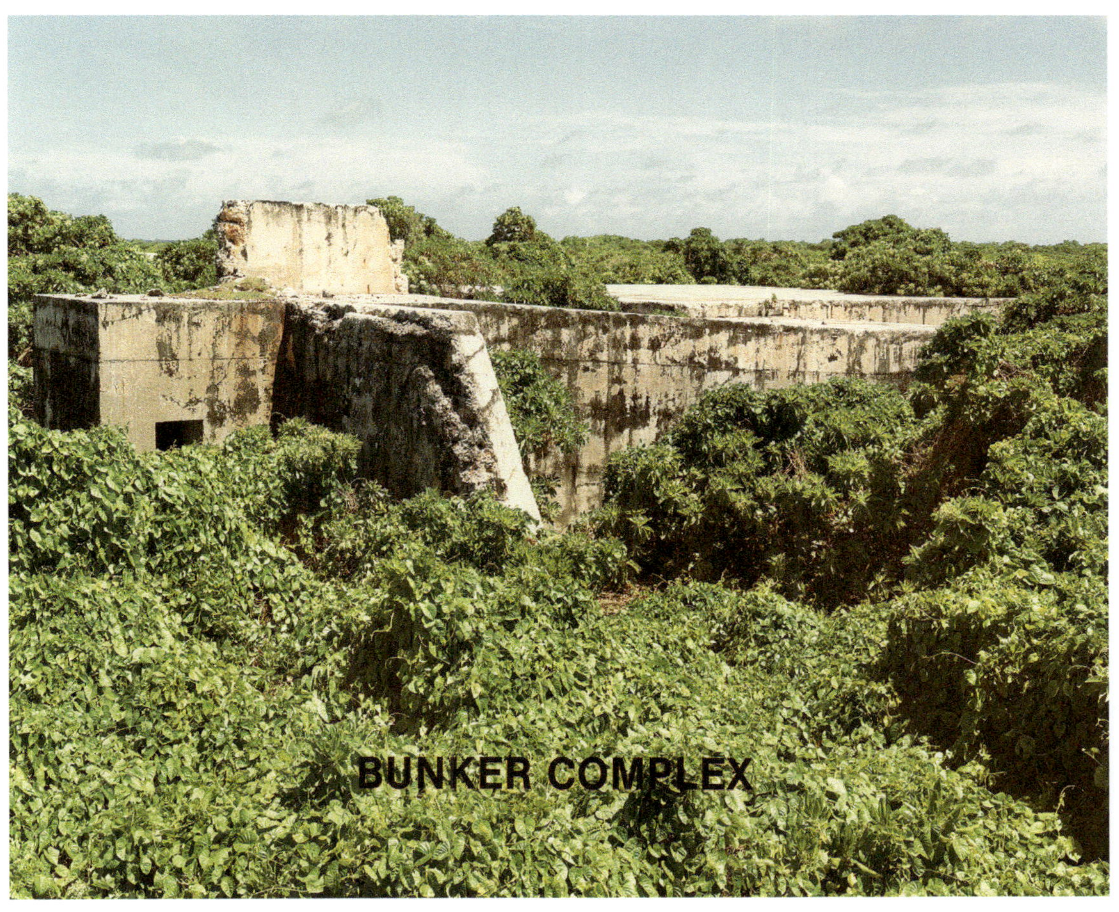

The bunker complex on Nam Island, Bikini Atoll, was built for the test known as Cherokee in Operation Redwing, 1956. This series of tests comprised seventeen nuclear detonations, from May to July. All the tests were named after Native American tribes: Apache, Blackfoot, Cherokee, Dakota, Erie, Flathead, Huron, Inca, Kickapoo, Lacrosse, Mohawk, Osage, Seminole, Tewa, Yuma, and Zuni. Cherokee was detonated directly overhead and was a weapon-related, thermonuclear detonation with a yield of 3.8 megatons. The only weapon test that was air-dropped ended up off target by four miles, and the airman first class responsible was reprimanded. The bunker, which was unmanned but contained sensitive and delicate instrumentation, needed to be massive. This reinforced concrete cube measured twenty-four feet on its exterior sides, while its one interior room was eight feet on each side; the walls—top, bottom, and sides—were eight feet thick. This complex might today be completely overgrown with radioactive vegetation.

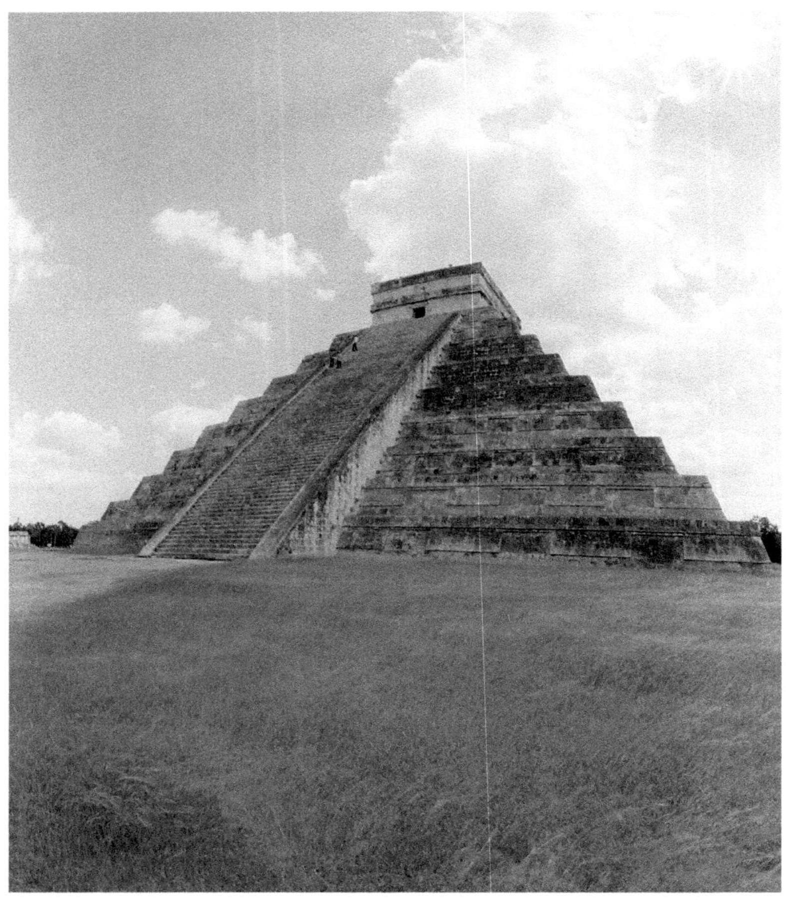

Chichén Itzá is near Merida in Mexico's Yucatán peninsula. Its heyday was much later than Palenque, thriving between 800 and 1300 CE. The scholarly consensus is still being negotiated about who inhabited Chichén Itzá, as the Itzá settled at the site after the heyday period. Chichén Itzá translates as "the mouth of the well of the Itzás." The architecture is a blend of Mayan and Toltec influences, although the Toltecs were located nearly eight hundred miles distant. This is a view of El Castillo, the step pyramid at the heart of the city. The sixteenth-century Spanish bishop Diego de Landa referred to it as the Temple of K'uk'ulcan, honoring the legendary ruler of the city and an ancient snake deity. To reach the top of the temple, adding the step taken to enter the sanctuary, the total number of steps comes to 365. Archeologists have discovered an earlier temple beneath El Castillo, with references to a stone throne in the shape of a snarling red jaguar. In Frederick Catherwood's lithographs, the pyramid was overcome with vegetation.

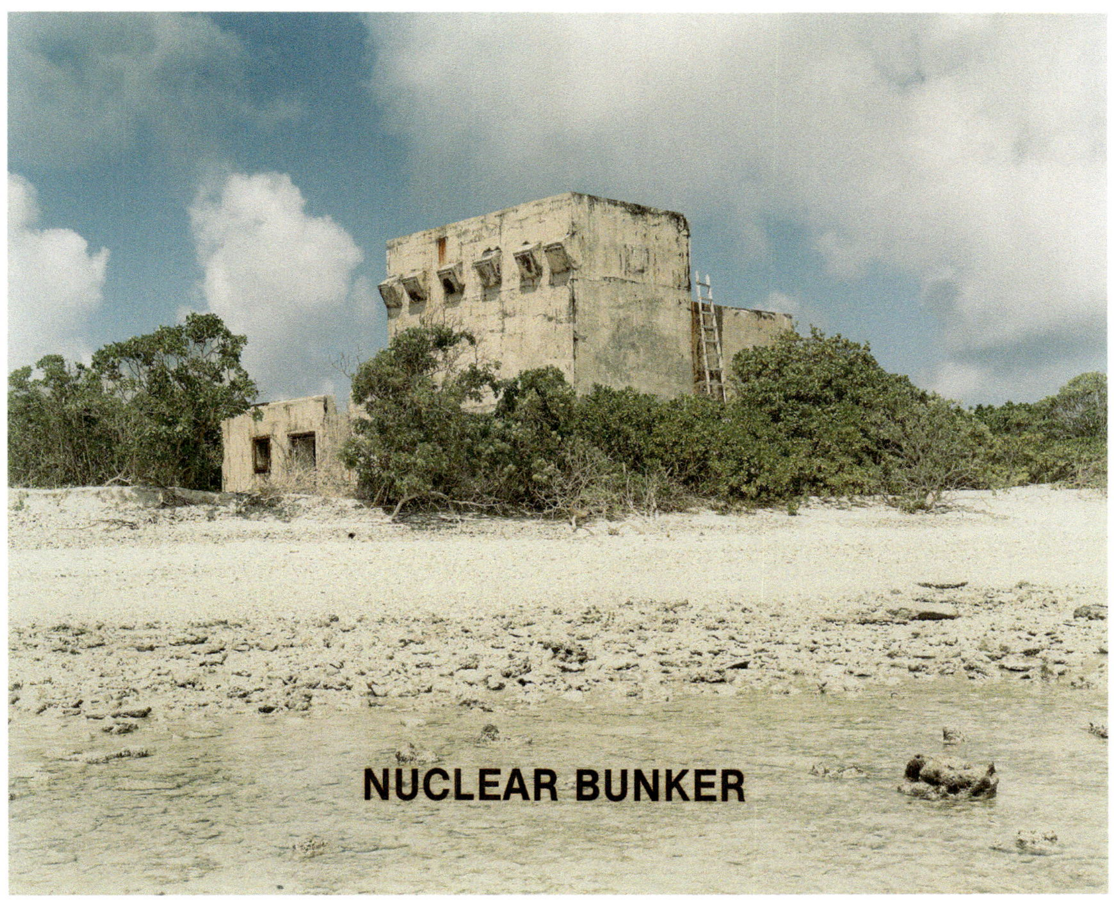

This nuclear temple was a University of California Radiation Laboratory photograph station bunker constructed in 1954 for Operation Castle on Aerkijlal Island, Bikini Atoll. Operation Castle consisted of six detonations—Bravo, Koon, Nectar, Romeo, Union, and Yankee—designed to evaluate the blast radius, the shock generated, and the fallout properties of nuclear weapons in the megaton range. The unanticipated amount of debris made it difficult to evaluate the fallout from individual blasts, but the tests were deemed successful as a critical lesson was learned: atmospheric testing could pose serious health issues to populations exposed to radioactive fallout. The Bravo detonation, conducted on February 28, 1954, was expected to produce a six-megaton blast, but it exceeded those parameters, yielding a fission explosion of fifteen megatons, the most powerful detonation in the US testing era. Note the six cement support housings for heavy-duty iron beams used to brace the bunker against the force of the nuclear blast. The bunker withstood the blast, and the beams were later removed. Photographs made after the detonation indicated that all the vegetation was eliminated.

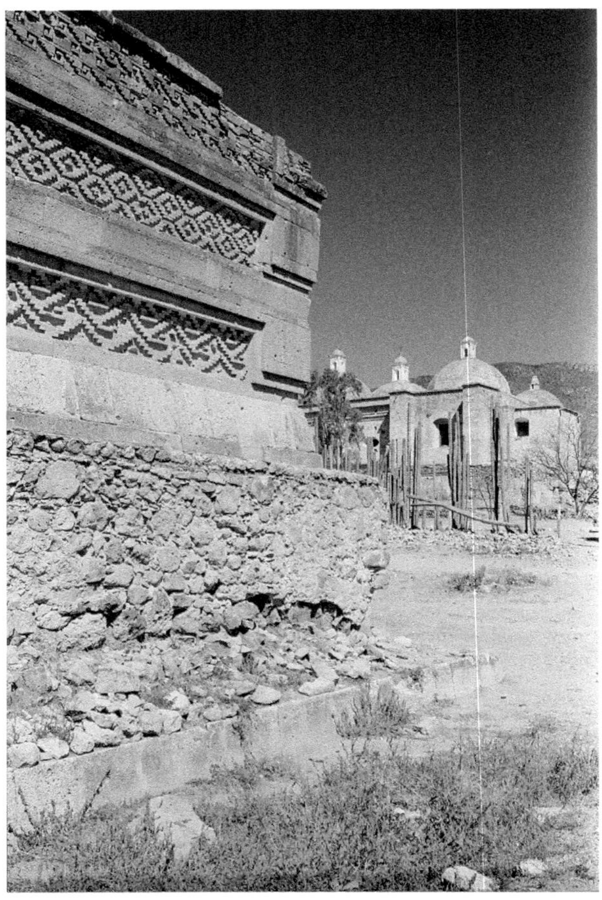

Mitla is a relatively smaller archeological site but one of the most significant Zapotec sites, located near Oaxaca, Mexico. Mitla is embraced within the small town of San Pablo Villa de Mitla. The name Mitla is derived from the Nahuatl name Mictlán, meaning "underworld." Its Zapotec name is Lyobaa, which means "place of rest." The buildings' elaborate and intricate geometric designs are reflected in local weavings, pottery, and roadway decorations, and the question remains whether the architecture influenced the crafts or vice versa. Either way, these strep-and-fret, meander, and key motifs, sometimes incorporating spirals and diamonds, have become a generalized graphic identity for the region. Mitla was settled first by the Toltecs, later by the Aztecs, and then disrupted entirely by the Spanish conquest. The site has five distinct zones built along a north-south axis, and centrally featured is the Group of Columns. The long rectangular halls were covered with a stucco background with a deep red coloring from the cochineal female scale insects found on cactus. The color red covers Mesoamerican architectural history, figuratively and literally.

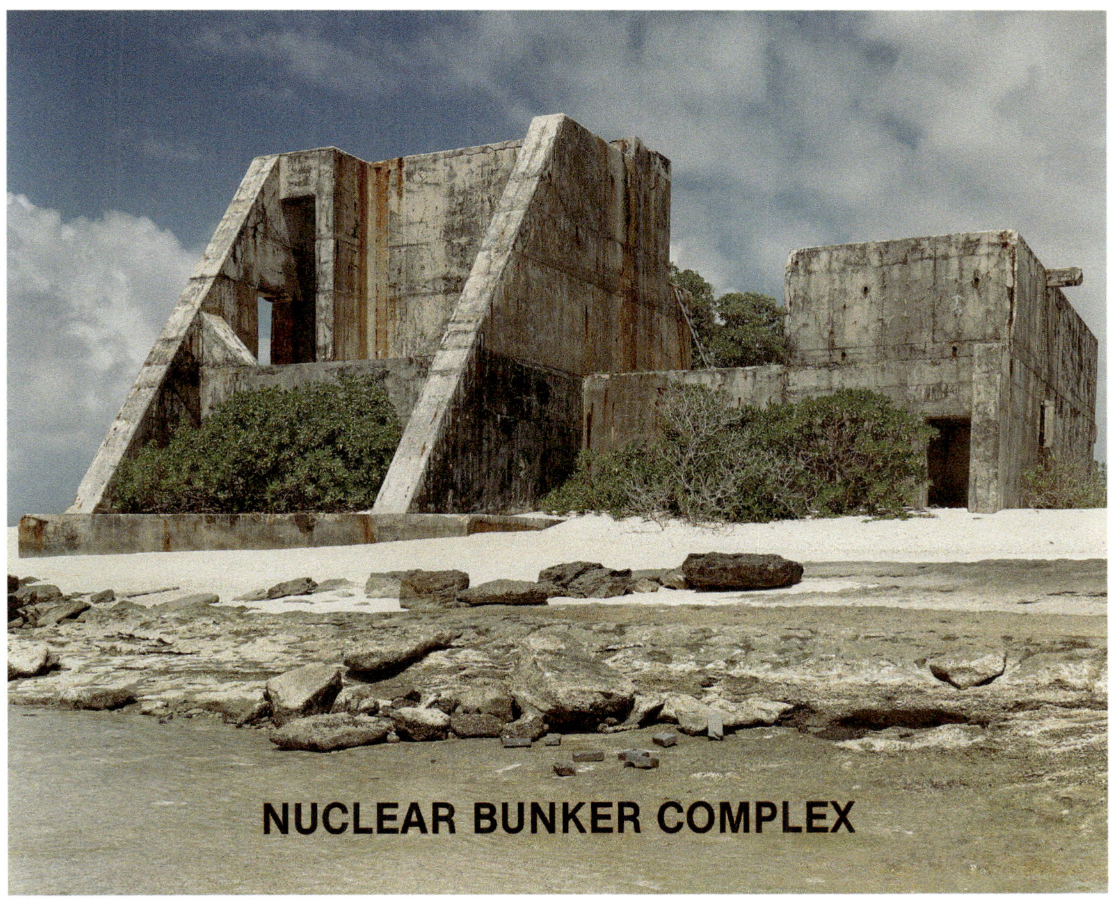

NUCLEAR BUNKER COMPLEX

This bunker complex was a photographic station and optical station used during Operation Redwing, 1956, and for subsequent detonations on Aomen Island in Bikini Atoll. Operation Redwing was a "next generation" series of weapons designed and subsequently detonated on both Bikini and Enewetak Atolls. These tests explored thermonuclear weapons, but the designs were significantly smaller than previous Castle series tests. These lightweight, smaller nuclear weapons were not more than twenty inches in diameter. Operation Redwing included both "clean" (low fission yield) and "dirty" (extremely high fallout) tactical weapons. All of the tests were laced with plutonium, one of the deadliest elements known to humankind. The forty-nine detonations that composed operations Redwing and Hardtack generated 48,846 kilotons, or, in relative terms, approximately 3,200 Hiroshima-size atomic bombs. The next-to-last detonation, code-named Tewa, was launched from a reef at Bikini Island and, when detonated, yielded 5,000 kilotons, equivalent to approximately 333 Hiroshima-size bombs. Tewa was incredibly powerful, and its blast was visible from Hawai'i, 2,500 miles distant. It contaminated 43,500 nautical miles of ocean. Several lead bricks can be seen in the center foreground at the water's edge. These were used in constructing radiation barriers.

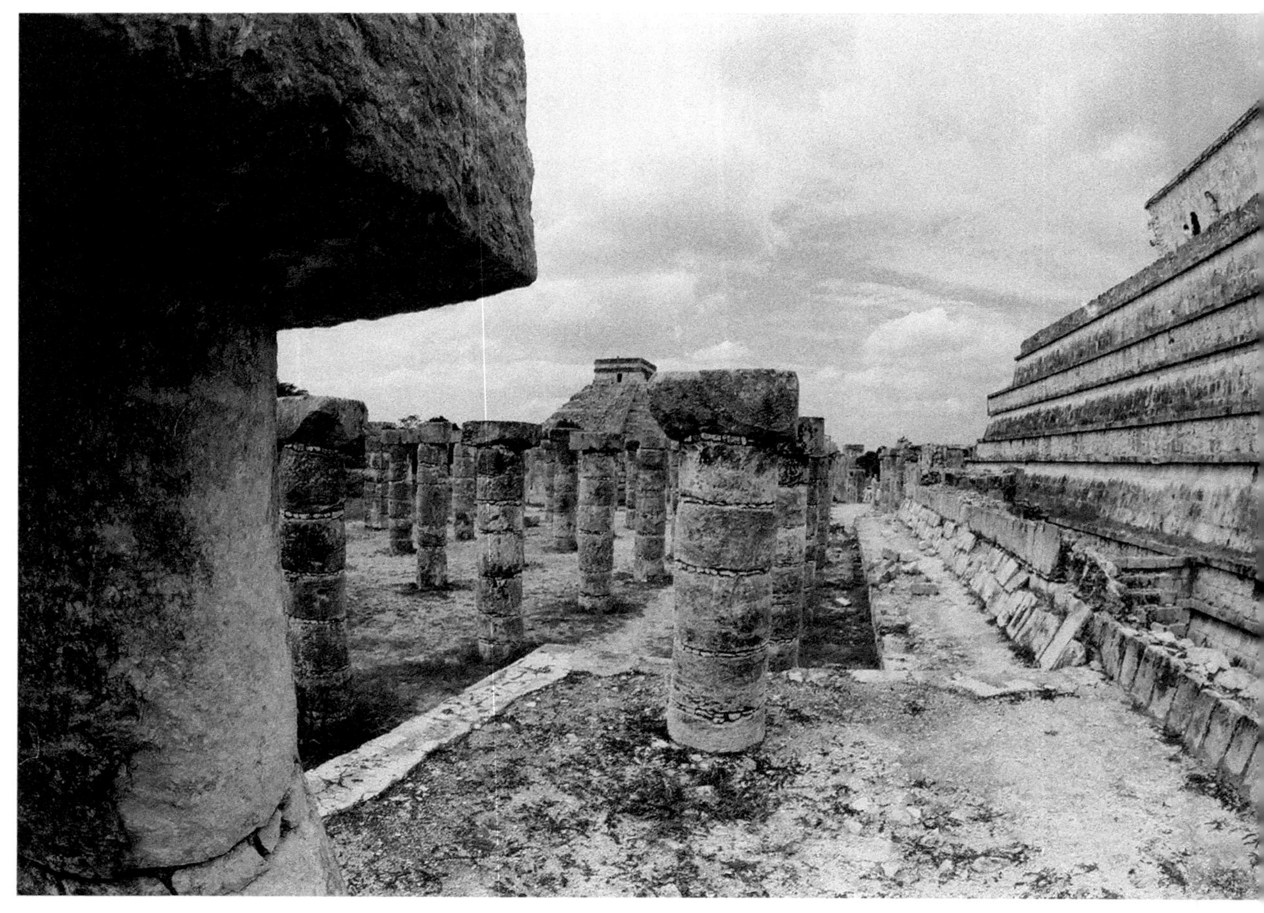

The embedded view from within the Temple of Warriors at Chichén Itzá leads to the Temple of K'uk'ulcan, in the distance, just left of center. The Temple of Warriors is a step pyramid, flanked with the stone pillars representing warriors. Two concepts of urban design were embraced, one astronomical and the other practical. Buildings were aligned in particular directions to cast shadows or feature specific events, mostly sunrises and sunsets. The Temple of K'uk'ulcan is situated such that the summer solstice sunrise aligns with the opposite corner's winter solstice sunset. The shadows created graphically generate through movement a zigzag shape that moves with the light, referencing the sky serpent's role in their cosmology.

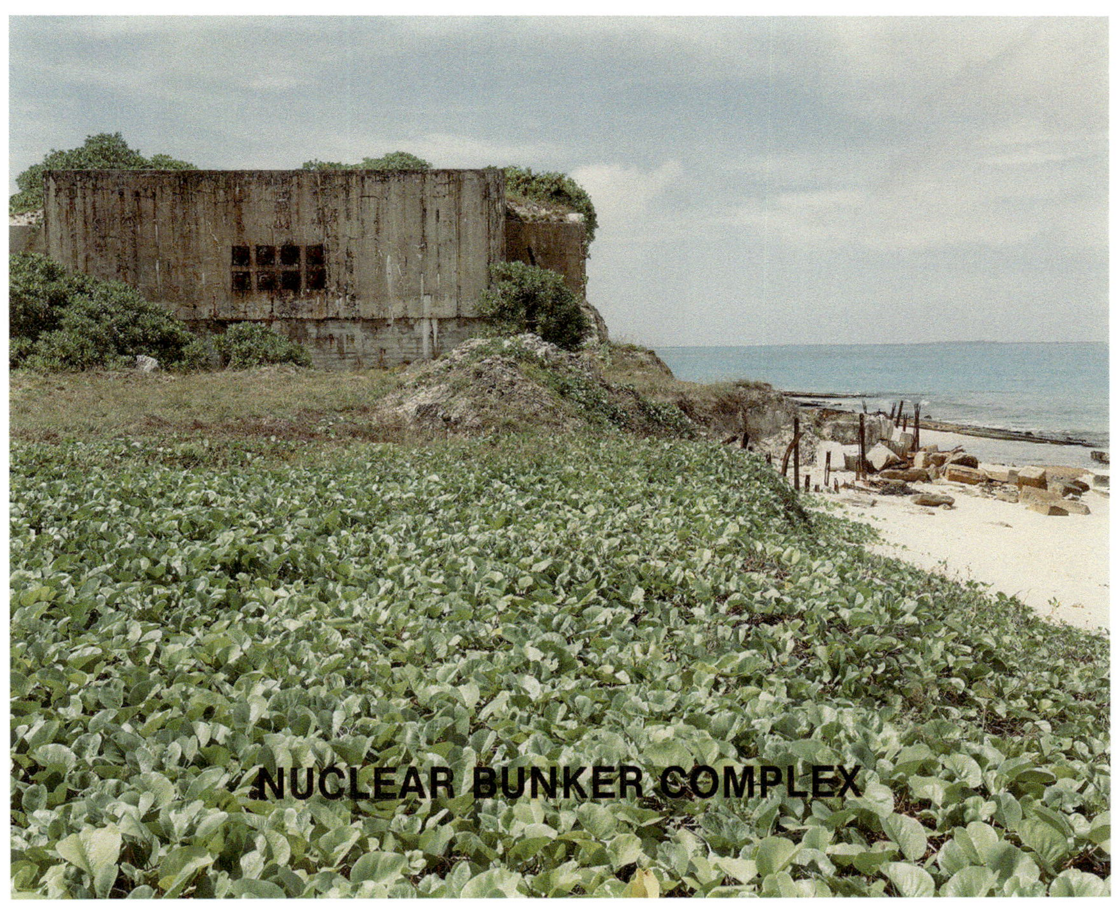

NUCLEAR BUNKER COMPLEX

This nuclear temple is Station 1310, an alpha recording diagnostic measurement station used in Operation Redwing in 1956 and Operation Hardtack in 1958, on Runit Island in Enewetak Atoll. Operation Hardtack featured thirty-five nuclear detonations, named after native American hardwoods and shrubs, such as Cactus, Butternut, Holly, Koa, Magnolia, Rose, Tobacco, and Yucca. The central focus was on intercontinental and submarine-launched ballistic missile warheads with high-yield strategic weapons. Two of the tests in this series were detonated above Johnston Island, approximately seven hundred nautical miles west-southwest of the Hawaiian Islands. Redwing's test sites were unusually diverse, including land-based, surface-to-water, underwater, balloon, and rocket detonations. Navy vessels assigned to witness the blasts experienced radioactive rain and contaminated seawater, which was used to "wash" the decks. Those who served became atomic veterans; this area is still radioactive.

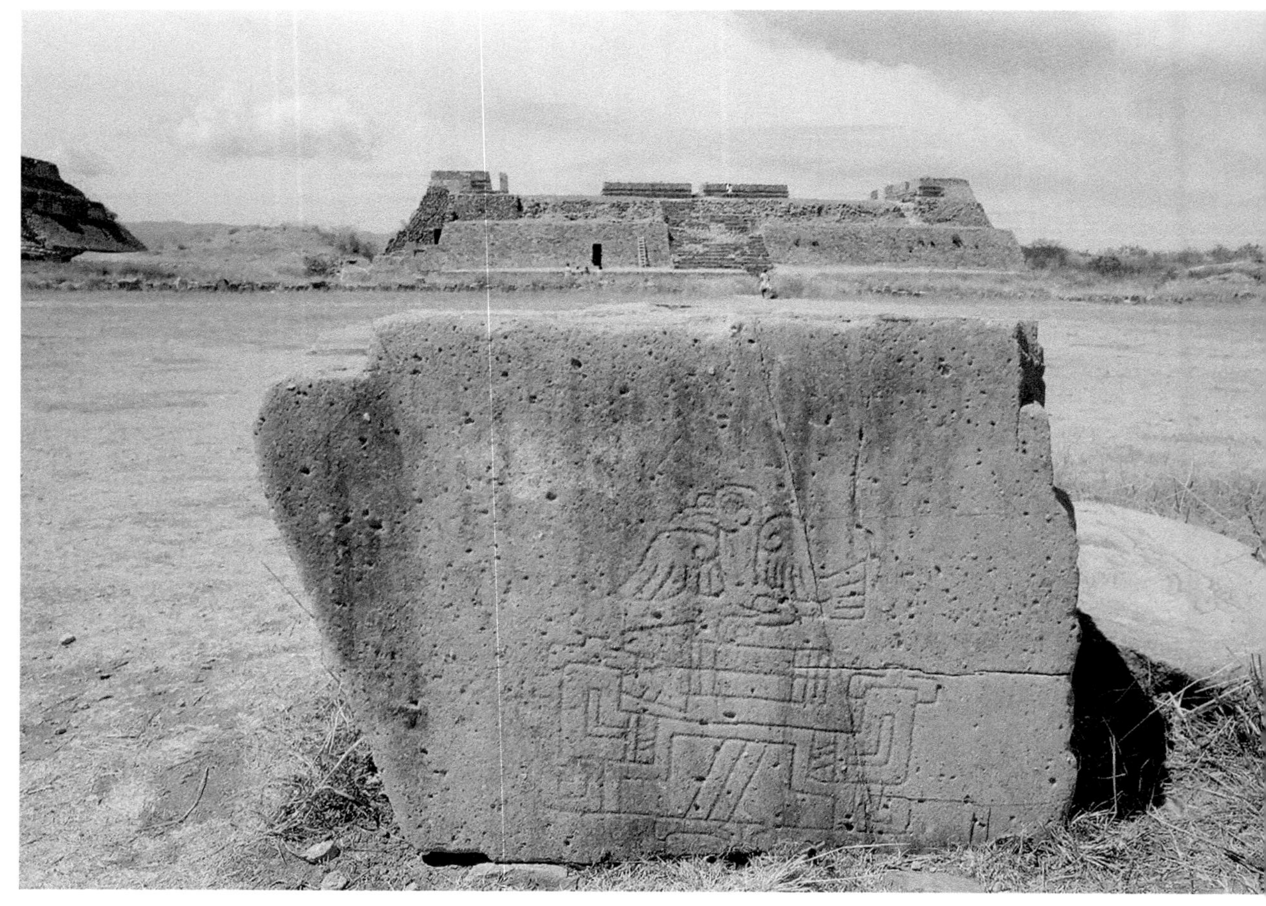

Monte Albán was a political center occupied over a period of 1,500 years by the Olmecs, Zapotecs, and Mixtecs. When the Zapotecs ruled, approximately from 500 BC to 850 BC, the site dominated the Oaxacan valley. Located on top of a prominent ridge, Monte Albán is just six miles west of Oaxaca. A cursory survey of the landscape from atop any of the temples or cliff edges reveals numerous mounds and similar shapes that are overgrown but definitely rectangular and pyramidic, if only to a certain baseline level. Monte Albán includes a grand center esplanade on a north-south axis, a spectacular ball court on the northeastern platform, one of the best-preserved tombs in all of Mesoamerican Mexico, and many bas-relief sculptures. Visually located above the bird stelae is the Edificio de los Danzantes (Building of the Dancers) across the large courtyard. Slabs were set into the platforms with glyphs representing days, names, and numbers. The stone slabs bear reliefs of figures in contorted poses resembling Olmec dancers, hence the name. Closed eyes and open mouths have been interpreted as symbols of captivity and ultimate sacrifice, usually performed in humiliating ways, such as through castration. After 850 CE, during the periods identified as Monte Albán IV and V, the sacred city entered an abandonment phase and was transformed into a fortified city.

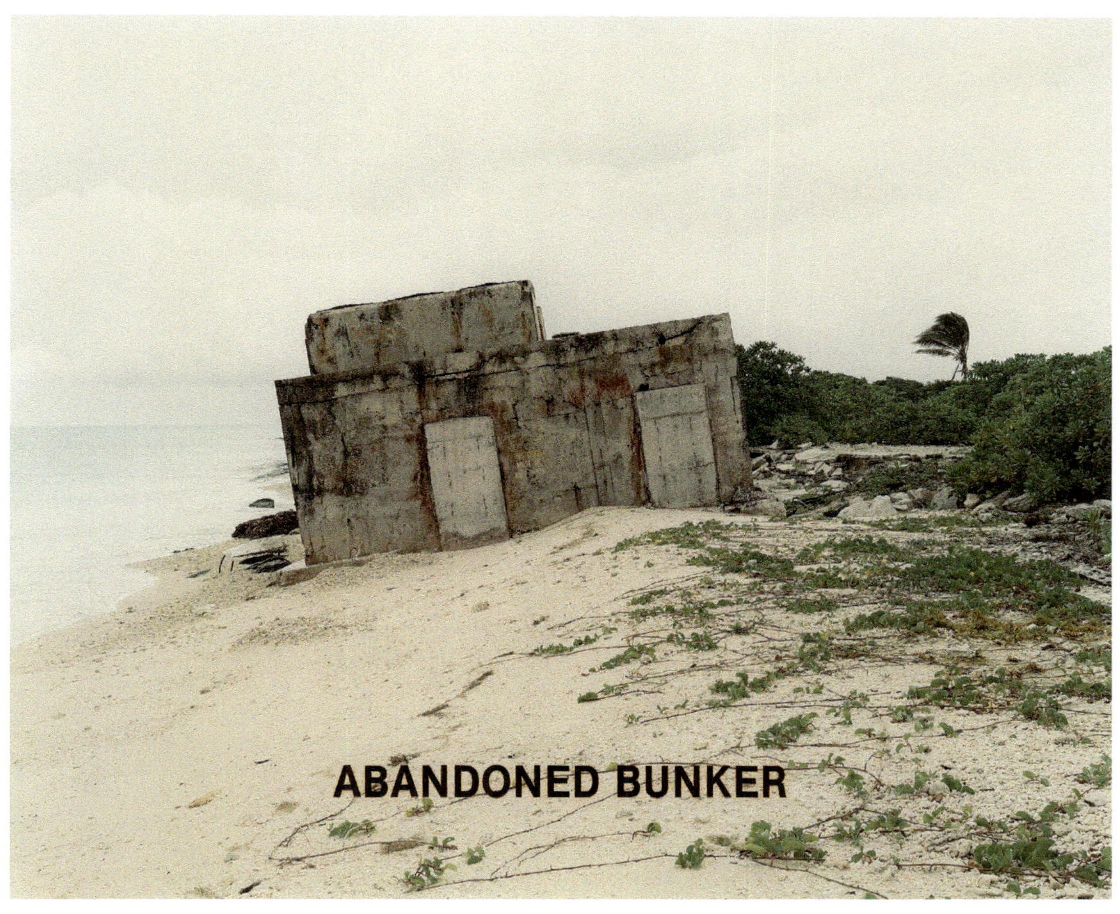

The nuclear temples throughout nuclear landscapes were rarely given lyrical or cosmological names, preferring the mundane, such as, in this case, Station 77. The left door was the entrance to the timing and firing distribution station; the right door led to the telephone switchboard; and the structure on the roof, Station 1511, housed camera mounts. These were constructed for Operation Redwing in 1956, on Runit Island in Enewetak Atoll. Shifting sands have caused this bunker to lean toward the water, a visual metaphor for not just the consequences of severe atomic testing but also the growing challenges of a rising ocean for the people of the Marshall Islands. External gamma radiation from the tests conducted between 1946 and 1958 has rendered the islands essentially unrecoverable. The Quince test, also part of Operation Redwing, misfired on August 6, 1958, spraying plutonium fuel across the island. Soldiers operating bulldozers and other earthmoving equipment pushed the radioactive soil into debris piles, reportedly destined for the lagoon. Soil collected and shipped from Area 10 of the Nevada Test Site replaced the contaminated soil, and other remediation efforts have been attempted. Yet the degree of radioactive contamination is well beyond safe limits, and this will continue for the foreseeable future. Reclaiming a culturally vibrant Marshallese lifestyle in a heavily polluted environment is a serious and complicated challenge, another facet of the nuclear legacy.

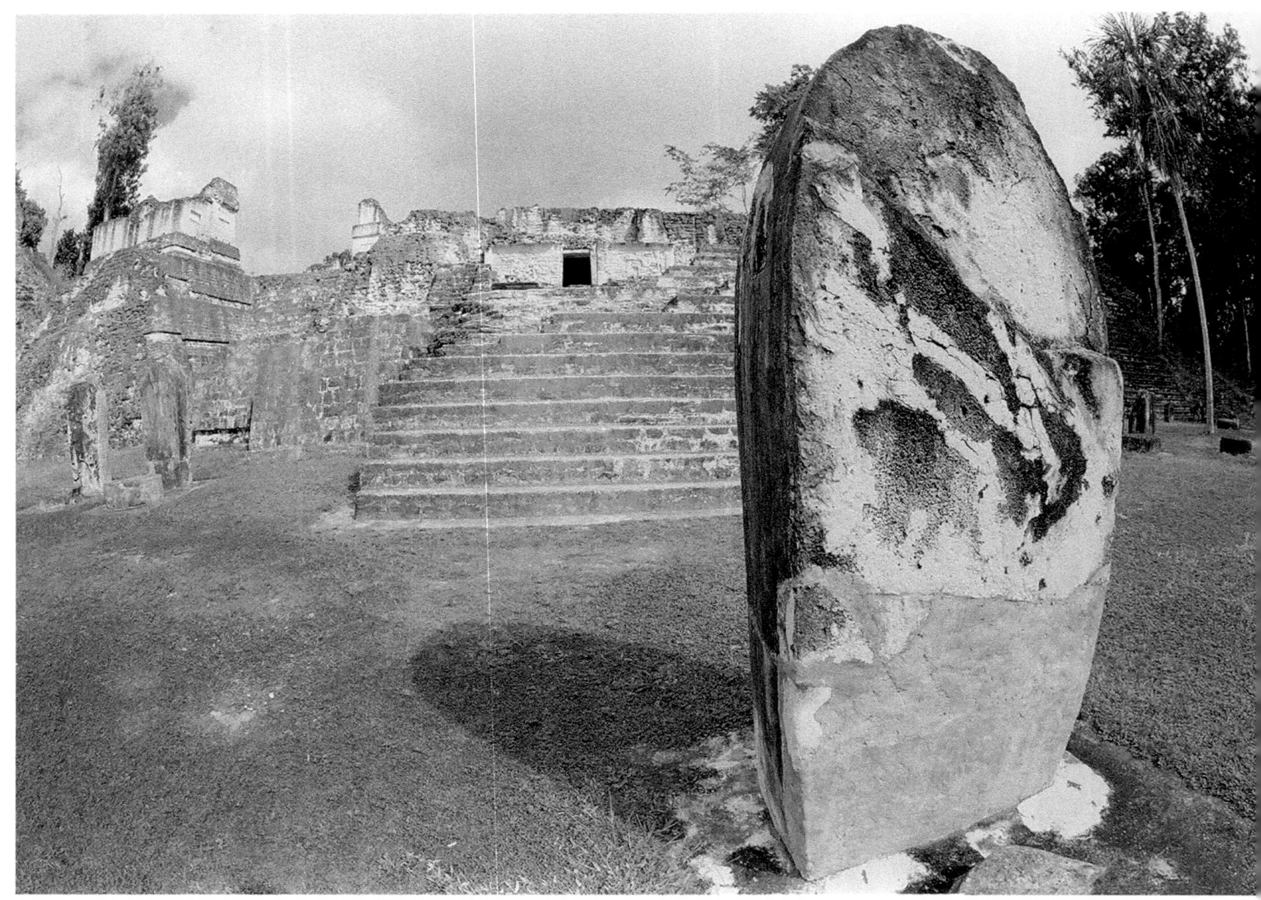

Guatemala's Tikal National Park covers approximately 358 square miles and has thousands of temples and other buildings. It was declared a national monument in 1931 and a national park in 1955, but at the time this black and white photograph was made, very few people visited the site given the arduous journey just to get there. The core of Tikal alone has more than three thousand buildings and covers nearly ten square miles. Today, Tikal is part of the Maya Biosphere Reserve, created in 1990 in part to protect the forests of the Petén, which are under severe pressure from population growth, illegal logging, and slash-and-burn agricultural practices. Most of the dramatic temples were constructed in approximately 750 CE, and at its height, Tikal's population has been estimated at one hundred thousand people. However, by the end of 900 CE, the city had been nearly abandoned. The causes of the collapse remain a mystery, although likely culprits include wars, famine, overpopulation, and resource depletion. The temple structures and defaced stone stelae were covered in vegetation until 1848, when a Guatemalan expedition officially discovered the ruins in the jungle. During the 1950s and 1960s, the Museum of the University of Pennsylvania and the Guatemalan Institute of Anthropology and History restored many of Tikal's structures to a prescribed level of architectural permanence. UNESCO designated the ruins a World Heritage Site in 1979.

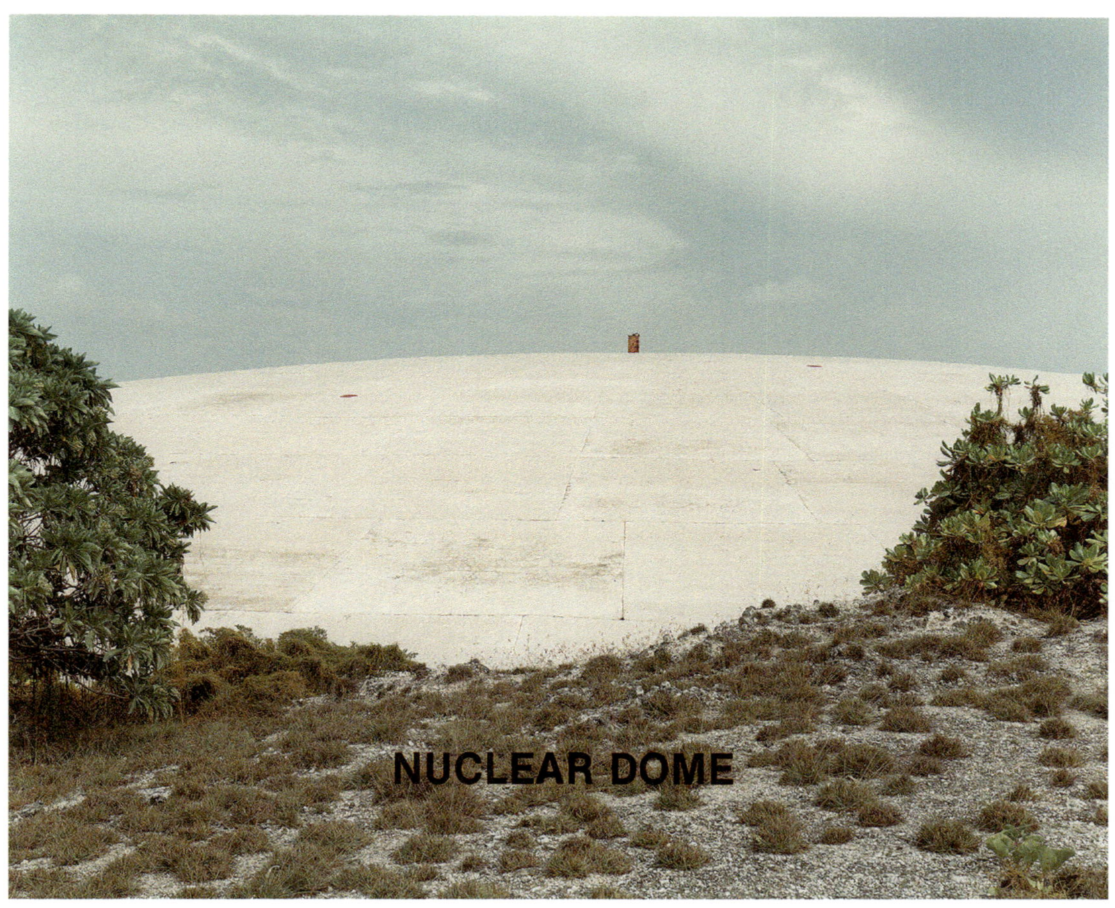

The nuclear detonation Cactus was an eighteen-kiloton weapons-related test that was fired on May 5, 1958, creating a crater 30 feet deep and 350 feet wide at the northern tip of Runit Island in Enewetak Atoll. During the period of clean-up, 111,000 cubic yards of radioactively contaminated soil and debris were entombed beneath an eighteen-inch-thick concrete dome. It took three years and cost $120 million to collect the debris. The crypt is constructed of 358 concrete panels that were built at the site. Later, male workers from the Department of Energy painted an oil can red and placed it at the top of the dome. They then painted a large pink circle around the oil can. From the air, this nuclear dome looked like a huge breast. Due to the circulation of this photograph, citizens in Colorado conducted a mail campaign insisting that the dome was insulting to women and should be cleared of any metaphorical references. While this is a much longer story, the final act was that a crew was sent to do just that. Just two years before this test, the Atomic Energy Commission had already defined the Marshall Islands as the most contaminated landscape in the world. With a rising sea level, the contaminants contained in the dome are vulnerable; a veritable soup of plutonium-laced groundwater is a time bomb of its own.

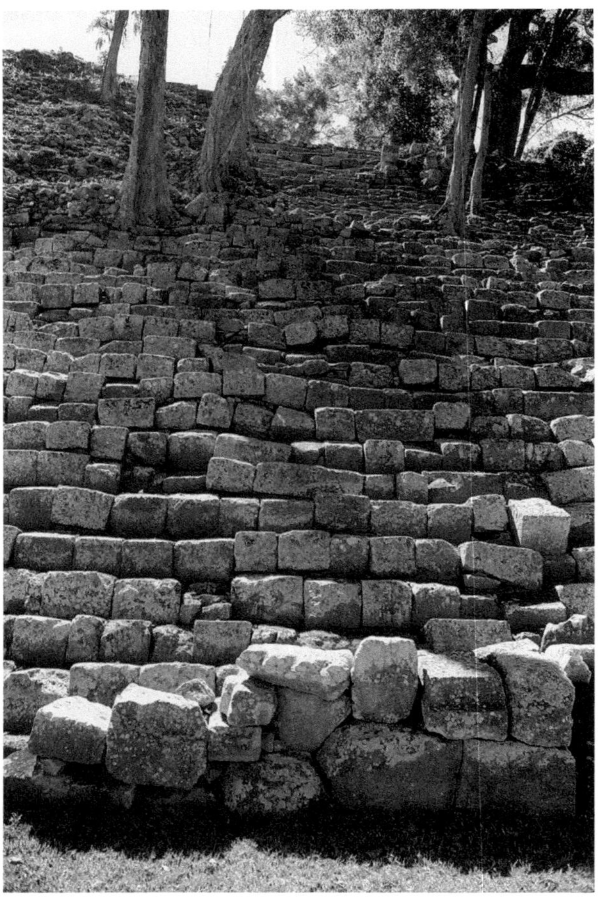

Copán is in western Honduras, close to the border with Guatemala. Flourishing between 426 CE and 820 CE, Copán was at the farthest southeastern edge of the Maya territories. Relatively small by Mesoamerican standards, Copán's city core was only thirty-seven acres. Small as it was, it had one of the most densely populated communities, with a great plaza to the north and a larger acropolis to the south. Using green-tinged volcanic tuff, Copán's artisans constructed the temple of the Hieroglyphic Stairway, with more than two thousand glyphs featured on sixty-three steps, one of the longest Maya inscriptions known. In 1839, Frederick Catherwood drew colorful, detailed drawings of an altar and stelae in the plaza, showing trees growing everywhere among the ruins. The site was thoroughly overgrown and required reconstruction. At first, the temple of the Hieroglyphic Stairway was reconstructed without any particular focus except how the stones fit together; only later did the pieces of the puzzle begin to make narrative sense.

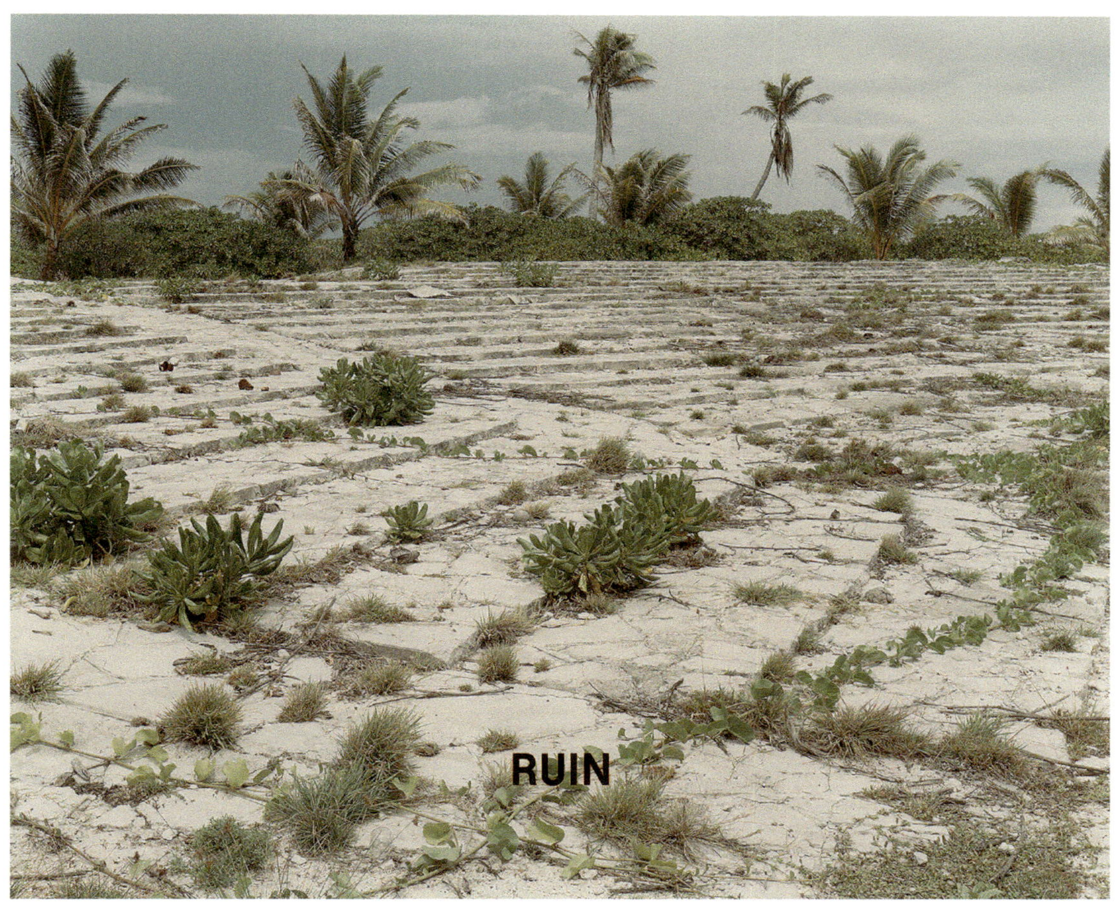

RUIN

As part of the entertainment facilities for test site personnel, a Greek theater was constructed on Enewetak Island during lulls in construction and testing. Although the concept of Greek theater had not been introduced or practiced in the Marshall Islands cultural milieu, either by the native Marshallese or by the military personnel, the metaphorical significance of a tragedy is apropos. In tragedy, the protagonist, usually a person of importance, suffers extreme sorrow especially as a consequence of a tragic flaw, moral weakness, or an inability to overcome a grave circumstance. Of course, the presentations at Enewetak's theater were entertainment of a different sort, but the allusion remains. How can anyone make sense of the nuclear era and its essential embodiment of death and a destroyed world when the presence of nuclear weapons has become part of a global consciousness? The nuclear temples, like Mesoamerican pyramids, have shared paradoxes—of death, of destruction and conquest, and ultimately of redemption. That last chapter remains to be written.

CHAPTER 11

Housewives Petitioning for World Peace

Ban-the-Bomb Activism in Cold War Japan

AKIKO TAKENAKA

In 1955, husband-and-wife artists Maruki Iri and Maruki Toshi revealed the tenth installment of their Hiroshima Panels—a series of fifteen large-scale folding panels on which they chronicled the horrors of nuclear bombings. Depicted on the panel titled *Petition* is a line of people waiting to sign a petition laying on a desk situated at the far right of the panel. At the desk is a mother with a baby on her back; we see her writing on a piece of paper. The attire of the people lined up behind her suggests a variety of occupations—housewives, students, construction workers, a doctor, and a nurse. The accompanying text reads:

> Stop the atomic bomb! Stop the hydrogen bomb! Stop war!
> The appeal of mothers in Tokyo's Suginami Ward spread throughout Japan.
> Children, mothers, fathers, elders, and workers of all kinds signed the petition.
> For the first time, a voice was given to the people's muffled cry, and millions signed the petition for peace.[1]

The petition campaign referenced in the panel collected over thirty million signatures—approximately one-third of the Japanese population—in fifteen months. It was a response to the Castle Bravo thermonuclear weapon test that the United States had conducted on March 1, 1954, at Bikini Atoll in the Marshall Islands. Central to this story was the Japanese fishing boat *Lucky Dragon No. 5*, which was situated eighty-five miles from the explosion site at the time. The explosion produced fallout in the form of pulverized surface coral, and the irradiated ash fell on the twenty-three crew members and their onboard tuna catch.[2] Feeling physically ill and nervous, the men navigated back to their home port at Yaizu, Shizuoka Prefecture, arriving early in the morning of March 14.

News of the nuclear incident broke in Japan two days later, on March 16. The *Yomiuri* newspaper, which broke the news, identified the cause of the illness as nuclear radiation.[3] By this time, however, the tuna had already been shipped to the Tsukiji fish market in Tokyo. The *Asahi* newspaper reported, in the evening edition that day, that scientists measured the radiation levels of what the paper called the "atom bomb fish [*genbaku uo*]" at Tsukiji.[4] The name stuck. The news, especially of the irradiated tuna catch, quickly sparked a nationwide panic. The price of tuna at Tsukiji fell 50 percent the next morning. Consumers avoided fish. But the problem did not end there. Castle Bravo was only the first in the series of nuclear tests dubbed Operation Castle that the United States conducted in the Pacific that year. In April, more tuna catches showed signs of radiation; radiation was also found in the rain that fell on Japanese soil.[5] The amount of radiation in rainwater increased in May. Newspapers warned the public to be cautious of their drinking water. Media fanned the flames with detailed, graphic depictions of radiation illness symptoms. On May 28, the Ministry of Welfare announced that a significant amount of radiation had been detected in various fruits and vegetables.[6] Concerns over food safety, coupled with the fact that this was the third time, after Hiroshima and Nagasaki, that the Japanese had been impacted by nuclear weapons, spurred social activism, primarily in the form of petition campaigns.

To this day the standard narrative in Japan, as depicted in the *Petition* panel, ties the *Lucky Dragon No. 5* incident to the antinuclear petition campaign that was said to have been initiated by ordinary housewives of Suginami Ward in Tokyo.[7] According to this narrative, the campaign subsequently spread nationwide and ultimately resulted in the establishment of the Japan Council against Atomic and Hydrogen Bombs (Gensuibaku Kinshi Nihon Kyōgikai, or Gensuikyō), one of two major antinuclear weapons groups in Japan. The Suginami movement is considered to have transformed the image of peace activism in Japan from that of a politically driven activity led by labor unions and the Japanese Communist Party (JCP) to a nonpolitical movement of ordinary people whose goal was to protect human lives.[8] But the Suginami petition drive was only one part of a much larger movement. Suginami was not the first locality to begin a petition campaign following the *Lucky Dragon No. 5* incident. Many other groups and organizations across Japan collected signatures in response to the irradiated tuna scare. Fishmongers initiated a petition movement at the Tsukiji fish market. Young villagers near the port city of Yaizu gathered signatures. Other wards in Tokyo had petition campaigns. But it is the Suginami housewives' campaign that remains strongest in the Japanese collective memory.

In the Cold War social climate, where activism against nuclear weapons typically was labeled communist, the Suginami campaign was able to maintain a nonpolitical appearance by framing the issue as that of domestic well-being. The accepted narrative was of housewives inspired by concern for the safety of the food their families consumed. As Ann Sherif points out, the story of a "feminized and domesticated movement was more politically palatable to newspaper readers than were the leftist activists who had been protesting in Hiroshima and Nagasaki since 1946."[9] But how were these women able to organize and maintain such a successful movement? How did they come to be in the spotlight? How did the Suginami movement develop into a nationwide movement?

In this chapter, I discuss the ban-the-bomb activism triggered by the *Lucky Dragon No. 5* incident with a focus on how and why the Suginami housewife narrative emerged. Though the Suginami campaign is remembered as grassroots activism initiated by housewives concerned about food safety, there in fact was a local male activist, the international law scholar Yasui Kaoru (1907–80), who had carefully planned and orchestrated the petition campaign, first in Suginami and then nationwide. He had plans to expand the campaign worldwide. Yasui carefully constructed the image of a women-led grassroots movement. Examining this movement allows us to better understand the way the two overlapping categories of women—mothers and housewives—were frequently used in association with the petition.

Yasui Kaoru and the Suginami Women

Reports of the Suginami petition campaign first appeared in the May 14, 1954, morning edition of *Tokyo Asahi* newspaper. The *Asahi* followed up with stories on June 21 and August 9. The articles identified Yasui Kaoru as the organizer, but there is no mention of the Suginami housewives. The evening edition of the August 5 *Asahi* newspaper featured the women for the first time with an article titled "Women's Power Demonstrated in Anti-Nuclear and Hydrogen Bomb Activism." This article, which appeared in the Home (*Katei*) section, also lists Yasui as the organizer. The "women" in the title were the members of the Suginami Federation of Regional Women's Organizations (Suginami Fujin Dantai Kyōgikai), but here again, there is no mention of ordinary housewives from Suginami.[10] In other words, there appears to be a consensus in media reports at the time that the campaign was spearheaded by Yasui Kaoru.

Yet, in pointed contrast, current collective memories of the petition campaign highlight the women. The *Petition* panel credits the Suginami women. In a further example, the official women's history of Suginami Ward describes the women as "housewives who jumped into the campaign with no previous experience in activism."[11] The *Mainichi* newspaper published in recent decades multiple articles related to the petition movement that credit the Suginami housewives.[12] Interestingly, Yasui's writings, from as early as August 1955, make frequent reference to "mothers [*hahaoya-tachi* and *okāsan-tachi*]" as the energy behind the movement, suggesting that it was Yasui himself who highlighted the women's participation in the petition campaign.[13] Who was Yasui Kaoru and why was he deliberately constructing an image of ordinary mothers spearheading the petition movement? And why did the mother narrative shift to the housewife narrative?

Suginami Ward, where Yasui became a peace advocate, was a relatively well-off left-leaning community. Yasui had been a professor of international law at Tokyo Imperial University and had written on what was then called "Greater East Asia international law" during the Asia-Pacific War (1931–45). He was purged from the university in April 1948 for his wartime publications and worked from home as a private lawyer until his purge was lifted in October 1950.[14] The time away from the university allowed Yasui to become fully engaged in his local community for the first time. He became involved in the PTA of the local elementary school (Momoi Daini Shōgakkō), which his daughter Yasuko attended. When the new Suginami library opened in 1952, he was appointed director. In November 1953, a community center was added to the library and Yasui took on its directorship. Yasui was invested in the education of women, especially mothers. He believed that women needed to pay attention to world affairs and think through political and economic issues. He argued that women needed this education to become good mothers.[15]

Once the community center opened, Yasui decided to convene a "reading group for housewives and mothers" with a "deliberate selection of difficult texts."[16] Yasui invited the women, explaining that "we can no longer trust the government from now on. We need to decide and act on our own. To do that, we must read. We must study what is happening in our society, in the world."[17] On November 7, 1953, Yasui held the first session of the Children of the Cedar (Suginoko-kai) reading group with twenty-four women, housewives mostly in their forties. Japan's wartime actions were constantly on his mind. Yasui may have been motivated by his reflection on and regret about his wartime writings, which supported the Greater East Asia Co-prosperity Sphere. Yasui was convinced that mothers were the strongest supporters of peace, but that they needed education to become effective agents of peace. "Mothers' hatred toward war is valuable," he wrote. "But that is not sufficient for protecting peace. They need to study social sciences and learn why war happens and analyze ways to prevent war."[18]

The reading group had a rigid hierarchical structure. Yasui sat at the front of the classroom with the women seated at rows of desks. He imposed strict rules. Many recalled that they did not really understand the content of the books or the discussions. Some later admitted that they did not read the books.[19] But many participants remember feeling a sense of empowerment from the meetings. Some women who studied in the group became activists. For example, Saitō Tsuruko (1909–2000), a mother of four who joined the group in August 1954 in the midst of the petition movement, remained active in her local organization, Kusanomi-kai, and became a trustee of the Lucky Dragon No. 5 Peace Association (Daigo Fukuryūmaru Heiwa Kyōkai) in 1982.[20] Perhaps it was their participation in the petition campaign rather than classroom education that ultimately gave the women a sense of empowerment.

The Suginami Petition Campaign

The April 5, 1954, meeting of the Children of the Cedar group was the first to take place after the *Lucky Dragon* incident. Yasui dedicated a large portion of the meeting to the topic. During the meeting, Ōtsuka Risoko, who had experience with an anticonscription petition campaign during the war, suggested collecting signatures. No decision was reached at that point, however. According to Ōtsuka's recollection, she and several other women gathered in Yasui's office after the meeting. Yasui told the women that he wanted to initiate a nationwide petition campaign but had not been successful convincing leaders of the citizens groups in which he was involved.[21]

Another incident is worth noting. On April 16, the Suginami Federation of Regional Women's Organizations (Suginami Fujin Dantai Kyōgikai, or Suginami Women's Federation)—an alliance of forty-two local women's organizations launched in January 1954 under Yasui's direction—hosted a meeting at the community center.[22] At the end of the meeting, Sugawara Tomiko, a fishmonger's wife who attended as a representative of the local commerce and industry association, stood up and asked the attendees to sign the petition by the Suginami Fish Merchants Union. At the encouragement of Yasui, also in attendance, every attendee signed.[23] Women remained after the meeting to discuss how to engage with the issue. One participant suggested a petition campaign, and the women decided to consult with Yasui. Serving as a liaison between the Suginami Women's Federation and Yasui, Ōtsuka wrote a letter urging him to start the campaign. Ōtsuka remembers Yasui later recalling that the letter was a big encouragement for him.[24]

The petition campaign had been on Yasui's mind, as we can see from his comment during the conversation following the April 5 Cedar group meeting. Also on April 16, Yasui had testified as an expert witness before the Foreign Affairs Committee of the House of Representatives of the Diet that, although taking the issue to an international tribunal was a possibility, the most effective way to appeal to the United States would be by shifting the global discourse.[25] In his later writing, he notes that he had wanted to initiate a mass movement, as he believed that it was "the only method to clearly demonstrate the intention of millions of ordinary people."[26] A worldwide petition campaign would certainly signal a shift in the global discourse.

To challenge the ongoing nuclear weapons testing, Yasui aspired to form a national movement that would later expand globally. He called on members of various citizens groups for a national petition campaign. For example, on April 19 at the meeting of the Citizens Alliance for the Protection of the Constitution (Kenpō Yōgo Kokumin Rengō), Yasui suggested a national petition campaign on the model of the Stockholm Appeal. Members voted to initiate the movement with a goal of ten million signatures but could not agree on a strategy.[27] Yasui later recalled that at that moment he realized that "the conditions were not yet there to develop a nationwide movement."[28] He then conceived a three-stage plan. The first step would be a local movement to take place between April and July 1954. The second step would be a nationwide movement from August to December. His third and final step was to be on an international stage. Yasui believed that the final step needed to begin by January 1955. Otherwise, the "timing would be lost," he wrote.[29] Yasui's strategy was to capitalize on the moment to advance his ongoing efforts to eradicate nuclear weapons.

The women of the Cedar group were the perfect candidates to initiate the first step: a local petition campaign led by members of the reading group that also involved members of the Suginami Women's Federation. Recognizing the interest among some of the women, Yasui decided to encourage them to start the campaign. After all, Yasui had created both the Cedar group and the Suginami Women's Federation. He coached the women through the campaign. But once the women began collecting signatures, Yasui framed his involvement as a response to the concern of many mothers who came to him for support, thereby creating the appearance of a women-led campaign. In his writing, he continued to refer to the women as mothers, emphasizing their domestic quality.[30]

It is curious that Yasui felt the need for a brand-new campaign. Petition campaigns had already started in many areas as early as March 17.[31] On March 31, the Women's Democratic Club (Fujin Minshu Kurabu) began collecting signatures using a bakery storefront in Kōenji, also in Suginami Ward.[32] Suginami resident and history of science scholar Tanaka Minoru also started a study group with members of his community and prepared for a petition movement.[33] The Tokyo Peace Conference (Tokyo Heiwa Kaigi) and Akita Peace Conference (Akita Heiwa Kaigi) started collecting signatures on April 13 and April 15, respectively. On April 18, members of the Umegaoka Housewives Group (Umegaoka Shufukai) embarked on a petition campaign.

It was not only the local organizations and peace groups that collected signatures. Fishmongers, whose businesses were greatly affected by the irradiated tuna, had also taken action. On March 29, Suginami fishmongers established the Suginami Fishmongers Council for Victims of the Hydrogen Bomb (Suginami Gyōshō Suibaku Higaisha Taisaku Kyōgikai). On April 2, approximately five hundred people from various businesses associated with fish (e.g., fishmongers, brokers, port workers' unions, and sushi restaurant unions) gathered in the auditorium of the Tsukiji market to discuss strategies. They agreed to present several demands to the governments of both Japan and the United States and to conduct a petition campaign.[34] On April 12, the Fishmongers Council submitted a petition urging a ban on hydrogen bomb testing to the Suginami District Council.

In the meantime, lawmakers around the country were working on formal resolutions. In mid-March, local legislative offices across the country began approving motions to ban nuclear experiments. During the 19th Diet meeting, both the House of Representatives (April 1) and the House of Councilors (April 5) voted to approve a resolution to appeal to the United Nations to "take measures to facilitate a ban on nuclear weapons and to prevent damage from experiments of nuclear weapons."[35] On April 17, the Suginami District Council voted on an appeal to ban nuclear weapons and sent the appeal to the Japanese government, embassies of the United States, the Soviet Union, and Great Britain, and the United Nations on April 22.[36]

It was not until early May that Yasui's campaign officially launched. On May 9, 1954, Yasui invited Suginami residents to the community center. The meeting resulted in the formation of the Suginami Conference for the Ban-the-Bomb Petition Movement (Gensuibaku Kinshi Shomei Undō Suginami Kyōgikai) with Yasui as the chairman. Members drafted the wording for the petition, which later came to be known as the Suginami Appeal.[37] The petition was an "appeal to the entire world to stop the manufacturing, storage, usage, and experiments of all nuclear weapons, including atom and hydrogen bombs."[38] It consisted of three slogans: (1) Let us all Japanese sign this petition to end atom and hydrogen bombs; (2) Let us appeal to all governments and people of the world; (3) Let us protect the lives and happiness of mankind.[39] Also on May 9, the Suginami Conference approved a timeline that aligned with Yasui's original plan.

The wording of the slogans was carefully planned. The first slogan was meant to include all Japanese regardless of party affiliation, unlike "conventional peace movements that tended to be limited to particular activists, or particular political groups."[40] The second slogan was an attempt to avoid the appearance of an anti-US movement, even though the nuclear testing that triggered the petition had been conducted by the United States. The third slogan asserted that the movement was driven by humanism, not politics.[41] According to Yasui, the main goal of the campaign was to be inclusive. But when we take into account the Cold War climate at the time, in which all antiwar activism, and ban-the-bomb campaigns in particular, were considered communist, we can see that Yasui's strategy was an effort to eliminate any impression that his campaign was driven by JCP members.

A similar strategy can be seen in the additional three points that the group approved: the group's catchphrase would be "Let us protect the life and happiness of mankind"; signatures would be collected by knocking on doors rather than standing at train stations and on street corners (and women were to undertake this task); and the group would focus only on opposing hydrogen bomb experiments.[42] Protecting the life and happiness of mankind is a noncontroversial goal for most. Knocking on doors may not be as efficient as standing at train stations during rush hour, but it creates a personal—not official—impression. And by having women take on the bulk of the signature collection, the campaign could maintain an appearance of women acting out of concern for food safety. The first issue of the group's newsletter, *Suibaku kinshi shomei undō Suginami nyūsu* (Suginami Newsletter for the Hydrogen Bomb Ban Petition Movement), instructed readers not to deviate from the agreed-upon slogan when collecting signatures and to avoid using terms such as *kenpō yōgo* (protection of the constitution) or *dokuritsu* (independence).[43] Here, too, we can see a deliberate attempt to make the campaign seem focused solely on banning a dangerous weapon and not driven by politics. The designation of words to not use also suggests the prevalence of words like *constitution* and *independence* in peace activism at the time.

Women's organizations were mobilized for the petition campaign. For example, the steering committee invited representatives of all the women's organizations in the Suginami Women's Federation to the first meeting on May 13 and requested their cooperation. All the representatives agreed to join the steering committee. By early June, steering committee members totaled 167, with 68 women among them.[44] The official petition campaign by the Suginami Conference began on May 14. During the campaign, the community center, the local PTA, and a women's organization each hosted a lecture to educate the residents on the importance of the petition.[45]

Once the petition campaign began, forms with signatures started flooding in. Yasui quickly embarked on the next step. The original document, the Suginami Appeal from May 1954, had already included their aspirational goal of unifying the various campaigns nationwide under the Suginami umbrella.[46] On June 20, the steering committee members met at the community center to strategize a nationwide movement.[47] Yasui announced on June 27 that the time had come to expand the movement to the national stage. On July 4, several members of the steering committee convened a meeting with representatives of Tokyo-based organizations that were either already participating in some form of petition movement or interested in starting a petition movement.[48] By this point, the number of signatures collected in Suginami amounted to 270,000, of which women had brought in approximately 190,000.[49] Yasui notes that radio and newspaper reporting on Suginami activism inspired and set the stage for the next phase—the national movement.[50] It is worth noting here that local lawmakers already had not only voted to approve the nuclear weapons ban appeal but also supported expanding the campaign nationwide.[51] In other words, although the campaign had successfully created the appearance of a grassroots movement, it had the official support of local lawmakers from the start.

On August 8, 1954, the National Conference for Anti-Atomic and Hydrogen Bomb Petition Movement (Gensuibaku Kinshi Shomei Undō Zenkoku Kyōgikai) conducted its inaugural meeting. The group agreed upon an official appeal, which was published in three magazines, *Sekai*, *Chūō Kōron*, and *Kaizō*. Yasui and Suginami Ward remained central to the national movement. The Suginami slogans that Yasui had drafted were incorporated into the nationwide movement, and the Suginami Community Center became its central office. On August 10, 1954, Yasui published the first issue of the national newsletter for the petition campaign.[52] By early October, ten million signatures had been collected. By December 13, the tally reached twenty million. On December 22, Prime Minister Hatoyama agreed to support the movement. The national movement was a success.

The Women of Children of the Cedar

I now turn to the women of the Children of the Cedar reading group so that we may better understand the gender dynamics in the Suginami petition movement. The women of the reading group have typically been described as "ordinary housewives" and "mothers with little experience in activism." But members who took on leadership roles in the campaign were mostly highly educated women, many with previous activism experience. Nonetheless, Yasui always referred to the women as mothers in his writings; he described them as "mothers who may not be able to accurately grasp the international trends if they tried to study by reading newspapers on their own."[53] Why was it necessary for Yasui to shape the discourse in ways that emphasized the ordinariness of the women involved? What kind of women were in the Children of the Cedar reading group?

Most of the women were indeed mothers. Word of the reading group had spread through the PTA at the Momoi Daini Elementary School, where both Yasui Kaoru and his wife Tazuko were active, and through word of mouth. Most of the early members had been born in the 1900s and 1910s and had not received the nationalistic education that children received in the 1930s and '40s. Almost all had at least a high school education. Some had graduated from a women's college. Some had long been interested in social issues; many were familiar with Marxist thought. Ōtsuka Risoko, for example, had participated in a Marxist reading group while attending a teacher's college for women.[54] Iwashita Ioe was introduced to Marxism while attending an Esperanto study group after graduating from high school. During the war, she was detained by the Suginami Police Department for a week because of the Marxist texts on her bookshelf.[55] Uemura Fumi was a graduate of Tokyo Women's College.[56]

The Sugawaras, the fish store owners who were central to the Suginami movement, also had a history of activism. For example, wife Tomiko, who had called out for signatures at the Suginami Women's Federation meeting, had been arrested and detained for nearly two months in 1928 for demanding better treatment of female bus conductors. Husband Ken'ichi had been an active member of various labor unions. In fact, the two had met through their union activities.[57] Even while operating the fish store, the couple engaged in various activities, such as demanding rice during the war and tax reform after the war. When the *Lucky Dragon No. 5* incident occurred, Tomiko was a representative on the Suginami District Council.[58] Just as many of the Cedar Group women were not ordinary housewives and mothers, Tomiko was not just the wife of a fishmonger. Nonetheless, she is remembered as the fishmonger's wife who needed her store to be able to sell fish again. The activist pasts of these women have been erased from the standard narrative of the petition movement. They are remembered as mothers and housewives who were worried about food safety.

Rewriting the Petition Campaign

Yasui's strategy to create a nonpolitical appearance was not limited to his mobilization of women. He strove to create the image of a petition campaign that was supported by political conservatives and liberals alike. The campaign needed signatures from members of the JCP, but the optics mattered. Elimination of any apparent ties to the JCP was deemed key. Yasui asked the local JCP branch for party members to join the movement as individuals, rather than as party members.[59] To enlist conservative support, he invited former student Makita Kiyoshi, a well-known businessman with trade ties to the United States, to take a leadership role in the campaign.[60] Makita later recalled that the strategy was to highlight his political conservatism so that people hesitant to get involved in what was typically perceived as a left-leaning movement would be more open to participating.[61]

These strategies were crucial to the success of the Suginami petition campaign. In fact, in the village of Yoshinaga, about ten kilometers to the south of Yaizu port, home of the *Lucky Dragon No. 5*, a petition campaign was cut short because of allegations of communist involvement. Just as in Suginami, women played a central role in Yoshinaga Village. Of the 2,000 signatures collected, approximately 1,700 had been collected by members of the local women's group.[62] The Yoshinaga attempt failed, nonetheless. The Suginami campaign succeeded, by contrast, because of careful optics. Yasui strategically placed the women in the forefront and utilized the media to create an image that the campaign was a grassroots effort by ordinary mothers. Women, including those who had been versed in political activism, were painted uniformly as ordinary mothers and housewives. In addition to creating the image of a women-led movement, Yasui also strategically highlighted politically conservative leaders.

Yasui was not alone in depicting the women as ordinary mothers and housewives. Female activists' writings on the "housewives' petition campaign" also characterize the petition collectors as naive housewives. One such example is a May 20, 1954, column in the *Asahi* newspaper by Matsuoka Yōko on members of the Umegaoka Housewives' Group (Umegaoka Shufukai) who began to collect signatures in April. (Matsuoka was a female activist and founder of the Women's Democratic Club who went on to play a central role in the women's liberation movement in the 1970s.) The narrative of the Umegaoka wives, as introduced by Matsuoka, closely resembles that of the Suginami women as depicted by Yasui. "I received a phone call from a woman I did not know," wrote Matsuoka, "who told me that they had collected signatures to protest hydrogen bomb experiments but did not know what to do next." Matsuoka decided to visit and met with about a dozen women who ranged in age from their twenties to their forties "huddled in a small room above a candy store." The women had read in an *Asahi* newspaper article that Mrs. Roosevelt had shared in an American newspaper some Japanese responses to the *Lucky Dragon No. 5* incident. They told Matsuoka that they were so moved they felt compelled to do something. They mimeographed petition sheets and walked around the neighborhood. They quickly collected 1,500 or so signatures but were at a loss as to the next steps. Matsuoka advised the women to send the signatures and a copy of the Housewives' Group newsletter to UN General Assembly president Vijaya Lakshmi Pandit. "The action of these housewives, who hastily acted just because it was 'something that was not good and needed to be stopped' . . . can be considered comically naive," Matsuoka wrote.[63]

Matsuoka's narrative of naive housewives is deceptive, however. In fact, the Umegaoka Housewives' Group's member profile was similar to the Cedar reading group: educated women with experience in activism. Why did Matsuoka, a seasoned activist, feel compelled to depict these women as naive housewives? Had she bought into the "ordinary mothers and housewives" myth that Yasui had played a role in creating? In fact, many writings from the time trivialize Suginami women's activism as mere personal undertakings. In Matsuoka's 1961 essay "In Order to Achieve Peace," for example, she outlines ways that the postwar world was not at peace. She mentions the wars in Korea and Vietnam, the presence of Japan's Self-Defense

Forces, and the continued suffering of the people of Hiroshima and Nagasaki. When Matsuoka's narrative reaches the *Lucky Dragon No. 5* incident and the resulting petition campaign, she writes: "Upon hearing that not only were twenty-three fishermen covered in 'ashes of death' but that fish too were irradiated, many women, now forced to reconsider what to cook for dinner that night, decided that the testing needed to stop and stood up for the petition campaign."[64] Here, she is suggesting that the women did not care about the ongoing war or the suffering that resulted until the impact was felt in their kitchens. Later media reports also used descriptors such as "housewives who need to protect their kitchen." Activists and media reports, then, domesticated the women's petition campaign as that of housewives and mothers only concerned about their dinner.

Housewives and Mothers as Activists

Yasui Kaoru referred to the Suginami women primarily as mothers. News reports at the time, when they did reference the women, described them as housewives. Later depictions of the Suginami women consistently categorized them as housewives. As a practical matter, most of the women fit into both roles. Due to the pronatalist policies of the wartime government, Japan's birthrate during the war was extremely high. Even in 1947, the total fertility rate in Japan was slightly below 4.7, suggesting that the vast majority of women who married had children.[65] The identification of women as housewives had to do with existing consumer advocacy activism by women who identified as housewives. The women who participated in activities to promote peace in the succeeding years and decades typically referred to themselves as mothers rather than housewives. I want to briefly analyze these two terms in the context of 1950s Japan as they relate to women's activism.

Hiratsuka Raichō (1886–1971), for example, used motherhood in her appeal for peace during the negotiations between Japan and the United States for a post–World War II peace treaty. On June 26, 1950, Hiratsuka, together with four other women, sent a letter to special envoy John Foster Dulles demanding comprehensive reconciliation of Japan with all Allied nations rather than just with the United States.[66] The women sent two follow-up letters, dated February 8 and August 15, 1951, signed by a larger number of women. The third letter concludes with the women's appeal for peace as mothers: "We are not politicians, diplomats, or businesspeople, to whom our thoughts and desires may seem unrealistic. But those who observe and consider from certain limited perspectives tend to forget about humanism. As women and as mothers, we protect precious human lives. We wish to think and act from a humanistic standpoint."[67] Hiratsuka's writings and speeches continued to highlight the peaceful nature of mothers both domestically and internationally. The idea of the peaceful mother would become solidified with the 1955 establishment of the Japan Mothers' Congress.

The "housewife" (*shufu*), on the other hand, became a powerful identity for women through consumer advocacy activism by the Japan Federation of Housewives' Associations (Nihon Shufurengōkai, or Shufuren) led by lawmaker Oku Mumeo (1895–1997). Shufuren, with rice paddle (*oshamoji*) and apron (*kappōgi*) as its symbols, advocated for product testing, food safety, and consumer education, among other initiatives. Shufuren, established in 1948, was already a well-known group, having accomplished some victories, including the eradication of defective matches. They had also conducted petition drives in opposition to price increases of rice (December 1950) and of electricity (June 1951 and April 1952).[68]

The activism that followed the *Lucky Dragon No. 5* incident developed out of concern both for food and environmental safety issues and for continued nuclear weapons testing. It therefore was at once a consumer advocacy movement and a peace movement. Some women most likely collected signatures as housewives who were worried about the food they put on the table, just like Matsuoka Yōko suggested. Others, including many of the women who studied with Yasui, thought about the larger implications of nuclear testing and especially what continued testing meant for international peace and security. Their dual identity as mothers and housewives neatly fit into this moment.

It is not clear how many of the Suginami women were members of Shufuren at the time of the petition campaign. But even if they had participated in previous petition campaigns as consumer advocates, they apparently needed to be categorized as "mothers with no prior experience in activism" in the mind of Yasui. This seems to be because the petition movement was, for him, not an act of consumer advocacy. Precisely because the Suginami petition movement was a highly political act for Yasui, the female participants needed to be domesticated as mothers with little experience rather than activist housewives.

The dual presence of the mother and housewife identities propelled the Suginami petition to success. The category of the housewife as consumer advocate had already been established at the time of the Suginami campaign through the successful activities of Shufuren.[69] It seemed natural, then, for many women to participate in a campaign for food safety. The identity of the mother as a peaceful being was gradually taking hold in the uncertainties caused by the Korean War and the US-Japan negotiations to end the Allied occupation. Yasui Kaoru was able to capitalize on this image of the peaceful mother to publicize his campaign. By framing the activism as aiming to protect life rather than oppose war, Yasui succeeded in expanding the campaign nationwide without political interference. At the same time, the presence of the housewife activists—who had successfully conducted petition campaigns in the past, but whom Yasui referred to as mothers without experience in activism—added much-needed energy and experience to the petition campaign. Because the Suginami campaign is remembered as an example of antiwar activism, the presence of housewife consumer advocates has been erased from our collective memory.

Notes

1. Translation is from the Maruki Museum website, accessed January 25, 2023, https://marukigallery.jp/en/hiroshimapanels/.
2. The boat was situated outside the danger zone that the US government had declared. But the explosion proved to be three times larger than what the planners had originally anticipated.
3. *Yomiuri Shinbun*, March 16, 1954.
4. *Asahi Shinbun*, March 16, 1954, evening edition.
5. Yamamoto Akihiro, *Kaku enerugii gensetsu no sengoshi 1945–1960: "Hibaku no kioku" to "genshiryoku no yume"* (Tokyo: Jinbun Shoin, 2012), 116–17.
6. Ōishi Matashichi. *Bikini jiken no shinsō: Inochi no kiro de* (Tokyo: Misuzu Shobō, 2003), 45.
7. See, for example, Kobayashi Yoshie, "Anti-nuclear Movement and Legacies of the Cold War," *Bulletin of Gunma Prefectural Women's University* 34 (2013): 113–23. Scholars have already debunked this myth in passing. My goal here is to critically examine how this myth was created to analyze the gender dynamics in play. See, for example,

Ann Sherif, "Thermonuclear Weapons and Tuna: Testing, Protest, and Knowledge in Japan," in *De-Centering Cold War History: Local and Global Change*, ed. Jadwiga E. Pierper Mooney and Fabio Lanza (London: Routledge, 2013), 15–30; Wesley Sasaki-Uemura, *Organizing the Spontaneous: Citizen Protest in Postwar Japan* (Honolulu: University of Hawai'i Press, 2001), 121.

8. Labor unions and JCP began engaging in peace activism around 1949. Fujiwara Osamu, *Gensuibaku kinshi undō no seiritsu: Sengo Nihon heiwa undō no genzō* (Tokyo: Meiji Gakuin Kokusai Heiwa Kenkyūjo, 1991), 2–6.
9. Sherif, "Thermonuclear Weapons and Tuna," 21.
10. *Asahi Shinbun*, August 5, 1954.
11. Suginami-ku Joseishi Hensan no Kai, ed., *Suginami no joseishi: Ashita e no suimyaku* (Tokyo: Gyōsei, 2002), 15.
12. *Mainichi Shinbun*, November 6, 1994, December 11, 1994, September 4, 1995, August 8, 1996, March 7, 2004 (two articles), July 23, 2012, and January 30, 2019.
13. For example, Yasui Kaoru, *Minshū to heiwa* (Tokyo: Ōtsuki Shoten, 1955).
14. Yasui's wartime work was understood to have supported Japan's role as the leader of the Greater East Asia Co-prosperity Sphere and suggested that Japan could be the liberator of Asia. His wartime writings include "Wakai Nihon no hitotsu no dōkō," *Nihon hyōron* 13, no. 10 (September 1938); and "Daitōa Sensō to Shina Jihen," *Kokusaihō gaiō zasshi*, August 1942.
15. Yasui Kaoru, "Tokubetsuku no shakai kyōiku," *Kusei shunjū* 2 (February 1954). Reprinted in "Michi" kankō iinkai, ed., *Michi: Yasui Kaoru sei no kiseki* (Tokyo: Hōsei Daigaku Shuppan, 1983), 159–69.
16. Based on recollections by Yasui's former student Hosoya Chihiro, interview with Hosoya Chihiro, December 9, 1981. Transcript available in Suginami Kuritsu Kōminkan o Sonzoku Saseru-kai, *Rekishi no taiga wa nagare tsuzukeru: Suginami Kōminkan no rekishi* (Tokyo: Suginami Kuritsu Kōminkan o Sonzoku Saseru-kai, 1984), 3:21–24. Hereafter cited as *RTNT*.
17. Ōsono Tomokazu, "Gensuikin no rūtsu: Suginami no shufu tachi wa ima," *Ushio* 277 (May 1982): 143.
18. Yasui, "Nan no tame no dokusho ka," *Suginoko* 7 (December 1959), reprinted in "Michi" Kankō Iinkai,ed., *Michi*, 172–73.
19. Interview date March 31, 2000. Transcript available in Chiiki Joseishi o Tsukuru-kai, ed., *Suginoko Dokushokai de mananda josei tachi: Gakushū kara jissen e* (Tokyo: Chiiki Joseishi o Tsukuru-kai, 2003), 45–49. Hereafter cited as *SDMJT*.
20. Nagahara Kazuko, "Hikaku no sekai o mezashite: Kusanomi-kai Saitō Tsuruko no kiseki," in *Genbaku to genpatsu sono saki: josei tachi no hikaku no jissen to shisō*, ed. Hayakawa Noriyo and Esashi Akiko (Tokyo: Ochanomizu Shobō, 2016), 63.
21. Maruhama Eriko, *Gensuikin shomei undō no tanjō: Tokyo Suginami no jūmin pawā to suimyaku* (Tokyo: Gaifūsha, 2011), 280.
22. Suginami-ku Joseishi Hensan no Kai, *Suginami no joseishi*, 172, 176.

23. Suginami Kuritsu Kōminkan, *Kōminkan no rekishi o tadoru: 1954–1989, 35 nenkan no kiroku* (Tokyo: Suginami Kuritsu Kōminkan, 1989), 21.
24. Ōtsuka Risoko to Hashimoto Ryōichi (date unknown), cited in Maruhama, *Gensuikin shomei undō no tanjō*, 290.
25. "Dai 19-kai Kokkai Shūgiin Gaimu Iinkai gijiroku," accessed through the National Diet Library Diet Minutes Database.
26. Yasui, *Minshū to heiwa*, 55.
27. Maruhama, *Gensuikin shomei undō no tanjō*, 283.
28. Yasui, *Minshū to heiwa*, 55.
29. Yasui, *Minshū to heiwa*, 56.
30. Former student Hosoya Chihiro also recalls that "although the ban-the-bomb movement is remembered as an organic movement initiated by the mothers of the Cedar group, Yasui was in fact the driving force behind it." Interview with Hosoya Chihiro, dated December 9, 1981, transcript in *RTNT*, 3:21–24.
31. Kobayashi Tōru, ed., *Gensuibaku kinshi undō shiryōshū*, vol. 1 (Tokyo: Ryokuin Shobō, 1995), xx. Hereafter cited as *GKUS*.
32. Maruhama, *Gensuikin shomei undō no tanjō*, 275.
33. Maruhama, *Gensuikin shomei undō no tanjō*, 276.
34. *GKUS*, 69–70.
35. The petition is reprinted in *GKUS*, 6.
36. Maruhama, *Gensuikin shomei undō no tanjō*, 289.
37. Transcript from this meeting and the list of attendees is reprinted in *GKUS*, 108–22.
38. Yasui, *Minshū to heiwa*, 57–58.
39. Yasui, *Minshū to heiwa*, 59.
40. Yasui, *Minshū to heiwa*, 59.
41. Yasui, *Minshū to heiwa*, 59–60.
42. Maruhama, *Gensuikin shomei undō no tanjō*, 308.
43. *Suibaku kinshi shomei undō Suginami nyūsu*, vol. 1, May 20, 1954, reprinted in *GKUS*, 119–20.
44. *Heiwa Tsūshin* 51, July 14, 1954, reprinted in *GKUS*, 77–98.
45. *Heiwa Tsūshin* 51, July 14, 1954, reprinted in *GKUS*, 77–98.
46. Maruhama, *Gensuikin shomei undō no tanjō*, 296–97.
47. Reprinted in *RTNT*, 4:52–57.
48. Transcript of the meeting is included in *Heiwa tsūshin*, no. 51 (July 14, 1954), reprinted in *GKUS*, 77–98.
49. According to another account, of the 270,000 collected by July 4, 1954, all but 16,000 were collected by going from door to door. *Heiwa tsūshin*, no. 51 (July 14, 1954), reprinted in *GKUS*, 77–98. Yasui notes that the number of signatures collected exceeded 285,000, of which "wives and mothers" collected over 200,000. Yasui, *Minshū to heiwa*, 61.
50. Yasui, *Minshū to heiwa*, 62.

51. Maruhama, *Gensuikin shomei undō no tanjō*, 325.
52. *Gensuibaku kinshi shomei undō zenkoku nyūsu*. The first four issues are reprinted in *RTNT* 4.
53. Yasui, *Minshū to heiwa*, 50.
54. Interview dated June 23, 1998, *SDMJT*, 36–38.
55. Interview dated March 31, 2000, *SDMJT*, 45–49.
56. Interview dated November 5, 2001, *SDMJT*, 13–14.
57. Interview dated May 28, 2001, Suginami-ku joseishi hensan no kai ed., *Suginami no joseishi*, 215.
58. A brief description of the couple's activism is included in Takeda Taijun, *Nihon no fūfu* (Tokyo: Asahi Shinbunsha, 1963), 71–78.
59. Maruhama, *Gensuikin shomei undō no tanjō*, 290–91.
60. Makita had been involved in trade deals through the US Ministry of Defense for "machinery necessary for production of weapons," and therefore could be considered a champion of the US-Japan alliance. Maruhama, *Gensuikin shomei undō no tanjō*, 294.
61. Makita interview with Yasui Tazuko and Itō Akemi, November 13, 1984, transcript in *RTNT*, 4:104–5.
62. Owada Michiko, "Daigo Fukuryūmaru no Bikini hisai to Hahaoya Taikai, Kuboyama Suzu," in *Genbaku to genpatsu, sono saki*, 21.
63. *Asahi Shinbun*, May 20, 1954, evening edition.
64. Matsuoka Yōko, "Heiwa o kakuho suru tame ni," in *Nihon no okāsan-tachi*, ed. Nihon Hahaoya Taikai Renrakukai (Tokyo: Awaji Shobō, 1961), 209.
65. "Trends in Number of Births and TFR: Japan, 1947–2007," available at https://www.un.org/esa/socdev/family/docs/egm09/figures.pdf.
66. Hiratsuka Raichō et al., "Hi-busōkoku Nihon josei no kōwa mondai ni tsuite no kibō yōkō," June 26, 1950, reprinted in *Gendai Nihon josei no shutai keisei*, ed. Chiba Yōichi (Tokyo: Domesu Shuppan, 1996), 2:133.
67. "Mi-tabi hi-busōkoku Nihon josei no heiwa seimei," August 15, 1951, reprinted in *Gendai Nihon josei no shutai keisei*, 2:143–45.
68. *Shufuren no ayumi*, official website of Shufuren, accessed July 11, 2020, https://shufuren.net/introduction/003-2/.
69. That the idea of the *shufu* had a strong social presence at the time can also be observed from the "housewife debate (shufu ronsō)" that began in early 1955. See, for example, Jan Bardsley, *Women and Democracy in Cold War Japan* (London: Bloomsbury, 2014), ch. 3; Ueno Chizuko, ed., *Shufu ronsō o yomu* (Tokyo: Keisō Shobō, 1982).

Voices of Deep-Sea Tuna Fishermen in the Japanese Anti–Nuclear Test Movement

YUKA TSUCHIYA MORIGUCHI

CHAPTER 12

The Japanese antinuclear movement flared up after the tragic death of Kuboyama Aikichi, chief radio operator of the Japanese tuna fishing vessel *Lucky Dragon No. 5*, which was exposed to radioactive fallout near Bikini Atoll in the 1954 US nuclear test in the Pacific. The so-called *Lucky Dragon* incident happened when the boat, with a crew of twenty-three men, was operating 160 kilometers east of the hypocenter of the Bravo thermonuclear test on March 1, 1954. The radioactive fallout rained down on the crew, and all of them showed symptoms of acute radiation sickness. They were immediately hospitalized upon returning to their home port, Yaizu in Shizuoka Prefecture, but Kuboyama died six months later. Although the immediate cause of his death was said to be hepatitis contracted through blood transfusion, his death symbolized the inhumanity of thermonuclear tests and stirred up great sorrow and anger among the Japanese.[1]

In chapter 11, Akiko Takenaka discusses and revises the conventional narratives depicting a movement mainly carried out by urban, middle-class housewives aligned with intellectuals, students, and teachers. Missing from such stories are not only gender perspectives, as Takenaka has aptly pointed out, but also the voices of the primary victims of the nuclear test: the Japanese tuna fishermen and their families. Where were the tuna fishermen during the upheaval of the antinuclear movement in the aftermath of the *Lucky Dragon* incident? Moreover, US nuclear tests in the Pacific did not end with the *Lucky Dragon* incident. Two more rounds of nuclear test series, Operation Redwing in 1956 and Operation Hardtack in 1958, continued to endanger tuna fishermen's lives. However, there is very little information in the existing literature, either in English or Japanese, about the reactions of the tuna fishermen and their families. This chapter explores this grossly overlooked aspect of the history of the Japanese antinuclear movement by examining the records of three Pacific coast towns of Japan—Misaki, Yaizu, and Muroto, all important ports for deep-sea tuna fishing operations. My observations are based on a series of interviews that I carried out in 2014–18 with retired tuna fishermen and their families, as well as research in local archives and publications in those three towns. The results provide a much more comprehensive and nuanced understanding of the Japanese antinuclear movement after the *Lucky Dragon* incident.

Silence

The 1950s and '60s were the heyday of the Japanese tuna fishing industry, especially because the export of frozen tuna to US canneries became a lucrative business. The tuna fishing business in this period operated under a dual economic structure. On the one hand, capital-rich seafood companies such as Nippon Suisan (abbreviated as Nissui) and Nippon Reizō (abbreviated as Nichirei) were building tuna ships of around five hundred tons or larger with modern freezing systems. These ships could navigate to distant fishing grounds without frequent refueling and store large amounts of catch in the freezing room at a very low temperature. They could thus continue expeditions without returning home for more than a year. Some of these large ships were mother ships accompanied by as many as a dozen catcher boats. The catcher boats either were loaded on board the mothership or formed a convoy that followed the mother ship all the way to the fishing ground, periodically receiving food and fuel from the mother ship. The fishermen employed by seafood companies worked on a contractual basis, receiving monthly salaries sent directly home, plus a commission depending on the volume of the catch in each expedition. Misaki port in Kanagawa Prefecture, about fifty-five miles southeast of Tokyo, was a typical example, as the deep and wide port structure could accommodate the large ships owned by seafood companies. Many fishermen from small villages moved to Misaki as migrant workers, sometimes accompanying their families, and were employed as crew. With crew on board, the large ships went on fishing expeditions for one to two years. To be sure, there were also smaller tuna boats in Misaki. However, no other port could accommodate as many large ships, nor was there any tuna port so close to Tokyo. For these reasons, Misaki became the mecca of the Japanese tuna industry.[2]

In contrast, there were more traditional tuna fishing towns that operated under a completely different economic system. Muroto in Kōchi Prefecture, located 470 miles from Tokyo and on a different island, was a typical example. Yaizu in Shizuoka Prefecture, about 140 miles southeast of Tokyo and the home port of the *Lucky Dragon No. 5*, was another. The traditional patriarchal order in the family, community, and fishing business was pervasive in those places. In my 2017 interviews with retired tuna fishermen and their families in Muroto, the interviewees told me that shipowners (*senshu*) were addressed as "master," and the chief fisherman (*sendō*) and crew members were knit into a vertical hierarchy. Fishermen were employed mostly through introductions from families and acquaintances. Their boats were typically around one hundred to three hundred tons. Their reward system was the traditional *buai-sei*, or commission system. The shipowners paid "preparation money" to the crew before their departure, which they would use to buy food, clothes, and other necessary items. When they caught a shipload of fish, they would return to any Japanese port where the market price of fish was good. The total sales, after deducting fuel and bait expenses, were divided between the shipowner and the crew members, 60 percent to the owner and 40 percent to the crew. The crew share was divided based on rank: the chief fisherman received four parts (*yo-nin-mae*), the chief engineer two parts (*ni-nin-mae*), a regular fisherman one part (*ichi-nin-mae*), and a novice fisherman a half (*han-nin-mae*). The preparation money "borrowed" from the shipowner was deducted from the salaries. When the fishermen did not receive enough to support their families, they further "borrowed" from the shipowner. Women were also integrated into the organic structure of the tuna fishing business. The shipowner, the crew, and their families consisted of a large "family" united by a common fate. Women raised children, grew rice and vegetables, tended to their houses, and did everything else during the prolonged absence of men. Tuna fishing expeditions lasted from six months to two or three years, depending on the size of the ship and the location of the fishing grounds. The whole community formed an organic cosmos where both men and women were an integral part of the tuna business and culture.[3]

There were reasons that fishermen in the first category—that is, those on large seafood companies' ships—did not participate in the antinuclear movement. In large-scale tuna fishing, the typical target was albacore, the species of tuna best for canning. The frozen albacore were exported mainly to the United States and used for canned tuna—Chicken of the Sea in the famous brand name by Van Camp seafood company. Albacore fishing grounds are scattered broadly worldwide, so modern ships with large fuel tanks and freezers sailed long distances, bypassing the Pacific nuclear testing grounds. Unlike fishermen on smaller vessels, they were not ordered to abandon their catch because of radioactive pollution, for they caught tuna far from the danger zone and exported directly to the United States. As a result, fishermen on those ships were less aware of the danger of radioactive fallout as compared to fishermen operating on smaller vessels. In my interviews with fishermen who migrated from Ehime Prefecture to Misaki port to get on board Nissui or Nichirei tuna ships, the interviewees stated that they "did not know anything about nuclear tests" or that they thought "the *Lucky Dragon* incident was already over" when they went on tuna fishing expeditions. In fact, however, US and UK nuclear tests in the Pacific continued until 1963, so some of my interviewees were actually on board while those tests were ongoing. Therefore, one reason for the fishermen's silence about nuclear tests can be summarized as their containment in large companies' ships, both literally and figuratively. Literally, they did not feel any immediate danger in large ships sailing far from the test site, even if they were unknowingly exposed to radioactive rain or contaminated seawater. Figuratively, they were contained in the global capitalist system as employees of large seafood companies. The price of albacore was not affected by nuclear tests, and neither were their salaries. Some of my interviewees even lived in Nissui's branch office in Argentina, where they caught albacore that was exported to the United States. Their life was remote from the antinuclear movement in Japan.[4]

Fishermen in the second category—that is, those on smaller tuna boats in Muroto or Yaizu—had totally different reasons for refraining from criticizing the nuclear tests. The traditional hierarchy made it difficult for them to raise any voice of protest. They did not want to offend the shipowners because their lives depended on the shipowners' paternalistic care. As mentioned above, rank and file crew members received only meager shares of the total profit, and they often borrowed money from shipowners. Also, the nature of small-scale tuna fishing expeditions made teamwork extremely important. When one or two dozen men spent many months in small vessels, vertical order and mutual cooperation were a matter of life and death. Their families also had to help each other while the men were at sea. In such an organic world, voicing political opinions might disrupt the social order and harmony. Thus, the fishermen and their families chose to remain silent.[5]

Moreover, it was the small-scale fisheries that were dramatically affected by the fall of the market prices caused by the nuclear tests. This reality could work either way, pushing the fishermen either to participate in the antinuclear movement or to remain silent. The majority of fishermen in Muroto and Yaizu chose the latter. Their boats were small (although some shipowners in Muroto and Yaizu built larger boats toward the end of the 1950s) and could not sail to the Atlantic Ocean or the African coast. Instead, they operated in the Pacific, near the danger zone. Moreover, because their freezers were small and could not store large volumes of frozen fish, they targeted more expensive species of tuna, particularly bluefin used for sushi and sashimi in the domestic market. When they brought the fish back to Japanese ports, however, the Ministry of Welfare inspectors were waiting with Geiger counters. When the spot check showed abnormal levels of radiation, they were forced to abandon the whole catch. Rumors of radioactive tuna spread throughout the nation, and consumers were thrown into panic. The University of Tokyo Hospital, where the *Lucky Dragon* crew had been hospitalized, was flooded with outpatients who felt sick from "eating fish from Yaizu." Misinformation circulated, and the market price dropped sharply. Everyone in the tuna industry, including fishermen and shipowners, wanted to erase the public memory of radioactive tuna as soon as possible.[6]

Figure 12.1 shows the desperate efforts that fishermen, fish dealers, and the government authorities in Yaizu were making a few months after the *Lucky Dragon* incident. These flyers reveal the dilemma that tuna fishermen faced: they were victims of nuclear tests, yet they also had their livelihood to consider. To convince consumers that tuna were safe, they could not complain about the hazard of nuclear tests.[7]

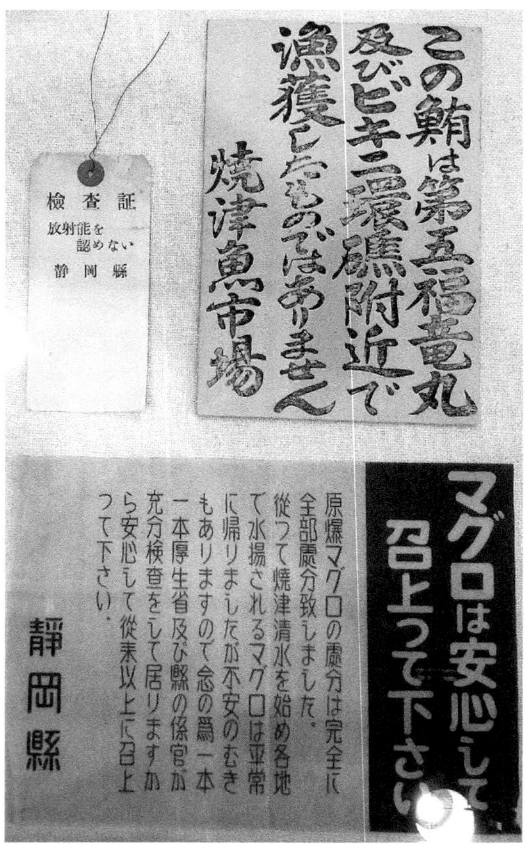

FIGURE 12.1. The upper poster, stating that "These tuna fish were not caught by the *Lucky Dragon No. 5*, or anywhere near the Bikini Atoll," was posted at the Yaizu fish market. The lower poster was distributed by the Shizuoka prefectural government, and reads, "Please consume tuna with no worries. All the radioactive tuna has been completely disposed of. Therefore, tuna fish unloaded in Yaizu, Shimizu, and other ports are safe. Because consumers are still concerned, the Ministry of Welfare and prefectural staff are examining each individual tuna for radioactivity. So please feel at ease and eat more tuna." Courtesy of Yaizu City History and Folklore Museum (Yaizu-shi Rekishi Minzoku Shiryo-kan).

In all three towns, Japanese discrimination against *hibakusha*, or victims of radiation, constituted another reason why tuna fishermen had to remain silent. The chief radio operator of *Kōei-maru No. 13*, another tuna fishing boat polluted by radioactive fallout, was living with his family in Misaki. When his wife tried to wash her husband's clothes at the public hydrant, she was stopped by her landlord. She eventually had to move back to her hometown with her children because of the neighbors' suspicion that their family was "contaminated." In Yaizu, the *Lucky Dragon* crew, many of whom were single young men, were shocked to hear young girls interviewed on a TV program saying that they did not want to marry any of them. When travelers from Yaizu checked into hotels and gave their addresses, they were politely told that there were no rooms for them.[8]

In sum, unlike urban, middle-class antinuclear activists, tuna fishermen and their families had complicated relationships with the nuclear tests. Although they were undoubtedly the direct victims of the tests, they had various reasons to not directly express their anger and criticism. If they wanted to live decently and avoid troubles with their neighbors and colleagues, they thought they needed to keep their mouths shut about nuclear issues. In some cases, however, anger outweighed prudence.

Misaki

Although Misaki port accommodated many large ships, there were also many small to medium-size tuna boats owned by independent shipowners. The 119-ton *Kōei-maru No. 13* was an example. The vessel was operating 230 miles east of the danger zone around Bikini Atoll on March 6–14, 1954. Since they started their fishing operations five days after the US nuclear test at Bikini and washed the ship thoroughly after they heard the news of the test, the crew were not concerned about radioactive pollution. However, when the vessel returned to Misaki port, examination by a Ministry of Welfare inspector showed an extraordinary level of radioactivity: 10,995 counts per minute on the lamp shade, 1,158 on the buoys, 252 on the deck, 112 from the yellowfin tuna, and 132 from the bigeye tuna. The fishermen were ordered to abandon their catch three hundred miles off the coast, where the fast and warm Kuroshio Current would quickly rot the fish meat and sink it deep into the sea. As he watched fifty thousand kilograms of fish sinking into the water, one fisherman murmured that he "felt as if he was throwing away his own son." The fishermen wanted to do something to express their anger and concern. On May 1 that year, they issued an "Appeal to Fellow Citizens," which stated:

> We are the crew members of the *Kōei-maru No. 13*. Our ship received radiation hazard and we were unaware of it. We are still receiving health checks at hospitals, which showed we had a white blood cell count of around four thousand to five thousand. Some of us feel exhausted. We cannot go on fishing operations, so we decided to leave the ship we have long been on board. . . . We received unfair treatment in many ways since we returned to our home port. We continued fishing for more than fifty days on the wide ocean with barely five hours of rest each day. We caught fish almost in exchange for our

> life and were ordered by the Ministry of Welfare to throw the fish away in the deep sea, where we had to sail for three days and nights. We had to throw fish, clothes, boots, and everything else into the sea. This is something we will never forget for the rest of our lives. Our fellow citizens! Words are not enough to express how we felt when our fish sank into the ocean one by one. Why do we have to go through such an ordeal, when all the Japanese people love peace from the bottom of our hearts? We really hate nuclear bombs. We really hate the United States. . . .
>
> Our fellow peace-loving citizens! . . . We will not give up. We will sit in the prefectural government, go on hunger strike, and battle to the end of our lives. We will fight until we receive real compensation. Give us compensation immediately and guarantee the livelihood of nuclear test victims! We appeal to our fellow peace-loving citizens all over the country to join us, especially laborers, farmers, and merchants, who have to work hard to earn a living. Protect the freedom of the high seas! Stop nuclear tests! And bring peace on the whole earth! If we cannot realize these demands, that virtually means death to us. Our fellow peace-loving citizens! Please support us![9]

Most of the *Kōei-maru* crew never got on board the ship again, and many went home to other parts of Japan. Since tuna fishermen in a big port like Misaki came from all over the country, once they were off board, it was difficult to reunite them. Thus the crew members who issued the "Appeal to Fellow Citizens" disbanded without any further action. *Kōei-maru No. 13* went on another expedition in 1956, composed mainly of different crew members, but was shipwrecked by a typhoon. All crew members died, including those who had participated in the appeal. Although the shipowner later received a portion of the US solatium—3,900 thousand yen (approximately US $11,000 at the exchange rate of those days), it is unclear how much was actually distributed to the fishermen, who had already left Misaki.[10]

According to the records of Miura City, more than 150 tuna ships belonging to Misaki port were exposed to radioactive fallout from the 1954 Bravo test series. Many tuna fishermen became ill and died young. However, since most of them were not natives of Misaki and went home to different parts of Japan when they fell ill, it was difficult to keep track of them. As a result, although sporadic antinuclear activities occurred in Misaki, it was difficult to maintain the momentum.[11]

Yaizu

When the *Lucky Dragon No. 5* returned to Yaizu port and crew members were hospitalized, their friends and families started the Villagers' Voice movement, a grassroots initiative to oppose nuclear tests and demand compensation. Residents of Yoshinaga Village, six miles south of Yaizu port and home to five of the twenty-three *Lucky Dragon* crew members, collected approximately two thousand signatures from the six thousand villagers in less than one month and submitted them to the village authorities and the Yaizu City's Ad Hoc Headquarters for Handling the *Lucky Dragon* Incident. According to the signature book stored at the Yaizu City History and Ethnology Museum, the majority (80–90 percent) of the signers were farmers, but sixty-one signers indicated "fisherman" as their occupation. Thus, the fishermen did not shy away from this movement.

The three express purposes of the petition were: (1) to express the villagers' support for the victims of the *Lucky Dragon* incident and their families; (2) to express gratitude for the warm support from all over Japan; and (3) to appeal to people all over the world to use nuclear energy only for the welfare of human beings and to ban testing and use of nuclear weapons.[12]

The movement started when a former classmate of the *Lucky Dragon* fishermen, Yamada Tomihisa, wanted to do something, knowing that his friends were suffering from radiation sickness. Yamada was not a political activist but a simple working-class young man. Born in 1929, he enrolled in technical school in Tokyo after graduating from an elementary school in Yoshinaga. After the war, he took a job at a hardware store in a neighboring town. He would later distance himself from the antinuclear movement when it became highly politicized and split over Communist versus Socialist Party lines. "An institutionalized peace movement run by political parties or unions," he believed, "could not serve ordinary people."[13]

After talking with his wife, Yamada met with four former classmates and discussed how they could support the victims. They contacted more of their former classmates and also consulted Ōba Etsuro, a junior high school teacher and leader of the Yoshinaga Village Youth Organization. Ōba played an important role in encouraging Kuboyama Suzu, the widow of Kuboyama Aikichi, to cooperate with the antinuclear movement. By May 1, the number of participants had expanded to forty, and they unanimously supported Yamada's proposal to collect signatures. They talked to Tomoda Tetsu, a candy shop owner and leader of the village women's organization. She was respected by villagers as a dynamic and reliable "big sister," and when she decided to cooperate with the movement, many villagers, especially women, followed suit.[14]

Interestingly, their activism was related to Japanese post–World War II democratization. The Japanese people embraced democratization promoted by the US occupation forces after many years of government control and censorship, and young people in Yoshinaga Village, influenced by such an atmosphere, engaged in various progressive activities.[15] They issued a journal, titled *Monthly Yoshinaga*, where they published poems, novels, and opinion pieces. Yamada was involved in this literary movement. Because of this context, expressing their opinions against nuclear tests came quite naturally to the young people in Yoshinaga Village.[16]

Although Yamada and the others embraced a progressive ideology and Ōba was a member of the leftist Teachers Union, the group carefully distinguished itself from any political party lines. Their activities were announced in two newspapers: the *Asahi*, a mainstream newspaper known for its moderate liberal stance; and *Akahata*, the Japan Communist Party's official paper. When village authorities became aware of the *Akahata* article, they summoned the women's organization leader and pressed for an explanation. Some signees were upset for being "duped" into cooperating with Communists. The local police started to keep them under surveillance. Yamada and his colleagues decided to wrap up the movement quickly to avoid further problems. On June 6, they held a ceremony at Yaizu High School auditorium and submitted the petition to the village office. Ōba contributed an opinion piece to *Sekai*, a well-known progressive journal, saying, "We do not want to attach any political meaning to the Villagers' Voice movement in Yoshinaga Village because it was promoted by friendship and the humanitarian awareness of the victims' former classmates."[17]

As mentioned earlier, Ōba played an important role in encouraging Kuboyama Suzu to voice antinuclear opinions publicly.[18] Born to a humble farmers' household and married into a fisherman's family, Suzu was not accustomed to public attention. Upon receiving 6.5 million yen (US $18,000 at the exchange rate of those days) as part of the two-million-dollar solatium, she was exposed to the jealousy and malicious gossip of fellow Yaizu citizens. Although other fishermen suffered from health impacts and the fall of fish prices resulting from the nuclear tests, they did not receive any compensation. Suzu was also tormented by media attention and pressure to become a symbol of the peace movement. She even had to send her two daughters to faraway private schools to avoid media attention and bullying by other children. Yet she gave voice to the anger and desperation that her husband had felt on his deathbed and expressed her sincere hope to ban nuclear weapons. Suzu spoke at women's club meetings and the national Mothers' Conference, a liberal women's movement embracing peace and democracy. As she did so, she was transformed from a simple housewife to a peace activist in her own right, while Ōba gave her moral support and edited her speech manuscripts.[19]

However, it was never easy for the *Lucky Dragon* survivors and their families, including Suzu, to express their opinions. In her interview with a *Shizuoka* newspaper reporter in 1993, Suzu said that although every time she heard about the news of a nuclear test she felt more confirmed that nuclear weapons should be banned, she was very annoyed at being put on a pedestal as a symbol of the peace movement. She cooperated with the antinuclear movement because her desire to oppose nuclear weapons was genuine, but she was upset when people called her a "red" even though she did not identify with any political party line.[20] Although the Japanese peace movement started as a broad coalition of citizens regardless of political affiliation, it was increasingly dominated by the Communist and Socialist Parties.[21] In 1961, the movement split along political party lines, with Communists approving of Soviet nuclear weapons, while Socialists opposed all nuclear weapons. The Communist and Socialist antinuclear organizations played tug-of-war over patronage of Suzu. On the anniversary of the *Lucky Dragon* incident on March 1, 1962, one group placed Suzu under house arrest in an attempt to prevent her from participating in the opposing group's memorial event. The other group then spirited her away and made her speak at their memorial event. Suzu became fed up with the peace movement and kept a distance from it. Although her message was read aloud every year at the anniversary event, she later told a *Shizuoka* newspaper reporter, "They were not my own words. People wrote messages on my behalf." Her daughter also testified that Suzu's life was turned upside down not only by her husband's death but also by media attention and the peace movement. The family was annoyed when the peace activists rallied at Aikichi's gravesite every year on the memorial day of his death. Suzu said, "That is not our family grave," and had another grave built for herself.[22]

Misaki Yoshio, a chief fisherman of the *Lucky Dragon No. 5* who used to participate in antinuclear rallies and ceremonies with Suzu, also felt that the peace movement had become a "heavy burden" for him. "It is difficult to explain," he said to the *Shizuoka* newspaper reporter; he felt that "the *Lucky Dragon* had become one of several factions of the peace movement" and no longer had "anything to do with the crew members." He believed that the "peace movement was of course good and necessary" but was afraid that ordinary citizens of Yaizu were suspicious of the *Lucky Dragon* survivors involved in the peace movement. Many citizens suspected that those activists had other motivations, such as gaining material profit or pursuing leftist political objectives. Since the livelihood of most Yaizu citizens depended on the fishing industry directly or indirectly, they felt their lives had been ruined by the incident, with falling fish prices, too much media attention to their hometown, stigma attached to the image of radiation sickness, and also the image of politicized, leftist residents. Their anger and frustration were directed toward the survivors, who in their eyes seemed to cooperate with leftist political activists. "Political parties and organizations take advantage of us—not only Kuboyama Aikichi and Suzu but the surviving crew," Misaki said in the interview.[23] The *Shizuoka* reporter tried to contact other *Lucky Dragon* survivors, but most of them refused to speak. They wanted to be left alone. Only Ōishi Matashichi, the *Lucky Dragon* chief freezing technician, was an exception. He became an antinuclear activist, published many books based on his experience, and gave lectures at schools and peace movement meetings.[24]

The antinuclear movement in Yaizu revealed the complicated relations between nuclear test survivors and the movement. Although the survivors, their families, and their friends were concerned about the nuclear tests and nuclear weapons, politicization of the antinuclear movement made it difficult to participate, especially in conservative fishing communities. Still, at least initially, Yoshinaga villagers raised their voices publicly, and a few strong-minded people such as Suzu, Misaki, and Ōishi continued their ties with the antinuclear movement in spite of complicated feelings.

Muroto

Muroto, another important tuna fishing port, is located on the Pacific coast of Shikoku Island, the smallest of the four main islands of Japan. Since most of the tuna ships there were small to medium size, weighing up to one hundred tons, those vessels had no other choice but to operate in the Pacific Ocean, even though the crew was aware of the hazards. Such a situation left dozens of ships from Muroto contaminated by various degrees of radioactive fallout. Many fishermen suffered from radiation sickness and were ordered to abandon their catch. *Katori-maru No. 11*, a medium-size tuna vessel owned by Tsurui Takaaki, was one such example. Tsurui participated in a lawsuit against the US government organized by Linus Pauling, a Nobel laureate in chemistry.

On April 4, 1958, Pauling filed a lawsuit in the Washington, DC, District Court, claiming that the radioactive fallout caused by thermonuclear tests infringes the fundamental human rights guaranteed by the US constitution. Pauling, believing that ordinary citizens who did not have expert knowledge about nuclear science had the right to voice their concerns about radioactivity, included an American housewife, Japanese fishermen, and French and British pastors in a group of seventeen plaintiffs. The lawsuit went all the way to the Supreme Court, where their claim was denied in October 1960.[25] Among the plaintiffs, three Japanese from Muroto—Tsurui Takaaki, the owner of *Katori-maru No. 11*; Matsushita Yaeji, the chief engineer of the same ship; and Nakatani Kiyoaki, president of the Murotomisaki Seamen's Union—were included.[26]

Pauling and the Japanese fishermen found each other through an introduction by A. L. Wirin, a Russian Jewish émigré lawyer who worked on a wide variety of Japanese American cases during and after World War II. He was an attorney for the Southern California branch of the American Civil Liberties Union and chief counsel for the Japanese American Citizens League during and after the war. He also defended the *Golden Rule* crew, who tried to enter the Pacific test ground in protest, and through his networks with Japanese antinuclear activists, Wirin contacted various Japanese individuals—including Nobel laureate Yukawa Hideki, Christian social reformer Kagawa Toyohiko, and the mayors of Hiroshima, Nagasaki, and Muroto. Among these contacts, Kagawa Toyohiko and three fishermen from Muroto responded positively.[27]

Many Muroto fishermen, among them Nakatani, Tsurui, and Matsushita, had been angry at the government order to abandon their catch because of radioactive pollution. Nakatani, as the Seamen's Union leader, gave a speech at an international convention of the antinuclear movement in which he eloquently explained the plight of tuna fishermen and thus became widely known among activists. He was asked to join Linus Pauling's lawsuit, and he agreed, together with his colleagues Tsurui and Matsushita.[28] Although nuclear tests were so upsetting for all Muroto residents that the City Council and the Fisheries Cooperative Association had already sent letters of complaint to the Japanese and US governments, it was a different story when individual citizens participated in lawsuits against the US government. Muroto was a conservative fishing community, and residents were generally suspicious of leftist political agendas. In fact, some Communist antinuclear activists came to Muroto after the *Lucky Dragon* incident and tried to encourage the residents to join their movement, but most were not persuaded.[29] The fishermen's participation in the lawsuit against a foreign government was exceptional, and it demonstrates the depth of their anger against nuclear tests.

These examples from Misaki, Yaizu, and Muroto show that tuna fishermen, their families, and their friends did participate in the antinuclear movement in various ways. However, their relations with the movement were much more complicated than those of their urban, middle-class counterparts. In Misaki, many of the fishermen were contained in large companies, making it difficult for them to clearly see the problem. In Yaizu, the stigma attached to the *Lucky Dragon* incident and the politicization of the movement created serious difficulties. In Muroto, the conservative social order made it difficult for fishermen to dissent. In all these towns, however, the fishermen raised their voices when feelings of anger and concern outweighed the reasons for silence.

A different picture of the history of the Japanese antinuclear movement emerges when the presence of the tuna fishermen is taken into consideration. The tuna fishermen were not absent from the movement. Unlike their urban, middle-class counterparts, however, activists in the fishing communities had different economic and social factors to consider. Particularly, small-scale tuna fisheries were severely affected by the falling market price of tuna, so the fishermen hesitated to do anything to scare away their consumers. In addition, their hesitation was related to the organic nature of the tuna fishing industry, where vertical order and communal harmony were respected, and with good reason. Moreover, because of the stigma attached to radiation sickness, fishermen wanted to hide any actual or potential exposure to radioactive fallout.

In July 2018, the Kōchi Regional Court dismissed a lawsuit filed by forty-five tuna fishermen and their families demanding state compensation for lost opportunities for medical treatment some sixty years prior. They had argued that government officials failed to disclose records concerning their exposure to radioactive fallout. The plaintiffs appealed to the Takamatsu High Court, but the case was again dismissed in December 2019. The High Court, however, expressed sympathy for the plaintiffs, saying that it was "understandable that they demand the same kind of relief that was provided for the Hiroshima and Nagasaki nuclear bomb victims," and "the possibilities for such relief should be considered" outside of the court.[30] The lawsuit by retired tuna fishermen in a remote town far from the metropolis took many Japanese people by surprise, as they had long forgotten the history of the nuclear tests. For the tuna fishermen and their families, however, the lawsuit was an expression of anger, sorrow, and regret that had long been suppressed. Without incorporating their stories, the history of the Japanese antinuclear movement will never be complete.

Notes

1. For more details, see the Tokyo Prefectural Daigo Fukuryū Maru Exhibition Hall website, accessed July 1, 2020, http://d5f.org/en/about.html.
2. The author's interviews with retired tuna fishermen in Ainan-chō, Ehime Prefecture, can be found in Tsuchiya Yuka and Miura Chiemi, eds., *Shiryōshū: Ehime-ken nanbu ni okeru maguro enyō gyogyō-sha e no kikitori chōsa* (n.p., 2017); Udagawa Masaru and Uehara Masahiko, *Nippon Suisan hyakunen-shi* (Tokyo: Nippon Suisan, 2011); Hoshi Tetsuo, ed., *Katsuo maguro gyogyō no subete* (Tokyo: Dōmei Tsūshin-sha, 1974), 112.
3. The author's interviews with retired fishermen in Muroto, Kōchi Prefecture, can be found in Tsuchiya Yuka and Miura Chiemi, eds., *Shiryōshū: Kōchi-ken Muroto-shi ni okeru maguro enyō gyogyō-sha e no kikitori chōsa* (n.p., 2019), henceforth cited as Kōchi Prefecture, 2019; Hoshi, *Katsuo maguro gyogyō no subete*, 86.
4. Author's unpublished collection of interviews in Ehime Prefecture, 2017.

5. Author's unpublished collection of nterviews in Kōchi Prefecture, 2019.
6. Kondō Yasuo, ed., *Suibaku jikken to Nihon gyogyō* (Tokyo: University of Tokyo Press, 1958), 2, 326; Yaizu Fish Wholesalers and Processors Cooperative Association, ed., *Yaizu suisanshi*, vol. 2 (n.p., 1985), 459, 477.
7. The *Lucky Dragon No. 5* Exhibits at the Yaizu City History and Folklore Museum. For more details, see the Yaizu City website, accessed July 1, 2020, http://www.city.yaizu.lg.jp/rekimin/. Explanations of the museum are in Japanese.
8. Miyake Yasuo et al., eds., *Shinsō-ban: Bikini suibaku hisai shiryōshū* (Tokyo: University of Tokyo Press, 2014), 231; Yaizu Fish Wholesalers, *Yaizu suisanshi*, 478.
9. Miura City, ed., *Bikini jiken Miura no kiroku* (n.p., 1996), 121–33. Translation by the author.
10. Miura City, *Bikini jiken Miura no kiroku*, 134–35.
11. Miura City, *Bikini jiken Miura no kiroku*, 154–57.
12. "Sonmin no koe," petition to the authorities, May 31, 1954, courtesy of the Yaizu History and Folklore Museum. Also in Katō Kazuo, *Yaizu heiwagaku nyūmon: Bikini jiken to Daigo Fukuryū-maru* (Tokyo: Ronsōsha, 2012), 182–83.
13. "Shimin tachi ga atsumeta gensuibaku hantai no koe," February 10, 2013, NHK Archives, accessed February 9, 2020, https://www2.nhk.or.jp/archives/shogenarchives/postwar/shogen/movie.cgi?das_id=D0001810406_00000.
14. Katō Kazuo and Akiyama Hiroko, eds., *Hiroshima Nagasaki Bikini o tsunagu: Yaizu-ryū heiwa no tsukurikata II* (Tokyo: Shakai Hyōronsha, 2012), 47–54.
15. For English-language sources on postwar democratization of Japan and progressive activities, see, for example, John Dower, *Embracing Defeat: Japan in the Wake of World War II* (New York: W. W. Norton, 1999); Takemae Eiji et al., *Inside GHQ: The Allied Occupation of Japan and Its Legacy* (London: Bloomsbury, 2002); Hiroshi Kitamura, *Screening Enlightenment: Hollywood and the Cultural Reconstruction of Defeated Japan* (Ithaca, NY: Cornell University Press, 2010).
16. Katō and Akiyama, *Hiroshima Nagasaki Bikini o tsunagu*, 47.
17. Katō and Akiyama, *Hiroshima Nagasaki Bikini o tsunagu*, 48.
18. Owada Michiko, "Daigo Fukuryū-maru no Bikini hisai to hahaoya taikai: Kuboyama Suzu," in *Genbaku to genpatsu, sono saki: Josei-tachi no hikaku no jissen to shisō*, ed. Hayakawa Noriyo and Esahi Akiko (Tokyo: Ochanomizu Shobō, 2016), 19–38.
19. Iizuka Toshihiro, *Shi no hai o koete: Kuboyama Suzu san no michi* (Kyoto: Kamogawa Shuppan, 1993), 145–63.
20. Shizuoka Newspaper, ed., *Daigo Fukuryū-maru, kokoro no kiseki* (n.p., 1993), 41–45.
21. For the domestic politics behind the Japanese antinuclear movement, see, for example, Toshihiro Higuchi, "An Environmental Origin of Antinuclear Activism in Japan, 1954–1963: The Government, the Grassroots Movement, and the Politics of Risk," *Peace and Change* 33, no. 3 (July 2008): 333–67.
22. Shizuoka Newspaper, *Daigo Fukuryū-maru, kokoro no kiseki*, 41–45.
23. Shizuoka Newspaper, *Daigo Fukuryū-maru, kokoro no kiseki*, 4–7.

24. Ishizaki Shōko, "Hibaku to dansei: Bikini hibakusha Ōishi Matashichi no kiseki," in *Genbaku to genpatsu, sono saki: Josei-tachi no hikaku no jissen to shisō*, 39–53.
25. Toshihiro Higuchi, "Tipping the Scale of Justice: The Fallout Suit of 1958 and the Environmental Legal Dimension of Nuclear Pacifism," *Peace and Change* 38, no. 1 (January 2013): 33–54.
26. "Press Release re: The Fallout Suits. April 4, 1958," Ava Helen and Linus Pauling Papers, Oregon State University Libraries, http://scarc.library.oregonstate.edu/digitalresources/pauling/.
27. *Yomiuri Shinbun*, March 26 and May 10, 1958; "A. L. Wirin," *Densho Encyclopedia*, accessed February 22, 2020, http://encyclopedia.densho.org/A.L._Wirin/. The plaintiffs were Norman Thomas (politician, USA); Karl P. Link (biochemist, USA); Leslie C. Dunn (zoology, USA); Clarence Pickett (pacifist, USA); Stephanie May (housewife, USA); William Bross Lloyd Jr. (editor, USA); Brock Chisholm (physiatrist, Canada); Toyohiko Kagawa (pastor, Japan); Kiyoaki Nakatani, Takaaki Tsurui, and Yaeji Matsushita (fishermen, Japan); the Rev. G. Michael Scott (pastor, UK); Dame Kathleen Lonsdale (chemist, UK); Bertrand Russell (philosopher, UK); Rev. Canon L. John Collins (pastor, UK); the Rev. Martin Niemoeller (pastor, West Germany); and Andre Trocme (pastor, France).
28. Details on the fishermen's participation in the lawsuit have been explored in Yuka Tsuchiya Moriguchi, "Suibaku jikken o meguru 1958-nen no soshō: Linus Pauling to Nihon no en'yō gyogyōsha o tsunaida hankaku shisō," in *Amerika kenkyū no genzaichi: Kiki to saisei*, ed. Itoh Shoko et al. (Tokyo: Sairyū-sha, 2023), 181–96.
29. Author's unpublished collection of interviews in Kōchi Prefecture, 2019.
30. *Mainichi Shinbun*, December 13, 2019, February 12, 2020; *Kōchi Shinbun*, December 13, 2019. Later, the plaintiffs filed two other lawsuits in Tokyo and Kōchi, and the cases are still pending as of February 2023. *Asahi Shinbun*, February 6, 2023.

PART THREE
TRANSPACIFIC ACTIVISMS

CHAPTER 13

A Long Road to Disability Compensation in Cold War America

NAOKO WAKE

The year 1990 marked a turning point for many American *hibakusha*, people exposed to nuclear radiation while in the military or on the job. With the passage of the Radiation Exposure Compensation Act, not only "atomic veterans" and "downwinders" irradiated on or near nuclear test sites in Utah, Nevada, and Arizona but also employees in the uranium mining industry, essential for nuclear weaponry development in the Cold War, became eligible for disability compensation. Combined with a 1984 act called the Veterans' Dioxin and Radiation Exposure Compensation Standards Act, which covered veterans exposed to radiation during the US occupation of Hiroshima and Nagasaki in 1945 and 1946, this 1990 act opened a way for US persons debilitated by radiation exposure—both soldiers and civilians—to be recognized. In contrast, another group of American hibakusha—Japanese American civilians who had been irradiated by the Hiroshima or Nagasaki atomic bombing in August 1945—were excluded from both acts' coverage. Today, these neglected hibakusha in America continue to rely on the Japanese, not their own, government's programs for treating their radiation illness.[1]

This chapter explores the historical roots of this negligence as both a legacy of the nuclear age that begs to be understood as a transpacific history of illness and a consequence of the racism and ableism that have persistently affected US hibakusha. Seen as members of a "perpetually foreign" race, Japanese American hibakusha attempted, yet failed, to make the US government recognize them as American casualties of American weaponry.[2] Marked by nuclear injury, Japanese American survivors were deemed "perpetually disabled" and unworthy of assistance.[3] If they overcame their illness, by contrast, they were seen as "model minorities" who were able to self-heal.[4] These assumptions have shaped the US disinclination to see US hibakusha as citizens deserving protection. Moreover, these processes of exclusion were significantly gendered, affecting male and female survivors divergently. The transpacific history of illness thus illuminates intersectionality among race, ability, and gender. By considering all these factors, we can begin to explain why Japanese Americans are left out of any formal apology or compensation.

A key to explaining this neglect, I argue, lies in the ways US hibakusha's illness and injury were suppressed throughout the 1950s and 1960s. These were the decades when prejudice against Japanese Americans as foreign coexisted uneasily with the emerging model minority myth. Asian immigrants in America in the first half of the century were "aliens ineligible for citizenship" partly because of their assumed physical and mental deficiencies.[5] Since the midcentury, however, they became model minorities, who outperformed whites by sheer perseverance. Both of these ideas defined US hibakusha's illness and injury, sometimes by making them invisible or inconsequential, and other times by rendering US survivors a useful tool for fighting the Cold War. Although many Japanese American survivors resisted such subjugation, their voices were frequently erased by inter- and intraracial tensions tied to ableism. US survivors' failure to obtain disability compensation, then, is best understood by looking at its historical roots in the 1950s and 1960s, which reveal both possibilities and limitations of the cross-national resistance to the nuclear from within the nuclear superpower.

An exploration of the understudied history of Japanese American hibakusha adds importantly to the scholarship on antinuclear activism. Unlike the famous Hiroshima Maidens, twenty-five young Japanese women who had come to America in the mid-1950s to have their bomb scars surgically treated, American survivors, many of whom are US born citizens, have been largely ignored by the US government and the public alike.[6] About one thousand US survivors of Hiroshima and Nagasaki reside in America today, but archival records about their history are limited. Given the scarcity of sources, I conducted interviews between 2010 and 2015 with about ninety hibakusha, their families, and their community supporters.[7] In their remembering, what may be called a counter-memory of the bomb has emerged. This counter-memory has been shaped by conspicuous silence about bomb illness and injury, because its cross-nationality does not fit into national remembering of the bomb driven by patriotic sentiment in Japan or America. The silence also has been shaped by changing assumptions about US survivors' race, ability, and gender through the latter half of the twentieth century. Thinking about the history of the resistance to nuclear power through the counter-memory of the bomb, then, illuminates the bomb's history in close relation to hibakusha identities shaped by and against US nuclear hegemony.

That nuclear hegemony offered no place for US survivors' cross-national experiences becomes evident if we look at their daily experiences in early Cold War America, where they were recent returnees from Japan. In what follows, I first examine problematic relations between US hibakusha and the US military. Because the military was largely a single-sex institution, my discussion focuses on male survivors. In the second section, I explore female survivors' experiences of illness related to changing ideas of gender, race, and ability as they rebuilt their families and communities. By organizing these sections by gender, I do not suggest that US survivors' identities are cleanly separated by dualistic gender categories. Rather, my organization reflects the remarkable power of gender found in the oral histories, shaping the contours and contents of US survivors' remembering. Gender in turn shapes what we can know about their cross-national experiences of, and resistance to, the bomb in midcentury America. Throughout, my intent is to suggest that not only gender but also race and ability are unstable, historically contingent categories, creating a gap between a variety of US hibakusha's self-understandings and rigid, often dualistic, understandings of illness, ability, race, and gender. The counter-memory of the bomb has thrived in this gap, suggesting the need to take seriously these categories of identity in our historical inquiry into nuclear weaponry.

In and Out of the US Military

A few thousand Japanese Americans—many of them second-generation US-born citizens called Nisei—were affected by the bomb. Hiroshima is the prefecture in Japan that sent the largest number of immigrants to America before the war. Nagasaki ranked ninth among prefectures as a source of transpacific immigrants.[8] Since it was common among first-generation immigrants to send their children to Japan for a few years of education, many Japanese American children were in Japan, and indeed, in their parents' hometowns of Hiroshima and Nagasaki, when the war broke out in 1941. There were other reasons why US citizens were in wartime Japan. Many, like Jack Motoo Dairiki, were visiting their grandparents and became trapped in Japan after Pearl Harbor.[9] This kind of story is important to tell: that immigrants traveled mostly for family reasons. They did not decide to be in Hiroshima or Nagasaki in 1945 for reasons of national loyalty or citizenship, as scholars of the bomb often assume about hibakusha.[10] Others, like Julie Kumi Fukuda, were family members of the "no-no boys," Japanese Americans who refused to declare loyalty to the United States while imprisoned in Japanese American incarceration camps.[11] By 1944, the number of no-no boys and their families requesting expatriation or repatriation to Japan neared twenty thousand. Of these, 368 individuals were deported before August 1945.[12] Of the large number of Japanese in America who hailed from Hiroshima and Nagasaki, an estimated one hundred of these deportees were in the prefectures in 1945. Still others, like Minoru Sumida, were sent to Japan shortly after the war's beginning in exchange for Americans in Japan. In Sumida's case, his US citizenship by birth was not taken into consideration.[13] For the purposes of these exchanges, US authorities simply defined Japanese Americans as Japanese—"Japanese" enough to be exchanged for more "American" citizens.[14]

An unknown number of those who survived the nuclear attacks returned to the United States. They were anxious to reunite with families they had left years before. Many suffered radiation illness quietly. The Cold War culture demanded a distinction between friends and foes along national lines. It was difficult for US survivors to find words for their cross-national experiences. George Kazuto Saiki, a survivor who came back to Hawai'i as a sixteen-year-old in 1949, was one of many who felt alienated. Although he was fortunate enough to be taken in by his sister, her family did not treat him well. As Saiki recalled, "When I came back [to Hawai'i], my sister did not welcome me. . . . She owned five houses where she used me as a servant. I took her children to a bath. I washed dishes. I also took out five houses' worth of trash, and cleaned their yards."[15] In addition to his household duties, Saiki endured ridicule by his neighbors. They were all Japanese Americans who spoke only English, said Saiki: "I didn't understand English [after spending many years in Japan]. . . . No wonder, then, did everyone ridicule me. . . . They were all Japanese Americans, but they had become Americans. Because all Japanese language schools had been closed down during the war. They gave me a nickname: Japan."[16] One consequence of the wartime persecution of Japanese Americans was linguistic discontinuity, which created a schism in the community and a kind of language disability in returnees. Saiki's daily experience, then, revealed *intr-a*racial racism that made returnees like Saiki foreign.[17] His remembering also shows a shift in gender roles in Japanese American households. Unable to communicate in English, Saiki played feminine roles in the kitchen, a domestic space traditionally reserved for women.

While US survivors rebuilt their lives, their relationship to the state was complicated by its need to mobilize all resources for the Cold War. US survivors' experiences as immigrants, and in some cases, their bomb experiences, were seen as resources to fight communism. Especially during the Korean War, many male US survivors were drafted into military intelligence because of their assumed bilingual ability. Beginning in 1950, the number of US military personnel on US bases in Japan rapidly multiplied, making translation an urgent necessity. But hibakusha's remembering suggests that their assumed language skills were largely a product of stereotypes. As Keiko Shinmoto recalled, her brother Shigeru, who came back to America soon after the bomb, was promptly drafted. This struck Shigeru as odd, because "he could not speak English. So he said, 'I don't know why I was drafted.'" Most likely, he was deemed useful because of an assumed bilingual ability. The problem, though, was that after years of living in Japan, Shigeru barely comprehended English. No wonder, then, that the family thought it fortunate that he survived the war without understanding the language of command. Behind this story of good fortune is a recognition that the state was unconcerned about Shigeru's lack of ability, which put his life in danger. Shinmoto's remembering, then, reveals not only *inter*racial racism but also how the military, then largely a single-sex institution, exposed male survivors to gendered ableism. Men's supposed abilities were actively sought by the military, resulting in the invisibility of hibakusha's actual ability as well as the integration of Japanese American masculinity into an American masculinity that served state interests. Previously, Japanese American men were often deemed physically slight, effeminate, and inscrutable. Now, they seemed unobtrusive yet scrupulous, making them excellent intelligence officers; their assumed bilingualism only added to this new image.[18]

George Kazuto Saiki, who had been ridiculed because he did not understand English, offers a further insight into the relationship among race, ability, and gender in the army. His experiences reveal how both the invisibility of hibakusha's ability *and* the integration of hibakusha's masculinity occurred arbitrarily yet persistently, and how their experiences capture a transitional historical moment when the stereotypes of Japanese Americans fluctuated between foreign and disabled and an extraordinarily able model minority. Saiki was rejected during an army induction examination in 1951. His English fluency simply did not match what the military required. In 1952, though, the examiner judged that Saiki was good enough after asking him in English what time it was. Saiki answered the question reflexively in English, which immediately resulted in a pass. The irony, however, was that Saiki had to take a language exam again after being sent to Tokyo. This time, it was a Japanese examination. Doubtful of a Nisei's Japanese fluency, his superiors were determined to station only the truly fluent in the capital's headquarters. The rest would be sent to the war front. This was not what Saiki expected; he had been told that he would be exempt from combat duties in Korea. Failing to pass the Japanese exam, though, Saiki spent sixteen months on the battlefield, where he continued to struggle to understand English. Like Shinmoto's, Saiki's case suggests how Japanese Americans were recruited often for reasons that did not match their actual ability. Saiki's experience also reveals how fragile this way of defining ability was. Within its own institutional parameters, the military exposed its own fallacious reasoning. Japanese American men could be a racial minority with exceptional abilities only insofar as these abilities met the standard set by Cold War priorities. If the standard changed, the stereotype could easily slide back into disabled.

Nothing showed this precariousness more clearly than the experiences of US hibakusha, for whom illness and injury played a central role in their relationship to the military. Take, for example, Minoru Sumida. Sumida had suffered major injuries in 1945 in Hiroshima, which left large visible scars on his arms and legs. Although he could function normally, these scars caused a prompt rejection at a medical examination for US military conscription. The rejection left Sumida feeling unfairly treated. He had come back to the United States, his country of birth, in 1958 for the sole purpose of enlisting in the military. Without enlistment, dual citizens like Sumida would lose US citizenship by their twenty-third birthday. Although he was able to maintain his citizenship in a way unrelated to army enlistment, he could not shake off his bitterness: "A week [after entering the United States], I went to a medical checkup for induction. They looked at my bomb scars . . . and I failed to pass." If the bomb had already made him disabled, why did he have to return so hurriedly? There was no answer. The only thing made clear was that the bomb had made Sumida disabled regardless of his actual ability. The price of escaping the label of foreignness was being labeled as disabled.

But nuclear scars on Japanese American bodies carried more than a single meaning. Male hibakusha might escape being labeled as disabled by being seen as foreign. Jack Motoo Dairiki, a Nisei born in Sacramento in 1930, was outspoken about his Hiroshima experiences after he returned to America in 1948. In 1952, Dairiki was interviewed by a radio program sponsored by the California Civil Defense, which used his story to assure state residents that "[even if] an atomic bomb [were] dropped . . . many will survive *if* they simply observe the fundamental rule of survival." The horrors of what Dairiki witnessed in 1945 were summarized in terms of training that had prepared him to duck and cover at the time of explosion and to take care of himself in case of injury. Daikiri's memory was construed as that of a man prepared for nuclear emergency.[19] Underpinned by gender expectations of the nuclear age, Cold War culture imposed a division between ally and enemy countries, stifling cross-national histories central to Japanese American experiences. Dairiki, as his story was told by the California Civil Defense, became a representative of the people of Japan. What made him available for the radio program—that he was an American-born citizen living in the United States—was not mentioned. He might be an able man, but he was foreign.

Only a narrow, arbitrary path existed for Japanese American male hibaksuha to escape being seen as disabled or foreign, as shown by Alfred Kaneo Dote. Two years after he returned to America in 1948, he was back in Japan again serving as a translator at military trials. In six months, he was transferred, this time to Korea. Like Dairiki's, Dote's bomb experience elicited curiosity. He lacked visible scars like Sumida's, allowing for a smooth induction. Thanks to his previous work experience, he was relatively fluent in English. Once in the army, a superior asked him to share his experiences as a survivor with the entire unit. Likely, this officer wanted to educate his unit about the bomb, in case it became a reality on the peninsula's battleground. Dote's survivorhood brought him another remarkable experience in the military. Before discharge, he was given a special physical examination. He was told of the result: "Well, there is nothing to worry about at this time!"—implying that, somehow, the new war healed the scars of the old one.[20] Disabilities inflicted on Americans in Japan during the Pacific War had been erased by serving in the US military in Korea.

Unlike Dairiki, there was no question that Dote was an American citizen serving the American army. Dote was spared the labels of foreign and disabled by being extraordinarily useful, a step toward a model minority. This was not a step he chose to take; rather, his superiors told him that he had taken it. Unlike others, who turned away US survivors as foreign or disabled, Dote's superiors happened to find his bomb experiences worthy, showing the power of arbitrariness. In this sense, Dote's experience circles back to Shinmoto's and Saiki's. They all functioned under capricious expectations about their abilities, which pushed them onto a narrow path toward inclusion. Outside the pathway, there always remained a danger of exclusion. By examining the Cold War as a transitional era for Japanese America, we begin to understand how hibakusha became invisible, or visible only when they served US national interests. The fact in the transpacific history of the bomb—that it affected people regardless of nationality—remained unrecognized. US hibakusha's illness and injury, too, became part of the counter-memory of the bomb consigned to the margins of national memories. These logics of exclusion as a necessary condition of inclusion were firmly established in the 1950s and 1960s.

In Family, Community, and Workplace

The previous section explored the intersection of race, ability, and gender with a focus on survivors in and outside of the US military. What about civilians? Did their family and community lives reveal similar logics of exclusion and inclusion? Indeed, US survivors' daily lives were shaped by the Cold War demand of containment, which I found particularly evident in female hibaksuha's remembering.[21] May Yamaoka's experience illuminates some of the challenges that US survivors faced, while Kazuko Aoki's recollections suggest reasons why women's memories frequently offer a useful entry into these challenges. In the early 1950s, Yamaoka worked in a federal government office in San Francisco. Although she had not told her coworkers her bomb experiences, the Korean War brought it out unexpectedly: "They [my coworkers] never asked [about my bomb experiences], and I never volunteered. . . . But when, I think after the Korean War . . . they showed an atomic bomb movie one day and . . . that's when they knew. Because I could not stand it, I ran out. . . . So they wondered why, so I told them why."[22] Even as she spoke, Yamaoka seemed eager to resume her silence: "I guess they . . . could not believe that I was in there [Hiroshima]. . . . I didn't say too much," she said.[23] In the predominantly white workplace, her desire to stay silent persisted.

The silencing of hibakusha took place not only *inter*racially but also *intra*racially. Kazuko Aoki remembered how she had been welcomed into a group of her husband's friends, his fellow internees at Jerome, Arkansas, during the war, when she had come to Hawai'i in 1959. Her husband had lost his brother to radiation illness, so Aoki felt he understood her feelings about the bomb. But when it came time to see his friends from the camp, his concern about Aoki's illness appeared to diminish. Aoki remembered, "The friends were closer to each other than they were to their parents and siblings. They got together all the time. But it was a bit hard on me . . . because I could not take a rest even when I wanted to."[24] At that time, Aoki was struggling with her health. She felt extremely weak, spending five to six hours a day bedridden. By 1960, she had developed thyroid cancer, one of the most common radiation illnesses.[25] But illness did not relieve her of the task of taking part in the other Japanese America, one that had taken shape in the United States during the war.

Equally important as this silencing is that stories of illness like Aoki's were told particularly richly by female hibakusha. I found striking the difference between how women and men talked about illness, injury, and disability. Often, women told intimate details in a way that men did not. Women lucidly recalled not only symptoms but also how they cared for them. I have argued elsewhere that this gendered remembering explains part of why US survivors' activism in the 1970s was women-centered.[26]

Storytelling and community organizing by women were the driving forces for hibakusha to break their silence. And yet, in the 1950s and 1960s, silence often indicated the constraints of inter- and intraracism.

This silence among American hibakusha was striking, particularly if we compare it to the growing visibility of Japanese hibakusha at the time. The Hiroshima Maidens, Japanese women whose faces had been disfigured by the bomb and who visited the United States in 1955 to receive reconstructive surgeries, highlight this gap between hibakusha on the different shores. A privately funded project, this act of "goodwill" offered an opportunity for Americans to express their guilt over the bomb without apologizing for it. These women also served as ambassadors of the Cold War alliance driven by US "liberal paternalism."[27] Young and female, they were "benign" and "helpless," a perfect vessel to carry the message of American benevolence.[28] The Hiroshima Maidens project, then, was a success insofar as it helped repair Japan-US relations. Japanese American hibakusha had little place in this alliance building. For the US government, helping US survivors heal would carry no diplomatic value; in fact, it might expose scars that were supposed to be healed by the Hiroshima Maidens. Instead of coming out, US survivors felt a need to fit in by suppressing their stories.

To further understand Yamaoka and Aoki's silence, it is useful to recall the notion of Japanese Americans as perpetually foreign. A legacy of the racist policies that defined Japanese as "aliens ineligible for citizenship" until 1952, the idea of Asians as never belonging to America persisted in the latter half of the century.[29] Japanese Americans experienced bias particularly as they grappled to rebuild their lives after the war. They had been released from the camps, but their national loyalty remained doubtful.[30] Questions about Japanese Americans seemed to multiply. They had been treated as enemy nationals; could they be Americans now? Moreover, could they become productive citizens after they had been made dependent on the state for so long? A close cousin of this questioning was the idea of Japanese Americans as perpetually disabled. As shown by disability scholars, the image of nonwhite immigrants as undesirable had been shaped by their assumed disability throughout the first half of the twentieth century. In the debate over the 1924 immigration act, for instance, proponents of the national quota system defined racial differences in terms of both mental and physical deficiencies, such as shapes of head, eyes, and legs, including many that did not interfere with functionality.[31] This association of race and disability made the restriction of Asian immigrants easy to continue after the war, when the United States tried to ameliorate its relationship with people of color nationally and internationally. Restrictionists argued that they were not driven by skin color; instead, they were simply using meritocracy based on ability. In fact, the 1965 immigration law officially made ability a selection criterion. Professional skills and financial capacity became proof of ability for those who wished to enter the country.[32] Unlike older, pre-1965 immigrants, the newer, post-1965 immigrants were preselected for desirable abilities that catered to US interests.

Some survivors' oral histories make clear how the ideas about their foreignness and disability propelled them to prove themselves. Mostly pre-1965 returnees, US survivors were not the alliance-building, thus assistance-worthy, Japanese; nor were they highly capable, post-1965 Americans. Interestingly, for female hibakusha, the road to inclusion offered opportunities not only for breaking gender boundaries but also for building interracial alliances, both of which I see as steps toward recognizing transpacific histories of the bomb. Unlike male hibakusha in and out of the military, their female civilian counterparts often found an unexpected agency for change in the process of becoming more included in US society. Equally important, their efforts to transform gender and racial relations often were construed as a story of Japanese Americans as a model minority.[33] For example, Joyce Moriwaki's recollections illuminated how female US survivors experienced gender relationships differently on either side of the Pacific, and how they felt that the difference made them belong more to the United States.[34]

Moriwaki was fortunate to find a job at an amusement park in Hiroshima as a teenager in the 1950s, but she did not fail to notice that there were hardly any desirable jobs available for women. When she came to Hawai'i in 1961, Moriwaki was pleasantly surprised by the treatment she received from her employers. "I thought I liked the job at the amusement park [in Japan], but things were even better in America," said Moriwaki. This was "because there was no discrimination" against women.[35] During the era when many white, middle-class women felt confined by the "feminine mystique," a statement such as Moriwaki's might have sounded overly optimistic.[36] However, many female survivors experienced their life in

America as decidedly liberating. This sense of liberation allowed Moriwaki to develop a feeling of attachment to the United States.

This kind of sentiment was provoked by race as well as gender. As a single mother of two children, Takeko Okano found a job at a bank after completing night school in San Francisco. She said, "At first, I applied for a job at a Japanese bank [in San Francisco]. But they didn't like a divorcee with two children . . . But when I went to a bank operated by white people, they did not care about those things. They were happy that I had a certificate."[37] Her employer found not only her status as a single mother but also her limited language ability inconsequential. "I think that non-Japanese people were nicer than Japanese people to me," Okano concluded. These "nicer" people gave her a decent job. She also became friends with Chinese American and African American coworkers, who stayed in close touch with her even after retirement.[38]

This kind of interracial affinity and alliance proved crucial when US hibakusha came together politically in the 1970s. Not only Asian Americans but also African Americans rallied in support of US hibakusha. When their activism led them to public hearings on the bills to provide medical aid to hibakusha in the California Senate and the US Congress, in 1974 and 1978 respectively, it was clear that these bills were made possible by interracial alliances. Politicians of color came in support, including Edward Roybal, Mervyn Dymally, and Patsy T. Mink. Again, women talked more freely about these developments. Men who had served side by side with racial others in the newly integrated army in the 1950s rarely discussed interracial affinity (although such discussions were not absent). All of this leads us to recognize the power of shared remembering in the making of the activism of the 1970s. Also, women's memories, more frequently than men's, showed the concrete ways in which breaking gender- and racial-boundaries played crucial roles in US hibakusha's resistance to the bomb and the lack of understanding about their illness. By breaking boundaries, women felt a sense of belonging to America, countering the stereotypes of Asian Americans as perpetually foreign and perpetually disabled. However, I also note that, asked about her concern about radiation illness, Okano laughed: "I have lived until I am eighty-seven."[39] This may seem an empowering statement. Against all odds, she had lived long. But she had been far from healthy. When I met her, she had just lost her son to cancer, which she thought might have been caused by her radiation exposure. The transpacific history of illness does not go away simply because Okano is still alive. In this light, Okano's statement about her long life might have been a cover for the bomb's debilitating effects and, by extension, the bomb itself. Her statement also risks making her seem a model minority capable of healing illness without any state recognition.

Memories of silence like Yamaoka's and Aoki's and stories of affirmative gender and race relations like Moriwaki's and Okano's suggest a thin line between exclusion and inclusion. If Japanese American hibakusha's ability was in question because of their race, as it was at midcentury, there was no reason for the US government to help them regain it. US survivors should remain silent about the bomb and hold onto any opportunity for inclusion. Alternately, they could believe that their nuclear scars were healed by fighting in the Cold War, as Dote was told, in effect generating a masculine form of the model minority myth. US hibakusha could also overcome their disability by working hard regardless of their gender and by building interracial unity, as Okano did. In fact, Japanese Americans who returned from the incarceration camps were encouraged by the US authorities to be "friends" with non-Japanese Americans.[40] In this light, the model minority myth might have made invisible female hibakusha's agency in pushing gender and racial boundaries by making their agency part of a racial ability to overcome adversity. They might still be seen as foreigners not fully integrated into the national body; nonetheless, they were believed to have abilities that made them a model for other minorities. If one minority group can overcome nuclear attacks, others should be able to overcome any hardships without the state's assistance. As assumptions about race and ability shifted, US survivors' cross-national experiences became a reason for treatment ranging from outright exclusion to highly conditional inclusion.

And yet, the gendered, ableist inclusion existed alongside the exclusion of Asian Americans as disabled and foreign. If US survivors came out as such and demanded recognition, they could be seen as doubly disabled. They were not only pre-1965 immigrants who lacked physical, mental, and socioeconomic abilities; they also had been exposed to radiation and were prone to illness. Although US hibakusha successfully gained recognition of their survivorhood from the Japanese government as a result of their activism in the 1970s, they failed flatly in getting the same recognition from the American government. In the 1980s, the Japanese government began sending Hiroshima physicians to conduct biannual health checkups for hibakusha in the United States.[41] The Japanese government also began issuing certificates to US survivors that made it possible for them to receive treatment for radiation illness free of cost in Japan. These are extraordinary accomplishments for a small group of hibakusha. One might argue, however, that by getting such support, US hibakusha indeed became perpetually foreign and perpetually disabled in the eyes of US authorities. They had been given benefits by a foreign government, which proved their disability by issuing them lifelong access to free medical care. Meanwhile, the US government steered clear of these responsibilities, reaffirming its position that Japanese Americans were foreign. Thus in 1990, when nuclear disability compensation was instituted, Japanese American hibakusha were not beneficiaries. One irony of this is that this legislation was expected to particularly benefit African American veterans and Native American miners. When the racial injustice of the nuclear era began to show signs of crumbling, no consideration was given to Japanese Americans. For all of their courage, US survivors' racial alliance building, spurred by gender boundary breaking, fell short of bringing state recognition to the transpacific history of illness.

The US definition of who deserves compensation for radiation-related disability has marginalized Japanese Americans, illuminating both a forgotten legacy of the Cold War and a blind spot in the history of antinuclear activism. By relying on the Japanese government to care for American hibakusha, the US government continues to miss opportunities to take ownership of the resistance to nuclear realities from within US national boundaries. Japanese American hibakusha oscillated between the stereotypes of being alien and disabled and a model minority, thanks to inter- and intraracialism, which thrive in gendered ableism. Consequently, Japanese hibakusha, not their American counterparts, are representative of hibakusha, making invisible the US resistance spurred by the bomb. This historical dynamic reveals how race, ability, and gender continue to falsely divide the history of the bomb and its discontents by imagined national borders.

Notes

1. Naoko Wake, *American Survivors: Trans-Pacific Memories of Hiroshima and Nagasaki* (New York: Cambridge University Press, 2021), chapter 6.
2. On the notion of Asian Americans as perpetually foreign, see Charlotte Brooks, *Alien Neighbors, Foreign Friends: Asian Americans, Housing, and the Transformation of California* (Chicago: University of Chicago Press, 2009); Caroline Chung Simpson, *An Absent Presence: Japanese Americans in Postwar American Cultures, 1945–1960* (Durham, NC: Duke University Press, 2002).
3. Although no scholars have discussed Asian Americans specifically as "perpetually disabled," disability studies scholars have richly noted the historical link between immigrants and the idea of disability. See, for example, Susan M. Schweik, *The Ugly Laws: Disability in Public* (New York: New York University Press, 2009); Douglas C. Baynton, *Defectives in the Land: Disability and Immigration in the Age of Eugenics* (Chicago: University of Chicago Press, 2016).
4. On the model minority myth, see Madeline Y. Hsu, *The Good Immigrants: How the Yellow Peril Became the Model Minority* (Princeton, NJ: Princeton University Press, 2015); Ellen Wu, *The Color of Success: Asian Americans and the Origins of the Model Minority* (Princeton, NJ: Princeton University Press, 2013).
5. Since the passage of the 1870 Naturalization Act, US citizenship had been limited to aliens of white and black races. At the turn of the twentieth century, the western states passed laws limiting property (especially land) ownership to aliens eligible for citizenship. See Erika Lee, *The Making of Asian America: A History* (New York: Simon and Schuster, 2015), 149, 172.
6. On the Hiroshima Maidens, see David Serlin, *Replaceable You: Engineering the Body in Postwar America* (Chicago: University of Chicago Press, 2004), chapter 2; Naoko Shibusawa, *America's Geisha Ally: Reimagining the Japanese Enemy* (Cambridge, MA: Harvard University Press, 2006), chapter 6.
7. Select interviews from the Naoko Wake Collection are also available in the Densho Digital Repository, https://ddr.densho.org/ddr-densho-1021/. I have also used two additional collections of US survivors' oral histories. The Shinpei Takeda Collection was created by artist Shinpei Takeda. The Friends of Hibakusha Collection was created by members of a support organization of US survivors.
8. Hiroshima-ken Henshū Iinkai, ed., *Hiroshima-ken ijūshi: Tsūshi hen* (The history of migration from Hiroshima Prefecture) (Hiroshima: Hiroshima-ken Henshū Iinkai, 1993), 8–9; Masaaki Kodama, *Nihon iminshi kenkyū josetsu* (Hiroshima: Keisuisha, 1992), 473.
9. Interview with Jack Motoo Dairiki, July 13, 2010, by the author.
10. Because of the assumption that hibakusha are Japanese citizens, many scholars continued to discuss the Hiroshima and Nagasaki bombings as exclusively affecting the Japanese long after the existence of Korean and American survivors became known in the 1970s. See Robert Jay Lifton and Greg Mitchell, *Hiroshima in America:*

Fifty Years of Denial (New York: Putnam's Sons, 1995); James J. Orr, *The Victim as Hero: Ideologies of Peace and National Identity in Postwar Japan* (Honolulu: University of Hawai'i Press, 2001).

11. Interview with Julie Kumi Fukuda (pseudonym), June 18, 1976, by the Friends of Hibakusha (FOH hereafter).
12. The children of "no-no boys" were required to leave the country if their parents were deported. Fearing separation, many adult family members tried to stay with the deportees by requesting expatriation or repatriation to Japan. Deportees numbered 54 in 1942, 314 in 1943. Jacob TenBroek, Edward N. Barnhart, and Floyd W. Matson, *Prejudice, War, and the Constitution* (Berkeley: University of California Press, 1954), 175.
13. Interview with Minoru Sumida, February 19, 2008, by Shinpei Takeda (ST hereafter).
14. On Nisei's struggle over their citizenship during the war, see Mary Kimoto Tomita, *Dear Miye* (Stanford, CA: Stanford University Press, 1995); Karl Yoneda, *Ganbatte: Sixty-Year Struggle of a Kibei Worker* (Los Angeles: Asian American Studies Center, University of California, 1983).
15. Interview with George Kazuto Saiki, June 24, 2013, by the author..
16. Interview with Saiki, June 24, 2013. A similar feeling of alienation from their families was expressed by many US survivors. See, for example, interview with Tim Nakamoto, June 23, 1991, FOH; interview with Miyoko Igarashi, June 23, 1991, FOH.
17. Spurred by the "racial turn" in US immigration history, scholars have explored the racism toward Asian Americans as something shaped by US racial hierarchy and white supremacy, shifting the focus of immigration history from ethnonational conflicts to racialization processes. See Anna Pegler-Gordon, "Debating the Racial Turn in US Ethnic and Immigration History," *Journal of American Ethnic History* 36, no. 2 (2017): 40–53. Works that explore intraracial racism include Eiichiro Azuma, "Brokering Race, Culture, and Citizenship: Japanese Americans in Occupied Japan and Postwar National Inclusion," *Journal of American-East Asian Relations* 16, no. 3 (2009): 187–94.
18. On the changing perception of Japanese Americans before and after the war, see Shibusawa, *America's Geisha Ally*, 72–73, 150–51.
19. Interview with Dairiki, July 13, 2010; Rinjirō Sodei, *Were We the Enemy? American Survivors of Hiroshima* (Boulder, CO: Westview Press, 1998), 66–69.
20. Interview with Alfred Kaneo Dote, June 25, 2012, by the author.
21. The effect of Cold War culture on Asian Americans has been richly explored in Cindy I-Fen Cheng, *Citizens of Asian America: Democracy and Race during the Cold War* (New York: New York University Press, 2013); Jodi Kim, *Ends of Empire: Asian American Critique and the Cold War* (Minneapolis: University of Minnesota Press, 2010).
22. Interview with May Yamaoka, July 17, 2010, ST.
23. Interview with Yamaoka, July 17, 2010. US survivors' silence about the bomb was particularly salient among hibakusha who married interracially. See, for example,

interview with Miyuki Broadwater, March 26, 2009, ST; interview with Lisa Gendernalik, July 17, 2011, by the author.

24. Interview with Kazuko Aoki, June 19, 2013, by the author.
25. Interview with Aoki, June 19, 2013.
26. Wake, *American Survivors*, chapter 5.
27. Shibusawa, *America's Geisha Ally*, 19, 34.
28. Serlin, *Replaceable You*, 90, 103.
29. See Brian Komei Dempster, ed., *Making Home from War: Stories of Japanese American Exile and Resettlement* (Berkeley, CA: Heyday Books, 2011); Greg Robinson, *After Camp: Portraits in Midcentury Japanese American Life and Politics* (Berkeley: University of California Press, 2012).
30. Simpson, *An Absent Presence*; Linda Tamura, *Nisei Soldiers Break Their Silence: Coming Home to Hood River* (Seattle: University of Washington Press, 2012).
31. Baynton, *Defectives in the Land*; Natalia Molina, *Fit to Be Citizens? Public Health and Race in Los Angeles* (Berkeley: University of California Press, 2006).
32. Hsu, *The Good Immigrants*, 217–19; Lee, *The Making of Asian America*, 286–87.
33. On the feminization of Asian Americans as a model minority, see Judy Tzu-Chun Wu, *Doctor Mom Chung of the Fair-Haired Bastards: The Life of a Wartime Celebrity* (Berkeley: University of California Press, 2005); Chiou-Ling Yeh, "A Saga of Democracy: Toy Len Goon, American Mother of the Year, and the Cultural Cold War," *Pacific Historical Review* 81, no. 3 (August 2012): 432–61.
34. Unlike other US survivors I examine, Moriwaki and Okano, in the following discussion, did not have family connections to America before the war. They were born in Japan to parents with no history of living in America, and they became American citizens as a result of postwar marriages to US citizens. I use their examples following US hibakusha's insistence since the 1970s that all US survivors be treated equally regardless of their citizenship by birth. In my estimation, those who fall into the category of postwar immigrants make up about a quarter of US survivors.
35. Interview with Joyce Ikuko Moriwaki, June 20, 2013, by the author.
36. Kirsten Fermaglich and Lisa Fine, eds., *The Feminine Mystique; Annotated Text Contexts Scholarship* (New York: W. W. Norton, 2013).
37. Interview with Takeko Okano, June 18, 2012, by the author.
38. Interview with Okano, June 18, 2012.
39. Interview with Okano, June 18, 2012.
40. Brooks, *Alien Neighbors*, 194–98; Robinson, *After Camp*, 3, 46.
41. The biannual health checkups of American hibakusha by Japanese physicians began in 1977, but the checkups were not sponsored by the Japanese government. Instead, the Hiroshima Prefectural Medical Association and other nongovernmental associations funded the first three checkups, in 1977, 1979, and 1981.

CHAPTER 14

Barbara Reynolds and the Politics of Transnational Antinuclear Activism

ELYSSA FAISON

At the edge of Hiroshima Peace Memorial Park stands a monument dedicated to the memory of American antinuclear activist Barbara Leonard Reynolds (1915–90). Erected only months after the Fukushima nuclear disaster of 2011, it is located in an area dedicated to celebrating the lives of foreigners who made a significant impact in Hiroshima. These include American journalist and philanthropist Norman Cousins (1915–90) and Swiss physician Marcel Junod (1904–61), each of whom played key roles in advancing the cause of Hiroshima *hibakusha*, or atomic bomb victims. The stone and plaque dedicated to Reynolds, the third foreigner to be so honored, display her image and a quotation attributed to her: "I, too, am a *hibakusha*." For the Quaker pacifist who had dedicated decades of her life to reminding the world how the atomic bomb dropped on Hiroshima toward the end of the Second World War had killed and maimed the residents of one of Japan's major metropolises in novel ways and without discrimination, the statement neatly summarized Reynolds's belief that nuclear weapons posed an existential threat to all of humanity.[1] In her activist work she sought to center the hibakusha of Hiroshima even as her pleas for peace were always framed as universal.

And yet, Barbara Reynolds was, in fact, *not* a hibakusha. The statement attributed to her was reportedly made to a Japanese colleague, Dr. Harada Tōmin, in 1963. At the time that the bomb dubbed Little Boy was released from the US military bomber Enola Gay to shatter the lives of those living and working in Hiroshima in 1945, Reynolds was a mother of three young children living comfortably in Ohio, supporting the career of her anthropology professor husband. She would not become converted to the cause of peace activism (and to Quakerism, which contributed to her identity as a peace activist) until after 1958—four years after the Bravo test at Bikini inspired a global antinuclear movement.

By the time Reynolds became converted to the cause of antinuclear activism in the late 1950s, the US military had been conducting nuclear tests in the Marshall Islands for over a decade, displacing thousands of Marshallese from their home atolls and exposing many to radioactive fallout. But as Reynolds understood, it was the Japanese who were familiar and relatable to Americans and other international audiences to whom she was appealing. By the time the US-led occupation of Japan ended in 1952, Americans could relate to the Japanese, who had become familiar in both war and peace, much more than they could relate to the inhabitants of atolls that made up one part of the sprawling United Nations Trust Territory of the Pacific Islands. Having lived in Hiroshima for years and developed deep personal connections with Hiroshima residents and hibakusha, she was committed to telling their stories and believed that their personal testimonials had the power to change minds about nuclear weapons and about war.

Why, then, did Barbara Reynolds identify herself as a hibakusha later in life? What did she mean by claiming that she, too, was a hibakusha? And how was that identification as a hibakusha understood by those in Hiroshima whose lives had been shattered on August 6, 1945, by the dropping of the first atomic weapon in war? Barbara Reynolds's story shows us how the political constraints of the Cold War and the unequal relationship between a defeated and recently occupied Japan and the new American superpower could create divergent political and activist priorities, even for people united in their advocacy of disarmament and peace.

The *Golden Rule*, the *Phoenix of Hiroshima*, and the Making of an Antinuclear Activist

Barbara Reynolds's transformation from a stay-at-home wife and mother and aspiring fiction writer living in Ohio into an outspoken peace and antinuclear activist based in Hiroshima, Japan, occurred in a broader context of US peace and antinuclear activism in the 1950s and the participation of American Quakers in that activism.[2] Peace organizations like the Women's

International League for Peace and Freedom (WILPF), the Fellowship of Reconciliation (FOR), and the American Friends Service Committee (AFSC) had been founded during and in response to the First World War. Although WILPF and FOR were international organizations, WILPF was founded by Americans Jane Addams and Carrie Chapman Catt, both central to the American women's suffrage movement, and dominated by members from the English-speaking world. FOR was founded by an English Quaker and a German Lutheran in 1914 as a Christian-based antiwar organization, with a US branch founded the following year. The AFSC, founded in 1917 by members of the Religious Society of Friends (Quakers), originally sought to aid religious objectors to war (and thus to conscription) by creating wartime service opportunities in which they could take part without betraying their pacifist principles.

All of these groups remained active through and beyond the period of the Second World War. Following the 1954 Castle Bravo hydrogen bomb test at Bikini Atoll, they focused aggressively on opposing nuclear testing, sponsoring petition drives and a "prayer and conscience vigil" in Washington in late 1957 along with other pacifist groups.[3] That same year, American journalist and philanthropist Norman Cousins, along with former AFSC executive secretary Clarence Pickett, founded the Committee for a Sane Nuclear Policy (SANE, today known as Peace Action). It was in the context of antinuclear activism in the United States connected to broader political, ethical, and religious movements that Reynolds came to engage in her own antinuclear work in Japan.

In the wake of these organized antinuclear activities, four men set out from Honolulu on a ketch called the *Golden Rule* in May 1958. Their goal was to reach the atomic testing grounds of Enewetak in the Marshall Islands, where the US government had announced hydrogen bomb testing would resume beginning that spring, to protest nuclear tests and advocate for disarmament. The crew consisted of three Quakers and a Methodist. The skipper, Captain Albert Bigelow of Cos Cob, Connecticut, was a former navy commander who had served in the Pacific theater during the war and was now a committed pacifist. Influenced by his involvement with the American Friends Service Committee, Bigelow was joined by fellow Quakers William Huntington and George Willoughby, with whom he had founded the group Non-Violent Action against Nuclear Weapons

(NVAANW), the sponsoring organization for the mission.[4] In addition to chairing NVAANW, Willoughby also served as executive secretary of the Central Committee for Conscientious Objectors. The youngest of the crew was a twenty-eight-year-old Methodist named Orion Sherwood who shared the Quakers' antiwar and antinuclear positions. The men had been moved to action as concerns grew worldwide about the potentially disastrous consequences not only of nuclear war but of nuclear testing itself, after the test blast of the first hydrogen bomb at Bikini Atoll in 1954. Among other things that made their voyage notable was the flying of a flag displaying what has come to be known as the peace sign, one of the earliest uses of the symbol in the United States.[5]

Alarmed at the group's plans to disrupt the nuclear test and at the possibilities their well-advertised protest held for mobilizing antinuclear sentiment nationally, the Eisenhower administration decided after a flurry of high-level consultations to have the Atomic Energy Commission issue a ban on Americans entering the test area. Ignoring the injunction, the crew of the *Golden Rule* set off from Honolulu on May 1, 1958, only to be intercepted and taken into custody. By May 7 the four crewmen had been convicted of criminal contempt of court for defying the ban and were given one year of probation.[6] Unchastened, the *Golden Rule* reconfigured its crew and set off once again in defiance of court orders on June 1, only to be boarded and arrested by the Coast Guard a second time. This time the entire crew was sentenced to sixty days in jail.[7]

What would compel a Quaker man like Albert Bigelow to attempt to skipper a small vessel into a nuclear test site as an act of political protest? At the time, Bigelow was fifty-one years old, a painter and architect, married with two daughters and four grandchildren. He was a former lieutenant commander in the navy, having commanded three combat vessels during World War II. After the war he worked as housing commissioner for Massachusetts (1947–48). He held the post of director of the Unitarian Service Committee starting in 1949, and had become a Quaker in the early 1950s. He and his wife were active in the Stamford Monthly Meeting in Connecticut, and he was involved in leadership of the New York office of the American Friends Service Committee.[8]

It was his membership in the Stamford Monthly Meeting and engagement with the AFSC that had led Bigelow and his wife, three years earlier, to agree to host two of the New York Hiroshima Maidens, who were in the United States to receive plastic surgery treatments. A joint effort of Norman Cousins, editor of the *Saturday Review*, and Methodist minister and Hiroshima bomb survivor Tanimoto Kiyoshi, the Hiroshima Maidens project brought twenty-five young Japanese women who had been disfigured by the bomb to the United States in 1955.[9] While Tanimoto organized the vetting of the young women who would eventually take part in the trip from Hiroshima, Cousins arranged for their surgeries to be undertaken at Mount Sinai Hospital in New York. To house the young women, many of whom would need to stay in the United States for over a year while their multiple surgeries were completed, he enlisted Quaker families from the New York City suburbs in New Jersey, Connecticut, and Westchester County, New York. In addition to Bigelow, fellow Quaker and crewman of the *Golden Rule* William Huntington also hosted one of the Hiroshima Maidens.[10] For a man like Albert Bigelow, already disheartened by the senseless killing he had witnessed during the war and stunned by the atomic bombings that appeared to have ended it, hosting two young survivors of the Hiroshima blast was a turning point toward peace and antinuclear activism. As he would write later, "The Hiroshima Maidens were 'truth made visible' to us in 1955."[11]

Albert Bigelow's radicalization as a Quaker peace and civil rights activist arguably began with the Hiroshima Maidens. But it was Barbara Reynolds who, having become radicalized by Albert Bigelow and the crew of the *Golden Rule*, would take up their task and subsequently return to Japan to sponsor a Peace Pilgrimage and the World Peace Study Mission, and found the World Friendship Center in Hiroshima. A chance meeting with the crew of the *Golden Rule* led her to become a Quaker and set her on a path of peace and antinuclear activism.

Born in Madison, Wisconsin, the daughter of an educator, Barbara Leonard met Earle Reynolds at the University of Wisconsin in 1935 and married him the same year. After a period living in Ohio, where Earle had a job as a professor of anthropology at Antioch College, by 1951 they were living in Hiroshima, where Earle had been hired to conduct a three-year study of the effects of radiation on human growth. A physical anthropologist and research scientist, he worked with the Atomic Bomb Casualty Commission (ABCC) with funding from the Atomic Energy Commission to undertake the study. He and Barbara had daily contact with atomic bomb survivors, and over the course of Earle's tenure at the ABCC, the family came to understand the depth of victims' suffering. Increasingly they came to question the United States' decision to use the bomb and, as the Cold War nuclear testing race got underway, to oppose such testing. For Earle, this understanding was scientific and rational: he knew that strontium-90, a radioactive isotope produced by nuclear fission, was "a bone seeker; that is, behaving similarly to calcium, it is much more active in children, whose bones are developing, than in adults."[12] And over the course of his time working in Hiroshima, he came to understand that the US government and its agencies—particularly the Atomic Energy Commission, which had funded his research and whose job he believed it was to inform the American public about the possible dangers of nuclear energy, was consistently downplaying the very real possibility of harm from nuclear fallout.[13]

Having finished his research work in Hiroshima by 1954 and with the family looking for an adventure, he decided to circumnavigate the globe in a small yacht called the *Phoenix of Hiroshima*.[14] The name was no mistake: throughout the 1950s the city of Hiroshima was frequently referred to in both the Japanese and foreign media as a phoenix rising from the ashes.[15] Along with their children, Ted and Jessica (sixteen and ten years old, respectively, at the time they set sail from Hiroshima), and Japanese crewmen from Hiroshima Mikami Niichi, Fushima Motosada, and Suemitsu Mitsugi, the family spent a total of three and a half years at sea.[16] While docked in Honolulu before their return to Japan in 1958, Earle, Barbara, the two children, and Mikami came into contact with the crew of the *Golden Rule*, whose ordeals of arrest and prosecution for disobeying the Atomic Energy Commission injunction they watched firsthand, attending each day's trial proceedings. Motivated by their concern about nuclear proliferation and their growing interest in Quakerism, they decided, following the jailing of the *Golden Rule* crew, to take up the torch and sail the *Phoenix* into the test zone in its stead.

A month after the second prosecution of Albert Bigelow and the rest of the crew of the *Golden Rule*, the Reynolds crew entered the nuclear test zone in the Marshall Islands in their yacht *Phoenix*. Earle was arrested by the US Coast Guard and returned to Honolulu. He was tried and convicted, and sentenced to two years in prison, a conviction that was eventually overturned by an appellate court as having been based on an invalid regulation—which had been Earle's contention all along.[17]

Before finally leaving Honolulu after the two-year ordeal of trials and appeals, Barbara and Earle both applied for and were accepted into membership in the Society of Friends. In April 1960 the family, now committed peace activists, and Barbara and Earle officially Quakers, returned to Japan, where Earle taught classes at Hiroshima Women's College and Barbara engaged in numerous peace and antinuclear activities, especially involving Hiroshima and Nagasaki atomic bomb survivors.

The Kawamotos and the Paper Crane Society (Orizuru-kai)

But much had happened in Japan and especially in Hiroshima with regard to antinuclear activism in the years since the *Phoenix* first set out on its journey. On March 1, 1954, the crew of the Japanese tuna trawler the *Lucky Dragon No. 5* (*Daigo Fukuryūmaru*) witnessed a secret hydrogen bomb test in the vicinity of the Marshall Islands. Upon arrival back at their home port of Yaizu, the crew, whose faces and hands had become blackened from exposure to radioactive ash, were sent immediately to the hospital. Eventually all twenty-three would be transferred to hospitals in Tokyo, where one of them, radioman Kuboyama Aikichi, would die after a couple of months of what Japanese physicians said was organ failure due to radiation exposure, and what American scientists trying to protect the secrets of the bomb would claim must have been hepatitis contracted from blood transfusions during his treatment.[18]

In addition to reading in the news each day about the medical conditions of the *Lucky Dragon* crew members and the eventual death of Kuboyama, nearly the entire population of Japan also had to contend with the fear that came from knowing that irradiated tuna and other fish had entered the market and been sold throughout the country after being off-loaded from boats that, like the *Lucky Dragon*, had been exposed to varying degrees of fallout from the Bikini test. Indeed, before the *Lucky Dragon* itself had been sequestered and its crew members taken to hospital, its catch had been off-loaded in Yaizu and sold. Where the bombings of Hiroshima and Nagasaki in 1945 had created a local sense of atomic victimhood, that sensibility became nationalized after the *Lucky Dragon* incident.[19]

The sense of outrage and despair felt worldwide in the wake of the Bikini hydrogen bomb test had a particular poignancy in the only country that had experienced atomic warfare. Hibakusha became the focal point of a new nationalized peace and antinuclear movement in the months and years after the Bikini test. In this newly charged environment, antinuclear activities took off. In addition to various international tours and projects in 1955 involving "atomic maidens" (the most famous being the Hiroshima Maidens project led by Norman Cousins and Tanimoto Kiyoshi), the World Congress against the A- and H-Bomb convened for the first time in Hiroshima, bringing together delegates from all over the world and contributing to an image of Hiroshima cultivated by city leaders as a "city of peace."[20]

This same year in October, a young girl named Sasaki Sadako died of radiation-caused leukemia. Her death became a focal point for Hiroshima activists, and especially hibakusha, who were concerned not only with promoting peace and opposing nuclear testing but also with improving conditions for survivors of the bomb. Sadako was one of many children in Hiroshima who died of radiation-related illnesses during the 1950s. The Orizuru-kai, or Paper Crane Society, notes as part of its history the deaths of a large number of children from a-bomb disease in 1954 and 1955, recording specifically the passing of nine-year-old Iwamoto Yoshie on October 23, 1954, of aplastic anemia; fifteen-year-old a-bomb orphan Hirota Noriyuki on October 24, 1955, of acute myelogenous leukemia; and Sasaki Sadako, who died the following day of subleukemic leukemia.[21] Sadako's story of folding paper cranes before her death captivated the public thanks to promotion of the story by the Orizuru-kai and helped her classmates successfully raise money to fund a monument dedicated to the children of the atomic bomb, which was erected in Hiroshima Peace Memorial Park in 1958.[22]

Peace activist Kawamoto Ichirō, founder of the Orizuru-kai, was a central figure in organizing students to get the children's monument erected. Kawamoto was sixteen years old and working in the town of Saka in Hiroshima Prefecture when the Americans dropped the atomic bomb on Hiroshima. Born in Peru to Japanese parents who had emigrated to South America, he returned to Japan after their death. Repeated trips into the city of Hiroshima to help survivors in the days immediately following the blast left him with significant radiation exposure and qualified him as a hibakusha. Even in these first days after the war's end, Kawamoto already had a reputation for sacrificing his own well-being to help others. An orphan himself, he befriended children whose parents had been killed by the bomb and others who suffered from radiation sickness or other injuries. He often fed and housed young people in need, despite the fact that he himself lived in modest conditions and barely had enough money to support himself.[23]

Kawamoto knew Sasaki Sadako personally because her father had a barbershop in his neighborhood. A two-year-old when the bomb was dropped, Sadako had shown no signs of injury or illness until shortly before her death at age twelve. Approached by a number of Sadako's bereaved classmates who wished to do something in her memory, Kawamoto organized them to use Sadako's story of folding paper cranes before her death to promote the construction of a memorial to children. Pamphlets and brochures distributed by his newly formed Orizuru-kai repeated and embellished upon the story of Sadako's efforts to fold one thousand paper cranes while she was in the hospital. Her story helped her classmates successfully raise money to fund the monument.

The Orizuru-kai, established in 1958, the same year that the Reynolds family sailed the *Phoenix* into the nuclear testing zone in the Marshall Islands, continued to attract new members who engaged in activities to support Hiroshima's children and promote peace even after the erection of the Children's Peace Monument in Peace Park. Under Kawamoto's leadership, one of the group's major efforts was to advocate for the preservation of the Atomic Bomb Dome, the name now given to the Industrial Promotion Hall that stood directly under the bomb dropped on Hiroshima, which was being threatened by local business and political interests who advocated razing it to make way for development and to eradicate what many saw as an unwelcome reminder of the suffering of the war.[24] During this period Kawamoto married a fellow hibakusha named Tokie, who joined him in his work on behalf of bomb survivors. Having followed with great interest the news about the voyage of the *Phoenix* and Earle Reynolds's trial in Honolulu, Kawamoto Ichirō and Tokie and members of the Orizuru-kai were at the airport to greet Reynolds with leis made of folded paper cranes when Earle flew back to Japan for a short trip to scout out academic

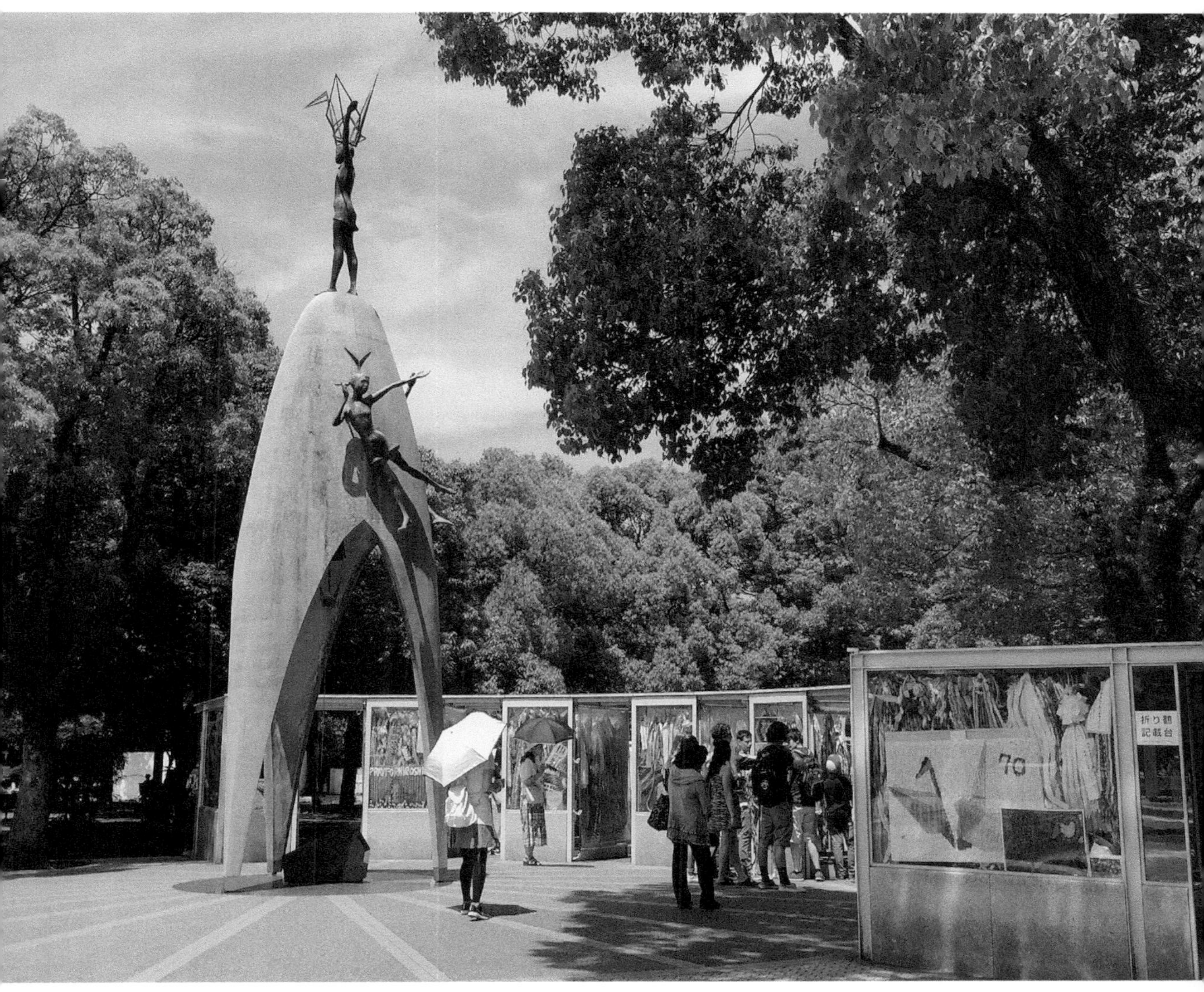

FIGURE 14.1. Children's Monument in Hiroshima Peace Memorial Park. Donations of folded paper cranes to the site have happened so consistently that special structures were installed to hold them in the mid-1990s. Paper cranes are removed and cataloged on a regular basis before being replaced with new donations. Photograph courtesy of the author.

job possibilities in January 1960. Such welcomes of notable foreigners and visiting peace activists became a staple of Orizuru-kai activities over the years.[25]

Diverging Priorities

When Earle and Barbara Reynolds arrived in Hiroshima upon sailing back from Honolulu in April 1960, the city was struggling to maintain an identity created by elites and government officials who wanted to brand Hiroshima as a tourist- and business-friendly city of peace. Meanwhile, an increasingly divided and potentially militant antinuclear movement was taking shape. Just as Hiroshima had changed and internationalized, becoming the new home to a variety of peace and antinuclear organizations in the mid-1950s, similarly Barbara Reynolds returned to the city changed, now an outspoken activist. In 1962 she organized and led a Peace Pilgrimage that took two atomic bomb survivors from Hiroshima to the United Nations and on a worldwide tour to educate a global audience on the dangers of nuclear war. In 1964 she organized the World Peace Study Mission, in which twenty-five atomic bomb survivors, accompanied by a dozen interpreters, traveled the globe to encourage world leaders to agree to nuclear weapons bans.

One of her greatest supporters in these efforts was the Hiroshima physician Harada Tōmin, who had been one of three Japanese doctors to accompany the Hiroshima Maidens in 1955 to learn advanced plastic surgery techniques and who participated in their surgeries at Mount Sinai Hospital. Having served as a medical officer for the Imperial Japanese Army during the war, Harada did not experience the atomic bombing of his hometown firsthand. He learned of the bomb and of Japan's surrender while a prisoner of war in Taiwan. Finally repatriated in March 1946, an emaciated Harada, still suffering the effects of malaria, returned to an obliterated Hiroshima to find that his wife and children had survived in the countryside. After erecting a small hospital amid the rubble of the bombed-out city, Harada began to see patients with mysterious symptoms. The long-term effects of radiation were not yet known, and Harada had not yet heard the term "atomic bomb disease" (*gen baku shō*), coined by Tokyo physician and radiation specialist Dr. Tsuzuki Masao. Before long he witnessed patients, especially young children, dying of radiation-related leukemia.[26] Harada served as chairman of Reynolds's World Friendship Center in Hiroshima for years and was a steadfast ally and colleague. Like Barbara Reynolds, he was not himself a hibakusha (and did not identify as such) but dedicated much of his life to working on their behalf and advocating for peace and disarmament. Harada Tōmin's collaboration with Reynolds represented a successful effort at forging transnational activist ties based on universalist antiwar and antinuclear principles.

But not all such associations would be as tranquil. After Reynolds's return from the World Peace Study Mission, a project hampered by disorganization and lack of preparation that came to an end with $50,000 in outstanding bills, a highly contentious and at times public debate broke out between Reynolds and Kawamoto Ichirō and his wife Tokie. Coming soon after Barbara and Earle had divorced on unhappy terms, this debate could not have been welcome.[27] Once close allies and collaborators on projects involving aid to atomic bomb victims—Kawamoto Tokie had even participated in the recent World Peace Study Mission—the Kawamotos and Barbara Reynolds were now, in June 1966, locked in a struggle over the use of paper cranes as a symbol for Hiroshima, the antinuclear movement, and the atomic bomb victims themselves. In a ten-page pamphlet distributed by the Orizuru-kai and almost certainly penned by the Kawamotos, the organization accused Barbara of attempting to profit off the backs of atomic bomb victims, who were, in their account, pressed into making folded paper cranes for Barbara to sell to foreigners. The cranes associated with their peace movement, they claimed, came almost entirely from the "Atomic Museum" (Hiroshima Peace Memorial Museum) and the Children's Monument, having been left there by visitors. They deplored Barbara's attempts to monetize the cranes in support of an international peace movement by attempting to produce crane-making kits for distribution globally, preferring that the use of the crane remain small-scale and local, concerned especially that people not forget the connection of the cranes to the story of Sasaki Sadako. They went even farther by suggesting that Kawamoto Tokie had not volunteered to go on the World Peace Study Mission but had in fact been bullied into it, presumably by Barbara, and that the disorganization of the mission forced participants to make and sell paper cranes during their travels just to have enough money to eat.[28]

The fight spilled over into local and national newspapers, where Barbara was accused of betraying the people on whose behalf she claimed to work.

At play here appears to have been a number of overlapping issues, including the perception of American imperialism. One accusation was that Barbara would send letters in English to atomic bomb victims who were barely literate in Japanese, much less English, with no thought of how they would read them. Barbara's penchant for large-scale projects similarly gave the impression, at least in this case, that she would think up and organize a plan but then leave the bulk of the labor for local groups to carry out.

This conflict between the Kawamotos and Barbara Reynolds took place amid a larger civic conflict over the commemoration of the atomic bombings in Hiroshima and Nagasaki that played out against the backdrop of Cold War anticommunist discourse in both Japan and the United States.[29] Reynolds may have been less aware of the underlying issues surrounding the perception of paper cranes made by atomic bomb victims being sold for profit. The Kawamotos in their newsletter noted with alarm that they had come to know of a merchant who opened a paper crane shop adjacent to Peace Park, near the Children's Peace Monument their organization had helped raise funds to build. Their opposition to this brand of commercialization went beyond their debate with Barbara Reynolds. The Kawamotos and their Orizuru-kai had started a campaign for the preservation of the Atomic Bomb Dome in 1960 and were becoming frustrated with the lack of movement on the issue by the mid-1960s. The battle lines seemed to divide between the city's business interests—who wanted the dome razed with an eye to potentially lucrative redevelopment in the area—and those who wanted to preserve the dome as a potential tourist site and a reminder of the suffering of the atomic bomb victims.

In this context, the accusations lodged against Barbara Reynolds represented more than just a personal dispute. Any suggestion of commercializing the symbols of atomic suffering undercut the campaign to preserve the dome and, with it, the agency and voices of the victims themselves. For her part, Barbara Reynolds always denied having sold paper cranes for profit. And indeed, her own objections to the commercialization of the sacred led her to fast as a form of protest against the rampant commercialization of the Christmas holiday taking place in the United States and globally. After much correspondence and several face-to-face meetings and attempted mediations with the Kawamotos, no clear resolution seems to have materialized. Barbara continued to produce and distribute versions of what she called the Peace Puzzle—a cardboard envelope containing paper and folding instructions to make a crane—and the Atomic Bomb Dome is still standing today.

This debate between the Kawamotos and Barbara Reynolds may appear quite trivial in the context of an emergent antinuclear movement in which firm battle lines were being drawn between communist- and non-communist-supporting individuals and organizations. In fact, Kawamoto's activities in the 1950s and '60s were indeed watched carefully by the Japanese police for any signs of communist support or affiliation. And in many ways, this debate was not something that defined a movement. But it does allow us to focus on two important aspects of hibakusha activism in Hiroshima. First, their activities were crucial to what became the global circulation of the most enduring symbols of Japan's peace and antinuclear movement. It was Kawamoto who crafted and promoted the story of Sadako and the paper cranes, initially for local and domestic reasons. That symbol remains central to activism focused on hibakusha, but it has also become universalized and deployed in contexts that strip it of its original, local meanings. Barbara Reynolds's efforts to circulate internationally the actual bodies and testimonies of hibakusha similarly had an enormous impact on global antinuclear discourse and imagery. Still today, while the numbers of living survivors of the Hiroshima and Nagasaki atomic bomb attacks are dwindling, many of them continue to publicly represent the cause of nuclear abolition.[30] Second, the fraught interactions between Barbara and the Kawamotos remind us that their activism was conditioned by their respective positions within the Cold War frame of American imperial dominance over Japan and much of East Asia. Just as the Kawamotos depended on Barbara for her access to money and influential foreign connections (such as Norman Cousins), Barbara in turn depended on cooperation from the hibakusha of Hiroshima to bring her message to a worldwide audience.

How, then, are we to interpret Barbara Reynolds's claim that "I, too, am a *hibakusha*"? Perhaps she meant it in a literal sense. Many scientists have proposed that the advent of the Anthropocene—a new geological boundary marker following the Holocene that is defined by globally discernible changes in the Earth's environment and climate linked to human activity—began with the nuclear age. A group of eminent geoscientists, oceanographers, atmospheric scientists, chemists, and historians of science has suggested in recent years that the detonation of the Trinity atomic test bomb on July 16, 1945, at Alamogordo, New Mexico, should serve as the precise starting point for the Anthropocene. The Trinity test, followed by the bombings of Hiroshima and Nagasaki and then decades of nuclear testing throughout the world, has been "the major cause," they note, "of distribution of human-made radionuclides over the globe. The small particles of radioactive debris from nuclear explosions (global fallout) were injected into the stratosphere where they circulate globally," descending back through the troposphere and scattering across the earth's surface.[31] This has resulted in the near doubling of atmospheric carbon-14 during the period of thermonuclear bomb testing from 1955 until the signing of the Nuclear Test Ban Treaty in 1963. These high levels of carbon-14 are traceable at the cellular level in humans and indeed all living organisms on planet Earth.[32] While the concept of the Anthropocene had not yet been discussed during Barbara Reynolds's lifetime, might she have understood in some other way that all of humanity had been fundamentally changed—materially as well as spiritually—by the bomb?

Or perhaps Barbara Reynolds referred to herself as a hibakusha metaphorically, the way Albert Bigelow spoke metaphorically of the *Golden Rule*. On the open ocean, Bigelow noted, the crew was "a self-reliant community, our very existence depended upon one another. We were all in the same boat. We were 'all in the same boat' with mankind too. In that 'boat' we all huddled together, cowering before a storm of our own making. We had loosed naked, uncontrolled horror upon the world."[33] As a peace activist Barbara Reynolds would surely have understood all of humanity to be interconnected, and as a devout Christian she believed all people were joined in the love of Jesus Christ.

Or perhaps she meant it the way her friend and colleague Dr. Harada Tōmin had understood her when she spoke to him the words that would become her epitaph:

> Around 1963 Barbara was sitting on a bench in Peace Memorial Park praying. At that time she was in the midst of a fast to protest the extreme commercialization of Christmas, but just to look at her no one would have guessed

> that she was fasting. I sat down beside her and asked, "What are you thinking about?" She replied without a moment's hesitation, "I too am a *hibakusha*." She offered no explanation. . . . Perhaps on that day in 1963 she was thinking, "The survivors are all suffering. Perhaps some have indeed overcome their suffering. In addition they all pray for peace for all of the people of the world. They are contemporary prophets. Unless I suffer with them, I can never become a person who helps bring peace."[34]

Or as Harada would later come to interpret it, "All of us are survivors of the bomb. Whether we were 3,000 miles or 10,000 miles from the atomic explosion is irrelevant. All human beings on the face of the globe, whether we realize it or not, are *hibakusha*, victims of the bomb."[35]

And yet to some, Barbara Reynolds's Christian humanitarian universalism—which saw Japan's hibakusha as prophets who spoke of the dangers of war and nuclear weapons to a collective human condition—did not always acknowledge the localized human condition of the very people she extolled as prophets. Reynolds's World Friendship Center Peace Puzzle card describes the mission of the center as "seeking to increase understanding and cooperation between all people of good will and expanding a welfare program to take care of the many lonely old people who have lost their families as a result of the atomic bomb." For Reynolds, the paper crane was purely a symbol of peace and had even lost its reference to children, much less to Sasaki Sadako. The debate with the Orizuru-kai indicates that despite Barbara Reynolds's key role in helping to internationalize the antinuclear movement and movements in support of atomic bomb victims through her connections in the United States and her travel worldwide, neither she nor the various groups and individuals with whom she worked could transcend the very real structures produced by a combination of Western imperialism that predated the war and newer configurations of Cold War rivalry that forced every position in Japan to be read as either pro- or anti-American.

This, however, does not mean that we have to take the Kawamotos' position that Barbara Reynolds was, in effect, a neo-imperialist. The scholar of Hiroshima memory Lisa Yoneyama, while embracing a view of the Hiroshima Maidens project as part of a larger discourse on American imperialism in Asia, also points to a central feature of Quaker involvement in that project and other humanitarian and peace efforts in Japan. As

Yoneyama puts it, speaking of the Hiroshima Maidens project, "Fraternal images at the national level concealed the fact that the Americans who had initially offered assistance to these women were critics of US military policies and were thus themselves part of an oppositional movement."[36] Here she is likely pointing to Norman Cousins's own antinuclear, antiwar, and anti-imperialist politics, but also the strong historical commitment to peace and nonviolence of the Society of Friends. While all of the Quaker families who hosted the young women of the Hiroshima Maidens project were white, suburban, middle-class Americans, and many of them were politically liberal, there existed among them as part of the Quaker heritage of peace and nonviolence a radical strain that manifested itself in the activism of people like Albert Bigelow, and after him Earle and Barbara Reynolds. The relationships forged between the Society of Friends and the Japanese people as a result of the Hiroshima Maidens Project and Barbara Reynolds's efforts on behalf of atomic bomb survivors took place on an individual and local rather than a national level. That is to say, Barbara Reynolds's activities on behalf of Hiroshimans and, as she understood it, the human race were not done in the name of US interests but expressly in opposition to those interests as they were understood at the highest levels of government; Reynolds's concern was more broadly with human rather than national interests.

For all that concern, Barbara Reynolds was not a hibakusha. She embodied through her life's work the tension between the universal and the particular—a tension that did not obtain for Hiroshima hibakusha like Kawamoto Ichirō and his wife Tokie. White American peace and antinuclear activists' belief in universal humanitarian values—and the "equality" of death and destruction they believed another nuclear war would bring—obscured the differential costs of American nuclear activities. The Cold War brought together Japanese and American peace and antinuclear activists in many of their mutual political efforts, but the differences between lived and theoretical hibakusha experience, as well as the power differential involved in international and personal US-Japan relations, could never be completely resolved.

Notes

1. In this belief Reynolds has never been alone. Recently nuclear humanities scholars N. A. J. Taylor and Robert Jacobs have argued that "Hiroshima" will likely continue to resonate with people beyond Hiroshima and Japan who may live perhaps millennia from now; or that in our own time, "people may too *experience* Hiroshima" through venues of commemoration. N. A. J. Taylor and Robert Jacobs, eds., *Reimagining Hiroshima and Nagasaki: Nuclear Humanities in the Post–Cold War* (New York: Routledge, 2018), 3.
2. Reynolds published her first book (her only mystery novel), *Alias for Death* (Coward-McCann), in 1950. After she and her family moved to Japan, she published a series of children's and young adult novels, including *Pepper* (Scribner's, 1952), about an orphaned baby raccoon; *Hamlet and Brownswiggle* (Scribner's, 1954); *Emily San* (Scribner's, 1955); and *Cabin Boy and Extra Ballast* (Scribner's, 1958).
3. Lawrence S. Wittner, *The Struggle against the Bomb*, vol. 2, *Resisting the Bomb: A History of the World Nuclear Disarmament Movement, 1954–1970* (Stanford, CA: Stanford University Press, 1997), 51.
4. The radical Quaker Lawrence Scott was another founder of NVAANW, which by September 1958 was replaced by the Committee for Nonviolent Action (CNVA) with Willoughby as its chair. Wittner, *The Struggle against the Bomb*, 54–57.
5. Mary Jo Lynch, "The Exchange: A Peaceful Controversy," *RQ* 10 (1971) 4: 337.
6. Press release, Religious News Service, May 26, 1958, DG13, Series E, Box 11: Fellowship of Reconciliation, Swarthmore College Peace Collection; Fellowship of Reconciliation (FOR), unpublished pamphlet draft, "Men against the Bomb: Eight Case Studies of American Non-violent Action," Nuclear/Germ Warfare Protests, Ser. E—NVA: Non-Violent Action, "Golden Rule" trip to Eniwetok, 1958, Swarthmore College Peace Collection.
7. "Summary of Events," DG76 Bigelow, Albert, Box 3, Swarthmore College Peace Collection. Albert Bigelow recounts these events in *The Voyage of the Golden Rule: An Experiment with Truth* (Garden City, NY: Doubleday, 1959).
8. Non-Violent Action against Nuclear Weapons press release leaflet, 1958, Fellowship of Reconciliation, Nuclear/Germ War Protests, Ser. E—NVA: "Golden Rule" trip to Eniwetok, 1958, Swarthmore College Peace Collection.
9. On the Hiroshima Maidens project, see Rodney Barker, *The Hiroshima Maidens: A Story of Courage, Compassion, and Survival* (New York: Viking, 1985); David Serlin, *Replaceable You: Engineering the Body in Postwar America* (Chicago: University of Chicago Press, 2004), chapter 2; and Caroline Chung Simpson, *An Absent Presence: Japanese Americans in Postwar American Culture, 1945–1960* (Durham, NC: Duke University Press, 2001), chapter 4.
10. Huntington's family hosted Sumimura Hideko, while the Bigelows hosted Enokawa Yoshie and Komatsu Sayoko. Letter from Helen Yokoyama to Ida Day, February 22, 1958, File Cabinet #5, Drawer 1: Folder "Correspondence: BY Yokoyama, Helen TO Ida Day, Peace Resource Center, Wilmington College."

11. Albert Bigelow Papers, handwritten autobiographical sketch, File DG 76, Swarthmore College Peace Collection.
12. Earle L. Reynolds, *The Forbidden Voyage of the Phoenix into the A.E.C. Prohibited Zone* (New York: David McKay, 1961), 31.
13. Reynolds, *The Forbidden Voyage of the Phoenix*, 31. See also David H. Price, "Earle Reynolds: Scientist, Citizen, and Cold War Dissident," in *Half-Lives and Half-Truths: Confronting the Radioactive Legacies of the Cold War*, ed. Barbara Rose Johnston (Santa Fe: School for Advanced Research Press, 2007), 55–75, which argues that Earle Reynolds's work with Japanese individuals and families living with and dying from traumatic bomb-related injuries made it difficult for him to continue with the type of "antiseptic" scientific work encouraged within the ABCC. Numerous letters that make up his correspondence held at the Peace Resource Center of Wilmington College also attest to his abiding concern that the government was withholding scientific information related to the effects of radiation from the American public.
14. Earle Reynolds recounts the journey of the *Phoenix* from its conception through the return of the boat to Honolulu in 1958 in Earle Reynolds and Barbara Reynolds, *All in the Same Boat: An American Family's Adventures on a Voyage around the World in the Yacht Phoenix* (New York: D. McKay, 1962).
15. Ran Zwigenberg, *Hiroshima: The Origins of Global Memory Culture* (New York: Cambridge University Press, 2014), 65.
16. The Reynolds family called the three men by the nicknames Nick (Mikami), Moto (Fushima), and Mickey (Suemitsu). After several altercations with Earle Reynolds, Fushima and Suemitsu left the *Phoenix* at the Panama Canal zone and boarded a vessel back to Japan in January 1958. Reynolds and Reynolds, *All in the Same Boat*. Earle and Barbara Reynolds had three children. The oldest, eighteen-year-old Tim, was attending boarding school in the United States and did not join in the voyage of the *Phoenix*.
17. Reynolds and Reynolds, *All in the Same Boat*, 281.
18. Ōishi Matashichi, *The Day the Sun Rose in the West: Bikini, the Lucky Dragon, and I*, trans. Richard H. Minear (Honolulu: University of Hawai'i Press, 2011), 63–65.
19. James J. Orr, *The Victim as Hero: Ideologies of Peace and National Identity* (Honolulu: University of Hawai'i Press, 2001). For the most thorough treatment of the *Lucky Dragon* incident, written by one of the crew members, see Matashichi, *The Day the Sun Rose in the West*. See also the essays in part 2 of this volume.
20. Zwigenberg, *Hiroshima*, 96.
21. "A-bomb disease," or *genbakushō*, was a term used in the months after the bombings of Hiroshima and Nagasaki to refer to the collection of external and internal symptoms such as burns and keloid scars, bleeding, anemia, fevers, and various radiation-related leukemias. The term, still used today, was coined by Dr. Tsuzuki Masao, a Tokyo radiology specialist who treated some of the first atomic bomb victims and was the lead physician in the treatment of the crew of the *Lucky Dragon* in 1954.

22. Cranes have long been associated with good fortune in Japan. Folk legend has it that folding a thousand paper cranes brings good luck, and such practice has often been associated with wishes for good health.
23. Robert Jungk, *Children of the Ashes: The People of Hiroshima after the Bomb*, trans. Constantine FitzGibbon (London: Paladin, 1985), 277–327.
24. Zwigenberg, *Hiroshima*, 216–21.
25. Kawaguchi Eiji, "Anheru no na totomo ni: Kawamoto Ichirō shoden," in *"Kaji no ha": Kajiyama Toshiyuki bungakuhi kenritsu kinenshi*, ed. Kajiyama Toshiyuki Bungakuhi Kanri Iinkai (Hiroshima: Keisuisha, 1993), 78–79. Members of the Orizuru-kai similarly greeted other American visitors, including Honolulu mayor Neal Blaisdell, his wife, and their entourage, who arrived in Japan in November 1959 to formalize and celebrate a new sister city relationship between Honolulu and Hiroshima. "Children of Hiroshima Welcome Blaisdell Party," *Japan Times*, November 10, 1959, 3.
26. Harada Tōmin, *Hiroshima Surgeon*, trans. Robert L. Ramseyer (Newton, KS: Faith and Life Press, 1983), chapter 2.
27. Earle and Barbara divorced in 1964. Earle later remarried to Akie Nagami from Hiroshima and continued his own peace and antinuclear activities, including sailing the Phoenix of Hiroshima to Vietnam in 1967. On Earle's activism, including the Vietnam trip, see David H. Price, "Earle Reynolds: Scientist, Citizen, and Cold War Dissident," in *Half-Lives and Half-Truths: Confronting the Radioactive Legacies of the Cold War*, ed. Barbara Rose Johnston (Santa Fe, NM: School for Advanced Research Press, 2007), 55–76.
28. *Crane* (newsletter), no. 57, June 11, 1966, Hiroshima/Nagasaki Memorial Collection, Peace Resource Center, Wilmington College, Wilmington, OH.
29. On the civic debates that took place in Hiroshima and Nagasaki in the 1950s related to how the bombings should be remembered and memorialized in those cities, see Zwigenberg, *Hiroshima*; and Chad Diehl, *Resurrecting Nagasaki: Reconstruction and the Formation of Atomic Narratives* (Ithaca, NY: Cornell University Press, 2018).
30. Most recently Japanese Canadian hibakusha Setsuko Thurlow, who was mobilized in her antinuclear activism as a result of the 1954 Bikini Castle Bravo hydrogen bomb test and the *Lucky Dragon* incident, emerged as a recognizable face of the antinuclear movement when she represented the International Campaign to Abolish Nuclear Weapons (ICAN) when it received the Nobel Peace Prize in 2017.
31. J. Zalasiewicz et al., "When Did the Anthropocene Begin? A Mid-Twentieth-Century Boundary Level Is Stratigraphically Optimal," *Quaternary International* 383 (2015): 201.
32. See, for example, Elisavet Georgiadou et. al., "Bomb-Pulse 14C Analysis Combined with 13C and 15N Measurements in Blood Serum from Residents of Malmo, Sweden," *Radiation and Environmental Biophysics* 52, no. 2 (May 2014), 175–87; and Quan Hua et al., "Atmospheric Radiocarbon for the Period 1950–2010," *Radiocarbon* 55, no. 4 (2013), 2059–72.

33. Albert Bigelow, *The Voyage of the Golden Rule: An Experiment with Truth* (Garden City, NY: Doubleday, 1959), 20. Perhaps it is no coincidence that Earle Reynolds titled the second of his two books chronicling the journey of the *Phoenix of Hiroshima*, published in 1962, *All in the Same Boat.*
34. Harada Tōmin, *Moments of Peace: Two Honorary Hiroshimans, Barbara Reynolds and Norman Cousins*, trans. Robert L. Ramseyer (Hiroshima: Gariver, 1998), 51.
35. Tōmin, *Moments of Peace*, 35–36.
36. Lisa Yoneyama, *Hiroshima Traces: Time, Space, and the Dialectics of Memory* (Berkeley: University of California Press, 1999), 202.

An Interview with Artist Will Wilson

ALISON FIELDS AND WILL WILSON

CHAPTER 15

Will Wilson is a Diné photographer and transcustomary artist who spent his formative years living on the Navajo Nation. His *Auto Immune Response* series (2004–present), discussed in chapter 16, pairs photography of a Navajo man navigating his postapocalyptic surroundings with installations of hogan greenhouses, weavings, and videos. In *Connecting the Dots* (2019–present), Wilson uses drone photography to document uranium contamination on the Navajo Nation. This interview took place on August 7, 2019, in Santa Fe, New Mexico.

ALISON FIELDS: Growing up on the Navajo Nation, what are the ways that the area's history of uranium mining impacted you and your family?

WILL WILSON: I don't think it was looming large in my mind at that particular moment. I just think the idea of an apocalypse, or that slow genocide that has already happened—it is present and occurring. And then also my space in it, from a really personal standpoint. Being this mixed-race kid who grew up at Navajo [Nation] and then also in San Francisco and dealing with the interesting racial politics that arose from that drove me to this idea of an environment gone askew. I'd certainly made the connection to a lot of 1970s postapocalyptic movies, and I think that kind of pop culture was something that was salient or interesting to me as a metaphor for what Navajo people were going through, what my life was going through at that particular moment.

One of the things that I remembered later as a kid was playing at a place called Rare Metals [near Tuba City, Arizona, Navajo Nation] that was a uranium processing mill in the 1950s and I think in the 1960s that a lot of my relatives spent time working at. And that site is now a Superfund site.

When I was a kid going to boarding school, it was this cool place you could go to and goof off and climb in the rafters of this postindustrial, abandoned space. There's this Joel Sternfeld image that I show in a lot of my lectures of Rare Metals, and he captured that. I'm sure he was aware of the whole irony of that space, this strange euphemism Rare Metals, which was this uranium-processing mill. That place is now fenced off and covered with tons and tons of rock. And I just shot it with my drone, which was pretty awesome, resulting in these really beautiful aerial images.

FIELDS: Can you talk about the link between the corn pollen and uranium powder in your *Auto Immune Response* (AIR) series?

WILSON: The sprinkling of the corn pollen in the morning is the Navajo daily prayer, as the sun is rising. The way that I've been told is that right before the sun hits, as the rays are coming, the holy people come and check out what's going on. Do you keep a clean space? Are you living within your means? Are you a good person? They are just checking in every morning. If you are there, and everything is right, and you are saying your prayers, then good things will happen, you are right in the world.

Recently, somebody was telling me that in Navajo creation there is a point in the story where people were offered two substances. They are both yellow, yellow dirt. They were told, this one is incredibly powerful and would generate all this energy, and this other one is also very powerful and can generate life, and you have a choice. Pick one and leave the other one alone.

I've had this dream for a long time of reproducing the gadget—the first atomic test object of the bomb and, instead of putting plutonium in the center core, to put a handful of corn pollen in there. Someday.

FIELDS: What do you imagine the starting point of the protagonist to be? What is the way he is engaging with this world or trying to figure it out?

WILSON: The closest analogy I can make is to a zombie movie where the protagonist wakes up in the hospital bed and doesn't really remember why he's there and how he's there, but suddenly it's time to figure out how to survive. That's where the more personal side of the narrative is, a source point for me thinking about what it has meant to grow up there as this kind of different person. It's still an issue— being half-white, half-Navajo in that space and that moving back and forth between this metropolitan of San Francisco to Navajo Nation in the 1970s and 1980s and all of the changes that were unfolding.

And then being from a pretty traditional family, a customary family. My grandmother never learned how to speak English. All the people in my generation, their first language is Navajo. I guess the other thing too is, I don't speak Navajo fluently, so it's always been this process of translation for me, growing up in that area. It's like writing a new story of my own making, to some extent. The story is there. There are multiple stories converging. That's interesting, because I'll write the backstory at some point.

FIELDS: Unlike other food-based art projects that deal with nuclear disaster, which focus more on the fear and anxiety embedded in a contaminated food supply, indigenous plants in *AIR* seem to provide the path for regeneration and survival. How do you see the balance of fear and promise operating in *AIR?*

WILSON: That's the other idea about time—a slow apocalypse, that as long as we're around, we're going to have to figure out a way to deal with it and respond to it.

I mean, the thing I've thought about a lot is that from my mom's generation to mine, there's been a huge shift. She grew up with her father with these amazing fields, and her mother had sheep, and her sisters had sheep, and most of the foods that my family ate came from the earth, directly from their labor. And that has shifted. The food shed became a food desert in one generation, really.

So, when I was thinking about transforming the *AIR* Research Lab into a greenhouse, that was behind some of that. And the seed that I sourced was from this place called Native Seeds/SEARCH. I was living in Tucson at the time, that's where they are based, and they had been collecting heirloom variety technology from the Southwest. They grow it on a little farm to make sure they have a continuing strain, and they bank the seeds. They also have a really cool program where they give out seeds to anyone who's Native for free, so you can just ask for it and they will help out.

FIELDS: As your series develops, your protagonist begins to cultivate plant foods in industrial greenhouses, moving to large-scale food production. You have had site-specific installations addressing this food production. How does your display change depending on the location of the exhibition?

WILSON: I've gotten to do it three times with that vision. The first time I did it I was in Tucson, Arizona. I had direct access to Native Seeds/SEARCH, so I was cultivating stuff that was regional. And then I also got to do it at the Denver Botanic Gardens, so we focused on the three sisters—corn, beans, and squash—Southwest regional, a little more toward Colorado. That was really cool because I got to tap into the resources of the botanical garden. They have these amazing greenhouses. The dream is that if this ever became a link to re-create maybe on Navajo Nation, maybe here [Santa Fe], I'd love to build some big greenhouses. And then I also got to do it here in Santa Fe, at the Santa Fe Art Institute. In that case, I used spices and food species that the residents of the art institute could tap into. But I do have this dream. I don't know if it will ever become a reality. Because the institution, the Santa Fe Community College, has a greenhouse program, a greenhouse management program. They have a set of greenhouses that are solar powered. They are particularly interested in algae for fuel production, but I think they are also interested in high-altitude, low-water species that can thrive here. I would love to do a project with the Navajo Nation, for example, that utilized some of their greenhouses and brought together elders, young people, around the idea of food and stories of food.

To those ends, I did a little pilot project. We went to the Navajo Nation Fair, I think in 2011 or 2012—and we set up a hogan there, and we had some of the plants in cultivation. My mom would find elders, or find folks to come in, and we would buy them a nice meal because right next to us was the Navajo Technical University culinary program. So, we'd buy people a lunch and have them come into the hogan. We had a little table set up, and in exchange for lunch, people would tell us a story about food.

FIELDS: On your website, you describe this as a pollinator—as a link to social action. How has that happened, or how do you see that happening in the future?

WILSON: I think in a lot of ways that artists are dreamers, but also we're really good at imagining solutions to really complicated issues. These are the kind of ideas that people who are a little more linear have trouble seeing or have trouble imagining.

I just met with Milton Tso, and he's the chapter president for Cameron [Cameron Chapter House of the Navajo Nation]—that's probably the community most affected by the uranium extraction in the West, of the Western Navajo Agency. He gave me a tour of some of the sites. He's been pulled into some activism in relation to his job because of the history and legacy of uranium extraction in the community and all of the families that were essentially poisoned—there's a number of wells that are off limits now, because they [the wells] have been impacted by toxic materials.

There's also a movement against allowing—there is a uranium mine on the rim of the Grand Canyon, and they want to haul the raw material to be processed to a site that's just above the Paiute Reservation in extreme southeast Utah or southwest Colorado, and that material would have to be shipped through Flagstaff and up [US Route] 89 through Cameron. The Flagstaff City Council recently passed a resolution—they didn't want to allow that to occur. So, we'll see, I think, to some extent eminent domain issues, who has the right to the roadway—at least in spirit. An [activist] organization called Haul No! was spearheading that effort and folded Milton into it. If he continues, if he runs again—his term's coming up at the end of the year—I'd love to collaborate with him more. We're just thinking about it.

I am going to continue photographing these sites when I can get out there. Plus, it's a great excuse for me to get out on the land. But I would love to offer that visualization of these red spots on a big map to whoever is interested. Particularly organizations like Haul No!

FIELDS: What are other ways this project has developed since it started in 2004, and what other ideas would you like to explore as it evolves?

WILSON: I don't know if this is speaking to that directly, but just this notion of land survey. It's a reason to be out there first and foremost. Hopefully I'll have a good body of images that is reconnecting me to that space in a different way and will introduce me to some of the players, in terms of people trying to figure out what to do and how remediation works out there. There's a moratorium on uranium extraction, but hopefully this will help firm that argument. I think that it's pretty widely accepted that it's not a good idea to restart this process. It's in the very beginning—I'll see where it takes me. Hopefully it will take me out there.

FIELDS: Do you see this land survey as an extension of the *AIR* series?

WILSON: I do and don't. At some point, maybe there will be really weird crossovers. And you'll be like, why is that guy wearing a gas mask in this place? There is also that mention of playing with time, between fact and fiction. It's interesting how much documentary and truth intersects with narrative on a broader scale. It's also just fun.

CHAPTER 16

Food Cultivation as Artistic Activism after Nuclear Disaster

ALISON FIELDS

Following the US development and deployment of atomic bombs in Japan at the close of World War II, the ensuing nuclear weapons testing programs across the American West and throughout the Pacific and Oceania, and nuclear accidents at power plants such as Fukushima Daiichi in Japan, the contamination of local food supplies has been one of the most tangible ways that people have come to experience and fear radiation. With wide-spanning impacts that include tainted tuna after the *Lucky Dragon No. 5* incident, malformed livestock found near the Nevada Test Site, radioactive salmon in the Columbia River near the Hanford Site in Washington, irradiated clams in the Marshall Islands, and contaminated rice paddies in Fukushima, Japan, the threat of radioactive food is global in scope. While foodways vary significantly by culture, the preparation and consumption of food is an intimate sensory experience, universally essential for survival.[1] As a result, concerns about food contamination are broadly relatable. Food also provides a means of visualizing radiation, giving invisible radioactive isotopes a recognizable form.

While the notion of radioactive food now broadly conjures anxiety, the Atoms for Peace program in the 1950s used the creation of atomic gardens—involving mutation breeding that used radioactive sources to develop thousands of new strains of plants—to explore the promise of atomic energy in food cultivation.[2] In a 1956 propaganda poster titled "How the Peaceful Atom Works," atomic research is credited with producing new strains of crops, larger crop yields, and savings in fertilizer costs, noting, "Food is one of the greatest problems of our time. The atom has contributed greatly to a completely new understanding of the life forces of growth and heredity so important to food production."[3] The poster's images include atom-radiated potatoes that remained fresh for two years, and a peanut plant grown from an atomic-treated seed, shown to produce one-third more peanuts than the most common strain. For a time, US citizens were permitted to obtain radioactive cobalt-60 sources, including Tennessee surgeon C. J. Speas, who irradiated his own seeds and sold them to home gardeners. He sold seeds to Muriel Howorth, the British founder of the Atomic Gardening Society, who became known for her advocacy of gamma ray gardens, her staging of isotopic pantomimes, and the irradiated peanuts she served at a dinner party for scientists and journalists.[4] Despite these private efforts and some lasting innovations in plant breeding and genetics, enthusiasm for the promise of atomic gardening gave way to more widespread concern about radioactive food.

Because locally produced food enters larger supply chains, anxieties about radioactive food extend beyond disaster areas. This was the case in the late 1950s, as the US Public Health Service began monitoring fallout in foods, and broad testing showed that the isotope strontium-90 was increasingly present in samples of milk.[5] The sharp rise of the isotope, which settles in the bones, was seen as a particular threat to American children. Editorial cartoonists and antinuclear activists circulated the image of a milk bottle marked with a skull and crossbones. In a 1962 speech at the National Conference on Milk and Nutrition, President John F. Kennedy acknowledged public concern about the impact of radioactive fallout on the food supply, centering on milk as a potential source of contamination. Pointing to guidelines created by the Federal Radiation Council, he assured his audience that the Public Health Service and other agencies provided constant monitoring of fallout in food. He concluded, "It is abundantly clear, that for the foreseeable future, there is no danger from the present amount of exposure. The milk supply offers no hazards."[6] Instead, President Kennedy described it as a necessary source of nutrition for children and adults. He underscored his support of the dairy industry by publicly drinking a glass of milk and noting its presence at every White House meal.[7] Despite such public assurances of safety, historian Spencer Weart notes that by the early 1960s radioactive fallout had come to stand in for nuclear weapons in the popular imagination. He writes, "By extension all radioactive isotopes, whatever their origin, were openly and permanently associated with horrible contamination. Any link to the ancient idea of life-giving radiation now seemed ludicrous."[8]

Across the globe, the lack of clarity about the potential harms of ingested radiation prompted individuals and groups to pursue their own findings. In *Food Safety after Fukushima: Scientific Citizenship and the Politics of Risk*, anthropologist Nicolas Sternsdorff-Cisterna defines this action as scientific citizenship: "A reassessment and reconfiguration of the citizen-state relationship, as citizens acquire the scientific literacy needed to critically examine expert advice, allowing them to challenge and circumvent the governmental response to a specific risk."[9] For instance, after the disaster in Fukushima, citizen scientists set up local food monitoring stations to independently check the radiation content of food.

Broadly, impacts from nuclear weapons testing and accidents at nuclear power plants have spurred numerous instances of food activism, resulting in efforts to make "the food system or parts of it more democratic, sustainable, healthy, ethical, culturally appropriate, and better in quality."[10] Building on issues raised by food activists, in this chapter, I examine how contemporary artists help visualize the intersections of anxiety, fear, ambivalence, promise, and regeneration in food cultivation following nuclear disaster. As artists from Fukushima and the Navajo Nation attest, the consequences of irradiated landscapes are wide reaching and deeply personal. Specifically, I discuss Japanese artists Ei and Tomoo Arakawa, whose performance *Does This Soup Taste Ambivalent?* involves serving soup from vegetables grown in Fukushima. I also address Diné artist Will Wilson's *Auto Immune Response* (*AIR*) series, particularly his *AIR Lab* iteration, which includes hogan greenhouses featuring indigenous plants as a mode of cultural survival on lands poisoned by uranium mining. While the two projects function differently, they both personalize the concern of contaminated food, include family involvement, and draw on environmentally and culturally specific foods. Through interactive performances and installations, these artists reflect on the uncertainty involved in assessing nuclear damage, while identifying scientific tools and cultural practices necessary for survival.

Does This Soup Taste Ambivalent?

In 2014, London's Frieze Art Fair launched the Frieze Live initiative, making space for performance-based installation art in the prestigious contemporary art show, held annually in Regent's Park. While over one hundred galleries submitted proposals, only six were chosen for Frieze Live. One of the selected works, created by UNITED BROTHERS and submitted through their Green Tea Gallery, *Does This Soup Taste Ambivalent?*, attracted special interest from the UK press in the weeks leading up to the event. The work of Japanese brothers Ei and Tomoo Arawaka, the performance was to feature the free distribution of soup prepared with vegetables grown in Fukushima, Japan, three years after its nuclear disaster. While the Japanese Farmers Association had certified the vegetables used by UNITED BROTHERS as safe, media took notice of the "radioactive" soup, publishing teasers that amplified the shock and dilemma of eating the potentially dangerous soup.

After Japan experienced the record-breaking Tōhoku earthquake and tsunami in March 2011, a multiple core meltdown occurred at the Fukushima Daiichi nuclear plant, which released gas that projected radioactive isotopes onto the surrounding landscape. The accident had an immediate impact on the local food supply. Within ten days, the Japanese government ordered that shipments of spinach and milk be suspended, citing contamination.[11] A number of farmers in Fukushima Prefecture—a heavily agricultural area known for its produce—were forced to abandon land in the evacuation zone. Outside of this zone, others continued to farm but saw demand for their produce decrease due to radiation fears. As media reports showed the radius of the radiation spread and thus the quantity of contaminated food expanding, public anxiety grew over government standards and testing, and many chose to not purchase food from the region. The presence of slow-decaying radioactive caesium, which dissolves in water and is absorbed by plants out of the soil, was the primary concern. While Fukushima farmers received compensation for banned shipments of their foods, elective consumer avoidance posed a greater loss, as prices decreased on produce from the area by up to 20 percent.[12]

The term *fūyōhigai*, originating in earlier Japanese nuclear accidents, refers to the economic damage caused by consumer avoidance, despite determinations of safeness.[13] According to sociologist Aya Kimura, *fūyōhiga* "broadly painted consumer food avoidance as prejudiced, disgraceful actions" that would cause pain to those in the afflicted areas.[14] Conversely, a national advertising campaign launched after the accident, Eat to Support, stressed the safety of food from Fukushima and encouraged customers to use their spending power to prevent economic and social damage to the region. In one advertisement, the popular singing group TOKIO is seen eating rice balls and a variety of produce, with the tag line "Let's continue to eat to support."[15] At some grocery stores in Fukushima, displays of vegetables grown and packaged locally were paired with a row of photographs of Fukushima farmers, humanizing the process of food production and creating a sense that the source is trustworthy. Bags of rice contain inspection codes with a phone number to contact an inspection center, where more information about the rice's production is available.[16]

Despite public efforts, many citizens continued to avoid food from northern and northeastern Japan for years after the accident. Chiaki Oku, an English teacher living in Fukushima Prefecture, makes an effort to buy food, particularly vegetables, from other areas of Japan. To explain her reluctance, she describes a gut aversion to the food: "I feel it."[17] Sternsdorff-Cisterna describes this common sentiment: "Food safety is both a question of science and affect," with safe food possessing both *anzen* and *anshin*. In Japan, *anzen* "points to the world of science and precision," while *anshin* "points to matters of the heart."[18] In relation to food safety, *anzen* provides scientifically measurable ways to evaluate safety, while *anshin* provides peace of mind. In *Does This Soup Taste Ambivalent?* audience members were assured of the food's safety in the measurable terms of the Japanese Farmer's Association guidelines, yet some still had an affective response that made them question whether they should eat the soup.

The UNITED BROTHERS performance was a family effort by the Arawakas, speaking to food contamination after the nuclear disaster but also about the psychological barriers created by these concerns—relative to both *anzen* and *anshin*. Born and raised in Fukushima but trained and primarily based in New York, performance artist Ei Arawaka envisioned the itinerant Green Tea Gallery as a bridge between his homes and a mechanism for international artists to engage with Fukushima.[19] With his brother Tomoo, who owned several tanning salons in and near Fukushima and long held a fascination with the art world, they formed UNITED BROTHERS and the Green Tea Gallery in the months after the nuclear accident.[20] At the moment of the disaster, Ei was in Tokyo, and his brother and mother were in their hometown of Iwaki, Fukushima, about sixty kilometers south of the power plant. He recalled being glued to the minute-by-minute updates and persuading his family to evacuate immediately.[21]

At the fair, the UNITED BROTHERS booth consisted of a simple round table with several pots of soup set up on hot plates, along with a stack of tan paper cups and napkins. On the white wall behind the table were photographs of the soup, tinted an eerie blue-green. Nearby, a series of documents provided basic information about Fukushima in English and showed the results, in Japanese, of the radiation testing conducted by the Japanese Farmers' Association on the soup's ingredients. The artists' mother, Miwako Arakawa, flew from Fukushima to London to prepare and serve the soup at 1 p.m. each day of the event. As Akiko Takenaka notes in chapter 11, mothers have often been incorporated into narratives of food activism in Japan, moving broad crises of food contamination into the personalized realm of cooking the family dinner.

The soup itself—a broth-based vegetable soup featuring daikon radishes and shiitake mushrooms from Fukushima as the main ingredients—was not the glowing concoction featured in the adjacent images. The radishes and mushrooms, sourced by Miwako in Iwaki, were selected because they could be purchased dried and easily transported in a suitcase. Reportedly delicious, the soup offered no visual signs of possible contamination. Some fairgoers simply saw the notice for free soup and ate it without any particular awareness of the context. For those who understood the premise, the reaction was more mixed. Some reacted with dark humor to trying the soup, like a man who commented, "My presumption is that there has been a recovery environmentally from [the nuclear disaster], I'm presuming that's the case, otherwise I'm going to have to wish my wife farewell."[22] Others downplayed the concern, noting that almost anything they ate could pose a risk, while still others could not bring themselves to try the soup. One blogger wrote, "Regardless of whether or not the soup will actually cause physical harm, to ask audiences to put their bodies at risk in order to fully participate in the exhibition is unfair. It is one thing for an artist to endanger his own body, but to create a piece of art based on the idea of the viewer choosing to endanger his or her own body seems too unreasonable."[23] Overall, far more visitors to the installation chose to eat the soup than not, with Miwako serving over one hundred cups a day.

Next to the table, a screen plays a science fiction film about an android from Fukushima. Tomoo produced the film with equipment purchased with compensation received from the power company for his business

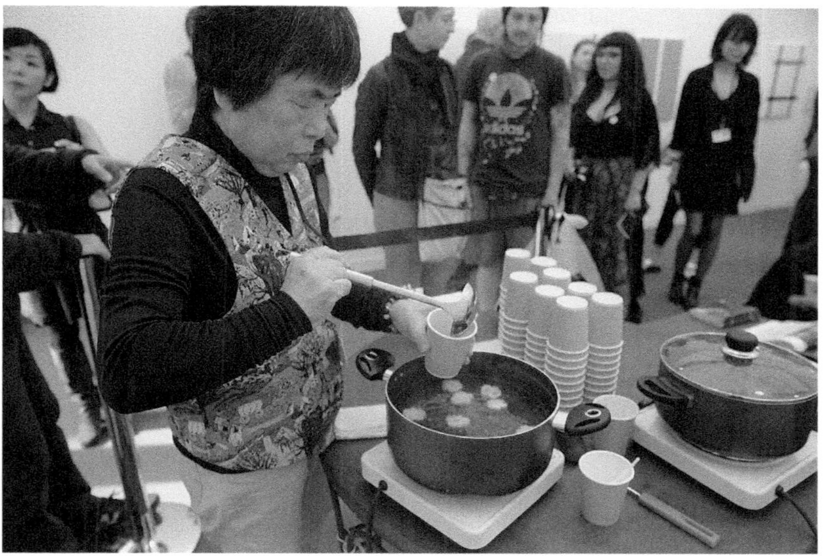

FIGURE 16.1. UNITED BROTHERS with Miwako Arakawa, *Does This Soup Taste Ambivalent?*, 2014, performance view. Photograph by Tomoo Arakawa. Image courtesy of Ei Arakawa.

losses after the disaster. While Ei described his brother's film as "B-movie chic" and "only enjoyable to the people who are in it," he acknowledged that the film's production engaged a number of professional artists, bringing them into conversation with the Green Tea Gallery's broader project.[24] While not overtly tied to the soup, the film provided a foundation for UNITED BROTHERS' multipart Fukushima Android Series Franchise, formed around topics of radioactivity, energy, and the power of art.[25]

By offering the soup for free to visitors, UNITED BROTHERS provided a counter to the highly consumerist space of the art fair. Served by their mother, it engaged social expectations of food preparation at the center of Japanese family life and connoted warmth and comfort. The Frieze catalog notes, "By tying the work to family and presenting it in a gallery or at an art fair as a gift, UNITED BROTHERS lend the ecological disaster an ethical dimension and an aesthetic quality that also comments on the status of art as a commodity."[26] Serving the soup represents an act of hospitality and sharing, but the act is laced with uncertainty. For instance, Miwako eats local produce in Iwaki and believed her soup was safe to share with Frieze fair visitors. However, despite her overall assurance of safety, she chose not to serve the soup to children who came to the booth.[27]

Miwako's decision not to serve the soup to children, despite her own willingness to eat it, shows that *anshin* does not only apply to oneself. Further, even when measurable data is procured, questions about the guidelines used or the comprehensiveness of the testing often remain. As Tessa Morris-Suzuki writes, "As time passes, the clearer it becomes that the Fukushima disaster not only poses challenges to the use of nuclear power but, at a fundamental level, raises questions about the construction and communication of scientific knowledge."[28] Foundational studies about the impacts of radiation after the US bombing of Hiroshima and Nagasaki in 1945, such as those conducted by the Radiation Effects Research Foundation (RERF), did not consider internal radiation. The RERF did not want to convey longer-term health impacts of radiation incompatible with the postwar American-led occupation of Japan. In studies following the nuclear accident at Chernobyl, it was challenging to provide direct links between internal radiation and particular diseases. While cancer is a frequent fear, evidence pointed more directly to cardiovascular disease as an outcome of internal radiation.[29] Scientists have disagreed about the conclusions of such studies and have debated the data used to set government standards for food testing. However, public discourse often overlooked these complexities, instead emphasizing food safety.[30]

Notably, the UNITED BROTHERS performance raises questions about risk assessment, the trust we place in expert opinion, and the psychological blocks that raise anxiety, even when data suggests a safe product. The performance does not ask for a particular action or outcome, or offer any judgment regarding decisions made, but rather encourages visitors to think about their own perceptions of safety and risk. Ei said, "I didn't want to offer so-called 'YES' soup to the people, in the way some politicians or civil organizations would do to simply promote food from Fukushima [in the wake of the disaster]. I thought this approach would exclude the people who disagree that food from Fukushima is safe. I came up with the 'ambivalent' position in order to create a platform for both opposing sides, as well as the middle ground who feel a dilemma about eating the food from Fukushima. My family and I are in this middle ground, I would say."[31]

The UNITED BROTHERS performance at Frieze Live, held nearly six thousand miles away and three years after the tsunami and Fukushima Daichhi nuclear disaster, presumably reached few audience members with direct knowledge of the event. Yet, the internal deliberation about whether to eat or not eat the UNITED BROTHERS soup made with Fukushima vegetables personalizes a conflict that has played out in Fukushima since 2011. Further, Ei suspects that Frieze promoters drew on the "symbolic power" of Fukushima in publicizing the performance, sensationalizing an affective response to potential radiation.[32] Once at the booth and provided with information about Fukushima and the results of radiation testing, the UNITED BROTHERS hoped to confront media narratives and provoke informed debates.

Auto Immune Response

At the 2011 Navajo Nation Fair in Window Rock, Arizona, at a community event far from the commercial space of the Frieze festival, Diné artist Will Wilson created another kind of interactive installation dealing with local foods. As an extension of his ongoing *Auto Immune Response* series, Wilson constructed a temporary hogan—a Navajo traditional and spiritual home—filled with plants growing from indigenous seeds and the scent of roasting mutton. Along with his mother, he invited tribal members to enter the hogan and offered them a free meal from the nearby Navajo Technical College culinary program. In exchange, he asked participants to share and record family stories about food. Like the UNITED BROTHERS, Wilson engaged his family in an act of hospitality. In this project, Wilson recognizes the evocative connection between scent and memory, and the importance of food as an anchoring point of cultural connection. This effort to document memories about Native foods speaks to one of Wilson's broader concerns as an artist—to interrogate the forces that have led to rapid cultural and environmental change on the Navajo Nation. This rapid change has had a profound impact on tribal foodways—the term indicating "the whole interrelated system of food conceptualization, procurement, distribution, preservation, preparation, and consumption shared by all members of a particular group."[33]

Over the past two centuries, shifting federal Indian policies fueled this transformation of Navajo foodways. Historian Devon Mihesuah notes that the tribe "went from cultivating beans, chilies, corns, melons, and squash to heartily accepting the introduction of sheep by the early 1800s."[34] While continuing to eat a varied diet of fruits, vegetables, and meats through the 1860s, the introduction of the reservation system made farming a challenge, and government rations introduced lard, sugar, and coffee into diets. In the 1950s, trading stores made processed foods even more available, and they were widely consumed.[35] The proliferation of these new unwholesome foods had a devastating impact on tribal health, contributing to a disproportionately high rate of autoimmune disease—the inspiration for Wilson's series title, *Auto Immune Response*. In addition to the toll on public health, a number of food cultivation practices were interrupted. In sum, Wilson notes that the Navajo Nation transformed from a "food shed to a food desert in a generation's time."[36] By inviting elders to share stories of food at the Navajo Nation Fair, Wilson created an archive of testimonies documenting this rapid change.

Another major driver of change on the Navajo Nation was the emergence of extractive industries in the twentieth century. The discovery of oil in the 1920s and the ensuing mining of vanadium, uranium, and coal transformed the Navajo landscape, which stretches across Arizona, New Mexico, and Utah. Uranium mining, central to the supply side of the nuclear weapons industry, had a particularly destructive impact on Navajo citizens and lands. The Manhattan Project secretly targeted the Colorado Plateau as a site for creating a domestic supply for uranium. As a hub during the US uranium boom from the 1940s to 1960s and a site of commercial mining until the 1980s, over 2,500 mines and mills extended across tribal lands.[37] The mining, processing, and transporting process spread radioactive materials across the reservation, contaminating the air and water. The Navajo Nation passed the Diné Natural Resources Protection Act in 2005, ending uranium mining and processing on tribal land. However, the health consequences of uranium mining are ongoing, companies operating at the edge of tribal land continue to pollute local aquifers, and the possibility of reopening mines remains. Some Navajo citizens have coalesced to resist the mining or transport of radioactive materials, in efforts such as Haul No!, an awareness tour held in 2017 along the proposed haul route of

Energy Fuels' Canyon Mine.[38] Wilson draws inspiration from such activist projects in his artistic practice.

Since 2005, Wilson's ongoing *Auto Immune Response* series of large-format, digitally altered photographs has examined the relationship between a postapocalyptic Navajo man, played by himself, and his beautiful but contaminated surroundings. Like the UNITED BROTHERS performance, *Auto Immune Response* engages a state of uncertainty tied to a nuclear event. In creating his postapocalyptic world, Wilson took cues from zombie movies where the protagonist wakes up completely unaware of what has transpired around him. With a twisting mushroom cloud looming in the background of *Auto Immune Response #1* and yellow dirt caked on his protagonist's hands, it is clear that the legacies of uranium mining on the Navajo Nation and nuclear testing in the Southwest are central to the destruction that has occurred.

But rather than defining specific catastrophes, Wilson focuses on the protagonist's response. The protagonist travels within the four directional boundaries of the Navajo Nation to determine what has occurred, what risks surround him, and how he can survive in this toxic environment. Most immediately, he must address his pressing need to secure food and shelter. To do this, Wilson's protagonist turns to scientific tools and prosthetic devices—including systems of irrigation, lighting, and food cultivation, along with his ever-present gas mask. The protagonist is also guided in his quest for survival by cultural knowledge, through acts such as the sprinkling of corn pollen in the Navajo daily prayer. Wilson describes this prayer as a connecting point with the holy people, a morning check-in to ensure that you are living in the correct way.[39] Through his efforts, the protagonist works to restore Hózhó, a Diné value of beauty and harmony, in a world that has become imbalanced.

While I have more fully examined the *AIR* series elsewhere, in this context, I wish to draw specific attention to an iteration of his project, the *Auto Immune Response Research Facility*, or *AIR LAB*, launched in 2010.[40] In *AIR LAB #1* and *#2*, Wilson constructed large steel greenhouses in the shape of a hogan. In the broader *AIR* series, the circular hogan, with its earth floor, clay and log walls, and portal to the sky, serves as the protagonist's home base and laboratory. Architecturally aligned with the cardinal directions, the hogan is an anchor to Navajo place and spiritual practice.[41]

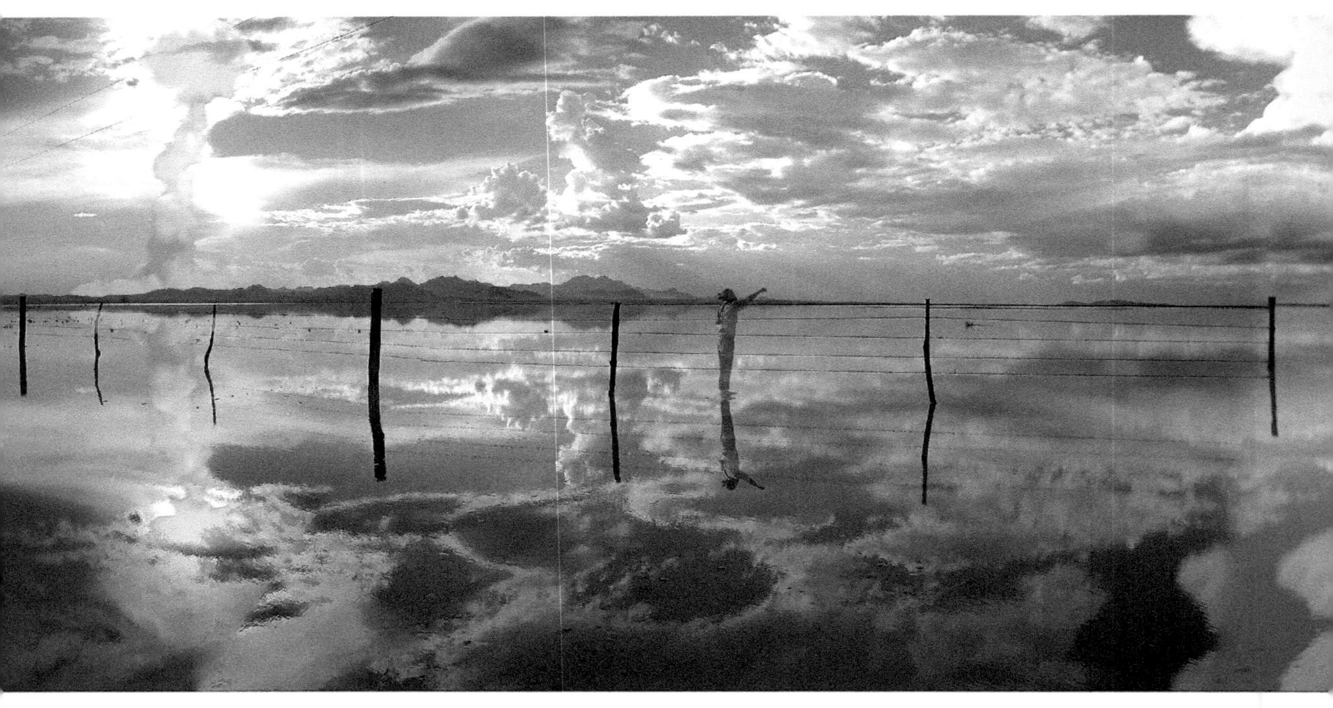

Poet Luci Tapahonso writes that the *hooghans* (hogans) date to the beginning of Diné time, when the holy people dwelled in Diné Tah and game and plant life was abundant. The hogans had two forms, "the round-topped female one for everyday living and the ceremonial, forked-top *hooghan*."[42]

In *AIR LAB*, Wilson's steel-frame hogans are fully open to the air. With rows of planters rising from ground level to the roof, the greenhouses use built-in irrigation systems to cultivate indigenous food plants. In 2010, Wilson exhibited *AIR LAB* at the Santa Fe Art Institute, and in 2011 at the Museum of Contemporary Native Arts in Santa Fe and the Denver Botanic Gardens in Colorado. As part of *Temporary Installations Made for the Environment* (TIME) in 2012, he installed *AIR LAB* at the Navajo Nation Zoo in Window Rock, Arizona. In these installations, Wilson paired his greenhouses with large-scale photographs from the *AIR* series, and in some cases, with photographs documenting the plant structure and cultivation process of food plants. Each installation was tailored to its site, with the food plants grown representing the specific region. In 2022, Wilson

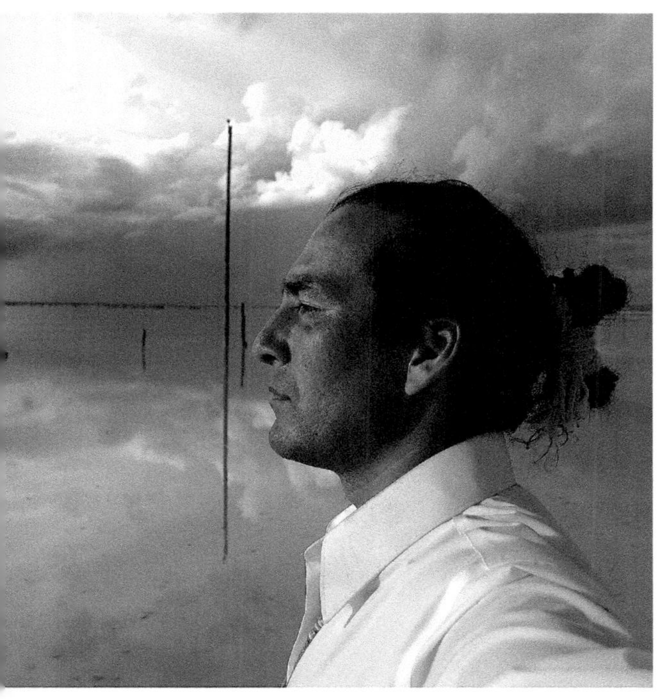

FIGURE 16.2. Will Wilson, *Auto Immune Response 1*, archival pigment print, 44 × 107 in. Courtesy of the artist.

installed *AIR LAB* at the Utah Museum of Fine Arts in the *AIR* exhibition curated by Whitney Tassie. Pairing the exhibit with works from his *Connecting the Dots* series, he worked with the University of Utah's Red Butte Gardens to cultivate Four Corners potato and plant species with the capacity to remove toxins from the soil.

In an artist statement, Wilson writes of the *AIR LAB* iteration: "This project served as a pollinator, creating formats for exchange and production that questioned and challenged the social, cultural and environmental systems that surround us." In an even more direct manner than his broader *Auto Immune Response* series, *AIR LAB* provides a link to social action.

To launch *AIR LAB,* Wilson worked with the nonprofit organization Native Seeds/SEARCH to obtain indigenous seeds. Founded in 1983 by conservation biologist Gary Paul Nabhan and based in Tuscon, Arizona, Native Seeds/SEARCH's mission is to "find, protect, and preserve" varieties of agricultural seed, recognizing their significance to cultures in the Greater Southwest.[43] In addition to food crops, Native Seeds/SEARCH also

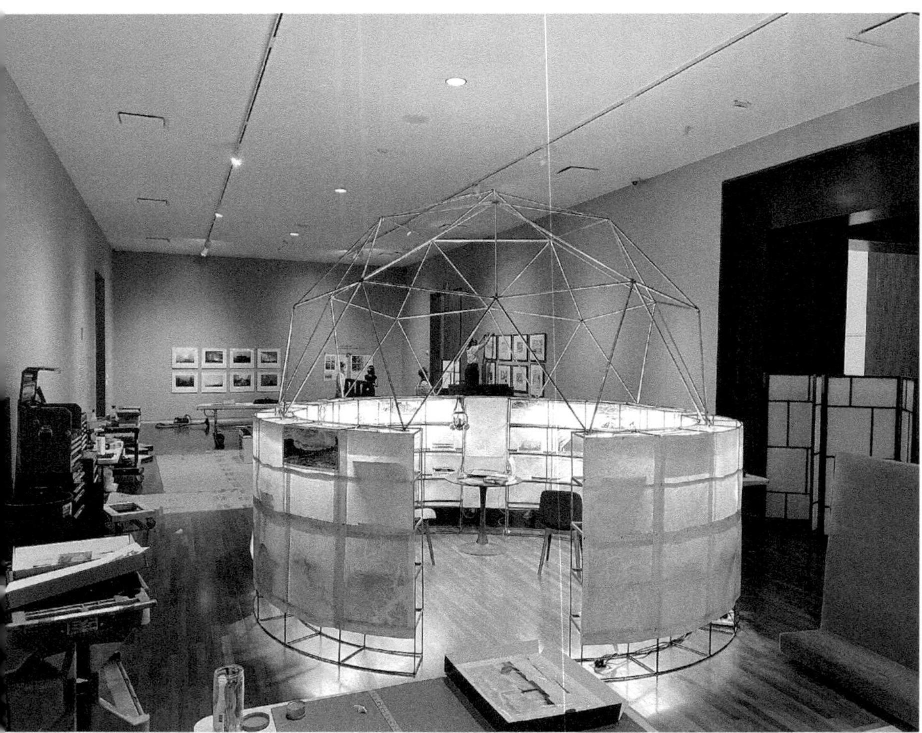

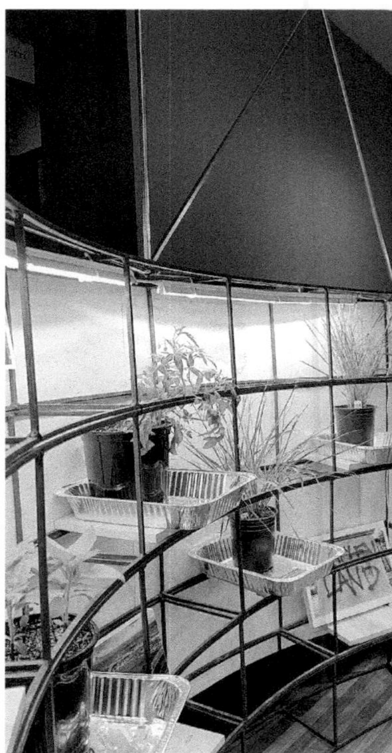

FIGURE 16.3. Will Wilson, *Auto Immune Response Laboratory*, installation view, Utah Museum of Fine Arts, 2022. Courtesy of the artist. See also plate 11.

preserves seeds used for dyes and fibers. While the organization protects over two thousand varieties of desert-adapted crops, its efforts go beyond preservation. Operating a conservation farm in Patagonia, Arizona, seeds from ancient crops and related varieties are made available to Native communities, both locally and globally.[44]

Wilson's partnership with Native Seeds/SEARCH on *AIR LAB* connects his series with broader, and interrelated, projects of food activism. Responding to environmental threats and health concerns, the Slow Food movement promotes local foods and traditional cooking, the permaculture movement encourages holistic thinking about natural ecosystems, and the Indigenous food sovereignty movement emphasizes food security and the right to "culturally appropriate food produced through ecologically sound and sustainable methods."[45] These movements have converged

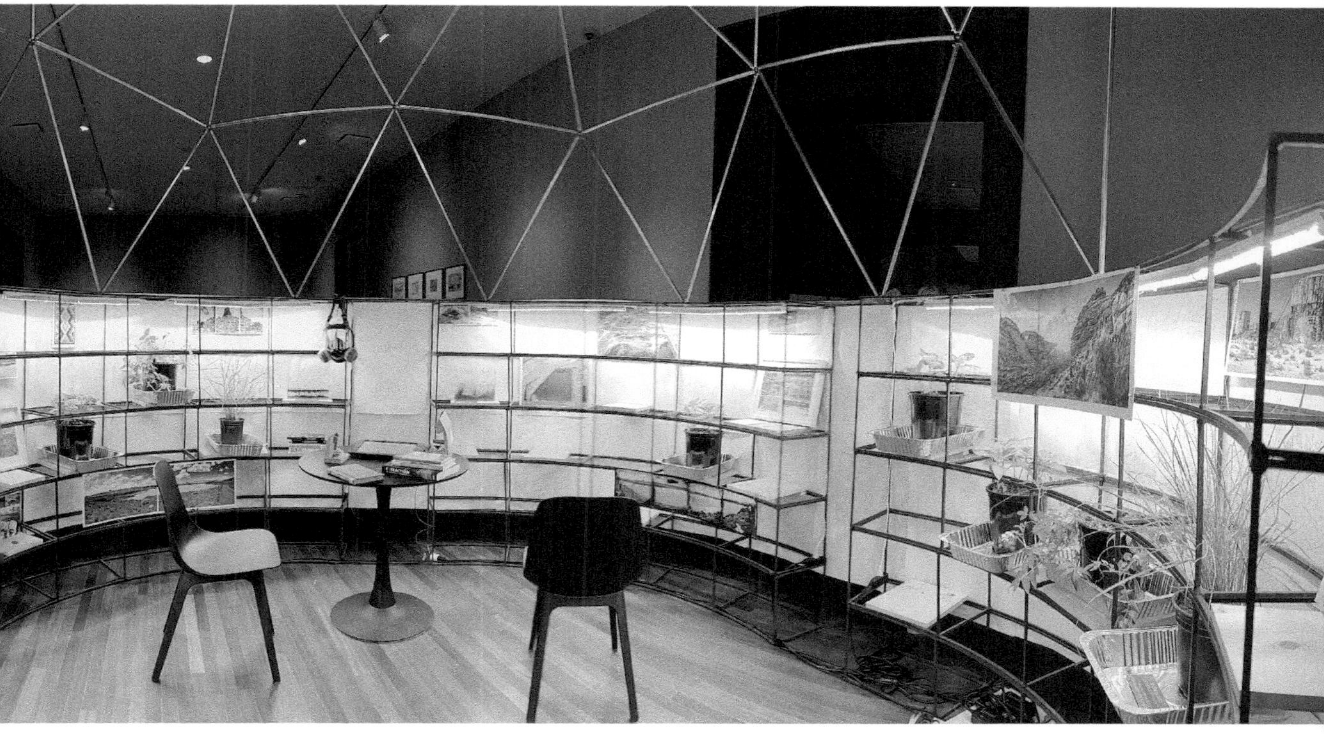

FIGURE 16.4. Will Wilson, *Auto Immune Response Laboratory*, installation view, Utah Museum of Fine Arts, 2022. Courtesy of the artist.

for unified goals. For instance, Native Seeds/SEARCH, in coordination with a consortium of nonprofit organizations, including the Center for Sustainable Development at Northern Arizona University, Slow Food USA in New York, Seed Savers Exchange in Decorah, Iowa, Chef's Collaborative in Boston, American Livestock Breeds Conservancy in Pittsboro, North Carolina, and Cultural Conservancy in San Francisco, worked to produce a project called Renewing America's Food Traditions (RAFT). This collaboration created an inventory of indigenous edible plants in America, including almost four thousand food varieties and species, in an attempt to revitalize varieties that are no longer used, to protect heirloom seeds, and to promote local and sustainable foods.[46] Heirlooms are food plants that have not been altered by modern breeding techniques and date back at least fifty years.[47] These seeds are specifically suited to their environments, have adapted to change, and are often tied to long-standing cultural practices. Because such seeds are adaptable and dynamic and tied to place, their cultivation can be understood as a lived expression of heritage and continuance.

Through the Native Seeds/SEARCH conservation farm and projects like RAFT, seeds that are recovered and protected are not simply stored but used. Scholar-activist Melissa Nelson, president of the Cultural Conservancy, explains that heritage is something that is continually evolving: "Indigenous and other traditional cultures know that if you want something to continue, to be sustainable, and be a vibrant, living entity, you have to have an active reciprocal relationship with it."[48] This value of reciprocity is central to *Auto Immune Response*. In Wilson's pilot project at the Navajo Nation Fair, food is offered in exchange for stories. In the photographic series, the protagonist's offerings of corn pollen reflect cultural practices of reciprocity. Finally, in *AIR LAB*, Wilson offers environmentally specific installations of indigenous food plants that evolve over time and can be shared and consumed. Wilson's *Auto Immune Response* offers an imaginative response for surviving not just a nuclear event but an environmental disaster that is tied to a specific environment and cultural practices. Through the protagonist's knowledge and cultivation of indigenous food plants, Wilson emphasizes restoration and growth. His protagonist's active measures for survival serve as a form of resistance to the environmental and bodily harm caused by uranium mining, nuclear testing, and rapidly changing ways of life on the Navajo Nation.

After the nuclear accident in Fukushima, owners of restaurants and grocery stores, and even producers of recipe books, publicly addressed and managed anxiety over radiation in food. Books like *Detoxing Radiation: The Power of Japanese Food: Brown Rice, Miso, and Seaweed* reinforced the idea that a traditional Japanese diet naturally counteracted radiation. While such claims were not scientifically supported, they gave consumers a sense of agency in addressing the concern of radiation.[49] As one reporter in San Francisco recalled, after the accident bulk bins of seaweed quickly sold out at her local grocery store, reflecting the belief that the natural iodine in seaweed would protect against radioactive iodine that might be traveling across the Pacific.[50] While the UNITED BROTHERS make no claim about the restorative powers of locally produced, culturally specific foods in *Does This Soup Taste Ambivalent?*, their performance asks audience members to think critically about how they perceive risk and the attitudes held and actions taken to ensure their own safety. The Arakawas rely on data to make any risk posed by the soup scientifically quantifiable; they hold the space of ambivalence to recognize that many affective factors impact beliefs about safety.

While Wilson's *Auto Immune Response* is less focused on identifying or quantifying risk, his *AIR LAB* iteration turns to indigenous food sources as the path for restoration and survival after nuclear disaster. While Wilson's protagonist does not face ambivalence, he must directly confront extreme uncertainty and imbalance, taking actions that will ensure safety and continuance. In Wilson's project, food is posed as a source of life rather than a source of contamination. Presented in very different venues, the UNITED BROTHERS inserted questions of food safety into the London art market and faced spectacle and jest in its promotion, while Wilson's installations were placed in museums and at community events within the impacted region. By considering these projects together, food from these diverse landscapes is shown to function as a symbol of promise, of ambivalence and fear, as an anchor for activism, and as a pathway for cultural connectivity and future survival.

Notes

1. Lana Dee Povitz, "Introduction," in *Stirrings: How Activist New Yorkers Ignited a Movement for Food Justice* (Chapel Hill: University of North Carolina Press, 2019).
2. Launched by Dwight D. Eisenhower's 1953 "Atoms for Peace" speech to the United Nations General Assembly, the Atoms for Peace program promoted productive, peaceful modes of harnessing atomic power.
3. "Atoms for Peace," National Archives catalog, accessed June 27, 2020, https://catalog.archives.gov/id/6948915.
4. Paige Johnson, "Safeguarding the Atom: The Nuclear Enthusiasm of Muriel Howorth," in "British Nuclear Culture," special issue, *British Journal for the History of Science* 45, no. 4 (December 2012), 566.
5. Spencer Weart, *The Rise of Nuclear Fear* (Cambridge, MA: Harvard University Press, 2012), 121.
6. "Got Milk? JFK Recommends It Highly in This Speech from January 23, 1962," YouTube, accessed June 27, 2020, https://www.youtube.com/watch?v=UJdOfVABRwM.

7. Weart, *The Rise of Nuclear Fear*, 121.
8. Weart, *The Rise of Nuclear Fear*, 121.
9. Nicolas Sternsdorff-Cisterna, *Food Safety after Fukushima: Scientific Citizenship and the Politics of Risk* (Honolulu: University of Hawai'i Press, 2018), 5–6.
10. Povitz, "Introduction."
11. Aya Hirata Kimura, *Radiation Brain Moms and Citizen Scientists: The Gender Politics of Food Contamination after Fukushima* (Durham: Duke University Press, 2016), 29.
12. Kimura, *Radiation Brain Moms and Citizen Scientists*, 31.
13. Naoya Sekiya, "What Is *Fuhyohigai*?," *Fukushima Journal of Medical Science* 57, no. 2 (2011): 93.
14. Kimura, *Radiation Brain Moms and Citizen Scientists*, 36.
15. Kimura, *Radiation Brain Moms and Citizen Scientists*, 37.
16. Ali Bunder, "Fear and Eating in Fukushima," San Francisco KALW Local Public Radio, March 30, 2015, https://www.kalw.org/post/fear-and-eating-fukushima#stream/0.
17. Bunder, "Fear and Eating in Fukushima."
18. Sternsdorff-Cisterna, *Food Safety after Fukushima*, 5–6.
19. Ei Arakawa has art degrees from the School of Visual Arts and Bard College and has shown work in major venues such as the Whitney Biennial, New York; the Tate Modern, London; Kunsthalle Zürich, Switzerland; Le Printemps de Septembre, Toulouse, France; the Museum of Modern Art, New York; and the DAAD Gallery, Berlin.
20. "Live: United Brothers," in *Frieze London Catalogue 2014* (London: Frieze Magazine, 2014).
21. *Does This Soup Taste Ambivalent?*, accessed June 13, 2020, http://blog.openingceremony.com/entry.asp?pid=10508.
22. "Tasting Fukushima Soup—Art and Ambivalence," BBC World Update, October 17, 2014, https://www.bbc.co.uk/programmes/p028v5nc.
23. Dee Dee Hughes, "The Art Equation: Radioactive Soup, Anyone?," *Daily Free Now*, accessed June 13, 2020, https://blog.dailyfreepress.com/2014/10/02/art-equation-radioactive-soup-anyone/.
24. Ei Arakawa, in conversation with Sherman Sam, *Ocula*, October 19, 2014, https://ocula.com/magazine/conversations/ei-arakawa/.
25. Green Tea Gallery, United Brothers Fukushima Android Series Franchise: Worldwide Premiere, January 23–February 23, 2019, http://freedmanfitzpatrick.com/exhibitions/green-tea-gallery/.
26. "Live: United Brothers."
27. *Does This Soup Taste Ambivalent?*, http://blog.openingceremony.com/entry.asp?pid=10508.
28. Tess Morris-Suzuki, "Touching the Grass: Science, Uncertainty, and Everyday Life from Chernobyl to Fukushima," *Science, Technology and Society* 19, no. 3 (2014): 333.

29. Kimura, *Radiation Brain Moms and Citizen Scientists*, 38.
30. Kimura, *Radiation Brain Moms and Citizen Scientists*, 44.
31. *Does This Soup Taste Ambivalent?*, http://blog.openingceremony.com/entry.asp?pid=10508.
32. Ei Arakawa in conversation with Sherman Sam, October 19, 2014.
33. Jay Anderson, quoted in James Deetz, *In Small Things Forgotten: An Archaeology of Early American Life* (New York: Anchor Books, 1996), 73.
34. Devon Mihesuah, *Recovering Our Ancestors' Gardens: Indigenous Recipes and Guide to Diet and Fitness* (Lincoln: University of Nebraska Press, 2020), 53.
35. Mihesuah, *Recovering Our Ancestors' Gardens*, 53.
36. "An Interview with Artist Will Wilson" in this volume.
37. Traci Brynne Voyles, *Wastlanding: Legacies of Uranium Mining in Navajo Country* (Minneapolis: University of Minnesota Press, 2015), xiii.
38. Haul No!, Facebook, accessed July 22, 2020, https://www.facebook.com/HaulNo/about/?ref=page_internal.
39. "An Interview with Artist Will Wilson" in this volume.
40. See Alison Fields, *Discordant Memories: Atomic Age Narratives and Visual Culture* (Norman: University of Oklahoma Press, 2020).
41. Janet Berlo, "Navajo Cosmoscapes—Up, Down, Within." *American Art* 25, no. 1 (Spring 2011): 11.
42. Luci Tapahonso, "The Diné Perspective," in *The Multicultural Southwest: A Reader*, ed. Gabriel Meléndez, Jane Young, Patricia Moore, and Patrick Pynes (Tuscon: University of Arizona Press, 2001), 101.
43. Native Seeds/Search, accessed July 20, 2020, https://www.nativeseeds.org/.
44. Gary Paul Nabhan, *Renewing America's Food Traditions: Saving and Savoring the Continent's Most Endangered Foods* (Hartford, VT: Chelsea Green, 2008), 2.
45. Lyric Aquino, "Indigenous Food Sovereignty Movement Gains Traction," Native American Journalists Association, September 19, 2019, https://najanewsroom.com/2019/09/18/indigenous-food-sovereignty-movement-gains-traction/.
46. Melissa K. Nelson, ed., *Original Instructions: Indigenous Teachings for a Sustainable Future* (Rochester, VT: Bear, 2008), 189.
47. David Buchanan, *Taste, Memory: Forgotten Foods, Lost Flavors, and Why They Matter: Restoring Diversity to Our Fields, Markets, and Tables* (White River Junction, VT: Chelsea Green, 2012), 5.
48. Nelson, *Original Instructions*, 188.
49. Kimura, *Radiation Brain Moms and Citizen Scientists*, 49.
50. Bunder, "Fear and Eating in Fukushima."

Contributors

MELANIE ARMSTRONG is associate professor in the Haub School of Natural Resources and director of the Ruckelshaus Institute at the University of Wyoming. She studies how social systems are built around shifting ideologies of nature, drawing theory and methods from political ecology, environmental history, and science and technology studies. She is author of *Germ Wars: The Politics of Nature and America's Landscape of Fear* and coauthor of *Environmental Realism: Challenging Solutions*. Her fifteen-year career with the National Park Service also provided a laboratory for exploring complex natural resource issues in the landscapes of the West.

HOLLY BARKER is a teaching professor of anthropology at the University of Washington and author of *Bravo for the Marshallese: Regaining Control in a Post-Nuclear, Post-Colonial World*. She began her work with the Marshallese when she served as a Peace Corps volunteer from 1988 to 1990 on Mili Atoll in the Republic of the Marshall Islands (RMI). After a brief stint with the Senate Foreign Relations Committee on Capitol Hill, she joined the RMI embassy in Washington, DC, where she was employed until 2008. While working full-time at the embassy in Washington, DC, she earned an MA in education and a PhD in anthropology from American University. She currently serves as one of three commissioners for the RMI's National Nuclear Commission tasked with pursuing nuclear justice for the people of the Marshall Islands, where she emphasizes capacity building for Marshallese students.

ELYSSA FAISON is L. R. Brammer Jr. Presidential Professor and associate professor of Japanese history at the University of Oklahoma. She is author of *Managing Women: Disciplining Labor in Modern Japan* and coeditor of *Sexing Class: Gender and Labour in Korea and Japan*. Recent works include "History: War Memory and Japan's Postwar," in *The Routledge Handbook of Contemporary Japan*, edited by Hiroko Takeda and Mark Williams; and "Socialist Feminisms," in *Handbook of Japanese Feminisms*, edited by Andrea Germer and Ulrike Wöhr. She is currently working on a book about atomic legacies in the United States and Japan.

ALISON FIELDS is associate director of the School of Visual Arts at the University of Oklahoma. She is the Mary Lou Milner Carver Professor of art of the American West and associate professor of art history. Fields received her PhD in American studies from the University of New Mexico. Fields is coauthor, with photographer Todd Stewart, of *Picher, Oklahoma: Catastrophe, Memory, and Trauma* and author of *Discordant Memories: Atomic Age Narratives and Visual Culture.* Dr. Fields serves as associate editor of the *Western Historical Quarterly.*

PETER GOIN, Foundation Professor of Art, Photography and Time-Based Media at the University of Nevada, Reno, is the author of *Tracing the Line: A Photographic Survey of the Mexican-American Border, Nuclear Landscapes, Stopping Time: A Rephotographic Survey of Lake Tahoe,* and *Humanature,* as well as a focused study on Nevada's petroglyphs and pictographs, *Nevada Rock Art.* Reflecting his long-standing analysis of Lake Tahoe's landscapes, Goin authored the award-winning *The Nature of Lake Tahoe: A Photographic History 1860–1960.* He served as editor of *Arid Waters: Photographs from the Water in the West Project.* Goin is coauthor of numerous other books, including the seminal *Black Rock* (with Paul F. Starrs), a dedicated investigation of the phenomenal desert region in northern Nevada, and *A Field Guide to California Agriculture* (also with Paul F. Starrs), which won the J. B. Jackson Prize for publishing excellence. With Lucy Lippard, he coauthored *Time and Time Again: History, Rephotography, and Preservation in the Chaco World* and with Gary Snyder, *Dooby Lane also Known as Guru Road: A Testament Inscribed in Stone Tablets,* and with Peter Frederici, *A New Form of Beauty: Glen Canyon beyond Climate Change.*

MARGO MACHIDA is professor emerita of art history (School of Fine Arts) and Asian and Asian American studies (College of Liberal Arts and Sciences) at the University of Connecticut. Born and raised in Hawai'i, she is a scholar, independent curator, and cultural critic specializing in Asian American art and visual culture. Her most recent book is *Unsettled Visions: Contemporary Asian American Artists and the Social Imaginary.* This book received the prestigious Cultural Studies Book Award from the Association for Asian American Studies in 2011. She also coedited the award-winning volume *Fresh Talk/Daring Gazes: Conversations on Asian American Art.* Dr. Machida is associate editor of *Asian Diasporic Visual Cultures and the Americas.* Recent publications include "Martin Wong: Renewing Our Conversation" in the *Martin Wong Catalogue Raisonné*; "Transcultural Sampling: The Reimagined Worlds of Carlos Villa," in *Carlos Villa: Worlds in Collision*; "Pacific Itineraries: Islands and Oceanic Imaginaries in Contemporary Asian American Art," *ADVA*; "Trans-Pacific Sitings: The Roving Imagery of Lynne Yamamoto,"

Third Text; "Devouring Hawai'i: Food, Consumption, and Contemporary Art," in *Eating Asian America: A Food Studies Reader*; "Convergent Conversations—The Nexus of Asian American Art," in *A Companion to Asian Art and Architecture*; and "Art and Social Consciousness: Asian American and Pacific Islander Artists in San Francisco, 1965–1980," in *Asian American Art: A History, 1850–1970*.

YUKA TSUCHIYA MORIGUCHI is professor of American history at the Graduate School of Human and Environmental Studies in Kyoto University. She received a PhD in American studies from the University of Minnesota. Her doctoral dissertation was published (in Japanese) as *Constructing a Pro-US Japan: US Information and Education Policy and the Occupation of Japan*. Her research since then has focused on US cultural/public diplomacy during the Cold War, especially through the lens of science and technology. Her most recent publication in this field is *Science, Technology, and the Cultural Cold War in Asia: From Atoms for Peace to Space Flight*. She has coedited three books: *Cultural Cold War and the Development of Knowledge in East Asia*; *Occupying Eyes, Occupying Voices: USIS Films and VOA Broadcasting in Japan in the Early Cold War Years*; and *De-Centering the Cultural Cold War: The US and Japan*. She is interested in Japanese seafarers' experiences of the US nuclear tests in the Pacific during the 1950s and the early '60s and has been conducting oral history interviews with retired fishermen.

JENNIFER RICHTER is assistant professor in the School for the Future of Innovation in Society and School of Social Transformation and the Consortium of Science, Policy and Outcomes at Arizona State University. She received her PhD in American Studies from the University of New Mexico in 2013. Her research interests are at the intersection of science and society, focusing on how federal policies are enacted locally. Dr. Richter focuses on energy justice, specifically in relation to nuclear renewable energy production, and how production affects communities. By examining how science and technology policies collide with local expectations and understandings of environment and economy, she explores the different scales of energy technologies and policies and their effects on people. Dr. Richter is coauthor of *Environmental Realism: Challenging Solutions* and has published recent articles in *Energy Research and Social Science*, *Journal of Geoscience Education*, and *Innovation: The European Journal of Social Science Research*.

SHINPEI TAKEDA is an artist and filmmaker working in a wide array of mediums involving themes related to memories and histories. He was born in Osaka, Japan, in 1978 and lives and works in Tijuana, Mexico, and Düsseldorf, Germany. In 2001, he founded the AJA Project (http://www.ajaproject.org/), a San Diego–based nonprofit working with refugee youth using photography and storytelling. In 2008, he cofounded Ghost Magnet Roach Motel (www.ghostmagnet.info), a noise punkformance unit in Tijuana, Mexico. In 2017, he founded a nonprofit based in Germany, Antimonument e.V., a platform for projects connecting memory and technology. His works and films have been shown in many countries, mainly Germany, Austria, Japan, Mexico, and the United States. For more information, see www.shinpeitakeda.com.

SEIICHIRŌ TAKEMINE is associate professor in the Department of Sociology, Meisei University in Tokyo. He received his PhD in International Studies from Waseda University in 2012. He has conducted field research concerning nuclear issues on the Marshall Islands since 1998. He is author of *Still Living with Nuclear Fallout on the Marshall Islands* (『マーシャル諸島終わりなき核被害を生きる』) and "Overlooked Invisible Victims of the US Nuclear Testing on the Marshall Islands: Why Were the Local People Exposed to Radiation?" in *Regional Ecological Challenges for Peace in Africa, the Middle East, Latin America and Asia Pacific*. He is the co-convener of a research committee on Global Hibakusha, a board member of Peace Studies Association of Japan, and an affiliated researcher at the Institute for Peace Science, Hiroshima University, and the Lucky Dragon Museum in Tokyo.

AKIKO TAKENAKA is associate professor in the Department of History at the University of Kentucky. She holds a PhD and MA from Yale University, a Science Masters in architectural studies from MIT, and a B.Eng from the Tokyo Institute of Technology. Her first book, *Yasukuni Shrine: History, Memory, and Japan's Unending Postwar*, is the only book-length scholarly work in English that critically examines the controversial war memorial. She is also the author of *Mothers against War: Gender, Motherhood, and Peace Activism in Postwar Japan*. She has published in journals including *Gender and History, Verge: Studies in Global Asias, Public Historian, Pacific Historical Review*, and *Review of Japanese Culture and Society*, as well as a wide range of edited volumes on topics from war memory and mass dictatorship to aesthetics and visual culture. She has guest-edited an issue of *Feminist Encounters*, "Feminist Politics and Activism in Reactionary Eras." She is a recipient of numerous awards and fellowships, including Fulbright, the Japan Foundation, and Michigan Society of Fellows.

NAOKO WAKE is professor of history and director of the Asian Pacific American Studies Program at Michigan State University. A historian of gender, sexuality, illness, disability, and memory in the Pacific world, she has authored *Private Practices: Harry Stack Sullivan, the Science of Homosexuality, and American Liberalism* and *American Survivors: Trans-Pacific Memories of Hiroshima and Nagasaki*. She has created the largest oral history collection of Asian American survivors of the

1945 Hiroshima and Nagasaki bombings in the world, housed in MSU's Robert G. Vincent Voice Library and in the Densho Digital Repository. Her current project concerns the histories of disability, archives, and literature in Asian America.

SHERRI WASSERMAN is a designer, writer/researcher, and multidisciplinary collaborator who constructs experiences at intersections of physical, digital, and informational landscapes. In addition to her extensive work on projects spanning from individual artist partnerships to initiatives for major institutions, she holds degrees in visual arts and history from Oberlin College, design and programming for emerging technologies from New York University, and science and technology studies from Arizona State University.

RAN ZWIGENBERG is associate professor of Asian studies and Jewish studies at Penn State University. He received his PhD in history from City University of New York and was a postdoctoral associate with the Council on East Asian Studies at Yale University. His research focuses on modern Japanese history, with a specialization in memory and intellectual history. His is the author of *Hiroshima: The Origins of Global Memory Culture*, coauthor (with Oleg Benesch) of *Japan's Castles: Citadels of Modernity in War and Peace*, and author of *Nuclear Minds: Cold War Psychological Science and the Bombings of Hiroshima and Nagasaki.*

Index

Page numbers in *italics* refer to illustrations.